MIDDLE EAST
CONFLICTS & REFORMS

Editors

Mohammed M. Aman, PhD

Mary Jo Aman, MLIS

Westphalia Press
An imprint of the Policy Studies Organization

Washington, DC
2014

Middle East: Conflicts & Reforms
All Rights Reserved © 2014 by Policy Studies Organization.
Mohammed M. Aman and Mary Jo Aman

CIP
Aman, Mohammed M.
Edited by Mohammed M. Aman and Mary Jo Aman.
Washington, DC: Westphalia Press, 2014.

ISBN-13: 978-1941472002
ISBN-10: 1941472001

Middle East & North Africa-Policy and politics
Arab Spring
Arab-Israel Peace
Aman, Mary Jo, Jt. editor

Printed in the United States of America

Westphalia Press
An imprint of Policy Studies Organization
1527 New Hampshire Ave., NW
Washington, D.C. 20036
info@ipsonet.org

Updated material and comments on this edition
can be found at the Westphalia Press website:

www.westphaliapress.org

To our parents
Mohammed and Loza Aman
Ronald and Goldia Parker

TABLE OF CONTENTS

Preface	vii
Part One: Leadership, Reform and the Arab Spring	1
Democracy and Islamist violence: Lessons from post-Mubarak Egypt, Jerome Drevon	5
In between the glorious past and wounded self image: What does Turkey have to offer for the Middle East? Bahar Senem Çevik	19
The wall of fear and the intelligence apparatus in Syria, Radwan Ziadeh	37
Iran and the Syria crisis: policies, problems, and prospects, Maysam Behravesh	45
"God save the king?": The evolution of protest in Jordan in light of the Arab Spring, Sarah A. Tobin	57
The Arab Spring and modernization of Islam: A major step towards the unification of human civilization, Susmit Kumar	71
Part Two: Policy and Economic Challenges	115
Arab Gulf investments into non-inclusive urban development in the Middle East: A partial precursor to the Arab Spring, Bessma Momani	119
Citizenship, national identity, and the future of "UAE, Inc.": Confronting the fragility thesis, Kenneth L. Wise	131
Middle East Union (MEU); A futuristic approach for democratic transition and economic development, Alan L. Moss	153
Ignorance, lobby, power and the formulation of U.S. foreign policy, Lawrence Davidson	167
Part Three: Civilizational and Sectarian Cooperation and Conflict	179
Socio-economic rights: A dialogue with Islam, Amitai Etzioni	183
Re-approaching-not merely reproaching-religious sectarianism within a tumultuous Middle East, Andrew M. Wender	195
Christian-Muslim relations in Egypt in the wake of the Arab Spring, Paul S. Rowe	209
Politics of conflict in Pakistan's tribal areas: Vulnerability reduction in violence-prone complex adaptive systems, Asim Zia and Kashif Hameed	223
Chill ground: Iranian–British relations during Khomeini–Thatcher years, Maysam Behravesh	237
Part Four: MENA Women's Rights: Triumphs and Setbacks	253
Imagining the new Egypt: Agential Egyptian activism/feminism, translation and movement, Maria Frederika Malmström and Anna Hellstrand	257
Working with patriarchy: Strategies for women's empowerment in comparative perspectives, Alessandra L. González	275
Gender segregation, effacement, and suppression: Trends in the status of women in Israel, Michal L. Allon	293
Gender and leadership style in the Middle East: Evidence from Egypt's civil service Jennifer Bremer and Ola Gameel Al-Talliawi	307
References	325
About the Authors	365

PREFACE

The Middle East is considered the cradle of civilization and the birthplace of the three monolithic Abrahamic religions. It has also been the center of great and historic conflicts that involved not only the countries and the peoples of the region, but also former and present global military and economic powers vying for the region's strategic location and fossil and economic resources. For these reasons, it was decided to devote an annual conference to address, discuss, and debate issues affecting the region. The Middle East Dialogue (MED) annual conference was conceived in 2010, with the first conference sponsored by the Policy Studies organization (PSO) and the Wiley refereed journal, the *Digest of Middle East Studies* (*DOMES*). The first MED conference was held on the 24th and 25th of February 2011, with the objective of bringing together, in the Nation's Capital, scholars, policymakers, civic and religious leaders from around the world to present, discuss, and debate issues and challenges facing the countries of the Middle East and North Africa (MENA) and their impact on American and global foreign policies and politics. From its inception in 2011, the MED conference has attracted speakers and participants world-wide. Topics of papers presented and panel discussions have covered timely issues affecting the region, such as political, social and economic reforms, human rights, women's rights, interfaith/sectarian dialogues, the Israel-Palestine disputes, the rise and fall of Arab governments, Iran's nuclear program, and MENA water resources, to mention a few.

The Second MED Conference in 2012 dealt with the dawn of the Arab Spring with its perceived high hopes for introducing democratic systems of government in the affected countries instead of the imposed military and authoritarian rulers like Ben Ali in Tunisia, Mubarak in Egypt, Qadhafi in Libya, and Saleh in Yemen. With the removal of these long-serving rulers and the free and fair election of new civilians to head governments in these countries there was new hope for introducing democracy to replace autocracy with long awaited economic and social reforms.

One year later, in February 2013, the theme of the MED Conference was "New Directions for the Middle East" as we addressed issues of peace, reforms, and women's rights. Unfortunately the summer of 2013 did not look as peaceful as we had hoped a year earlier. The Egyptian military coup imprisoned the first democratically elected president, and a bloody confrontation with the party in power, the Muslim Brotherhood, brought the country to a standstill. Most recently, the present Egyptian temporary government declared the Muslim Brotherhood a terrorist organization. In Tunisia, the leader of the opposition party was assassinated; in Libya, the chaotic situation and armed confrontations are on the rise, and the Syrian civil war continues to escalate with no end to the bloody conflict in sight.

The six Arab Gulf States, members of the Gulf Cooperation Council (GCC), feared the Arab Spring, and its possible threat to the region's monarchies. They took collective actions to stamp out the Shi'a uprising in Bahrain and took individual steps to appease their citizens financially, and to promise some form of nominal democratic citizens' participation. The tragic and chaotic post-Arab Spring events and failed democracies in the affected countries may have eased the pressure on, and worries of, the relatively more stable GCC monarchies.

The papers presented in this monograph were selected from the third MED Conference held on February 21, 2013 at the historic Whittemore House in Washington, D.C. Also included in this volume are select and edited papers from another, similar conference held during November, 2012 at Al-Akhawayn University in Ifrane, Morocco, with topics covering the areas of public administration and leadership in the MENA region. This amalgamation of papers aims to strengthen and enrich the contents of this series, as the papers should be of interest to scholars, and decision makers interested in the MENA region.

This two volume series is divided into seven parts, with this first volume in the series titled **Conflicts and Reforms** and contains the following four parts:

- **Part One**: Leadership, Reform, and the Arab Spring;
- **Part Two**: Policy and Economic Challenges;
- **Part Three**: Civilizational and Sectarian Cooperation and Conflict; and
- **Part Four**: MENA Women's Rights: Triumphs and Setbacks.

The second volume in the series titled **New Directions in the Middle East** contains the following three parts: **Part Five**: Israel/Palestine Divide; **Part Six**: Communication, Media, and the Arab Awakening; and **Part Seven**: Management and Conflict Resolution.

Each of the two volumes and the seven parts contained therein are prefaced with separate prefaces and introductions written by the Editors and summarizing the contents of the published papers in each volume. Brief biographical information about each contributing author and co-author(s) appears at the end of the volume under the heading "About the Authors."

While the Arab Spring has occupied much of the global media's attention in recent years, its aftermath has received mixed reviews and analysis from international media commentators, policy and academic experts, among others. The fall of older autocratic rulers did not produce young democrats or reformers. Instead, ethnic and religious strife has gained a foothold; economic paralysis and insecurity make some Arab citizens long for the "good old days" of authoritarian and military regimes and a false expectation of normalcy, economic security, and political stability. Domestic unrest, lack of safety and security for all citizens, a shortage of the necessities, such as food and petrol, damaged infrastructure, and power blackouts have turned hope into despair, and the Arab Spring into a nightmare where military and state-security forces rule.

In the four parts of this first volume the authors deal with such persistent issues as democracy and whether the MENA countries are ready for the change from the single man or family rule to a shared system of government in which all citizens have a voice in a participatory and inclusive system of government. Questions are also raised and answered about Islam, the dominant religion in the MENA region, and democracy and are they compatible. Issues of religious and ethnic sectarianism as seen in Bahrain, Syria and Egypt are examined in light of the latest events surrounding the Arab Spring and the demands for fairness and equal representation. In other parts of the volume the authors point to the stagnant economy, corruption, concentration of wealth among the very few as well unemployment among a growing population of young people. These are major ingredients in the continued malcontent in the MENA region that goes beyond any Arab season or generation. Similar attention is given to the rights of women and the necessity of overcoming the gender barriers and giving women equal rights and opportunity to be full partners if MENA countries are to move forward and join other countries that have advanced socially as well as economically as a result of gender integration and eliminating these and similar barriers facing their citizens.

The views expressed by the authors are their personal views and do not represent the views of institutions with which they are affiliated, the Policy Studies Organization (PSO), *DOMES*, or its editors. Because of its balanced treatment and the nature of the delicate issues presented about the most sensitive region of the world, this monograph will be a valuable addition to every academic course, office, and library collection where expert and novice readers alike can be introduced to varied points of view.

The editors wish to thank the authors and co-authors who contributed to this volume and responded kindly to our editorial comments and questions. Our sincere thanks to the MED2013 Conference planners, organizers, sponsors, panelists, panel chairs, and discussants. They all made this conference and the publication of this book possible. Special thanks to the leadership and staff of the PSO, and in particular, its President and Co-Chair of the MED Conferences, Dr. Paul J. Rich; Executive Director Daniel Gutierrez-Sandoval; Whitney Shepard, Director of Development and Programs; Matthew Brewer, Director of Outreach and Open Source Materials; and Devin Proctor, Director of Media and Publications for their strong support of and dedication to the MED Conferences and their publications. Special thanks to the University of Wisconsin-Milwaukee for its continued support of the MED Conferences and to graduate assistants Tina Jayroe, and Brittany Khateeb for their assistance.

We hope that the authors' writings and observations as presented in this volume will help lift the MENA region from its current position to a much better level of advancement that could bring ever-lasting peace, stability and prosperity to *all* of its citizens.

The Editors

MIDDLE EAST
Conflicts & Reforms

PART ONE

Democracy, Reform, and the Arab Spring

Recent developments in the aftermath of the Arab Spring and the hope for introducing democratic systems of government, particularly in the affected countries, have ignited the old and Orientalists' debates about MENA (Middle East and North Africa) countries transitioning to democracy, and question if Western-styled democracy is incompatible with Islam. The post-dictatorial regimes were toppled by the peaceful and sometimes violent demonstrations in the streets of Tunisia, Egypt, Yemen, and Libya, and brought to power Islamists who are more concerned about ideologies than they are about tackling these urgent social, economic, and employment issues facing their fellow countrymen and women. Islamists are now in power and the question they face is what to do with the newly acquired authority in meeting the demands and aspirations of the average MENA citizen. The recent tragic events in Egypt and the overthrow of the Muslim Brotherhood regime by the military resulted in a politically divided Egypt with an uncertain future.

Using data retrieved from field research in Egypt and repeated interviews of leaders and members of the two main former militant groups, *al-Jama'ah al-Islamiyah* (the Islamic Group) and *Jama'at al-Jihad* (the Jihad Group), as well as interviews with militants of the *Salafi jihadis* and their supporters in Cairo, Dr. Drevon explores the contentious relations between the absence of democracy in the Middle East and the use of armed violence by Islamist groups in light of the Arab Spring. Drevon's stated objective is "to decipher the evolving positions of former and current groups who used or promoted violence and to relate them to broader academic debates on violence and democracy on the one hand, and on de-radicalization on the other hand." He points out that published research demonstrates that the large majority of former Islamist militants in Egypt reject any sort of violence in post-Mubarak Egypt, even if they have not renounced their religious legitimization of violence in the past. It also reveals that even if they maintain a religious opposition to democracy in Egypt, the opening of political opportunities and their progressive joining of the political process has favorably led most of them to accept democratic practices in reality. Furthermore, it adds that the voice of those currently promoting violence in Egypt has been marginalized and that their main objective has been the promotion of armed violence in Syria. Last, it stresses two potential security threats unrelated to the opening of political opportunities in post-Mubarak Egypt and to the general debate on democracy and violence.

If there is one nation in the region and the Muslim world that benefitted from the Arab Spring, it must be Turkey, even though it has suffered its own June 2013 internal political unrest. Positions taken by the Turkish government prior to and immediately following the fall of the four authoritarian Arab regimes (Tunis, Egypt, Libya, and Yemen), and most recently the civil strife in Syria, has gained Turkey a much improved status and leadership role in the region as a defender of people's demands for freedom and democratic reforms. Some reformists have looked at the Turkish system of government as a most suitable model for a predominantly Muslim democracy that has also had a recent history of its armed forces intervention in its domestic politics. Yet, some have raised questions about Turkey's claims of democratization, citing political strategy towards the Kurdish question and Sunni-conservative hegemonic policies pursued during the third term of the Justice and Development Party (JDP).

In his paper about the new leadership role recently being played by Turkey's government, Dr. Çevik uses a social psychology and psychoanalytic framework to discuss the fundamentals behind the Turkish inspiration - the socio-political effects of the Arab Awakening in relation to the Turkish identity. Such identity, the author claims, is misplaced between "the glorious past and wounded self-image." She argues the necessity of a new political language with the Middle East which Turkey can offer and construct new channels for dialog. According to Dr. Çevik, the Turkish experience of co-existence among democracy, secularism, modernity, and Islam should serve as an extraordinary example for the Arab Middle East.

Unlike what happened in Libya, where the rebellion against the dictator Mu'amar al-Qadhafi was assisted by NATO's airstrikes and a massive delivery of weapons to counter his mercenaries resulted in the elimination of his regime, the Syrian revolt has been the most violent and, so far, the most unsuccessful in ousting the al-Assad regime. Historians and foreign policy experts will study and argue about the reasons as to why NATO military support was not used in the same way in Syria in support of the uprising against the al-Assad regime. Why Bashar al-Assad has lasted so long may be due to several factors—among them what Dr. Radwan Ziadeh refers to as the "Wall of Fear"—referring to the hated Syrian Intelligence Apparatus. Ziadeh's case study can be applied to the kind of "wall" every authoritarian Arab regime has relied upon for decades; many continue to do so in order to maintain their grip on power at any cost, and to subjugate their own people. According to Dr. Ziadeh, the security/intelligence service in Syria is comprised of a massive bureaucracy responsible for maintaining a policy of oppression, and a monopoly on truth. In what he described as Syria's Orwellian system of surveillance, there is one secret police operative for every 256 Syrians. There is not just one, but at least four separate massive intelligence bodies: military, air force, political, and general. He predicts that the Syrian security apparatus and its intelligence forces will be the greatest obstacle to any hope of transitional justice in Syria. Because of their long history of human rights violations, the leaders of the intelligence bodies guilty of crimes against humanity should be, along with President al-Assad, brought before the International Criminal Court under the Rome Statute. Dr. Ziadeh concludes that "once these forces are rehabilitated and reformed, which will necessitate a long, arduous process, ... then the Syrian people can begin to knock down the wall of fear that has paralyzed free expression and a dignified life for as long as many of us Syrians can remember."

The Arab Awakening (or Arab Spring) has reached countries that thought it could never happen to them. Such countries are the oil-rich GCCs (Gulf Cooperation Council), Iran, and Syria (the events of June 2013 have placed Turkey on the threshold of such a description). The current civil war in Syria resulted in further deterioration in the relations between the Syrian Baa'th regime and neighboring countries, along with well-establish hostilities towards Iran and Hezbollah, Syria's only allies in the region.

Iran's pursuit of a nuclear program remains front and center of the potential armed conflict and the current major crisis threatening the entire Middle East. The United States' led economic sanctions against Iran have had a severe effect on the country's economy and the falling value of the Iranian currency, among others. Iran's oil exports, estimated to be 90% of its total export revenues, places it as the world's fourth largest oil producer. Therefore, the American Western-led sanctions on the country's oil and natural gas exports revenue continue to have severe economic, and probably political, repercussions. There is the expectation that the recent Iranian election of June 2013 that resulted in the selection of the moderate and experienced political cleric, Hassan Rouhani may have a positive impact upon Iran's foreign policy and its relations with the West, as well as its Gulf neighbors.

Maysam Behravesh gains an insight from the mainstream constructivist theory of international relations to examine the Iranian geopolitical approach to the Syrian conflict and the problems it constitutes for its national security and international image. Dr. Behravesh analyzes Iran's involvement in the raging political ethnic and civil strife in Syria and how Iran has been an influential player in Syria ever since the outbreak of popular protests against the al-Assad government in March 2011, and particularly in the aftermath of a full-blown security crisis. In an explicit demonstration of a realpolitik-based foreign policy, Iran has made tremendous diplomatic, financial, logistical, and military efforts to retain the Baa'thist regime and prevent the loss of its sole state ally in the region. Seeking to shed light on the changing nature of the Syrian crisis, Bahravesh investigates the evolution of Iranian strategy toward the Arab Spring-induced revolt and offers a contextualized analysis of its geopolitical perils and problems for Tehran. He further explores the most viable scenarios the conflict may witness in the future. He concludes that unless Iran undertakes a proactive function in resolving the crisis—that is, by facilitating al-Assad's departure—it will have little, if any share in the unfolding redistribution of power in the new Middle East.

Dr. Sarah Tobin discovered from her field research in the Hashemite Kingdom that, unlike the Arab Awakening in Tunis, Egypt, and Libya, the protest in Jordan has experienced a series of alterations in governmental and legal enforcements. She explains the alterations in the series of protests in Jordan that ran into three phases: the first phase was the Arab Spring of 2011 in which there were multiple protests and agitations, which are widely understood as limited—or even unsuccessful—in their effect. The second phase includes the 2012 protests of Article 308 of the penal code, or the "Rape Law," which redefined the terms by which protests were held without governmental permissions, and established culture change for women as a viable aim for protest. The third phase was characterized by the most recent protests against the International Monetary Fund (IMF) enactment of reductions of subsidies on imported gas, in which residents with vested economic interest protested in larger numbers. She argues that these phases of protest and their changes in aims and mobilizations render protest in Jordan a protracted, discursive vehicle by which the "citizen" is actively being redefined.

What has become known as Islamic militancy and political Islam movements and whether this fits with Samuel Huntington's "clash of civilizations" is a subject debated by Dr. Kumar. He points out that these movements may be a violent prelude to the modernization of Islam, and a major step toward the integration of human civilization. He points to two factors: the global economic depression and global Islamic fundamentalism that, he believes, "are going to redefine human civilization in the same way that the Great Depression and the two World Wars redefined human civilization—by resulting in a unification of European countries that have been fighting each other for thousands of years." He further predicts that global Islamic militancy aspires for a temporary establishment of an Islamic empire in the Middle East and North Africa, with fundamentalist Islamic parties seizing power in democratic elections, as has happened in Egypt, Libya, and Yemen. It seems that these new ruling regimes will try to turn back the clock by imposing strict Islamic rules with the hope that in the end, this may lead to the formation of secular and democratic nations in the region that may follow the Turkish model.

Democracy and Islamist Violence: Lessons from Post-Mubarak Egypt

Jérôme Drevon

Abstract

This paper explores the contentious relations between the absence of democracy in the Middle East and the use of armed violence by Islamist groups in light of the Arab Spring. Its main objective is to decipher the evolving positions of former and current groups who used or promoted violence, and to relate them to broader academic debates on violence and democracy on the one hand, and de-radicalization on the other. This research demonstrates that the large majority of former Islamist militants in Egypt reject any violence in post-Mubarak Egypt even if they all have not renounced their religious legitimization of violence in the past. Second, it reveals that even if they maintain a religious opposition to democracy in Egypt, the opening of political opportunities and their progressive joining of the political process has favorably led most of them to accept democratic practices in reality. Third, it adds that the voice of those currently promoting violence in Egypt has been marginalized and that their main alternative has been the promotion of armed violence in Syria. Last, it nevertheless stresses two potential security threats unrelated to the opening of political opportunities in post-Mubarak Egypt and to the general debate on democracy and violence. First, local grievances in Sinai have led to violence in the past and are still to be dealt with. Second, the current political deadlock can potentially lead to localized and specific armed activities that could start a cycle of violence. This research is based on field research in Egypt and uses repeated interviews of leaders and members of the two main former militant groups, *al-Jam'ah al-Islamiy'ah* (the Islamic Group) and *Jama't al-Jihad* (the Jihad Group) as well as interviews with militants of the *Salafi jihadi* trends and their supporters in Cairo.

Introduction

Post-9/11 debates on the disputable correlation between the absence of democracy in the Middle East and the use of armed violence by Islamist groups were reignited after the Arab Spring. More than ten years ago, al-Qaeda's attacks on the United States were subsequently followed by the assertion that the undeniable source of violence lay in the prevalence of autocracy in the Arab world, and that reforming Middle Eastern regimes would eventually lead to the demise of armed militancy. The American president at that time, George W. Bush, famously favored this view and promoted a so-called freedom agenda that called for the liberalization and democratization of the region. In academic circles, congruent analyses similarly contended that violence in Middle Eastern countries stemmed from a mixture of repression and exclusion from the political process. Conversely, other academics and practitioners discarded the veracity of this claim and rather advocated for the consideration of other diverse factors unrelated to the political nature of Middle Eastern regimes to explain political violence, including, but not limited to the nature of Islam or religious cults, internal socioeconomic disruptions in these societies, and the impact of foreign policies of Western countries. The Arab Spring–a term that was coined in 2011 to describe the succession of protests and internal strife in the Middle East and North Africa–unsurprisingly resumed this debate and regenerated the previous divide. Presently, democratization supporters oppose the scepticism of the faction that posits the Arab Spring will reinforce the radicals and foster their opportunities to use violence.

This line of fracture has been reflected in the debates on al-Qaeda and its future in the region. Contrasting understandings of al-Qaeda—its nature, strategy, and popular appeal—led to profound differences between analysts. The divide emerges from distinctive interpretations of the impact of macro changes on the organization in different States. Some argue that the Arab Spring represented the symbolic demise of al-Qaeda and its ideas. These popular uprisings would have proven that al-Qaeda's strategy failed, and that non-violent resistance could yield more significant results in a shorter time. Besides, they argue that the uprisings paved the way for the political inclusion of moderate Islamist political parties that would eventually eradicate the appeal of the proponents of violence. On the other hand, other analysts advance that the Arab Spring reinforced the radicals—many of whom were freed from jail in Egypt, Libya, and Tunisia—gave them the freedom to organize themselves and recruit, and allowed them to create safe havens in several neighboring countries.

In this light, Egypt is a crucial case study that can inform the study of other countries in the region and enrich theoretical debates on democracy and Islamist violence. Egypt was indeed the birthplace of two of the most prominent Islamist armed groups, Jama't al-Jihad and al-Jama'ah al-Islamiy'ah; and Egyptian ideologues and military commanders have played a pivotal role in various other organizations and movements, including, most prominently, in al-Qaeda. Thereafter, the 2011 Egyptian revolution led to the peaceful removal of former president Hosni Mubarak, and the opening of new political opportunities for Islamist parties as well as the possibility to change state institutions by peaceful means. Former militants were freed, many of whom joined the political process. The previous justifications for armed violence against the state and its representatives apparently disappeared.

This paper intends to demonstrate that the large majority of former Islamist militants in Egypt reject any resort to violence after the 2011 uprising even if they have not renounced their previous ideas. Moreover, it endeavors to show that even if they still maintain the ideological commitments that they held in the past, the change of political opportunities in Egypt and their progressive joining of the political process has favorably led most of them to accept democratic practices in reality. Hence, this research adds that voices promoting violence have been marginalized in Egypt and that their only alternative has been the advocacy for jihad in Syria, which constitutes a potential security threat for the future. This research is based on field research in Egypt and uses repeated interviews with leaders and members of the two main former militant groups, al-Jama'ah al-Islamiy'ah and Jama't al-Jihad, as well as interviews with militants of the Salafi Jihadi movements and their supporters in Cairo.

Debates on Islamist Violence and Democracy

The academic debate on the disputable correlation between political violence and authoritarian regimes has been a persistent debate in the literature, and is by no means limited to studies of Islamist violence. The literature on civil wars, insurgency, political violence, social movements, and terrorism has long investigated the relationship between a combination of political exclusion at the macro level and varying patterns of repression. These studies have investigated different patterns of exclusion and repression based on a large array of factors, including ethnic, religious, and political. They have, moreover, covered broad geographical areas in Africa, the United States, Asia, and Europe and different types of regimes and repressions.[1] They have generally proven that even if violence is multifaceted and originates from various sources (multilayered ideational and material parameters are usually considered), authoritarian regimes themselves do galvanize the radicalization of individuals and groups, and resort to violent tactics and strategies.

Scholarly debates on Islamist violence have closely followed these discussions and produced similar claims. The main innovation championed by some studies pertains to the religious nature of violence that has often been allegedly considered exceptional to Islamist militancy.[2] Academics have therefore promoted two different sets of claims. The first contention relates to the fundamental impact of state domestic policies toward political opposition groups and Islamist movements specifically. Sympathetic scholars stress the primary role played by a combination of political exclusion and repression on Islamist groups. Hafez (2003), Burgat (2003), and Burgat and Dowell (1993), for example, endorse the hypotheses that the use of violence by Islamist armed groups in Algeria and Egypt was an outcome of these policies. Similar studies of the radicalization of individuals and ideologues in Middle Eastern countries favored congruent views.[3] Alternatively, the presupposed apocalyptic and distinct nature of Islamist violence, Western foreign policies, and other domestic factors disconnected from exclusion and repression have been assertively proclaimed to be the primary causes of Islamist violence.[4] These discussions comprise the fourth wave of terrorism debate (Rapoport, 2004), the new terrorism thesis (Morgan, 2004; Tucker, 2001), the impact of Western foreign policies, and domestic-centred approaches. This debate has been significant and vital after the Arab Spring and ought not be considered to be restricted to a handful of conscientious scholars, and merely theoretical in nature. The future of unfolding developments in the Middle East and the future of Islamist violence are directly entrenched in this question. If violence is a mere reaction to authoritarianism, then it will eventually fade away. On the other hand, if violence emanates from other material or ideational parameters, the collapse of old regimes will implausibly cause its disappearance.

The Arab Spring and its aftermath have been logically marked by this question, as reflected by the vigorous debates on the future of the al-Qaeda organization. The central contention springs from two pivotal factors: first, the disappearance of high-level figures of the organization, primarily marked by the assassination of Osama bin Laden on May 2, 2011; and second, by the succession of upheavals in the Middle East and North Africa that led to civil wars in some cases, and relative change of political authority in others. The previous divide among analysts is similarly reflected on this issue. The disappearance of bin Laden would have arguably represented the end of an era symbolized by the Saudi's charismatic, real or symbolic leadership of the jihadi movement worldwide. The vanishing of the rather unchallenged leader would have led to the organization in a state of disarray, led by a contested figure, Ayman al-Zawahiri, who supposedly lacks the consensual character of his predecessor. Adding insult to injury, the Arab Spring would have simultaneously represented the failure of al-Qaeda's strategy of armed confrontation with the West and Arab regimes, and demonstrated that peaceful resistance could achieve more than the organization could have ever hoped. Meanwhile, others contrastingly argue that the death of Osama bin Laden would not be as considerable as assumed, considering that the Saudi leader had been in hiding for years and was allegedly disconnected from any direct organizational role in al-Qaeda's franchized groups. Besides, the Arab Spring would not symbolize the demise of al-Qaeda and its ideas, but rather, would present the organization an unprecedented array of opportunities in many countries. First, al-Qaeda would benefit from a favorable conjuncture in countries such as Tunisia and Egypt whose leadership was mostly peacefully removed from power. The opening of the political field, the liberation of Islamist militants and the diminishing pressure from the security services would help the organization promote its ideas and proselytize its cause. Second, the organization would also prosper where peaceful uprisings failed, and lead to the militarization of oppositional factions. In that regard, Syria would supposedly play a significant role. The advent of strong self-defined salafi jihadi armed groups such as *Jabhat al-Nusrah* and *Ahrar al-Sham* would indeed be essential to the re-legitimization of al-Qaeda's sponsored paradigm of armed violence. Al-Qaeda's future prospects are therefore intertwined with the potential correlation between democracy and violence in the Middle East. It is consequently crucial to decipher the general implications of the Arab spring in the region.

The 2011 Uprising

On January 25, 2011, a popular uprising ignited 18 days of mostly peaceful demonstrations and strikes that led to the abdication of former Egyptian president Hosni Mubarak. Coined the "Revolution of January 25," this non-violent opposition to the Egyptian leadership was inspired by similar protests in Tunisia and built on genuine domestic grievances. These demonstrations aggregated diverse components of Egyptian society, from various religious sensibilities, to various socioeconomic status and level of education. The position of different political and social movements *vis-à-vis* the revolution has nevertheless been a contentious issue until now.

The role of Islamist actors more specifically has been constantly questioned and debated since then. Many opponents of the Islamic trend have indeed accused Islamist movements, preachers, and leaders of opposing the revolution from its inception. Broadly defined, Islamists would have, according to this view, deemed popular demonstrations against the leader un-Islamic and reprehensible. Using the concept of *khuruj 'ala al-hakim* (rebellion against the Muslim ruler), they would have strongly opposed any resistance to the Egyptian leadership, while benefiting from the opening of political opportunities shortly after its removal. This argument, nevertheless only partially holds true, and does not comprehensively account for the position of all the components of the Islamic trend. It further conceals the justifications, real or questionable, of the position of some of them.

Rather than dwelling upon the position and subsequent evolution of non-violent Islamist actors, the following focuses on the position of former and current militant groups and figures. In that regard, any study of their viewpoint has to be preceded with a brief recontextualization of the years that led to the revolution. It has to decipher their ideological positions, their organizational structure, and consider any potential point of rupture from their past.

First, al-Jama'ah al-Islamiyya was in organizational and intellectual disarray before the revolution. The group was fractured along several lines: geographical, ideological, and organizational. Its members were dispersed across Egypt, in various jails and even overseas (N. Ibrahim, personal communication, September 10, 2012; A. Hamad, personal communication, September 6, 2012). After the completion of the ideological revisions whereby the leadership of the movement wrote extensive publications renouncing former Islamic justifications of violence, the Egyptian State began to ease the pressure on the group, and freed thousands of its members after 2006. Prior to the revolution, several individual leading members, including Karam Zuhdi and Najih Ibrahim, were no longer incarcerated, while others, including Abud and Tareq al-Zumur were still in jail. At the time, prominent and secondary members of the Islamic Group could also be found abroad in different countries and settings, from political refugees in Europe to the tribal belt along the Afghanistan–Pakistan border.[5] However, this geographical fracture was not the only dividing trend inside this movement.

The movement was also divided ideologically between an accommodating position and a more hostile approach toward the Egyptian regime (A. Hamad, personal communication, September 6, 2012). In 2011, this division was reflected in the perceived legitimacy of the January uprising. Prior to the revolution, all the members and leaders of the Islamic Group did not genuinely accept all the aspects of the ideological revisions (A. Hamad, personal communication, September 6, 2012). For instance, the current mufti of the group, Abd al-Akhr Hamad, argues that he refused many religious arguments asserted in the revisions and continued to oppose Hosni Mubarak and the legitimacy of his regime before the revolution.[6] Yet, he insists that his opposition to the ideological revisions did not make him an advocate of violence and that he strongly opposed the use of force in Egypt (A. Hamad, personal communication, September 6, 2012). Other members and leaders of the Islamic Group confirmed the same premise. They argued that the position towards the Egyptian regime by the two champions of the revisions, Karam Zuhdi and Najih Ibrahim, was opposed by many members of the Islamic Group (A. Hamad, personal communication, September 6, 2012). Despite their consensus on the legitimacy of the ceasefire, many members indeed believed that the two leaders of the group went too far in proclaiming that Hosni Mubarak was a Muslim leader and that his regime should be accommodated. These divisions were reflected during the 2011 revolution. The two previously mentioned historical leaders of the Islamic Group did not express public support for the popular uprising (N. Ibrahim, personal communication, September 10, 2012), while individual members of the group joined the demonstrations as individuals. In the meantime, Abud and Tareq al-Zumur openly encouraged the protest from their cells, which resulted in consensus on the legitimacy of organizing popular mass protests at that time.

On the other hand, the Jihad Group was in limbo and disarray and could not therefore adopt an official public position on the uprising. The group was divided geographically, organizationally, and ideologically. Organizationally, this group had never been formerly structured, either in Egypt or in abroad even before the revolution. It had remained a conglomeration of cells loosely united around a common belief that the regime in Egypt had to be toppled through a military coup and replaced by an

Islamic state (A. Amir al-Jaysh, personal communication, June 8, 30, July 7, September 4, 2012; K. Habib, personal communication, July 30, 2012; O. Qassem, personal communication, July 1, 2012). High ranking figures were scattered in Egypt and abroad and were isolated from one another. Osama Qassem, often considered among the most important religious scholars of the group, confirmed that when he was in jail, he had no contacts with other cells outside and that no common decision could be made. He further affirmed that other high ranking members in jail were also divided and did not agree on tactical and strategic objectives (O. Qassem, personal communication, July 1, 2012). What is more, in 2006, the ideological revisions led by a former leader of the group, Sayyid Imam, did not–according to most accounts[7]–result from consensual discussions among members of the Jihad Group, but were imposed by the security services and therefore, the Jihad Group could not adopt a unified common position on the 2011 uprising. Some members and high ranking figures participated as individuals, while others adopted a more passive stance—fearing a possible backfire in case of a failure of the uprising to yield any result.[8]

The Post-Revolution

The post-revolution era witnessed several developments whose outcome yielded important theoretical lessons for the academic debate on Islamist political violence in authoritarian regimes as well as for the future of Egypt. First, thousands of Islamist prisoners were released by the military authorities–the Supreme Council of Armed Forces (SCAF)–and then by President Mohammed Morsi. They included foot soldiers, mid-ranking and leaders of the Islamic Group, the Jihad Group and unaffiliated individuals. In addition, other militants were freed during the revolution when some prisons were stormed by unidentified individuals. Second, the Islamic Group and the Jihad Group joined, at different levels, the political process and created political parties. The former officially created the *Hizb al-Bina' wal-Tanmiy-'a* (Construction and Development Party) while individual members of the latter united around *Hizb al-Salama wal-Tanmiy'a* (Safety and Development Party). Third, a self-proclaimed salafi jihadi trend appeared in Egypt, composed of former Jihad Group members and youth unaffiliated with militant groups in the past. They have organized public demonstrations and opposed the democratic process that followed the removal of Hosni Mubarak. Fourth, Islamist-led violence rapidly developed in the Sinai Peninsula. Military patrols, as well as police stations, and the oil pipelines from Egypt to Israel were attacked many times by unspecified militants. Last, the Syrian civil war has been used by several groups of individuals to mobilize young sympathizers and send some of them to fight in Syria. These five factors are to be examined in detail here.

First, the most symbolic decision of the military authorities was the liberation of thousands of Islamist prisoners, including the historical figures of former Egyptian militant groups. The group of prisoners released included members from different organizations; groups that were arrested a few years before the revolution because of their sympathy with al-Qaeda and the salafi jihadi movement in general; high ranking leaders of militant groups involved in the 1981 assassination of former President Anwar al-Sadat in 1981; and others who have been in jail for nearly 30 years. Among the latter were the cousins Abud and Tareq al-Zumur[9] who were freed on March 2011. Also included were other emblematic figures of the Islamic Group and the Jihad Group, such as Mohammed al-Zawahiri,[10] Sayyid Imam,[11] Rifai Taha and Hamzah.[12] Immediately after the revolution, the cases of several prisoners were still pending in the judgements on the returnees from Albania and Afghanistan, but all were finally cleared of the charges against them.

The opening of political opportunities then led to intense discussions inside the Islamic and Jihad groups and yielded conflicting outcomes for both groups. First, the Islamic Group reconstituted its internal structure and re-organized fully. Internal elections were held at the local level, and a new leadership was elected (A. Hamad, personal communication, September 6, 2012). Then, the general assembly of the movement decided to join the political process and created the political party, Hizb al-Bina' wal-Tanmiyah (Construction and Development Party). All members of the movement consensually accepted this decision and recognized the legitimacy of the democratic opening in Egypt (N. Ibrahim, personal communication, September 10, 2012, A. Hamad, personal communication, September 6, 2012). On the other hand, the Jihad Group remained divided and failed to reach a general consensus on a *modus operandi* to adopt after the removal of Hosni Mubarak. Individual members created a new political platform, the Hizb al-Salamah wal-Tanmiyah (Safety and Development Party), that has so far failed to be recognized as a political party by the State. (A. Faraj, personal communication, June 11, July 1, 2012, K. Habib, personal communication, July 30, 2012, O. Qassem, personal communication, July 1, 2012). The party was initially led by a former leader of an Islamist cell in the 1970s, Kamal Habib, before his resignation in 2012. The group has failed to either attract all the members of the Jihad Group or to reach a consensus on a political program (K. Habib, personal communication, July 30, 2012).

In defiance of these choices, some of the dissidents of the Jihad Group who refused the legitimacy of the democratic process created their own platform and officially established the salafi jihadi movement in Egypt. They denounced the creation of political parties by Islamist groups and their participation in the elections, and claimed that democracy could be accommodated even under the objective of implementing Islamic Law in Egypt. Despite their exaggerated place in the media and on the Internet, they only represent a small faction among former jihadis and marginal figures who did not have a prominent place in militant groups. Their leaders, represented by Ahmad Ashush, Mohammad al-Zawahiri, Marjan Salem, Adel Shahto and Muhammad Higazi, represent a limited number of individuals. They have managed to amass around them hundreds of young individual sympathizers of the salafi jihadi persuasion previously unaffiliated with jihadi groups.[13] Regardless of their uncompromising refusal of the democratic process, however, they have not called for the use of violence in Egypt, but rather focused on ideological proselytization.[14]

Fourth, the most precarious and pressing security issue in post-Mubarak Egypt has been associated with the security vacuum in the Sinai Peninsula. Historically, conflicting relations with the state, combined with the grievances of the local Bedouin population and a strengthening of local groups' progressive connection to militant groups in the Gaza Strip have led to an increasingly unstable situation. Unknown militant groups attacked various symbols of the Egyptian State and, in an unprecedented development, an Egyptian military base, leading to the death of 16 Egyptian soldiers in August 2012. The subsequent outrage and the renewed warning of the international community then led to a stronger involvement of Egypt in this issue. More generally and despite the potential risks for the future, violence in the Sinai Peninsula remains, for the most part, a local issue with its own internal dynamics (Pelham and Royal Institute of International Affairs 2012). It represents a security risk that is locally contained.

Finally, the Syrian conflict that started in 2011 has affected Egypt as well, and has been used by radicals to promote their agendas and mobilize fighters. The first reactions were mostly centered on the Syrian opposition and consisted of small demonstration by dozens of supporters of the Syrian opposition in downtown Cairo, near the headquarters of the Arab League. Thereafter, salafi social and political movements joined them and expressed their support of the Syrian uprising. They ranged from public figures, politicians, and preachers, to salafi jihadi sympathizers. They organized demonstrations next to the Syrian embassy in Cairo, including a sit-in, and, later, against the Russian and Iranian diplomatic representations.[15] In the meantime, with the help of individuals in Egypt, the increasing attention to the mostly unaffiliated Egyptian youths being mobilized and sent to Syria. Depending on the networks of the latter, they joined other larger groups, from Free Syrian Army (FSA) affiliated armed groups to salafi jihadi groups such as *Jabhat al-Nusrah*.[16]

Theoretical and Empirical Implications for Egypt and the Region

Two years after the 2011 uprising, Egypt offers a timely opportunity for academics and practitioners to review the importance and role of ideology in the use of violence by Islamist actors and to comprehend the local as well as the broader and more generalizable lessons of regime change. In this regard, the post-revolution era offers three generalizable lessons in this topic area, with one specific to Egypt. The three generalizable lessons pertain to the previously discussed alleged correlation between ideology, democracy, and violence.

First, field research in Egypt and extensive interviews of leaders and militants has established that the ideologies of these groups are enduring and stable. All leaders and members of the Islamic Group and the Jihad Group have not comprehensively rejected the principles they adopted in the past, even if they deplore sporadic instances where violence has been used excessively. Nevertheless, their current practices and approaches to jihad and politics prove that their interpretations of these principles and their translation in reality have notably changed and revealed an undeniable pragmatism.

Second, ideologies of violence still remain in Egypt and are promoted primarily by the so-called salafi jihadi movement. This new emerging campaign after the revolution has promoted its principles (including violence) based on its opposition to secular states deemed oppressive and un-Islamic. Yet, paradoxically, its leaders have not favored the use of violence under the current conditions and have preferred peaceful proselytization.

Third, for the past few years, Syria has represented the central hub for young partisans of armed violence in Egypt. The extreme violence of the Syrian conflict, the wide regional and national sympathy for the opposition, and the absence of alternatives supported the case of armed militancy in Syria. Many youths were mobilized in support of the uprising, and some fled there to join the military opposition to the regime.

Finally, post-Mubarak Egypt also offers one additional lesson: even if the overwhelming majority of former Egyptian militants involved in armed violence against the former regime reject the use of armed violence now, this rejection does not mean that violence cannot return if the current deadlock persists and if the opposition between the government and its opponents deteriorates further—as demonstrated by the proliferation of violent attacks between the supporters of both sides in the past few months.

To begin with, interviews with members, commanders, and leaders of the Jihad Group and the Islamic Group have revealed that many of them continue to hold onto most ideas that they fought for in the past and have not genuinely renounced them. The opening of political opportunities and the abatement of pressure from the security services on former Egyptian militants offers the first real chance to review the true impact of the ideological revisions of the two groups and assess their reliability and accuracy. Hence, while most members acknowledge and reject some excesses of their own use of violence in the past, they maintain that violence was "Islamically" acceptable and legitimate under the former regime. They still believe that Hosni Mubarak was an oppressive leader whose rule was unjust and un-Islamic, and most argue that he could not legitimately be considered a Muslim.[17] According to the most prominent religious leader of the Islamic Group, Abd al-Akhr Hamad, and Osama Qassem of the Jihad Group, the use of violence in Islam against a leader who does not apply Islamic law and has no intentions of doing so is legitimate in theory (A. Hamad, personal communication, September 6, 2012; O. Qassem, personal communication, July 1, 2012). Second, both groups further support a comprehensive application of Islamic law in Egypt and strongly reject the principle of democracy, arguing that sovereignty in an Islamic state belongs to God and not to the people. Their respective political program emphasizes this demand, and both see political participation as the main path toward an Islamic state in Egypt (A. Hamad, personal communication, September 6, 2012; O. Qassem, personal communication, July 1, 2012).

Their ideological consistency ought not to conceal the manifest flexibility of the translation of these ideas into these groups' practices. The survival of their long-term ideological commitments to jihad and democracy has not made their political positions immune from the pragmatism that stems from political participation. The comparative analysis of the Islamic Group and the Jihad Group reveals that a party that is supported by a strong and legitimate leadership is certainly amenable to the adoption of moderate choices as a political party. Hence, while the Jihad Group never managed to adopt a clear political platform and witnessed ideological divergences in its leadership when its first Secretary General Kamal Habib resigned (K. Habib, personal communication, July 30, 2012), the Islamic Group not only federated all its members in a political party, but also adopted several positions that were, *a priori,* opposed to its ideological views. For example, its political wing refused to support the candidacy of Hazem Abu Ismail in 2012 during the presidential elections–this is a candidate who openly rallied his supporters around the idea that he would apply Islamic law in Egypt–and preferred the more moderate Abul Futuh. Its leaders affirmed at the time that their analysis of the political situation in Egypt confirmed the need for a candidate of consensus that would not further divide the country (A. Hamad, personal communication, September 6, 2012). The impact of these discrepancies between ideology and political practice has yet to be further evaluated.

This important lesson for policymakers and academics has major implications for the possible exclusion of political parties based on platforms opposed to democracy and more generally, on the debate regarding the so-called "radicalization" of radical Islamist movements. First, the experience of the Islamic Group shows that a political party based on a religious program which excludes any acceptance of democracy can acquiesce in practice with political practices required by democratic systems and potentially include them in its political program in time. This would tend to denote that political movements which openly reject democracy should not be excluded from political participation. Rather, their participation around a unified leadership should be encouraged. Second, this example proves that the academic debates on de-radicalization that have mushroomed for the past few years have to be re-evaluated and reconsidered. The cases of these two Egyptian groups revealed that these groups have not comprehensively renounced their former ideologies, but rather, have only marginally criticized some specific points. A strict focus on ideological reorientation therefore seems ineffective and unfruitful, contrary to the promotion of political participation. The latter indeed appears to be more likely to have more reliable and long lasting consequences on these groups. Thus, the distinctive evolution of their political practice is not contingent upon the pressure of the security services or the provision of external rewards, and more likely to be internalized by these groups.

Second, the revised viewpoints of the large majority of members and former members of the Islamic Group and the Jihad Group shall not eclipse the existence of ideologies prone to violence in Egypt. The main proponent of these ideologies, the emerging and still loosely defined salafi jihadi, is resolute in its staunch opposition to any political process based on democratic elections, and commands jihad as an armed struggle in domestic and foreign contexts. Nevertheless, two additional elements tend to endorse the adoption of a cautious approach to the actual menace posed by this trend. First, their inflated presence on the Internet and in the writings of Western pundits should not misrepresent their real importance. The salafi jihadi movement is only constituted by dozens of activists formally associated with the Jihad Groups, and most of their young followers have not been involved in militancy in the past. They are mere sympathizers socialized by online publications, and their level of genuine commitment to violence is still to be evaluated.[18] Second, their theoretical ideological commitments are not sufficient to understand their positions in practice in Egypt. An ideological lens based exclusively on theological arguments is not adequate to illustrate their current opposition to violence in Egypt and the underlying reasons. Discussions with their sympathizers and members rather disclose that they do not consider violence legitimate as long as preaching is possible, and believe that violence can be used only as a reaction to State policies perceived as oppressive. Moreover, they argue that the conflict in Syria and the broad legitimacy enjoyed by armed opposition to the Syrian regime facilitates the promotion of violence abroad.[19]

Third, the most pressing issue in Egypt and the region pertains to the on-going armed conflict in Syria and its possible implications in the future. The perceived legitimacy of armed violence against the Syrian regime has eased the mobilization of Egyptian youths in Egypt, and instead facilitated the transfer of an undetermined number of them to northern Syria. A year-long field research with some of them has demonstrated that most were disconnected from militant groups in Egypt, but only progressively became acquainted with their ideas and subsequently with the jihadi trend. Their adoption of salafi jihadi ideas progressively accompanied their involvement with the Syrian conflict. Thereafter, individuals and groups of friends used local contacts supported by regional networks to arrange their travels to Turkey and Syria in order to join armed groups–affiliated or not–with the FSA.[20] This process is, to some extent, similar to the participation of thousands of Muslim fighters in the war against the Soviets in Afghanistan in the 1980s. The lessons of the 1990s have to be assimilated to prevent a similar outcome. At that time, the praise for Muslim fighters that prevailed until 1992 switched to strong condemnations and to their denunciation as renegades and terrorists who threatened the national security of Arab regimes. In many cases, the fighters who went to Afghanistan explained that the impossibility of going back to their home country after the withdrawal of the Russian forces and the pressure of the security services on them instigated their adhesion to a militant group that could provide them with an alternative.[21] Consequently, Arab regimes, including Egypt, should strive to reincorporate most Arab fighters who are presently in Syria and dismiss a sole focus on a military solution when they return.

Finally, the security situation in Egypt is still potentially precarious. The previous argument on armed violence in Egypt and its rejection by the large majority of Islamist actors does not mean that violence cannot erupt again if the current deadlock remains. Former members of the Jihad Group indeed acknowledge that even if they currently reject violence, the increasing proliferation of armed attacks by government and opposition supporters raises the idea among some of them that they could use violence against the opposition if they later decided to remove President Morsi from power.[22] They are not currently preparing themselves, but a prolonged stalemate, accompanied with armed provocations from both sides could encourage this idea and kindle a more violent conflict.

Notes

1. The present study does not intend to cover this literature exhaustively. Interested readers can refer to the literature covered in Bjørgo, 2005; Lia and Skjolberg, 2004; Schmid, 2011.
2. The following studies stress for instance the particular role played by religion in violent conflicts (Hoffman, 1995; Juergensmeyer, 2003, 2008; Selengut, 2003; Stern, 2004).
3. See for instance various studies of the radicalisation of the Islamist intellectual Sayyid Qutb as a result of torture in Egyptian prisons (for example in Calvert, 2010).
4. Cf. notes 2 and 3.
5. For example, the second son of Sheikh Omar Abd al-Rahman, the incarcerated leader of the Islamic Group in a U.S. prison, Ahmad, was killed by an American drone in November 2011. According to his brother Muhammad (personal communication, August 31, 2012), Ahmad was at that time fighting alongside the Taliban Pakistan.
6. Some of his arguments are detailed in his text Muraja'at hawl al-muraja'at available at http://www.tawhed.ws/r?i=8ja7dzs2.
7. Interview with various members of the Jihad Group including those previously quoted.
8. Interview with various members of the Jihad Group including those previously quoted.
9. Both played a central role in the assassination of Anwar al-Sadat in 1981 and were the most symbolic prisoners in detention before the revolution.
10. He is the brother of Ayman al-Zawahiri, the current leader of al-Qaeda. In the past, he only had a secondary role in the Jihad Group, according to its members.
11. He was the leader of the Jihad Group from the late 1980s to the beginning of the 1990s.
12. Both were the successive leaders of the military wing of the Islamic Group. Later Rifai Tahah was also the head of the Islamic Group abroad.
13. According to the author's field work with young Salafi Jihadi sympathisers in Cairo.
14. According to the author's field work with young Salafi Jihadi sympathisers in Cairo.
15. According to the author's field work.
16. According to this author's fieldwork.
17. Personal communication with members of the Islamic Group.
18. According to this author's fieldwork.
19. According to this author's fieldwork.
20. According to this author's fieldwork.
21. Personal communication with members of the Islamic Group.
22. Personal communication with members of the Jihad Group.

In Between the Glorious Past and Wounded Self-Image: What does Turkey Have to Offer for the Middle East?

Bahar Senem Çevik

Abstract

The Middle East is currently going through a transition period that will not only determine the new identity of the Middle East, but also the future of a more democratic and politically stable region. Regardless of the present identity conflict, Turkey poses as one of the most influential attractive powers in the changing Middle East. This paper will borrow a social psychology and psychoanalytic framework to discuss the fundamentals behind the Turkish inspiration–the socio-political effects of the Arab Awakening in relation to the Turkish identity which is misplaced between the glorious past and wounded self-image. The paper also argues the necessity of a new political language with the Middle East that Turkey can use to offer and construct new channels for dialogue.

Introduction

Turkey, the only secular democracy with a predominantly Muslim population in the Middle East, has gone through a distinctive quest for identity in the last century. The fall of the glorious Ottoman Empire, foreign occupation, the Greek–Turkish War, and the establishment of the republic are all identity markers in the collective Turkish mind creating psychological wounds to the self. The new Turkish identity distanced itself from the Ottoman identity emphasizing secularism, equal rights for all citizens, and democracy. To create the modern Turkish identity, all symbols relating to the Ottoman Empire were abandoned. More importantly, any reminder of the trauma pertaining to the loss of the empire was denied. Contrary to the Ottoman identity which was perceived as backwards, Oriental, and religious, the modern Turkish identity has been constructed as Western, modern, and secular. It was as if modern day Turks existed only within the Turkish republic, with no recollection of the past. Hence, there was an immense split in the Turkish identity in refusing to acknowledge the Ottoman inheritance.

Despite the shared history, culture, and religion, Turkish modernization, secularism, and the abolishment of the caliphate caused a rupture between Turkey and the Arab world. The long lost ties between Turkey and the Middle East have just been reestablished with the efforts of the Justice and Development Party (*Adalet ve Kalkınma Partisi*—AKP). The Islamic and conservative roots of the AKP enabled the initiation of a communication process with the Middle East. More importantly, as a trusted neutral state, Turkey has been an actor that could bring parties in conflict to the same table. The moderate tone and success of the AKP in establishing a stable economic growth, jobs, and opportunities, not only for the elites, but also for those perceived former victims oppressed by the system impacted the Arab perceptions of the AKP. Turkish Prime Minister Erdoğan's personal apprehension of the Israeli–Palestinian conflict and the Gaza Strip also won the hearts and minds of the Arab streets as they witnessed that their own governments' hands were rather tied. Owing to the economic growth, political, social, and economic ties with the European Union (EU) and most importantly, being a Muslim democracy, Turkey influenced the Middle East in cultural, economic, and political terms.

Although many argue that Turkey has become a role model for the Arab Middle East, this is not the case. Turkey can be described as an inspiration for the Arab Middle East, where similarly for a long time, the EU has been an inspiration for Turkey. Turkey, standing as a secular democracy with conservative values still stands as the foremost inspiration throughout the Arab Awakening and will continue to be, as long as the AKP continues improving democracy. Thus, it is not only a Turkey that is changing the Arab Middle East, but a Turkey that will need to provide a more open society in order to continue being an inspiration.

One key factor in sustaining the current Turkish communication with the Arab Middle East is to recognize the traumas and collective memory of the Arab communities. The re-established ties with the Middle East are still undeveloped. For that reason, any perceived threats to the boundaries of the Arab identity, such as aggressive political rhetoric, can hinder the ties and amplify nationalist sentiments. During the Arab Awakening, Turkey has had the opportunity to restore her self-image by reconnecting with her past. Turkey's tarnished self-image and humiliation concerning the loss of glory was recently substituted with self-confidence as the Arab Middle East professed admiration for Turkey. However, the new found Turkish confidence has been showing signs of an assertive political rhetoric which is aggravating societal expectations.

Before elaborating on the socio-political implications of the modern Turkish identity and its relation to the new developments in the Middle East, a short discussion on psychological identity of the individual and the group is necessary.

A Theoretical Framework

Large groups, such as nations and ethnic groups are formed by the collective of individuals sharing common goals and traits. The psychosocial identities of individuals constituting large groups begin at birth, taking shape during infancy through the interaction between the infant and the primer caregiver; then becoming permanent at adolescence. As the child develops an individual identity, his or her large-group identity is also constructed by the influence of external objects such as primary care givers, parents, and family. Large-group identity becomes more meaningful in the developmental stage, during adolescence and becomes an indispensable part of identity by creating a sense of belonging. On an individual level, the child learns that projecting his/her negative feelings onto those he/she likes or knows is unacceptable, and therefore projects aggression to external objects or others which is often directed by the adults in the social environment. External objects are mostly stable, and permanent, and also are shared by the other people in the same large-group. These types of external objects can also be identified as "suitable targets" (Volkan, 1994). These feelings and behavior are then reflected to the outside as primitive defense mechanisms such as externalization and projection (Freud, 1993). This is a process in which a crucial element of identity development takes place by constructing an outside "other," in which one can project all the negative feelings and attributes. The enemy serves as a reservoir that can deposit good and bad attribution of either the self or the others. Creating the "other" is linked with the perceived self-image. It is unbearable for an infant or individual to think that they have unwanted (bad) parts. Therefore, individuals and societies that demonstrate similar psychological behavior not only externalize and project bad parts, but also socially compare themselves to others.

The linkage between individual and group dynamics is seen in shared rituals and symbols of identity which emphasize a group's distinctiveness (Ross, 2000). A group can be described as "a collection of individuals who perceive themselves as members of the same social category, share same emotional involvement in this common definition of themselves, and achieve some degree of social consensus about the evaluation of their group and of their membership in it" (Tajfel & Turner, 2004, p. 283). All societies are formed by their individual members and thus carry the psychology of these individuals to a level of group consciousness. Freud (1949) describes the individual as a component of the identified groups. In this sense, group psychology is the oldest human psychology, given that people are socialized within certain groups. He further argues that individuals and societies demonstrate parallel behavior, where individuals in a group are more likely to approve things or behavior that they normally would not. On group belonging, Alford (1994) states that the sense of belonging is similar to the stage of life when there is a bond between the mother and the child. Tajfel and Turner (2004) suggest that there are several motivations for group belonging which can be categorized as individual need for self-esteem; associating positive or negative connotations to social groups; categories and memberships; and finally evaluation of one's own group. Tajfel and Turner's argument proposes that individuals strive for group belonging that will enhance their self-esteem. In a psychoanalytical sense, individuals' need to attach to a group demonstrates itself under what Volkan (1997, p. 27) calls "large group identity."

Although each individual is different, each brings together a certain group behavior that can be described as large-group. Large-groups are described as a large number of people sharing specific particular emotional and intellectual attitudes that differentiate them from different groups (Volkan, 2006). Individual behavior also influences group behavior. When an individual identifies with a group, he/she is most likely to behave or feel differently. For instance, people tend to follow the attitudes of the majority to reassure themselves that they are included in a group. Although individuals belonging to the large-group generally never meet each other, they are still bound by "sameness" (Volkan, 2004). It can be suggested that large-groups are alive and have a level of collective consciousness that is constructed and carried on from one generation to another. Based on these definitions, ethnic, national or religious groups may be categorized as large-groups. Large-group identities invest in specific habits, attitudes, prejudices, customs, traditions and values. While these attributes are perceived as being positive, customs, traditions and values of other or unknown groups may be perceived as being inferior or negative. Hence, Volkan describes the seven threads of large-group identities as follows: shared reservoirs for images associated with positive emotion; shared good identifications; absorption of others' bad qualities; absorption of leaders' internal worlds; chosen glories; chosen traumas; and formation of symbols that develop their own autonomy (Volkan, 2004). These qualities of the large-group altogether shape how we perceive the "other" and how the "other" perceives us, as perceptions are developed through how we define ourselves and our large-group. As the symbolic features of group identity pass on from one generation to another, leaders may interfere with how the large-group perceives the outer world. During times of crises, economic recession or mass humiliation, the group can regress and leaders of large-groups can mobilize individuals to scapegoat or even attack those who are perceived and presented as "others" (Volkan, 2006). Similar to individuals, large-groups also try to maintain or repair the identity through rituals. It is necessary to point out that, unlike crowds or masses, large-groups share a common history or collective memory that is shaped by historical events. Large-groups have a specific characteristic. In this sense, historical glories, traumas and humiliations define the present day psychology and collective identity of such large-groups. It is also important to note that the large-group identity is a present reflection of collective historical memory, and that this collective memory is generated from facts as well as emotions rooting from societal perceptions. In this sense, the individual psychological need for the other is also present in the collective mind.

What Mack (1990) calls "the enemy system," is a state developed and sustained in the mind. Mack suggests that group cohesion is maintained through the real or constructed enemy, the "other." Thus, the "other" is extremely important for construction, sustainability and cohesion of large-groups such as nations and ethnic identities. A large-group defines itself in the mirror image of the "other." Every nation or large-group is engaged in a struggle to sustain its identity markers. Thus, a way to achieve group cohesiveness is creating the "other" alongside developing a common purpose closely knit to this "other" (Stein, 1990; Moses, 1996). Alford (1994) asserts that excluding, insulting, humiliating, ignoring or criticizing an outside group enhances group cohesion. Good parts of the self and object images can also be externalized into a suitable target which is shared by the members of the large groups, for instance, swine serve as a reservoir for the bad self aspects of Muslims; or David's Star serves as a reservoir for the good self aspects of Jews. In terms of international relations, any criticism from an external source serves as a cohesive agent to hold onto the identity. In this manner, these suitable targets are utilized to form an enemy or ally which would become a shared part of the individual or large-group identity (Volkan, 1988). During times of crises and stress, individuals or members of large-groups can also tend to reactivate this process through externalization of good and bad aspects of self so that the members of the large group can create a devaluated or feared enemy, or an idealized ally.

It can be argued that as the collective mind has a certain psychology, nations also sometimes act on an irrational psychological basis at times of crisis. Therefore the psychology of international relations is interconnected to the individual and group psychological motivations. The linkage between the Turkish collective psyche and the recent developments in the Middle East will be further elaborated in the following sections.

Constructing the Modern Turkish Identity: A Historical Split

Turkey, the natural heir of the Ottoman Empire, was established in the aftermath of the First World War, having endured various collective traumas such as loss of empire, human resources, dignity and independence. Following a difficult course of struggle for independence, the people of the once glorious Ottoman Empire founded the Turkish Republic based on pillars almost the opposite of what it was before. Unlike the previous system, the modern republic had three major pillars: modernity, secularism and democracy which initiated the creation of a new identity. In contrast to the Ottoman Empire, the rulers of the modern republic adopted secular nationalism with the removal of political and public visibility of Islam in order to create a modern state with its institutions (Ahmad, 2008). During the course of establishing the state, the new Turkish identity disregarded and devalued almost everything that was linked to the old, rusty Ottoman identity. Owing to the need to establish a new identity and forego historical grievances of the large-group, Turkish society stripped itself of most symbols which echoed the past as if it were an adolescent trying to find a new identity, something different from that of its parents. One of the most distinctive purification processes took place in language, when Arabic and Persian were eliminated from school curriculums–words of these origins were replaced by purely Turkish ones–and the Latin alphabet was introduced as a means to create a new identity. While Shaw and Kural-Shaw (1977) argue that this linguistic nationalism cut young Turks off from their Ottoman heritage, Volkan (2004) describes this process as psychological purification. The author argues that:

> ...a large-group will cast off certain elements-symbols, ideologies, leaders, even subgroups or neighbors-that no longer seem useful or appropriate, or that seem to impede or threaten the growth and revitalization of identity. Such purification rituals, some of which begin to emerge while the group is still engaged in war or war-like conditions, represent attempts to modify or recreate identity, to increase cohesion, and to foster a sense of sameness among members that is more durable, relevant and effective. (p.108)

The reasoning behind the efforts of purification can be traced back to the psychology of mass humiliation. Humiliation is an unbearably massive blow to the self-esteem or self-perception of an individual as well as a large-group. Any humiliating incidents to those identities with an exaggerated self-image, such as the effect of capitulations which provided privileges to Western powers are likely to be more wounded. It can be argued that even the establishment of modern Turkey by Ataturk, a charismatic and visionary leader, could not fully undo the humiliation resulting from the fall of the Ottoman Empire (Moisi, 2009).

Since the empire was a hegemonic power of its time, the identity was constructed on glorifying symbols or "chosen glories." As this glory perished by the turn of the century, Turks were shamed and stripped of the self-image grandeur and left with the wounded, discomforted, and weak self-perception. Though as a reparative leader Atatürk became a savior to uplift and mend the Turkish people (Volkan, 1988). Likewise, Volkan & Itzkowitz (1984; Volkan, 2007) argue that Turks could not properly mourn their previous losses because an extraordinary charismatic leader, Mustafa Kemal Atatürk, was almost received as a savior and gave Turks a new identity and self-esteem repairing humiliated remains of the empire. In fact, the sudden loss of an empire, the purification process, and modernization were quite a transition for the public to take in a very short period. The reforms constituting the Turkish modernization ranged from clothing to changes in the alphabet, laws, and education. Only by means of these reforms could Turkey break away from the non-working Ottoman tradition and damaged self-image. One of the major consequences of top down modernization later came into light in terms of a conflict between secular and conservative movements (Altunışık & Tür, 2005). The Turkish modernization dating back to the last decades of the empire (Shaw & Kural-Shaw, 1977) — mainly the Young Turk era—created an immense split in the identity because of the fracture between modernists and Islamists. This fracture is also seen in the conflict between reformists and Ottomanists, namely the First and Second Group, in the First Grand National Assembly (Teazis, 2010). As the National Struggle (*milli mücadele*) constituted an Islamic tone, most people saw this struggle as a religious struggle; however, realizing the confrontation of the Kemalists, hope was lost (Ahmad, 2008). Later discussions and arguments of Islamist elements in Turkey reflect this perceived insult. One of the most important breaking points in the Islamist and secular factions is the radical reform in the abolishment of the caliphate which also played an important part in the relations with the Middle East and shaped the perception of Turkey in her immediate neighborhood. It can be argued that the identity discussions emerging from the last decades of the Ottoman Empire are still present in the Turkish society, more or less on a symbolic level. Despite abandoning symbols pertaining to the past, the majority Muslim population could not easily forego old habits. The Turkish modernization has been viewed as an elitist and top-down modernization containing the Islamic or religious tone in the society. In the meantime, Turkey found her political and cultural alliance with the West. Regardless of the fact that Turkey struggled to gain her independence from Western powers, Turkish policymakers chose to side with the West observing that a developed nation (*muassır medeniyet*) could only be achieved through adopting Western values. As the political elite chose a more Western path, modernity gradually became "Westernism" or admiration for the West. It is not surprising that conservative factions in the society that were loyal to old habits, Sultanate and Islamic ways became reactive to such policies. As a result, it can be argued that modernizing efforts and the values that the modern republic stood for became symbolic "others" for these factions (Çevik, 2009), while the conservative grassroots and rural society were identified as backward, and the Turkish secular elite qualified as the in-group "others." In psychological terms, Islamists were suitable targets of externalization and shared reservoirs for seculars while seculars were the suitable targets of externalization for Islamists. The outcome of such societal fragmentation has been revealed in blaming one another for all political, economic, and social troubles. As conservatives held seculars responsible for cultural corruption and perishing identity, seculars held the conservatives responsible for "secularism is about to perish." In doing so, both groups have held on to symbols that represented their distinctive identity. Volkan argues that when a loss is not internalized at a time of loss—meaning that when one does not accept the loss and initiate a grieving process—a linking object is chosen that keeps the person holding on to the lost object. To illustrate, following the death of a loved one, the loss may be denied and objects such as a tie, a watch, or a book that have emotional meaning may be kept as a keepsake. As a result, mourning of the loss is postponed, becomes perennial and can easily later regenerate at times of crisis. Large-groups also go through the same process or denial and perennial mourning (Volkan, 1990; Volkan & Zintl, 1993). Large groups refer to their linking objects when faced with an identity crisis, such as the one taking place in Turkey, when each group has its own linking objects. For instance, the conservative poet Necip Fazıl Kısakürek and the secular poet Nazım Hikmet have both become identity markers or symbols of political identities. In the same way, former prime ministers Adnan Menderes versus İsmet İnönü or "tyrant" Abdülhamit versus "Great Sultan" Abdülhamit are also societal dichotomies that are persistent in the public debate (Zürcher, 2010). Such debates still occupy public discussions encompassing a variety of topics such as whether the 1960 *coup d'état* was a democratizing move to save secularism, or whether it was against the national will; and other discussions on whether Sultan Vahdettin was a traitor. Besides, secular factions tend to take up Atatürk, the national flag, and Tenth Year March as symbols and linking objects that glorify the Atatürk era or the republic as a myth. On the other hand, Islamist factions are taking up religious elements such as the Prophet, scripts and anything that has social relevance to the Ottoman identity. Consequently, there seems to be an irrational emblematic clash between Atatürk and religious symbols, resembling a conflict between secularism and Islam.

In a general sense, Islamist political factions feel that for many years the state has oppressed them in such a way that they could not participate in the political process (Ahmad, 2008). In fact, Atatürk's reformist efforts were achieved at a price where conservative masses were deprived of religious education (Shaw & Kural-Shaw, 1977). This may have resulted in the reactive attitude of the Islamist masses toward Kemalist reforms, but should not be analyzed as the only source of reactionism in a reductionist manner. Thus, as one faction of society identified with the West, Western values, and modern Turkish Republic, another faction identified with the Middle East, more conservative values, and the Ottoman Empire. While some parts of secular groups identify only with the modern Turkish Republic, some conservative or Islamist groups only identify with the Ottoman Empire. In fact, the glorification of the Ottoman era with a sense of nostalgia among Islamist and conservative factions is, upon occasion dubbed as "Neo-Ottomanism."

Despite the implication of the early republican political elite that Turkey was not connected to the Ottoman Empire, Karpat (1992) points out that Turkey is the natural heir of the Ottoman Empire in cultural, strategic, historical, and religious terms. Unfortunately, following the death of Atatürk, the revisionist Turkish modernization became an ideology that refused to find a common ground with the past and established a rapprochement with history. More importantly, the positive self-image and optimistic assessment of the future resulting from the psychological impact of the Turkish independence slowly diminished in the post-Atatürk period. As Turkey lost her founding father, society was left without the charismatic leader enhancing the self-image of the public (Volkan & Itzkowitz, 1984), which resulted in a revisit to the wounded self-image. Eventually, as the Turkish collective psyche continued to be trapped in past traumas, modernist elements of society clung to the glory of the first decade of the modern Turkish Republic, while others clung to the glory of the forefathers, blaming secularism for being deprived of their historical identity. Most importantly, these conflicting political factions devalued one another and refused to realize that one is not the alternative to the other, but rather complimenting identities that have a long history of collective consciousness.

Though at the time of nation building and modernization, it was sometimes necessary to break ties or put distance between the past identities—not only a political and physical distance, but also a psychological one which remained present until the mid-1990s. Because of this split, Turkey has been facing a serious identity conflict where the "other" is actually within society itself with reflections in the international arena (Çiftçi, 2010). However, with the landslide victory of the conservative Justice and Development Party, Turkey in recent years has initiated identity discussions which have promoted rapprochement with the past and the present. As discussed previously, adolescence is a period of identity conflict. In a large group setting such as Turkey, society is just like an adolescent trying to find the wholeness, or what Erikson (1968) calls sense of inner identity. This inner identity is a combination of the learned identity and the desired identity. This process of self-definition and re-definition is illustrated by what Turkey has been going through in the last decade.

Unlike the *status quo* politics of the secular political parties, the AKP has constructed its foreign and domestic policy with inspiration from the Ottoman Empire. Nevertheless, the success of the AKP on solving the Turkish identity crisis will depend on whether it can equally incorporate different thoughts and ideologies. Simply put, the "new Turkey" notion is most likely to thrive if the Turkish identity can find a balance between the Ottoman and Republican glory. More importantly, different political factions, both conservative and secular, will need to learn how to live together and find a common ground to establish dialogue in a way that can also serve as an inspiration to others in the region that are just beginning the process of democratization. This analysis will be discussed in more detail in the following sections.

New Alliances and New Priorities

Turkish foreign policy has long reflected the aphorism "Peace at Home, Peace in the World," which is very much connected to the Turkish identity and traumatizing past. During the early years of modern Turkey, policymakers remained neutral to international conflicts and tried to stay away from such situations, taking into account the recent traumatic events endured by the citizens of the long-lost Ottoman Empire (Altunışık & Tür, 2005; Oran, 2012). Turkey, born out of the ashes of the Ottoman Empire, was devastated by war, economic, and social challenges which resulted in a search for a new policy course (Barkey, 2010). In the Balkan Wars, millions of Muslim refugees from the Balkans and the Caucasus, lost lands, and foreign occupation can all be attributed to this collective trauma. Turkish collective consciousness thus became very aware and suspicious toward any political or social breach later on. It can be argued that such a societal defense was constructed to distance all domestic and external threats similar to the way individuals react to threats to their identities. As such, Ahmad (2008) points out that Turkey remains apprehensive about various political openings that resemble the Treaty of Sevres, which was the initial treaty that partitioned Anatolia. Such a phobia is well grounded because of the historical recollections of the dismemberment of the Ottoman Empire. Turks today perceive the collapse of the Ottoman Empire to be the result of unjust plots conjured up by Great Powers and their client states which resulted in the infamous Sevres Treaty. According to Barkey (2010), the Sevres trauma was occasionally invoked in contemporary Turkey—especially during the early years of the republic when the Sevres trauma was still very fresh in the collective memory, and therefore it is understandable that policies were quite deliberate.

Regardless of signed agreements with several neighbors in the early republican period (Ahmad, 2008), Turkish foreign policy remained semi-isolationist as a mean to refrain from external threats and to maintain its self-confidence. In that sense, isolation was due to strategic, practical and historical causes (Karpat, 2012). Deringil (2004) argues that this strategy stems from historical experiences and beliefs and the necessity to heal wounds. In a sense, the regime was consolidating itself while dealing with the anxiety of loss, and thus, isolation was necessary. It was a time to give a boost to the self-image because another strike to the fragile self could be disastrous. However, as the young Republic faced the threat of World War II, the policymakers chose "active neutrality" as a means to find balance between opposing camps and better safeguard her position (Deringil, 2004). Turkish foreign policy has been, more often than not, shaped by regional security concerns such as the Communist expansionist threat, terrorism, and regional conflicts. Thus, Turkey's NATO membership can be traced back to two motivations, one being security concerns and the other being modern Turkey's identity (Kirişçi, 2001a). Still, the isolationist and active neutrality policies were dominantly Western-oriented in line with Turkey's Western and modern identity.

As the Turkish political system adopted a multi-party regime, together with democratization and industrialization ruling, political parties became more aware of the need to find ways to establish relations with nations other than the traditional Western allies (Uzgel, 2012). This political trend was illustrated in the assertive policies towards the Caucasus after the fall of the Soviet Russia and Özal's liberal openings. Since then, Turkey has been trying to find her position in the new global political arena. In doing so, Turkish isolationist policy strategies began to shift to a more engaged policy in the 1990s, and at the turn of the century with the decreased security threats (Larrabee, 2011). Turkey initiated a new route to connect with her neighbors and region by trying to open up dialogue and cultural interaction. At that time, global shifts in politics and threats once more placed Turkey in a key position. After the tragic events of 9/11, Turkey became a much more interested party in regional politics as it was once more promoted as a role model and sample for a democratic Middle East in an-anxiety driven post-9/11. However, Turkey's main role began with the AKP's landslide victory in 2002 which brought a major change in the society as well as politics. Because of the changes in the global system, Turkey could not carry on a passive foreign policy toward the Middle East. The shifts in domestic politics and economical parameters also eased such a policy transition as the periphery was now integrated with the center politics. The psycho-social motivations of the conservative roots of the AKP and conservative businesses have also been quite convenient in following a more proactive policy toward neighbors and the Middle East (Şahin, 2010). Turkey's new-found pro-activism is based on the set of guidelines put forward by Foreign Minister Davutoğlu in his widely acclaimed concept "strategic depth." Strategic depth as a foreign policy strategic vision takes into account Turkey's historical, geographical, demographical, and cultural background. This vision is built on a strategic mentality in which society realizes its cumulative power in historical and cultural terms (Davutoğlu, 2011). Since the mid-2000s, Turkey has put the concept of strategic depth at work trying to reconnect with her roots and former territories. Turkish pro-activism and interest in the Middle East peace process and its mediator role has increased its attractive power and demonstrative effect (Dinç, 2011). Most importantly, Turkish politicians have been openly criticizing Israeli policies on new settlements and aggressive policies on Gaza. Such a political rhetoric has laid the groundwork for Turkey's regional role. With the uprisings in the Middle East, Turkey's pro-activism has been transformed into an ever growing interest in the Turkish experience. This well earned regional influence has two psychological dimensions, one related to the collective Turkish psyche and the other related to the Arab collective psyche.

Turkish Inspiration for the Middle East and a New Political Language

Although Turkey is and will be a part of the Middle East due to geographical and historical grounds, a Turkish inspiration or discussion of a role model has never been such a critical discussion as the one taking place during the Arab uprisings.

One of the most crucial historical traumas pertaining to the Turkish collective psyche and the Middle East is the widespread perception that the Arabs betrayed the Turks at a time when there was a war against Christian "enemies." This perception is generally accepted among secular factions of the society that it has been indoctrinated by the formal education system—stemming from both actual reality and constructed realities. On the other hand, Turks as well, represented a negative image in the Arab mind, mostly in Islamist and some nationalist factions. It can be inferred that Arab communities had a certain disappointment in the modern Turkish Republic because of changing the Arabic alphabet—the holy language of Islam—to the Latin alphabet and the abolishment of the caliphate (Karpat, 2001; Uysal, 2011). Some factions in the Arab Middle East also had a feeling of being left behind by the Turks and blamed the Ottomans for the underdevelopment of the Middle East. Although relations were somewhat stable with the Arab world, there was almost no cultural interaction, or rather, a disapproval on both parts which is very much related to the nation building of Turks and Arabs (Awad, 2003). The interpretation of Turkish secularism in the social and political sphere influenced relations with the Middle East which resulted in a general feeling of superiority compared to the Arab countries.

Such a political environment and collective memory regarding Turkey's ordeal with Islam and secularism could not be seen as a role for the Arab Middle East where religion played a much different role in society than Turkey. Indeed, Turkey's close ties with the other secular and democratic nations in the Middle East and Israel was perceived negatively in the general Arab public opinion. As a matter of fact, Turkey and Israel reached the zenith of bilateral relations in the late 1990s, which is described as a "strategic partnership," a relationship based on security concerns (Inbar, 2001). Nonetheless, Turkey's efforts to expand to new markets enabled a more active foreign policy approach to gain momentum as Turkey's regional security concerns diminished.

As Turkish politics have become more accustomed to Islamic or conservative tendencies—by electing a party with Islamic roots—Arab public opinion has visibly changed. The ruling Justice and Development Party plays a very important role in rapprochement with the Middle East. Serving as a bridge between the West and the Muslim world, Turkey's AKP administration began the process of what could be called a historic reconciliation or rediscovery (Larrabee, 2007). It would probably not be possible for other administrations to achieve this rapprochement because of the lack of trust on the part of the Arab countries. Turkey has become the living proof that economic excellence, democracy, modernity, and Islam can actually co-exist. It can be suggested that Turkey has already gone through her own "awakening" or "spring" to find a balance between different factions in the society and to politically represent Islamic movements. In a way, Turkish democracy proved that all political movements, whether secular or Islamic, can be represented in the political system. Political representation and integration of conservative factions might have possibly eliminated the threat of a societal uprising similar to that of the Middle East. However, it should be noted that Turkey is an extraordinary example of co-existence between Islam, democracy, and secularism which is owed to the historical transformation of Turkish identity. Almost a century of Turkish experience and the process of finding an inner balance illustrates that Turkey can offer a new rhetoric of hope in the region.

Another element of the Turkish inspiration lies in Turkey's EU bid. The mutual distrust between Turks and Arabs seems to be diminished partly because of the problems in Turkey's EU bid. The stagnant relations between the EU and Turkey have also pushed Turkey to find new regional partners with continuous relations with the West. Therefore, the secluded and globally isolated Middle Eastern countries, at a time when Islamophobia is on the rise, view Turkey as a gateway to the West.

Turkey's regional initiative started with Syria and continued with other nations. Despite its ups and downs, Turkey has been quite successful in rediscovering the Middle East. This rediscovery is attributed to several factors. There are several reasons behind Turkey's apprehension in the Middle East. It can be suggested that Turkey has found a new path in the Middle East due to her economic development, more advanced democracy, political stability, and unique identity. All these elements make Turkey an attractive power in the region. Kirişçi (2011b) coins the composition of these elements as Turkey's "demonstrative effect." As the general framework of the paper focuses on identity, this section will elaborate the discussion on Turkey's identity as a comparative advantage.

Keyman and Öniş (2007) argue that "in the post 9/11 world, Turkey and its historical experience of modernity has constituted a significant case for the possibility of the co-existence of Islam and democracy" (p. 8). As a matter of fact, the ruling AKP has been demonstrating that Islam and democracy—or even Islam, democracy, and modernity—can all coexist peacefully. It should also be mentioned that this case is what makes Turkey an exception in the Middle East. Keyman and Öniş (2007) propose Turkey as an alternative modernity which may well describe the quite exceptional identity of Turkey. As a matter of fact, the alternative modernity that Turkey poses with a balance of democracy, modernity-secularism, and Islam is Turkey's strategic asset. Turkey's growing soft power in the Middle East is represented in Turkish soap operas that attract millions of viewers within the Middle East. These soap operas are not only Turkey's soft power tools, but are also a demonstration of why Turkey is an attractive power. In terms of identity, Turkey offers what the Middle East has been striving for—a democratic, modern, and Muslim identity with strong ties to the West and Western values.

Turkey's EU bid is clearly an opening for the Middle Eastern countries. In this sense, Turkish soap operas represent a demand from the Middle East because the stories and lifestyle symbolize the identification object as well as the desired object. In many ways, Muslim Turkey is culturally similar to the Arab Middle East, but Turkish modernization is what makes Turkey unique. In fact, it can be suggested that the economic and industrial development in Turkey is rather linked to an open society that, compared to other Muslim nations, has a longer tradition of democracy and human rights. Consequently, Turkey should embrace the past and present, realizing that the current success in regional and global politics would not have happened without the vision of Atatürk and the succeeding influential leaders in Turkish political history, such as Menderes, Özal and Erdoğan. Any disconnection between the past and present identity will most likely hinder the sustainability of Turkish inspiration.

Today, the collective memory of the traumatic history between the Turks and Arabs seems to be on the road to recovery. The current good relations could only be realized when Arabs and Turks stopped becoming an object of externalization for one another. Turkey is not only trying to reconnect with her past, but also is willing to demonstrate her ability to solve regional conflicts.

Turkey's role as a mediator is correlated to the perception of Turkey in the Arab streets and whether Turkey can be a trusted party that genuinely supports the causes of the Middle East. The uprisings in the Arab Middle East are a call for honor, dignity, political representation, and a reversal of deprivation and humiliation (Hashemi, 2011; Şahin, 2011; Yılmaz, 2011). Unfortunately, almost none of the Arab nations has been able to stand up against the colossal problems in the Middle East. The Palestinian question is the foremost important element in representing Arab honor. For that reason, the uprisings in the Middle East were also a demand from the public to stand up for Arab honor. Until the Arab Spring, Arab honor and pride was represented oddly by Iran's President Mahmoud Ahmadinejad, crediting his anti-Israeli rhetoric. In the meantime, the Iranian government failed to respond to the unexpected Arab Spring movements, while Turkey with her ever growing soft power took the role of a regional influence by responding to the requests of the Arab streets. Initially, Erdoğan's "One Minute" frenzy in Davos and the Mavi Marmara flotilla incident upgraded Turkey's credit in the region as a supporter of the Palestinian question. Unlike Arab leaders, Turkish Prime Minister Erdoğan openly took a stance against Israel's policies toward Palestine and became an international voice for Palestinian human rights as well as other humanitarian issues; thus, winning the hearts and minds of the Arab communities.

As mentioned earlier, a humiliated Arab world showed signs of regression mainly due to the events of the 20th century. This regression could only be reversed by the support of a charismatic leadership. It can be suggested that because of the lack of a leadership in the Arab Spring movements, a political vacuum, and the increasing soft power of Turkey, the charismatic Turkish Prime Minister Erdoğan has become a symbol to repair this humiliated identity. Erdoğan was welcomed to Egypt and Tunisia by a large crowd indicating their identification with a charismatic leadership. Erdoğan seems to symbolize the narcissistic extension of the victimized and aggrieved societies. Recent developments following the Egyptian elections and crisis at the beginning of 2013 introduced a new reality to the Middle East uprisings. A Turkish–Egyptian alliance in facilitating a dialogue presents a brand new vision for the Middle East where an Arab Muslim and non-Arab Muslim nation cooperate for the Middle East peace process without huge competition among leadership (Orsam Minutes, 2012).

Economic development, political stability, consolidation of advanced democracy, and unique identity are all equal elements in promoting the Turkish inspiration. Nevertheless, Turkish identity and democracy are extremely crucial in setting up a comparative advantage. Turkish policymakers and society should find a balance, a mixture of past and present identities. Just as an individual has good and bad parts in the inner self, a nation, ideology, or regime can also have good and bad parts. Although it will not be possible to eliminate and separate these good and bad parts, a more objective stance can be taken. In terms of Turkish politics, the Ottoman Empire was not all perfect or not all rotten, just as the republican era was not all good or all bad. The resolution of tensions among domestic political divisions will evoke a more stable nation, and in effect, a more stable region. In this sense, improvements in freedom of speech are necessary steps for Turkey to take to sustain regional influence and set a positive example. Democracy is an essential part of Turkey's role in the Middle East as an inspiration. Turkey, as the dominantly Muslim nation with the most advanced democracy, has a distinctive journey of democratization which is yet to be completed. Turkey has gone a long way in political and social democracy, but there are still steps needed to be taken in terms of the Kurdish question, and minority and human rights.

As Turkey demonstrates her willingness to strive for more democracy and economic progress, it is more likely that it can remain a regional influence, and more importantly, an inspiration, a hope. Besides, Turkish policymakers should also look into ways to grow in the areas of science and technology that will give hope and a sense of achievement for the Muslim communities. The path to liberal democracy and the EU membership process still deserves much attention in shaping Turkey as an inspiration (Oğuzlu, 2011).

With the Arab awakening, Turkey has been praised for setting an example of a consolidated democracy and political system, both by the West and the Arab Middle East. This new found admiration has been quite flattering for Turks as the Turkish large-group identity faced degradation at the hands of the European Union and her own leaders. Weak coalition governments, corruption, and inflation rates also effected this humiliation, while most Turks felt the need to be taken seriously, to be respected. Turkish society yearned for success, which represented the glory of the Ottoman and the early republican era (Çevik, 2012). For instance, the European championship of the soccer team, Galatasaray in 2000, was perceived and framed as Turkish success over Europe. It was as if Turks were retaliating against the European attitude towards Turkey's membership. As mentioned previously, the Turkish self-image experienced deep wounds in the last century. The ruling AKP has partly recovered and is restoring the Turkish self-image. In this manner, the Arab uprisings have served the interest of restoring Turkish self-confidence. However, as Turkish self-confidence has been rising, the Turks run the risk of over-confidence which is evident in the rhetoric of the political elites, as well as the gap between Turkish capacity and rhetoric (Dinçer & Kutlay, 2012). With the regional and global praise for Erdoğan, AKP, and Turkish influence, the Turks have also rediscovered their long lost grandiose self-image. Together with the grandiose self, a sense of nostalgia on fulfilling the Ottoman destiny has been more and more visible in the society.

Self-confidence is necessary to strategize and implement proactive policies, but over-confidence may easily have a blinding effect. Turkish over-confidence is illustrated in Turkish Prime Minister Erdoğan's speech in 2011 during his visit to Cairo promoting secularism as a way forward in political democratization. Although, in essence the message did not mean to interfere in Egyptian domestic issues, there were criticisms on the perceived meaning of 'secularism' in Egypt which apparently means non-religious. Also, Erdoğan's vow to pray at the Damascus Umayyad Mosque might have possibly raised eyebrows in the Arab Middle East. Such an assertive political rhetoric may cumulate anxiety and frustration in the Middle East. In fact, psychologically speaking, when one large group interferes or crosses the psychological boundaries of another large group, a feeling of shame, humiliation, and loss of dignity may arise. In this context, Oğuzlu (2011) asserts that Middle Eastern nations have their own internal dynamics, and a proposal of a role model will conflict with their self-esteem. In this case, Turks and Arabs, as distinct and different large groups with coinciding but conflicting histories, should be aware of such a process. Each group has diverse symbols rituals, myths, and representations about themselves and one another. More importantly, the admiration expressed for the Turkish leaders might also be a result of the absence of a charismatic Arab leadership (Abou-el-Fadl, 2012). In this sense, if the vacuum is filled by an Arab leader or nation, there is a possibility for Turkey to be pushed to the sidelines. Similarly, trauma and humiliation play a major part in defining the large group identity. The Ottoman domination of Arab lands; re-carving the Middle East (Sykes Picot); occupation of the Arab lands after the San Remo Conference; establishment of an Israeli state; the Six Day War; and the Camp David accords are all historical ordeals of the Arab collective mind. Likewise, the *Nakba* [Arab defeat in 1948 by Israel] can be categorized as the chosen trauma of the Arab world. As a result, a perceived insult to the Arab large group identity by a non-Arab nation can have a crushing effect on the already wounded self-image. Coupling this affect with the over-confidence of Turkish foreign policy might regenerate negative responses in the Arab collective psyche pertaining to the Ottoman Empire. Such a rhetoric and political action is likely to generate a nationalist sentiment and enhance group cohesion (Çevik, 2012).

A mutually respectful political rhetoric is indispensable in the Middle East transition. The basic human psychology has the need to trust. This basic trust is a crucial component in building relationships with others (Erikson, 1968). Just as the primary caregiver is a trusted object that can be relied upon, in political terms, a nation with an attractive power, an inspiration, should also establish a trustable relationship. Basic trust that promotes the message of "equal but different partners" will enable a more open and sincere dialogue in the Middle East. In this context, Turkish foreign policy strategy to stand by the public demands of the Arab streets has been the cornerstone of trust between Turkey and the Arab public. The occasional over-confidence of Turkish political rhetoric has possibly hindered this new found trust and thus, negatively impacted the communication channels. However, building a mutually trustable relationship will also sustain the restored self-image of Turks and Arabs alike. Another basic need is respect, which the Arab and Turkish societies desire and expect. The regenerated dialogue between the Arab nations and Turkey should be one of mutual trust and respect.

Conclusion

The Middle East is clearly not the same as it was before. The new Middle East will give more visibility to Islam in both the political and social spheres. Apparently, religion will play a major role in the future of these societies. One of the most intriguing questions is whether the Middle East will become radicalized after the Arab Awakening. The Turkish experience of co-existence among democracy, secularism, modernity, and Islam is an extraordinary example with a unique history. Because of large group differences, the recollection of historical memory and sociological variations, it is in the best interest of the region for Turkey to be an inspiration, not a role model. An inspiration can illuminate the process of democratization in the Middle East transformation, and assist these nations in finding their own identity. In doing so, Turkey is transforming as well in areas such as democratization, human rights, freedom of speech, and more importantly, a balance in identity. Although there is still a long way to go, the new found self-confidence has been a healing process for Turkish society, which was almost like a call for dignity and restoration of the wounded self. In this manner, Turkish society can clearly relate to what the Arab Middle East has gone through with respect to large group psychology. Likewise, the Arab Middle East has experienced mass traumas and is still an object of humiliation, as the Palestinian Question has yet to be resolved.

With a proactive foreign policy that was initiated with the Islamic oriented AKP, Turkey has become a trusted partner. Cultural, economic, and political dialogue between the Arab nations and Turkey has been changing static perceptions on both sides. As the Middle East embarks on a new journey, Turkey can enjoy her newfound prestige provided that she continues her own earnest journey of finding her true self.

The Wall of Fear and the Intelligence Apparatus in Syria

Radwan Ziadeh

Abstract

The security/intelligence services in Syria are comprised of a massive bureaucracy responsible for maintaining a wall of fear, a policy of oppression, and a monopoly on truth. Syria's Orwellian system of surveillance composed of four intelligence bodies—military, air force, political, and general—is so massive that there is one secret police operative for every 256 Syrians. This security/intelligence apparatus is the bedrock of the regime and a symbol of its overall corruption. Responsible for mass human rights violations, including torture and extrajudicial killings, these services exercise an inordinate amount of control over legal and policy decisions. The security/intelligence monster in Syria is in need of a comprehensive overhaul to restore accountability and to change its mission from maintaining the security of the regime to guaranteeing the security of the Syrian people.

Introduction

While the ascendancy of President Bashar al-Assad heralded a new era of reform for Syria in the minds of many, the changes Bashar al-Assad orchestrated served to further consolidate his surveillance apparatus and tighten regime control. What was lauded in the early 2000s as a purging of Syria's old guard was, in actuality, a nominal reshuffling that effectively strengthened the president's control over the security/intelligence system by dismissing any officials who posed a threat to his primacy. Under al-Assad, this security/intelligence complex has grown in both size and power, compounding corruption in the process. This apparatus is the crux of the regime's ability to maintain a wall of fear in Syria, quashing dissent through monitoring, followed by military action against citizens, often targeting political dissidents.

This paper seeks to illuminate the extent of the influence of the Syrian intelligence forces in virtually all realms of life by elucidating its structure and history to the greatest extent possible. Furthermore, it will give an overview of the intelligence forces' perpetration of mass human rights' atrocities against protesters and political activists during the Syrian revolution that began in 2011.

The Ascendancy of the Syrian Intelligence Apparatus

Throughout the period of Syria's Third Republic, which began in 1963, security (military and intelligence) elites have enjoyed unwarranted influence in policy and decision making, crowding out Baa'thist intellectuals. This pattern has continued for decades: security/intelligence elites—the true proprietors of power in Syria—marginalize intellectual would-be policymakers, allow them to fester and fight among themselves, and seize opportunities to grab power.

The process of policy and decision making in Syria is not as complex as it is secretive. Despite the fact that many overlapping agencies within this security/intelligence structure may influence policy, the president is the ultimate decider. The 1973 Syrian Constitution instituted by Hafez al-Assad dictates that the president is responsible for leading society and state, for issues of foreign policy, and for commanding and controlling the armed forces. Essentially, the president sits above all other state institutions, with any checks or balances from judicial or legislative structures rendered useless by purposefully designed bureaucracies. While power during the Third Republic has increased for the president, it has also favored a group of elite cronies, a small group of trusted individuals mostly from rural military backgrounds. This handful of elites has only further consolidated its reign over all aspects of life in Syria over the years, building the wall of fear higher and higher.

The Ba'th Party's coup that ushered in the Third Republic in 1963 coincided with the rise of the military faction within the party. This military group would go on to control the party's political activities, choosing its leaders based on its own interests. Thus, this military system would rise to a position in which it overrode and impeded the effective functioning of other civilian state institutions.

The Structure of Syria's Intelligence Services

Since the beginning of this period, military, security, and intelligence operations have all overlapped and have functionally served as one entity (their roles are often redundant). This security mega-apparatus is composed of the General Intelligence Directorate, the Political Security Directorate, the Department of Military Intelligence, and the Air Force Intelligence Directorate. At the same time, each of these branches is massive, providing one member of the intelligence services for every 153 adults in Syria.

The security/intelligence complex's individual bodies are structured so as to ensure ultimate protection for the regime, especially for the president, meaning that the identities and activities of members of different branches are often kept secret. The sheer size of these bodies coupled with the fact that their functions often overlap, allows the president to achieve said ultimate protection by not relying too much on any single agency. Since their true purpose is to protect the president and his power rather than to impose public order and safety, the redundancy of these agencies' purposes is insignificant, and it actually serves to bolster the president's security.

Of the aforementioned bodies, general intelligence serves mainly as state security and is under the supervision of the Ministry of the Interior. Political intelligence is also administrated by the Ministry of the Interior. Military intelligence and the special segments of the air force tasked with intelligence and security function nominally under the Ministry of Defense. Air force intelligence has historically been the closest to and most trusted by the al-Assad presidents, and is notorious for carrying out some of the most brutal interrogations and even frequent torture and detainment of political opponents of the regime. Air force intelligence is among the parties most responsible for maintaining the wall of fear in Syria.

The General Security Directorate is often referred to by its old moniker, "State Security," and it comprises an investigative branch, and information security branch, an internal branch, and an external branch (Human Rights Watch, 2011b, p. 92). This body is responsible for monitoring civilian activities, both inside and outside Syria.

Political intelligence, or the Political Security Directorate, monitors political activity, looking to identify and quash any dissent that might threaten the regime. In addition to monitoring political dissidents, this body also keeps track of foreigners residing in Syria and their interactions with locals (Syria's Intelligence Services, 2000).

The Department of Military Intelligence comprises the military investigative branch, the Palestine investigative branch (responsible for monitoring the activities of Palestinian organizations), the communications security and surveillance branch, and the "security branches" (Human Rights Watch, 2011b, p. 91).

Finally, the Air Force Intelligence Directorate is composed of an investigative branch and a special operations branch. The most ominous branch of the intelligence apparatus, air force intelligence was utilized by Hafez al-Assad as his "personal action bureau," as he was once air force commander (Human Rights Watch, 2011b, p. 23). Air force intelligence maintains vast detention facilities.

The leaders of these different branches are often chosen through patronage networks and ties, meaning that the heads of these intelligence/security bodies are close trusted friends of the president. According to Human Rights Watch, "in theory, the National Security Bureau oversees the four intelligence agencies. In practice, however, the agencies operate with a high degree of autonomy, answerable mainly to President Bashar al-Assad" (Human Rights Watch, 2011b, p. 90). Under Hafez al-Assad, these groups, with the exception of the air force intelligence, were responsible for carrying out their surveillance tasks locally under the supervision of the local leadership of the Baʿth Party. As these bodies became more influential, competition among them intensified, causing each group to expand exponentially. Again, because of the benefits offered by holding a close personal relationship with the president, the leaders of these branches often made sure that their respective intelligence/security bodies went beyond their assigned duties, inserting their influence into political and administrative dealings.

The push to expand in both size and power, as I write in my book *Power and Policy in Syria*, buttressed the pyramid that insulates the president from insecurity. The growth of this pyramid—comprising the government administration, the Baʿth Party, and the security/intelligence forces—facilitated the expansion of an "Orwellian system of surveillance" (Ziadeh, 2011). Over time, the administrative and party aspects of the triumvirate have faded into the background, while the security/intelligence forces have seized the opportunity to fill a void of influence over political decisions.

While the existence of these different sides of the pyramid creates the illusion of checks and balances, thus lending legitimacy to the regime, they actually exist, as I mentioned previously, simply to insulate the president while ensuring that no single part of the pyramid can easily threaten the regime. Furthermore, Hafez al-Assad was known to restructure and shuffle any military or intelligence sectors posing threats or displaying questionable loyalty. As a result, these institutions have become bulwarks of loyalty for the regime through reliable patron–client bonds.

The Security/Intelligence Complex and Syrian Foreign Policy

The primacy of the security/intelligence forces is evident in Syrian foreign policy: the minister of foreign affairs is usually, by law, responsible for making decisions regarding foreign policy. If the decision in question has military or security components, however, the legal role of this minister may be superseded by the security/intelligence apparatus, topped by the president in his position as commander of the armed forces. Personality also trumps position in foreign policy protocol; in other words, an individual with lower official rank may override someone with a higher position, like the minister of foreign affairs himself, in advising foreign policy decisions. The operative factor is the person's proximity to and rapport with the president. The president's trust confers power. These patterns and practices illuminate the dynamics at play: those who have cultivated close personal relationships with the president often come from military backgrounds, meaning that members of the security and intelligence forces can wield significant influence over foreign policy.

To illustrate the extent of the influence enjoyed by the security/intelligence complex, one can examine the relationship between Syria and Lebanon. Under both Hafez and Bashar al-Assad, leaders of the Syrian military intelligence were responsible for cultivating ties with Lebanese organizations. For instance, when Fuad al-Sinyurah was Prime Minister of Lebanon, Syria enjoyed relatively warm relations with Lebanese organizations like Hezbollah and the Amal movement due to the work of the Syrian military intelligence forces in consultation with the president. The close Syria–Lebanon relationship was not, in fact, a product of work by the ministry of foreign affairs. Likewise, Syria's role in the region was irrevocably altered when it withdrew its military and intelligence forces from Lebanon in 2005. Thus, this military/intelligence apparatus is truly the crux of the Syrian government under the al-Assads–junior and senior.

As a direct result of so many of the country's resources' being dedicated to the intelligence services, other imperative areas of life have been neglected and have suffered in terms of development. The al-Assad regime has essentially hijacked the country's future in order to preserve its own primacy. The regime has co-opted virtually every sphere of public activity; for instance, labor unions serve as an extension of the intelligence forces, by mandate monitoring the activities of the union members and reporting relevant information to the regime (Ziadeh, 2011). Thus, the realms of civil society, non-governmental organizations, education, and civic life in general have stagnated and even regressed due to their institutional co-optation by regime interests via the intelligence apparatus.

Intelligence Forces, Human Rights Atrocities, and the Syrian Revolution

The four bodies composing the Syrian intelligence apparatus have been instrumental in suppressing the Syrian revolution that began in 2011. A Human Rights Watch report entitled "By All Means Necessary: Individual and Command Responsibility for Crimes Against Humanity in Syria" asserts unequivocally that "all of the main intelligence agencies have been implicated in the killing of unarmed protesters and the arbitrary arrest and torture of detainees" (Human Rights Watch, 2011b, p. 91). The report also presents evidence that "military commanders and officials in the intelligence agencies gave both direct and standing orders to use lethal force against the protesters…as well as to unlawfully arrest, beat, and torture the detainees" (Human Rights Watch, 2011b, p. 7).

Leaders of the intelligence forces, along with President Bashar al-Assad by virtue of his position as commander of these forces, have perpetrated crimes against humanity by ordering or authorizing the use of deadly force against unarmed civilian protesters. The Human Rights Watch report interviews some 60 members of the military and intelligence forces who have defected since the start of the revolution. One of the former intelligence agents who defected from the branch of Air Force Intelligence in Dara'a said that "the commander in charge of Air Force Intelligence in Dara'a, Colonel Qusay Mihoub, gave his unit orders to 'stop the protesters by all possible means,' which included the use of lethal force" (Human Rights Watch, 2011b, p. 9). A defected member of Air Force Intelligence's Special Operations said that "Colonel Suheil Hassan gave orders to shoot directly at protesters on April 15 during a protest in the Mo'adamiyeh neighborhood in Damascus" (Human Rights Watch, 2011b, p. 9).

In addition to the authorization of the use of lethal force, the intelligence services embarked upon a campaign of mass arbitrary arrests, torture, and executions. Those interviewed for the Human Rights Watch report confirmed the practice of arbitrary arrests at protests and checkpoints as well as "'sweep' operations in residential neighborhoods across the country. Most of the arrests appear to have been conducted by the intelligence agencies, while the military provided support during the arrest and transportation of detainees." The report continues, stating that these defectors' accounts confirm the "massive campaign of arbitrary arrests…including many children" (Human Rights Watch, 2011b, pp. 10–11).

From among those interviewed for the Human Rights Watch's report, it was mainly the members of the intelligence agencies who had knowledge of the practices within the detention facilities. The remainder of the defectors, mostly members of the military, said they had only been involved in transporting the detainees to said facilities. The interviews in the report also confirmed the practice of "summary execution of detainees or deaths from torture in detention" in Douma and Bukamal. Also, the report states, "A defector who had been posted in the eastern town of Bukamal, by the Iraqi border, said that he saw 17 bodies of anti-government activists including a number that had surrendered to an intelligence agency several days earlier" (Human Rights Watch, 2011b, p. 12). Many of those detained were children, and the arrests in general were arbitrary, often with no formal charges levied, and with no notification of the families. Some detainees have returned, while others have not reemerged. The report notes that "many of those cases constitute enforced disappearances" (Human Rights Watch, 2011b, p. 21). One defector from the Special Operations branch of Air Force Intelligence told Human Rights Watch that he estimated the total number of detainees to be over 100,000. These high numbers were reached by way of "sweeps" that often followed protests, which entailed large-scale arrests as well as looting and destruction of property (Human Rights Watch, 2011b, p. 46).

Furthermore, there is evidence that commanders in the intelligence and military forces denied medical treatment to injured protesters, and those protesters who were brought to the military or a military-controlled hospitals "were also subjected to mistreatment and beatings by intelligence agents and hospital staff" (Human Rights Watch, 2011b, p. 12).

Some defectors also told Human Rights Watch that "officers or intelligence agents" killed members of the military who refused to follow orders to shoot at protesters. Defectors also confirmed that some of them were detained and tortured for this refusal, and even for having participated in protests "during leave or before they started their military service" (Human Rights Watch, 2011b, p. 13). Meanwhile, the official regime line claimed that armed gangs were responsible for the deaths of these military personnel. Indeed, some of the military casualties were caused by protesters and members of the armed resistance; however, it is entirely feasible that some of these casualties were actually deliberate killings of those who refused to follow orders (Human Rights Watch, 2011b, p. 67).

The intelligence forces, according to the report, "have also arrested lawyers, activists, and journalists who endorsed or promoted the protests, as well as medical personnel suspected of caring for wounded protesters in makeshift field hospitals or private homes" (Human Rights Watch, 2011b, p. 21). In addition to these practices, security forces also mounted sieges of entire residential areas, as they did in Dara'a, "cutting off all means of communication and subjecting residents to acute shortages of food, water, medicine, and other essential supplies" (Human Rights Watch, 2011a, p. 44).

One of the defectors, who was a member of Air Force Intelligence in Dara'a said that his group was ordered to enter a mosque in Dara'a where protesters often gathered and that Colonel Majed Darras ordered them to kill those gathered (Human Rights Watch, 2011b). Most of the defectors interviewed for this Human Rights Watch report were members of the military rather than the intelligence forces, although their accounts corroborate the notion that the intelligence forces were the individuals responsible for overseeing the violations, for giving the orders, sometimes for actually firing at protesters, and also for ensuring that military personnel obeyed the orders. Taken together, the testimonies from defectors seem to show that the Special Operations units of Air Force Intelligence were responsible for ordering and overseeing the mass arrests, torture, and custodial deaths (Human Rights Watch, 2011b, p. 9).

Conclusion

The security/intelligence apparatus functions as the crux of the regime: it cements the pyramid of isolation that supports President Bashar al-Assad, and it is directly responsible for terrorizing the Syrian populace by committing crimes against humanity. The revolution that began in 2011 and is still ongoing has brought greater international attention to these violations, but in reality, torture, mass arbitrary arrests, and enforced disappearances have been the modus operandi of the intelligence services since the beginning of the Third Republic. These forces are the heart of the wall of fear that has discouraged the blossoming of civil life in Syria. Those leaders of the intelligence bodies guilty of crimes against humanity should be, along with President Bashar al-Assad, brought before the International Criminal Court under the Rome Statute.

In light of these revelations, the intelligence forces will be the greatest obstacle to the process of transitional justice in Syria. Indeed, when the violence and atrocities currently being perpetrated in Syria finally come to a halt, a process of reconciliation and rebuilding must begin to forge a country that guarantees freedom and human rights to all its citizens. The culture of impunity and decades of malpractice that have permeated the intelligence forces will certainly serve as an obstacle to the development of other areas of civilian as well as military life in Syria. Indeed, the mandate of the security and intelligence bodies must be to protect the people of Syria, not the regime. Once these forces are rehabilitated and reformed, which will necessitate a long, arduous process, then the Syrian people can begin to knock down the wall of fear that has paralyzed free expression and a dignified life for as long as many of us Syrians can remember.

Iran and the Syria Crisis: Policies, Problems, and Prospects

Maysam Behravesh

Iran is going to go down in Syria with the ship ... [and]as an American, it would not break my heart to see Iranians beaten in Syria.
  - Fred Hof, Former US State Department advisor on Syria[1]

Abstract

Iran has been an influential player in Syria ever since the outbreak of popular protests against the al-Assad government in March 2011, and particularly so following their radicalization into a full-blown security crisis. In an explicit demonstration of a *realpolitik*-based foreign policy conduct, Iran has made tremendous efforts, ranging from diplomatic and financial to logistical and military, to retain the Ba'athist regime in power and prevent the loss of its sole state ally in the region. Seeking to shed light on the changing nature of the Syrian crisis, this paper investigates the evolution of Iranian strategy toward the Arab Spring-induced revolt and offers a contextualized analysis of its geopolitical perils and problems for Tehran. It also explores the most viable scenarios the conflict may witness in the future, concluding that unless Iran undertakes a proactive function in resolving the crisis—that is, by facilitating al-Assad's departure—it will have little, if any, share in the unfolding redistribution of power in the new Middle East.

Introduction

When the revolutionary uprisings—later known as the Arab Spring—of the Middle East and North Africa (MENA) broke out in Tunisia on the eve of 2011, the Islamic Republic of Iran (IRI) embraced them with open arms. The Iranian government projected the protests as a wave of "Islamic Awakening" which was soon to dismantle pro-Western dictatorships in the region. By tracing its roots back to the "Islamic Revolution" of 1979, the government moved to consolidate the ideologically confrontational narrative, particularly when Tunisia's "Dignity Revolution" spread to the streets of Cairo and Alexandria in January, leading to the ouster of Egyptian President Hosni Mubarak from power less than a month later. The revolutionary tide that proceeded to engulf Libya, Yemen, and Bahrain before long was largely in Iran's favor until it arrived to the eastern shores of the Mediterranean in March 2011 and thrust itself upon Iran's Syrian brothers. The Syrian revolt was the Arab Spring's moment of revelation for Iran. Revolutions defy prediction and the IRI had almost entirely failed to take this into consideration both in its geopolitical calculations vis-à-vis the MENA uprisings and in its endeavor to construct a consistent narrative for them.

Caught up in a strategic dilemma following the radicalization of the Syrian protests into a full-blown security crisis, the leadership in Tehran faced two equally painful choices: (1) to continue to lend political support to the revolt as it had openly done in the cases of Tunisia, Egypt, Yemen, and Bahrain and thus facilitate its long-time Alawite ally's loss of grip on power, or (2) to express opposition to the uprising and risk losing the moral high ground, and along with that, its credibility in the Muslim world. It opted for the second, and at the same time tried to justify it by recourse to the old familiar theme of upholding resistance against Zionism and Israeli occupation. The Syrian rebellion was detached from the rest of Arab revolutions in the Iranian corridors of power and was portrayed as a plot hatched by foreigners to undercut the "axis of resistance" in which Ba'athist Syria under al-al-Assad had been playing the function of a vital link between the Islamic Republic and its Lebanese proxy Hezbollah. In spite of the soaring costs and growing risks of such a complicated approach, Iran's syndromic obsession, one may argue, with sustaining the rule of Bashar al-Assad (or at least a likeminded figure from within the regime as sympathetic to the IRI) has yet to fade away.

This paper attempts to tease out the various dimensions of Iranian policy toward the Arab Spring-induced revolt in Syria, to offer a contextualized analysis of the security perils and strategic problems it has caused for Tehran, and to explore the most viable scenarios the crisis may witness in the future. This study contends that what the IRI leaders perversely continue to neglect is the increasing likelihood of their Syria game turning into a perilous zero-sum gamble with profound repercussions for Iran's already undermined strategic standing and security. This piece suggests that if Syrians manage, in their attritional and costly quest for change, to find a way out of their current plight and to build a future of their own, it will almost undoubtedly be one without al-al-Assad and his cohort. This will most likely render Iran the greatest loser both of the war now and of the peace then. Hence, the vital need for Iran to change its policy if it really wishes to avoid strategic paralysis and irrelevance in the region.

Iranian Treatment of the Syrian Crisis

The uprising in Syria started more or less in the same manner as other protests in the region, with a protestor from the northeastern governorate of al-Hasakah immolating himself in the footsteps of Tunisia's Mohamed Bouazizi and public calls being made on the social media outlets for mass demonstrations against the government (Williams, 2012). A short while later in mid-March, a better mobilized group of demonstrators took to the streets in the southern city of Daraa, presaging a widening of protests that were mostly focused in their early phase upon greater civil liberties, termination of government corruption, improvement of the economic situation, and the release of political prisoners. Having witnessed two other revolutions that had commenced softly but finally succeeded in bringing down the ruling regimes, the al-Assad government chose a rather different path and largely resorted to embryonic suppression, characterized, among others, by fatal torture and sexual abuse of several protestors in custody (Amnesty International, 2011).

Notably, the shock-and-awe response partly bore the hallmarks of a systematic military campaign in Hama back in 1982, when under the rule of Bashar's father, Hafez al-Assad, the Syrian army violently put an end to an Islamic uprising led by the Muslim Brotherhood against the government. The bloody operation, successful as it was in effectively curtailing an almost decade-long opposition and consolidating the Ba'athist regime's foothold, left at least 20,000 dead in the central western town (Fisk, 2010). It also appeared an impulsive show of resolve by Damascus to its Arab rivals, who having lost two precious allies in Tunisia and Egypt, were anxious to see a spread of popular protests to their Shi'a-governed neighbour. Equally noteworthy were the similarities one could detect in the type of reaction to the methods al-Assad's most influential friends in Tehran had used to halt post-presidential election rallies and quell the Iranian Green Movement less than two years earlier. It may not be a sheer coincidence that some hard-line quarters affiliated with the Iranian leadership refer to the Syrian uprising as "*al-Sham* sedition" or "*fitnah*" (Salami, 2013) in parallel with the label "Green sedition" officially coined for the 2009 street protests.

The most reliable and long-standing partner of the al-Assad regime, the Islamic Republic, has been under the regional and international spotlight since early signs of trouble surfaced in Syria. Given its entrenched tradition of basically survivalist foreign policy, it was predictable that Tehran would side with the government in Damascus, deviating from the approach it had taken to other Arab Spring uprisings. However, the display of support manifested itself at the beginning mostly in the form of arrested denial of popular dissent. A general examination of official speeches and news stories in the Iranian state media, which were avidly reflecting the revolutionary developments in the Middle East and North Africa, points to a remarkable coverage deficit vis-à-vis the Syrian events for most of 2011; except for cases where the government claimed to have been victimized by "foreign-backed terrorists" and "criminal gangs."[2] With the intensification of protests throughout the Arab nation into pockets of armed resistance, and the formation in late July of the Free Syrian Army (FSA) largely by former military officers who had switched sides, Tehran could no longer afford to downplay or deny the existence of a full-fledged opposition intent on initiating a fundamental change of the prevailing political order. In a move that highlighted Iran's amplified role in the burgeoning conflict, the U.S. Treasury Department declared sanctions against Qasem Soleimani, commander of the Iranian Quds Force (QF)—the military arm of Islamic Revolutionary Guards Corps (IRGC) which is in charge of operations overseas—and Mohsen Chizari, another senior IRGC-QF officer, who were accused of aiding and abetting the Syrian government in violation of human rights and repression of revolutionaries (US Department of the Treasury, 2011).

Nevertheless, its first official denunciation of the anti-regime demonstrations in Syria and implicit confirmation of alignment with Bashar al-al-Assad came on June 30, 2011, when Ayatollah Ali Khamenei, Iranian Supreme Leader, dubbed the uprising "deviational" for its pro-American character in an address to a gathering of government officials in Tehran, asserting that "the hand of America and Israel is evident in Syrian events, and the logic and criterion of Iranian nation stipulate that wherever slogans are chanted to the advantage of America and Zionism, the movement is deviational" (Khamenei, 2011; also cited in Abdo, 2011). As the initially rights-oriented struggle was increasingly militarized following the influx of predominantly Sunni and occasionally al-Qaeda-linked Jihadist fighters from around the wider Middle East and Central Asia to fight the al-Assad regime, Iran found itself in an internationally more justified position to back its sole regional ally. The severity and scale of the conflict on the ground were reaching alarming levels, concerning decision makers in Tehran that developments may spiral out of control. Indicative of likely factional differences over the Islamic Republic's unmistakably one-sided policy toward the crisis, Foreign Minister Ali Akbar Salehi urged Damascus in late August to heed the "legitimate demands" of its citizens, while warning its Arab neighbors against the security repercussions of a possible "vacuum in the Syrian regime" (as cited in Bakri, 2011).

Assessments made by Western intelligence agencies and diplomats were pointing to the increasingly active presence of Iranian elite groups, who in coordination with their Syrian counterparts, were trying to rein in the rebellion. There were similar reports about Iran's efforts to provide the Syrian security forces with sophisticated training, anti-riot gear, and Internet surveillance technology (Coughlin, 2011; Crilly, 2012;

Tisdall, 2011). Tehran's decision to ratchet up support for Damascus was also an endeavor to counterbalance its regional Sunni nemeses, which viewed Syria as an occasion to beat Iran and a battleground where the future equation of power and influence in the region would be determined. By that time, Syria had been suspended from the Arab League due to disproportionate use of violence against civilian protestors. The pursuit of an emboldened strategy by Iran was concurrent with a subtle normative shift from selective denial to tentative demonization in the IRI's narrative reconstruction of the revolt. Along parallel lines, a hardening of tone and attitude on the part of Iranian officials towards the predicament could be seen. Mohsen Rezaee, the current secretary of Iran's Expediency Discernment Council and a former IRGC commander-in-chief, proclaimed in an interview with the Lebanese Hezbollah-affiliated *al-Manar* television that "Syria, Hezbollah and Hamas are our red line[s] and we will not allow any trouble to affect them, for they constitute the frontline of the world of Islam against Israel, and we advise Americans to abandon the path they've chosen" (Rezaee, 2011). The Israel factor was bound to play a significant part in the Islamic Republic's vindication of attempts to preserve the by-then-favorable status quo in Syria.

There were new hopes in 2012 that the appointment of Kofi Annan in February as the United Nations–Arab League joint peace envoy for Syria would help alleviate the raging crisis. Introducing an internationally acclaimed six-point peace plan, he strived to achieve a political solution mostly with the help of great powers in the UN Security Council and key regional actors closely engaged with the developments. His efforts were effectively marred, however, by a fundamental conflict of interests and a prevailing atmosphere of mistrust between Russia, China, and Iran who, on the one hand, were in favor of al-Assad's staying in office, and the United States, Europe, Saudi Arabia, Turkey, and Qatar, who, on the other, threw their weight behind the opposition from the outset. Despite the increasing consolidation of rebel groups in the key conflict zones and the mounting international condemnation of the systematic violence government-affiliated forces employed to contain them,[3] the uncertainty and geopolitical stakes were too high for Iran to change course. Diplomatically, it did help Annan advance his peace initiative, but only to make sure that al-Assad would survive. Practically, Tehran deepened its involvement by reportedly deploying elite military forces and commanders in flashpoint areas and transferring more advanced weaponry to the government (Charbonneau 2012; Fassihi, 2012b; Gordon, 2012).

The bombing at the Syrian national security headquarters on July 18, 2012, was a turning point in the whole trajectory of the war, as it illustrated the opposition's deep penetration into the state apparatus whose rising degree of vulnerability was being ever more exposed. A hardly reparable blow to the government, the incident left a number of high-ranking officials dead, including al-Assad's brother-in-law and Deputy Defence Minister Assef Shawkat, Defence Minister General Dawoud Rajiha, and Assistant Vice President General Hassan Turkmani, and wounded others. It also sent a stark message to Iranian leaders, convincing them to establish channels of communication with the opposition forces in the hope of bringing the conflicting sides to the negotiation table or at least slacken the conflict's accelerating momentum in favor of the government as any erosion of the al-Assad regime's core could mean getting one step closer to the disintegration of the "axis of resistance" against Israel and potential loss of Hezbollah ("Iran, Syria relations main axis of resistance," 2012). The capture by the Free Syrian Army of 48 Iranian males, who according to rebels belonged to the Revolutionary Guards and were on a "field reconnaissance mission" in Syria when they were caught, added to the urgency of getting in contact with the opposition (Cave & Saad, 2012; Fassihi, 2012a).

A complex three-pronged strategy, which has since continued to largely inform the Islamic Republic's tactical policies toward Syria, was crystallizing: Tehran would continue to espouse the al-Assad government at all levels while trying to reach as far as possible to various rebel groups on the ground. A third component was to work diplomatically with the new UN peace envoy Lakhdar Brahimi as well as with those regional actors that in one way or another were providing support for the rebel forces. Such a costly and curious strategy was underpinned by the perception on the part of Iranian leaders that they needed to hedge their bets just in case al-Assad lost control entirely or was targeted in an unexpected rebel offensive (Oweis & Abbas, 2012). It also depended considerably upon the continuation of Russia's complicated efforts to sustain the status quo. Despite the huge risks and strategic implausibility of the approach, it succeeded at least in securing the release of IRGC hostages a few months later in a prisoner swap deal that resulted in the Syrian government freeing over 2,100 detainees in return.

Yet, Iran has also deployed a back-up strategy independent of the Syrian government as well as the opposition, which may well explain the scope of its scepticism about the orientation of developments in Syria and the high level of threat perception it has toward the changing regional landscape. Anticipating the growing possibility of the country disintegrating into sectarian and ethnic territories, it is seeking in close coordination with Hezbollah to establish asymmetric control on the ground by planting militia networks and proxies that would remain under Tehran's command and act independently of other parties involved in the conflict. The "Jaysh al-Sha'bi" force, which consists of around 50,000–60,000 militia fighters and is distinct from Syrian paramilitary forces (*Shabiha*), represents a working example of this sophisticated worst-case-scenario-based strategy (DeYoung & Warrick, 2013).

Geostrategic Vulnerability Exacerbated

It is much easier to talk about the repercussions of Iran's policy vis-à-vis the civil war in Syria for its national security and strategic interests than the policy itself. Now, about two years into the revolt, which has claimed the lives of over 60,000 Syrians and forced around 700,000 to flee the country, Tehran's treatment of it has, by many measures been a failure rather than a success, leaving it strategically more vulnerable in the wider Middle East. Domestically, it has sharpened widespread discontent that was already simmering owing to severe economic hardship as well as paralyzing political corruption and mismanagement. Regionally, it has alienated Iran's few friends and antagonized many of the Sunni Arab states. And internationally, it has helped foster greater mistrust in the course of nuclear negotiations and elicited harsher sanctions over Tehran's controversial atomic programme. The Islamic Republic has also had its revolutionary image stained in the Muslim world by a display of double standards and is rapidly losing what has been left of its popularity with certain segments of the Arab street including Palestinians.

Almost from the start, Iran's Syria policy was the subject of strident popular criticism among many Iranians who resorted mostly to social media to vent it. The first open expressions of internal dissatisfaction, however, erupted in early October 2012, when a steep plunge in the value of the Iranian national currency *(rial)* sparked protests in the capital. Itself in harsh economic pain (which is in significant part the consequence of comprehensive international sanctions), Iran has consistently carried on funnelling considerable financial and military support for the al-Assad regime—partly as an effort to relieve the potentially destructive impact of western oil embargo against Damascus and keep it afloat. It is noteworthy that one of the chief slogans street protesters in Tehran chanted, "leave Syria alone, give us a thought instead," was an admonition to the authorities that, if anything, charity begins at home. Strikingly, in the latest attempt of the kind, it signed an economic contract with Syria on January 16, 2013, supplying it with a one billion dollar line of credit to be sponsored by the state-owned Export Development Bank of Iran (EDBI) ("Yek bank-e Irani," 2012). As a result of such policies, many inside Iran cannot help regarding Syria as another national burden of the same ilk as Palestine and Lebanon.

In terms of the regional political dynamics, a fundamental divergence of interests and policies served to pit Iran against most of the other Muslim states, not least Turkey and Egypt with which it had endeavored hard to develop effective relations over the past two years in a bid to break out of its isolation. While Tehran's economic ties with Ankara have largely remained intact for clear reasons, the much-needed diplomatic cooperation to address international concerns over the Iranian nuclear programme has noticeably suffered. Another relevant factor driving a wedge between the two neighbors appears to be the suspicions that Iran is sheltering members of the Kurdistan Workers' Party (PKK), as well as Kurdistan Communities' Union (KCK) (Bozkurt, 2012), with the chief intention being to keep Turkey preoccupied with issues of border security and hold Ankara-backed rebels at bay in the northern parts of Syria. Turkey's invocation of its NATO leverage and the ensuing deployment of Patriot missile batteries near the Syrian border have additionally pushed the relationship closer to the brink. Obviously, the Islamic Republic views the defense shield as a prelude to establishing a no-fly zone over Syria, and more importantly, yet another Western bid to further close in on its nuclear facilities.

But for the stern dispute over the Syrian crisis, Iranian–Egyptian relations had so far been re-established after more than three decades of diplomatic freeze. Egypt's [then] Islamist President Mohammed Morsi and other senior Muslim Brotherhood officials have repeatedly pointed to the IRI support for the al-Assad government, continuing to subject any full resumption of bilateral ties to Tehran's cooperation with other regional states to secure a political transition in Syria (Batrawy, 2012; Dehghan & Harding, 2012; Golovnina & Perry, 2013). Of course, one may not rule out Iranian qualms about Egypt's close engagement with Saudi Arabia, more or less normal relations with Israel, and significant dependence upon the United States' military and financial help for the time being, but it is almost evident that the Islamic Republic's unwillingness to sacrifice its Alawite allies for Muslim Brothers has stood as an impediment to a comprehensive rapprochement. Most unexpected along these lines, however, is the reconsideration on the part of Palestinian resistance groups, not least Hamas, to distance themselves from their long-time patron and swing toward its anti-al-Assad nemeses (Black & Sherwood, 2012; "Meshaal: Erdogan is not only Turkey's leader," 2012). This would cost Iranian leaders an affinity they had long invested upon and taken pricier pains over the past eight years to build by showing radical opposition to Israel.

Lastly, with respect to toughening pressure and growing threats of military action against Iran, it can be safely argued that its Syria stance is working to the detriment of its nuclear ambitions, perhaps erasing any residual leniency in the international community about Tehran's atomic activities. A number of European Union documents and U.S. State Department cables released by WikiLeaks long before the March 2011 uprising show that the al-Assad government has managed to extensively develop its chemical weapons programme with substantial logistical and technological assistance from Iran in recent years (Ball, 2012; International Institute for Strategic Studies, 2012; WikiLeaks, 2006, 2008). Moreover, former Israeli officials have suggested that Tehran is trying to transfer parts of Syria's massive arsenal of nonconventional weapons to Hezbollah, primarily out of concerns that the imminent collapse of al-Assad may disrupt the supply lines to the Lebanese resistance group, at least for the foreseeable future (Ephron, 2013).

Some of the more sceptical quarters in Tel Aviv and Washington may readily interpret, or otherwise wish to portray such a move as indicative of Iranian determination to put its annihilation rhetoric against the "Zionist entity" into practice the moment it gets the bomb. Pertinently, when it comes to the menace of these armaments, top Israeli authorities tend to rhetorically juxtapose Syria's unconventional arsenal with the Islamic Republic's nuclear endeavors. A part of Prime Minister Benjamin Netanyahu's speech to mark the International Holocaust Remembrance Day on January 27, 2013 is worthwhile quoting here: "We must look around us, at what is happening in Iran and at its proxies and at what is happening in other areas, with the deadly weapons in Syria, which is increasingly coming apart…There is a cluster of threats, and their reality continues to evolve" (as cited in Reed, 2013, Lappin, 2013). This said, the crucial puzzle remains as to whether the potential fall of al-Assad will persuade Iran to adopt a more cautionary approach in the face of external warnings or struggle more forcefully than ever to secure the ultimate deterrent.

Toward a Post-al-Assad Syria?

Much to the apprehension of Iranian leaders, the Syrian regime's chances of survival are arguably waning. On the one hand, though the rebel groups are divided by their various, and in some cases even conflicting allegiances and visions of how a future Syria should look. They are all fighting, first and foremost, to put an end to the rule of al-Assad, their common enemy. On the other, Russia seems to be getting more and more disappointed with the highly unstable state of affairs prevailing in Syria and the government's inability to bring it under control. The most explicit articulation of this scepticism came during a CNN interview with Russian Prime Minister Dmitry Medvedev on January 27, 2013 where he called al-Assad's resistance to reform an "important, but not fatal" error and asserted that "[t]he chances for him surviving are slipping away as days and weeks go by" (as cited in Smith, 2013). The reported transfer of Bashar al-al-Assad and his close circle of confidants to a warship under Russian superintendence in the Mediterranean (Miller, 2013; "Report says al-Assad residing on warship," 2013) also signifies the deteriorating security in the capital Damascus and rising fears of an abrupt rebel takeover.

Altogether, this opens up a number of possibilities for the future course of events and what will become of the Syrian state and society. The first scenario consists in the continuation of the situation as it stands now, namely, al-Assad's enduring rule amidst a civil war that is engulfing the whole territory; a possibility certain quarters in the Islamic Republic appear to have pinned faith upon ("Mo'aven-e vezarat-e kharejeh-ye Iran," 2012). However, given the daily escalation of conflict, mounting international pressure for al-Assad to relinquish power, and increasing official defections, it would be abundantly wishful to take his long-term survival for granted. The second scenario would be the dissolution of central command under al-Assad and the creation of a destructive power vacuum, which the opposition might not manage to fill immediately. That is a situation that can give rise to the rule of warlords and, if prolonged and unchecked, lead to the disintegration of Syria. The third alternative would see forces headed by the Syrian National Coalition overcome the government, build up on the state institutions, and establish a representative central establishment of their own with international assistance. All told, there is no escaping the fact that the tipping point of uprising has long passed in disfavor of the pre-Arab-Spring status quo and there will be no return whatsoever of business as usual in Syria as Iran favors and struggles to restore.

Conclusion

Iran has already started working with the opposition and some of its international backers to ensure any regime replacing that of al-Assad will consider its strategic interests and demands, particularly as far as antagonism against Israel and alliance with Hezbollah—or more broadly the balance of power in the region—are concerned. One should note, however, that if this *realpolitik* engagement has failed to yield meaningful results so far, it is because the Islamic Republic is pushing in the wrong direction. It is still seeking, against all the odds, to retain a measure of the old guard, which the majority of Syrians are quite unlikely to grant after so much blood has been spilled, mostly at the hands of the government. Iran has almost lost the war in Syria, and also the battle for hearts and minds in the region. Yet, it still has the opportunity to reverse the past course and thus, instead of endeavoring to perpetuate al-Assad's rule, take the lead and help facilitate his exit. Only then may it win any peace afterwards and expect others to respect its concerns. Put in broader terms, unless Iran undertakes a proactive function in resolving the crisis—that is, by enabling al-Assad's departure—it will have little, if any, share in the unfolding redistribution of power in the new Middle East.

Notes

1. Cited in Slavin, B. (2012, 13 December). Former US official urges military intervention in Syria. *Al-Monitor*. Retrieved from http://www.al-monitor.com/pulse/originals/2012/al-monitor/former-official-urges-us-militar.html

2. The Islamic Republic News Agency (IRNA), Fars News Agency (FNA), and Press TV serve as good instances of such a practice.

3. The year 2012 saw some of the gravest massacres since the outbreak of the uprising that had degenerated by July into a veritable civil war according to the International Committee of the Red Cross (ICRC). The massive casualties in the Western city of Homs on February 4 following a military siege, the mass slaughter of 108 people in Houla villages on May 25, the massacre of approximately 78 people in Mazraat al-Qubeir on June 5, and the Daraya massacre in late August with a death toll of at least 400 were among the conflict's most notable mass atrocities and widely attributed to military and paramilitary forces (*Shabiha*) loyal to Bashar al-Assad. For further details, see "Hundreds of casualties" in Syria's Homs. (2012, 4 February). *Aljazeera*, Retrieved from http://www.aljazeera.com/news/middleeast/2012/02/201223231333768854.html; Nebehay, S. (2012, 29 May). Most Houla victims killed in summary executions: U.N. *Reuters*. Retrieved from http://www.reuters.com/article/2012/05/29/us-syria-un-idUSBRE84S10020120529; Sherlock, R. & Samaan, M. (2012, 8 June). Syria massacre: UN observers greeted by smell of rotting flesh. *The Telegraph*. Retrieved from http://www.telegraph.co.uk/news/worldnews/middleeast/syria/9320654/Syria-massacre-UN-observers-greeted-by-smell-of-rotting-flesh.html; Mahmood, M., Harding, L., & agencies in Damascus. (2012, 28 August). Syria's worst massacre: Daraya death toll reaches 400. *The Guardian*. Retrieved from http://www.guardian.co.uk/world/2012/aug/28/syria-worst-massacre-daraya-death-toll-400; and Castle, T. & Unsworth, T. (2012, 14 June). Syrian Army systematically killing civilians: Amnesty. *Reuters*. Retrieved from http://www.reuters.com/article/2012/06/14/us-syria-amnesty-idUSBRE85D08520120614.

"God save the King?" The Evolution of Protest in Jordan in Light of the Arab Spring

Sarah A. Tobin

Abstract

Protest in Jordan has experienced a series of alterations in governmental and legal enforcements, in goals and ethics for change demanded in protest, and in the visibility for such protests that continue to render acts of protest worthwhile and important. This series of alterations in protest can best be understood in three phases. The first phase is the Arab Spring of 2011 in which there were multiple protests and agitations, which are widely understood as limited in their effect or even unsuccessful. The second phase includes the 2012 protests of Article 308 of the penal code, or "Rape Law," which redefined the terms by which protests were held without governmental permissions and established culture change for women as a viable aim for protest. The third phase is characterized by the most recent protests against the International Monetary Fund's (IMF) enactment of reductions of subsidies on imported gas, in which residents with vested economic interested protested in larger numbers. In this paper, I argue that these phases of protest and their changes in objectives and mobilizations render protest in Jordan a protracted, discursive vehicle by which the "citizen" is actively being redefined. As such, there are expanded spaces for political, economic, and social and cultural agency on the part of this reimaged citizenry. This alters and amplifies the challenges for the terms of Hashemite and royal stability, and it ultimately challenges the terms by which political processes can and will move forward.

Introduction

As the Arab Spring of 2011 turned to an "Arab Autumn" or "Arab Winter," the objectives, forms and styles, and impetus for mobilization in protest began to change. In Jordan, we saw that the Arab Spring was largely judged in terms of what it was not and did not accomplish. The Arab Spring in Jordan did not mobilize the population en masse, nor did it effectively agitate for sustained, long-term political and economic reforms. Arab Spring protests in Jordan were often understood as a seemingly ineffective and relatively unpopular tool for political and economic change. Simultaneously and surprisingly, protests continue with regularity even into 2013. This is because protest in Jordan has experienced a series of alterations in governmental and legal enforcements, the goals and ethics for change demanded in protest, and the visibility for such protests that continue to render protest worthwhile and important, even if not for the initial political and economic reforms of the early Arab Spring.

This series of alterations in protest can best be understood in three phases: the first is the Arab Spring of 2011 in which there were multiple protests and agitations, frequently by ethnic Jordanians, for political and economic reform on the part of the government, which are widely understood as limited in their effect or even unsuccessful; the second includes the 2012 protests of Article 308 of the penal code, or "Rape Law," which allows rape charges to be dropped if the perpetrator agrees to marry the victim, and he agrees not to divorce her for the following three years. These protests redefined the terms by which protests were held without governmental permissions and established culture changes for women as a viable aim for protest, rather than primarily governmental reforms by and for a largely male audience. The third phase is characterized by the most recent protests against the International Monetary Fund (IMF) enactment of reductions of subsidies on imported gas, in which Palestinian, Iraqi, and Syrian refugees and other residents with vested economic interested protested in larger numbers.

In this paper, I argue that these phases of protest and their changes in goals and mobilizations render protests in Jordan a protracted, discursive vehicle by which the "citizen" is actively being redefined. As such, there are expanded spaces for political, economic, and social and cultural agency on the part of this reimaged citizenry. This alters and amplifies the challenges for the terms of Hashemite and royal stability, and it ultimately challenges the terms by which political processes can and will move forward.

The Arab Spring in Context

Any glance at the region's news will find the Middle East still in the throes of uncertainty and instability prompted by the Arab Spring. While nearly every country in the region has seen some kind of protest or action, including marches and rallies, Tunisia is arguably the most "successful" case of popular protest followed by relatively peaceful and democratic regime change. However, the assassination of secular opposition leader, Chokri Belaid in early February 2013, has prompted many to rethink the long-term possibilities for cooperating with the relatively moderate Islamist party Ennahda. The closer one draws geographically to Jordan, however the less certain the outcomes of the Arab Spring and the movements forward.

The case of Egypt often serves as a reference point for Jordanians when they discuss what they do not want out of an Arab Spring or post-Arab Spring national experience. As one informant told me, "If Egypt suddenly became a place where everyone is happy and prosperous, there'd be a revolution in Jordan" (Tobin, 2012, p. 107). Closely associating Egypt with lower standards of living and political and economic insecurity—particularly after the democratic election of Mohammed Morsi—persisted. Largely, Jordanians were keen to see stability maintained because an alternative leadership and the potential for military rule was considered far worse than what most residents of Jordan experienced on a daily basis. Furthermore, with the amplification of sexual harassment, assault, and gang rape of women in Tahrir Square, Jordanians were keen to keep women visible and safe in protests, which further distanced them from the more reprehensible aspects of Arab Spring and post-Arab Spring life of their near neighbors.

The case of Syria also draws points for comparisons among Jordanians. As a country with a shared border, the comparisons are quite potent in forming opinions about protest and political action. In 2012, I wrote about the ways in which the Syrian secret police were understood by Jordanians to be more secretive, alarming, intrusive, and insidious than the Jordanian intelligentsia: "The consensus was that the Jordanian police will kick you but will not kill you" (Tobin, 2012, pp. 106–107). Furthermore, by this point in the Arab Spring, it was already known that the Syrian secret police would round up their own people en masse for interrogations, torture, and even executions, which are all fears Jordanians did not share about the outcomes of their own protests. And, as the last year has played out, the concerns with the power and ferocity of the al-Assad-led Syrian secret and not-so-secret police were justified, prescient even. With hundreds of thousands of Syrians now living in refugee camps and around Jordan (United Nations High Commissioner for Refugees, 2013), and the country now in the throes of a Civil War, Jordanians are both horrified by these potential outcomes of protest, but highly skeptical of the power for these outcomes in their own neighborhoods. They have historical, political, social, and economic experiences with protest in Jordan, which further inform this position.

History of Protest in Jordan

Understanding the history of protest in Jordan puts the Arab Spring and the post-Arab Spring protests into a greater context. The historical context offers a wider analytical lens that reveals much about the legal status of the act of protest, the demographics of the participants, the aims and interests of the protest, and the state-society as well as the lesser-reported society–society relations.

Jordan has a history of protests that go back to the country's very foundations. The government's first constitution of 1950 guaranteed the populace the right to assemble, and labor and union activism flourished (Adely, 2013). Until the Constitution was suspended in 1957, labor unions and trade unions were active in their demands-oriented struggles, and they facilitated the first International Confederation of Arab Workers in 1956 (al-Hourani, 2013).

During the Jordan Crisis of 1957–1958, the Hashemite rulers briefly intertwined the nation's political, economic, and national allegiances with those of Iraq, experienced an attempted coup, and dissolved British control in Jordan. These crises pushed Jordan to realign their interests with the United States, primarily as a means to stave off Communist and Islamist influences (Tal, 1995). It was a short period of tremendous upheaval and political contraction. As a result, King Hussein imposed martial law, suspended parliament, dissolved political parties, and arrested and vanquished leftist and nationalist political opposition.

The late-1980s and 1990s saw some of the most important public assemblies and protests in Jordan, which occurred during a period of "political reopening" ("History of Jordan," n.d.). As the United States limited its foreign aid to Jordan, King Hussein responded by introducing limited political reforms and liberalizations that were aimed to generate support for new economic policies, particularly neo-liberal shifts and IMF-backed loans (Choucair, 2006). This included the 1989 reestablishment of the Right to Assemble and the lifting of Martial Law. As a result, price inflation and a lack of political freedoms were often the rationale given for protests at locations that varied from universities in cities such as Yarmouk to rural areas known for religious and social conservatism, such as Ma'an. Coming out of the Civil War of the 1970s and the intense political and border definition and redefinition with Israel, the late-1980s and 1990s were a period of upheaval and uncertainty. During this time, a diverse set of political parties emerged, as did an interest in free press and a public culture of debate. The Right to Assemble proved to be a vital lynchpin for the populace's participation in securing an ordered and relatively peaceful public society.

In 2001, the 1989 Right to Assemble was modified to a permit-based system for assembly, in which the protestors needed to notify the government of planned gatherings, including who would be protesting, when, and where. The government official hearing these notifications might have balked at certain locations for protest or numbers of people gathering, but the populace held much decision-making power in protest planning and execution. This changed in 2003 when the permit-based system was expanded to a permissions-based system. Now, the power to decide lawful protests resided most fully on the shoulders of the government. Furthermore, the law stipulates that it is unlawful to criticize the King of Jordan or call for his deposition. Insulting the King is illegal, and—at least until relatively recently—a commonly honored part of the law.

When protests are conducted outside of the governmental, permissions-based processes, arrests can and are made. As Schwedler (2013) points out, however, rarely are people charged with violating the laws that regulate public gatherings. Instead, people are charged with "damaging state property, threatening state security, or insulting a foreign regime—completely separate charges from the public gathering law" (Schwedler, 2013, p. 2). The Hashemite rulers selectively use the laws that regulate public gatherings as a means to pay homage to public democratic processes and veneers of free speech and also as a means to garner support for otherwise unpopular economic policies, which are consistent with the 1989 constitutional enactments.

Despite these substantive barriers to organizing and conducting public gatherings, Jordan's 20th century has seen tremendous numbers and types of protests, most of which never make international headlines. These include protests against Israel or against U.S. foreign policy in the region. They may include actions that speak to domestic policy in education and labor. In fact, in 2011 there were over 800 labor protests and actions in Jordan (Adely, 2013; Amman, 2012). These ongoing series of protests and public gatherings all speak to the role that protest and protesting have played in defining, funneling, and regulating state–society and society–society discourse. This is what defines protests in Jordan: it is a discursive means by which the government is able to hear and respond to the interests of the populace in a highly regulated format, and a means for the populace to popularly and democratically voice concerns and agitate for change. All of this tends to occur without a fundamental threat to structures of stability and balances of power, which is not surprising to those who are familiar with a Jordan "Forever on the Brink" of economic and political disaster (Lynch, 2013). Protest is, in short, a protracted discourse about participation in political life, economic justice, and modes of sociality in contemporary society and everyday life. The lens of protest as discourse reveals much about the Arab Spring in Jordan and about the ways in which the discourse between the Hashemites and the populace—in protest—has changed. (Jordan Labor Watch, 2012).

Phase One: Jordan's Arab Spring

The Arab Spring in Jordan garnered much attention, primarily for what it was not (Tobin, 2012). Parliamentary elections were held on November 9, 2010, and the first protest in what could be understood as the Arab Spring took place on January 28, 2011 with 3,500 people. Compared to the tens or even hundreds of thousands of Egyptian protestors that had taken to Tahrir Square in Cairo at this time, and even taking into account that the population of Jordan is a fraction of population in Egypt, the 3,500 protestors in Jordan may have raised a few eyebrows, but still seemed quite small.

On February 1, 2011, King Abdullah responded by sacking the first of what would become four prime ministers, all of whom were summarily dismissed from their positions during the course of the last two years. In turn, the populace took to the streets in protest again on February 2 and 4, 2011. In response, King Abdullah offered up to $500 million for salary increases for government employees and in subsidies for food staples and fuel.

On February 18, 2011, and again on February 25, 2011, Jordan saw protests that more than doubled the size of the first. Between 7,000 and 10,000 people came out to protest for governmental reforms, which would make the parliament more representative, and they agitated for the King to relinquish his power to appoint the prime minister. To these demands, King Abdullah promised reforms within a three-month timeframe.

It is worth mentioning that in these early stages of the Arab Spring, the discourse lay solidly between the ethnic Jordanians and political or passport-holding "East-Bankers" ("Jordanian-Jordanians") and the Hashemite government. The population in Jordan is ethnically quite diverse. Most Jordanians are not ethnic Jordanians and passport-holding "East-Bankers." Though census data has not been collected, it is estimated that approximately 50% of the populace are ethnic Palestinians. Many of them, but certainly not all, carry Jordanian passports. Furthermore, it is estimated that another 20%–25% of the population are not ethnic Jordanians, Palestinians, or Jordanian passport holders. They include mainly Iraqi and growing numbers of Syrian refugees, but also some foreign workers (both Arab and non-Arab), as well as other small minorities groups such as the Druze. In these early stages, the protestors were overwhelmingly pro-regime and pro-democratic reformers–permission-seeking and peaceful, and largely made up of East-Bankers. These passport-carrying, political citizens frequently constitute those who are working within the political system to impact change and are desirous of continuous stability. They are loyal subjects in this Hashemite Kingdom, and they reap the rewards for it. They are the first recipients of these economic and political gestures of reform. Oft-cited employment discrimination renders Jordanian-Jordanians most likely to work as higher prestige and more secure government employees, while Palestinians are more likely to work in the private sector. Gerrymandering enables Jordanian-Jordanian over-representation in the

Parliament (National Public Radio, 2013). As a result, Jordanian-Jordanians would be the most keen to see the implementation of these early economic and political reforms promised. The Arab Spring, certainly in its earliest manifestations, was very much a discourse of loyalty and reward between political citizens as Jordanian-Jordanians and the Hashemite rulers.

These divides in terms of interests and allegiances of the citizenry were made most prominent in the Dakhliya Circle protests of March 2011. For two days in March, the Circle of the Interior Ministry became a space for uncertainty and contest between Jordanian-Jordanian loyalists and a mix of opposition forces. On March 24, opposition forces of primarily ethnic Palestinians with mixed passport holdings modeled the highly publicized protests in Tunisia and Egypt, eschewed the necessary permissions to protest, and occupied this central traffic circle with claims of a sit-in for an indeterminate period of time. Loyalists and anti-reformists showed up with a counter-protest. There were chants and slogans painted on large signs, and the two groups raised their voices for their own causes.

What amounted to a shouting match on the first day of this protest, took a turn towards violence the second day. After Friday prayers, the two sides started throwing rocks at each other. At this time, the government closed off the circle from traffic and sent in the riot police to quell the disputes between the two groups. The presence of the riot police, however, prompted fears of governmental repression by Egyptian-style *baltigiya* (thugs), and by the end of the day, the protest was over and the two sides dispersed. Over the course of these two days, there was one fatality, which the government's Medical Examiner determined was from "natural causes." Also, there were 62 civilians and 58 police injured.

In many ways, this apex of the Arab Spring protests is not so much about a certain populace agitating for political and economic reformation as much as it is revealing of the deep divides among the Jordanian citizenry. Not all Jordanians are Jordanian-Jordanians, and protest demographics, political loyalties, and government-dolled resources and rewards reflect this.

Two days later, on March 27, 2011, King Abdullah called to avoid "any behavior or attitude that would affect our unity" (*Al-Jazeera*, 2013). However, one of the challenges to building a unified, cohesive society based on political affiliations in Jordan is that these differences in citizen status and everyday practices of nationalism run deep. Recent political campaigns by the Hashemites have focused on trying to overcome ethnic differences through a series of campaigns. Between 2003 and 2006, there were three national campaigns of "Jordan First," "National Agenda," and "We Are All Jordan." However, these campaigns were largely seen as inauthentic and propagandist; they did not address the very real and, for many, very tangible manifestations of inequalities from the polls to the bank, and from family histories to national narratives.

On September 22, 2011, King Abdullah spoke on National Public Radio to discuss the Arab Spring events of the year. He said:

> What bothers me in a lot of countries is [that] society is being led by the street, as opposed to the light at the end of the tunnel. But we have got to remember that the Arab Spring began—and there's [sic] challenges all over the world, including your country—because of economic difficulties: unemployment, poverty. We have the largest youth cohort in history coming into the workforce in the Middle East. And that is how the Arab Spring started. I mean, Tunis started because of the economy, not because of politics....
>
> What keeps me up at night is poverty and unemployment. We have, in the past 10 years, managed to establish a credible middle class. But any shifts in oil prices, economic challenges, that middle class becomes very fragile. (National Public Radio, September 22, 2011)

As demonstrated by this First Phase of the Arab Spring and post-Arab Spring period, political citizens and loyalists were agitating for and receiving minimal change through largely legal and peaceful means. This was ultimately a narrow discursive exchange that involved few people and mainly elites. However, as this quote of King Abdullah's and the Dakhiliya Protests demonstrate, this small—and important—segment of society hardly captured the wider interests of populace, residents, and citizens. Still, the First Phase brought people to pay attention to their own political and economic interests—their rightful place as citizens, broadly defined—in relation to not only the ruling government, but also each other. The Second Phase captured this movement in defining and redefining the citizen.

Phase Two: Protesting Article 308

During the summer of 2012, protests emerged in light of several, high-profile enactments of Article 308 of the penal code, or "Rape Law". According to Jordanian law, the rape of a child under the age of 15 is punishable by death. However, the death penalty and other punishments for the rape of youth either under or over age 15 are exonerated by enactments of Article 308.

Utilizing and defending Article 308 in Jordan is not uncommon, though many find it offensive. Nonetheless, many human rights activists indicate that there is no political desire or will to alter the laws surrounding gender inequities and sexual crimes (IRIN, 2013). In 2010 alone, there were 379 reported cases of rape and assault of girls under age 15, which were resolved by Article 308 (Hattar, 2013). Dr. Hussein Khazai, a sociologist at the University of Jordan, came out in support of Article 308 with supporting "evidence" that women are sociologically different from men and have the ability to overcome the ordeal if they have the desire to do so, which is achievable by fulfilling their social roles as wives and child bearers (Hattar, 2013).[1] Jordan's first female coroner, Israa Tawalbeh, came out vocally in support of Article 308, saying there is:

> nothing wrong in Article 308 as such. The problem is how some local and international human rights groups interpret the law. Actual rape cases are rare in our society. Sometimes, girls under 18 lose their virginity to force their families to accept marriage to their boyfriends. The law categorizes this as rape. [It] solves problems for some . . . I think the law fits our society and reality. It protects the girls by forcing attackers to marry them. (Hattar, 2013, p. 1)

Comments invoking the "protection" of girls are often used as a code to mean protection against honor killings. In honor killings, the honor of the family—broken by a female's sexual misconduct, broadly construed—once lost, can be restored through the death of the female or, less commonly, the legal binding of the two persons in marriage. Jordan is considered to have a relatively high-rate of honor killings, including one-third of all murders in 1999 (Cuomo, 2013), which constitutes approximately 15–20 women per annum (*IRIN*, 2013). Perpetrators of honor crimes are typically offered lenient sentences, if charged at all. The female's "sexual misconduct" in these cases can also include being a victim of rape. Article 308 provides women a marriage to their rapist when, at least in theory, their only other alternative would be death. The logic is that it is better to be seen in Jordanian society as a divorced woman than a raped women.

There were several high profile cases that were brought to light in 2012, which prompted the protests. In April 2012, a 19-year-old male kidnapped a 14-year-old girl from Zarqa, and then took her to the desert where he proceeded to rape her for three consecutive days, when a police patrol happened to find them. The male was arrested and imprisoned, and the girl was put into a holding cell to protect her against an honor killing potentially rendered by her family. According to one report, the 19-year-old male was already married, and his wife was in on the scheme (Pearlman 2013). The male avoided his death sentence by agreeing to marry the girl, in accordance with Article 308. Later in 2012, an 18-year-old female's father struck a deal for her to marry her unemployed rapist, who was already married to a woman who was a beggar in her attempts to care for their six children. In June 2012, a man talked a 15-year-old girl into entering an empty apartment where he proceeded to rape her. He sought to marry the girl to avoid prosecution. Cases like these were brought to light at an alarming rate.

Later that month, Jordanians began taking to the streets in protest. On June 25, approximately 200 people, primarily women, but some men as well, linked arms along Queen Alia Street in Dakhliya Cirle—the same site as the controversial protests of 2011—holding signs that read "You're killing us with your honor;" "I am not your honor;" "Rape has become a national duty;" and "My life is more important than family honor." The protests continued at this site and in disruptive locations such as the commercial thoroughfare of Rainbow Street near First Circle throughout the summer.

Highly contested, these protests were conducted without government permits, highly visible, disruptive to traffic flows, and—in a shift from Arab Spring protests—aimed to create a groundswell of public support for changing the culture of society more than the legal structures in place. These were protests against patriarchy more than against politics. As a result, disliked and unwanted protestors were not subject to governmental suppression or political violence, but rather to symbolic violence through the insults, harassment, and defamation by fellow citizens. Protestors' pictures were altered and slandered on Facebook and other online social media sites. Threats of rape to protestors were in abundance, and even death threats were launched against them.

In addition to the lack of governmental permits for protesting, these protests were notable as Facebook and other social media were eschewed for person-to-person contact in organization and engagement. In some ways, these protests harkened back to a pre-Arab Spring preference for mobilization through personal contacts rather than through social media, while at the same time demonstrating innovation by using protest as a discourse to engage in culture change of fellow citizens by fellow citizens. In particular, these protests sought to expand the citizenry—an equal citizenry—along gendered lines, rather than lines of ethnicity or passport holdings. Women too could engage in protest and use it a means to funnel, solidify, and legitimate their side of the discourse.

Phase Three: Protesting Gas Prices

During the 1980s and the Iran–Iraq War, Jordan extended significant political and economic support to Iraq, including the use of the Port of Aqaba as Iraq's main supply route. Jordan received a prime part of the deal, including oil at extremely heavily subsidized prices.

In 2012, Jordan sought an IMF loan of $2.3 billion to help cover its $5 billion budget deficit. Jordan is a resource-poor country, relying on imports for 95% of its energy needs, and since 2003 has been relying upon inexpensive gas from Egypt. As a result of the Arab Spring in Egypt, in particular, these imports have become unreliable. The pipeline that carries gas to Israel and Jordan from Egypt has been attacked and in need of substantial repairs more than a dozen times, which has stopped reliable shipments. As a result, the Jordanian government has had to switch to the more expensive fuel oil to generate electricity. And, in what is primarily seen as a political act of desperation, Jordan has even received offers from Iran for free gas for the entire Jordan populace. These disruptions and unstable sourcing problems have cost the Jordanian government $7 million per day, which is the primary reason for the $5 billion deficit.

In September 2012, the Jordanian government attempted to reduce subsidies on imported gas by 10%. There were overnight protests that prompted the government to reverse their policies the next day. After some deliberation, however, the Hashemites took to it again in November 2012. This time, the reduced subsidies resulted in a 14% increase at the pump, from $3.80 to $4.25 per gallon of gas. The reduction in subsidies also resulted in a 50% increase in cooking gas canisters, from $9 to $15.

Not surprisingly, the populace took to the streets without governmental permissions. During the first night of protests, demonstrators exhibited a violence that had not yet been seen: tires and garbage were burned, roads were blocked; counter measures enacted by the riot police included tear gas and water cannons. Between this first protest on November 13, 2012 and December 1, 2012, there were nearly daily protests. The result of this two weeks of action included 3 killed, 71 injured, 158 detained, and over 100 people charged with incitement against the government, rioting and—for the first time—illegal gathering (RT, 2013) A few were also charged with incitement to change the government, which carries a death sentence (Rudoren, 2013).

These were, however, non-permitted protests that brought together ethnic Jordanians with full political citizenship, ethnic Palestinians that could or could not have the same political rights, and refugees from Iraq and Syria, most of whom were unlikely to have much more than temporary residency permits. Here, the protestors also represented a range of Islamist and non-Islamist affiliations, as they were "people of all backgrounds, including women without veils and men without beards" (Levs, al-Assad, Razek, Alkhshali, & Karadsheh, 2013), and "many affiliated with Muslim, Arab nationalist, Marxist, communist and youth opposition groups" (*Al-Jazeera*, 2013). It was for the first time in these protests that this diverse demographic called for regime change, and called upon King Abdullah to step down. With echoes of Tunisia and Egypt, the protestors called out "The people want the fall of the regime!" or *Ash-shab yurid isqat an-nizam!*

The subject of the protests, demographics of the protestors, and their willingness to call for King Abdullah's deposition indicated that protest is no longer a discursive matter on narrowly defined political issues for a small fraction of ethnic Jordanians who retain the rights and privileges of full political citizens. As primarily non-Jordanians, most of the protestors do not enjoy the same privileges, and as a result, do not feel as encumbered or obligated to pay homage to the King. Rather, protest has emerged here as discourse between all the residents of Jordan and the economic policies that marginalize them globally and compound their economic marginalities locally.

Conclusion

As seen during the last two years, the culture of protest in Jordan has been one of changing discourses and, as a result, an expanding definition of "the citizen" (Goode, 2013), a category to which more and more people in Jordan are now laying claim. At the advent of the Arab Spring, the first protests reflected a more narrowly defined citizen, one who works within the political system, is loyal to the regime, and benefits from a preferred political status. This reflected a kind of political citizenship at play, complete with the right to reside in the country, and to vote in elections.

However, with the protests against Article 308, protest became defined as a discourse by and between the populace, as women especially laid claim to their equal rights as a kind of "cultural citizen." This gendering of cultural citizenship brings women the right to know and to speak, as well as rights for participation, representation, and public recognition. The protestors' aims of changing the culture, rather than agitating for political reform speak to the interest in developing an equal footing in society according to cultural standards, rather than only in the eyes of the law. It is at this point that we also see the beginnings of an erosion of permit-seeking protests with little to no repercussions. In these protests we see that not every gathering necessitates government involvement. In the case of the protests against the culture surrounding Article 308, it could be argued that because the protest did not agitate for political reform, the Hashemite rulers found little ground to worry. Though the protests were unpermitted and took place in Dakhiliya Circle—just as the March 24–25, 2011 protests did—it could also be argued that the content of the protests was not fundamentally threatening in the same way that protests for constitutional reform would be. In fact, the Hashemite rulers would likely be hard pressed to come out in public support of Article 308, for fear of negative Western reception. Though, on the other hand, by not getting involved, King Abdullah missed out on an opportunity for political reform that could have brought him some much needed positive attention.

The expansion of discursive elements in protesting Article 308 also prompted other segments of society to imagine and envision themselves as a legitimate part of the citizenry, even if their ethnicity or passports do not technically support such enactments. This citizen can be understood as an "economic citizen" with rights to work and economically prosper. This category applies to those who may be long-term residents of Jordan with little hope of attaining full political citizenship, such as some Palestinian refugees, and Iraqi and Syrian refugees. In fact, the cutting of gas subsidies impacts these oftentimes-impoverished communities' everyday lives much more immediately than parliamentary elections and new prime ministers.

The challenge of the economic citizen is, however, that the political impetus to work within the system and to refrain from calling for King Abdullah to be deposed is removed. Although, refugees are required to live by the laws of the land in which they reside, they are not involved in the formation of political or cultural processes to the degree that natives are. In fact, without the ability to participate in political processes, they are disenfranchised and may look to other avenues to participate in agitating for change and expressing their most immediate interests.

This expansion and redefinition of the citizenry carries implications for enhanced agency. This analytical progress of "the citizen" demonstrates that people in Jordan are very much embracing notions of self-determination and freedom of expression. It is a notable observation if for nothing more than the fact that many of these protestors have not necessarily been in Jordan for decades or generations. As such, this means that these refugees are carrying their interests with them, from a previous political, economic, and social context and into another.

As a result, we can understand the need for protest in terms of a broken social contract (Barrett, 2011). As Barrett (2011) reminds us, "Lucre begets loyalty." But we must think of lucre here as capital broadly defined to include political and cultural capital, and not only financial interests. When a social contract of political exchange and agreement is broken, the resulting protests make sense; this is a model often encountered in the literature. This then raises the question as to what a social contract of cultural exchange and agreement might look like and what kind of protests would result were this contract broken. The model of protesting Article 308 provides insight into how these processes are often highly gendered, with desires for equal citizenship also reflecting cultural practices. Finally, the protests against decreased gas subsidies constitute an important moment where a social contract on economic agreements is also rendered in terms that simultaneously emphasize and marginalize the state. On the one hand, the policies enacted by King Abdullah and the IMF-backed loan put the Hashemite government front and center as the interlocutors of this social contract. That is, King Abdullah signed this policy into action. On the other hand, these policies impact simultaneously many who legally and technically reside outside of much of the regulatory state apparatus. Refugees, by definition, occupy a minimal status neither entirely inside nor outside any given state. As such, these policies also bring together more closely the IMF and the Palestinian, Iraqi, and Syrian refugees. The resulting claims for an economic citizenship expressed in protests are both a commentary on the broken social contract policies within the hosting state—such as between refugees who pay sales tax to the state but no longer benefit from the gas subsidies as they live on the economic margins—and reflective of a broken social contract with larger neo-liberal policies that aim to remove state involvement and bring the transient populations into more free-market interactions unmediated by the state. Citizenship and the cultures of protest here are reflective of a wider variety of types of relationships with the state's Hashemite rulers, others in society, and forces that reside far beyond the country's geographic borders.

The limitations of King Abdullah and the Hashemite rulers to serve as a sufficient "umbrella state," encompassing all manner of populations and bringing them into the fold as equal political, cultural, and economic citizens was revealed most prominently during the Parliamentary Elections on January 23, 2013. Forty percent of eligible voters came to the ballot box in large support of the regime. Of the remaining 60% of eligible voters that did not cast a vote, many opted to choose a purposeful ballot boycott instead. This kind of political action demonstrates the inability of the regime to reach people in a meaningful way that encourages their participation within the election system. However, the election boycotts are ultimately aiming to establish an emergent, and dueling, system that could incorporate all kinds of citizens more expansively and therefore more effectively. As the Arab Spring turns into the Arab Summer, Autumn, and Winter, the Hashemites would do well to reorient and expand their own understandings of who their citizens are and work to address these differentiated types of needs in an expanded discourse with them all.

Notes

1. Apparently, Dr. Hussein Khazai has since changed his mind on these sociological points: Cf. http://www.alghad.com/index.php/article/550750.html

Arab Spring and Modernization of Islam: A Major Step toward the Unification of Human Civilization

Susmit Kumar

Abstract

Two factors, the global economic depression and global Islamic fundamentalism, are going to redefine human civilization in the same way that the Great Depression and the two World Wars redefined human civilization—by resulting in a unification of European countries that had been fighting each other for thousands of years. The global Islamic militancy may lead to a temporary establishment of an Islamic empire in the Middle East and North Africa, with fundamentalist Islamic parties taking power in democratic elections. These ruling parties will try to turn back the clock by imposing Shari'a rules. But in the end, it will lead to the formation of secular and democratic nations, such as Turkey, in the region. Until World War I, Turkey, whose population is 99% Muslim, had been the seat of the Ottoman Empire (1299–1922), an Islamic empire, and the Islamic caliphate. Since 1923, it has become a secular, democratic nation. Hence, the current rise in Islamic militancy worldwide does not reflect Samuel Huntington's "clash of civilizations," but is instead a violent prelude to the modernization of Islam, and a major step toward the integration of human civilization.

Introduction

The first decade of the 21st century saw the world plunging into both serious political and economic crises which seem reminiscent of the first half of the last century when the world faced both economic (Great Depression) and political crises (two World Wars). The rise of Islamic fundamentalism and the global financial crisis of 2007/2008—sometimes labeled, and referred to here as the Great Recession—came as a surprise for world powers and seem to have no solution.

The rise of Islamic fundamentalism extremists worldwide took most by surprise when on September 11, 2001, they intentionally crashed airliners into the World Trade Center and the Pentagon, killing more than three thousand people. On that day, U.S. National Security Adviser, Condoleezza Rice was scheduled to outline a Bush Administration policy that would address "the threats and problems of today and the day after, not the world of yesterday" (Shakir, 2006). The focus was largely on missile defense, not terrorism from Islamic radicals. The address was designed to promote a missile system as the cornerstone of a new national security strategy. It contained no mention of al-Qaeda, Osama bin Laden, or Islamic extremist groups, according to former U.S. officials who saw the text. The speech was postponed in the chaos of the day. It mentioned terrorism, but did so as one of the dangers from rogue nations such as Iraq, who might use weapons of terror, rather than from the extremist cells now considered to be America's main security threat (Wright, 2004).

Until 2010, nobody would have thought of the drastic changes, known as the Arab Spring, happening in Middle Eastern and North African Islamic countries. After the fall of dictators such as Hosni Mubarak of Egypt, Ben Ali of Tunisia, Ali Abdullah Saleh of Yemen, and Muammar al-Qadhafi of Libya, every ruler in this region now looks vulnerable. Al-Qaeda is not limited only to Afghanistan and Pakistan; rather, it has become a franchise. The combination of religious medievalism and sociopolitical instability indicates that a transitional period is under way.

Until 1900, no one could have predicted that democracies would replace kingdoms in most European countries, or that Asian and African countries would have gained independence within five to six decades. Because of the two World Wars, most European kingdoms were replaced by vibrant democracies, and colonial rulers had to leave most of Asia and Africa due to the destruction wrought on their economies. Similarly, we will see in this paper that the present political and economic crisis is a major step toward the integration of human civilization.

Although these crises take a heavy toll, they bring changes within a few decades which otherwise would have taken several centuries. In order to give birth to a beautiful child, a woman has to go through the pain of labor. Even with the loss of millions of lives, these events work as a catalyst for the evolution of human civilization.

Science and technology has made tremendous progress in the last half of the 20th century, drastically reducing travel time among various continents from months to hours. Owing to the Internet and the World Wide Web, information now travels in seconds throughout the globe. This has also led to the integration of a global economy; a mouse click can transfer money to any part of the world. All these developments have sped up the evolution of human civilization at a rate that was previously unthinkable.

In this paper, I first discuss post-cold war theories given by political scientists, and then the history of Islam, and why Islam needs modernization, and how that would take place. I will also discuss how a drastic change in the global economy would affect the transition in MENA (Middle East and North African) countries. I will show that the current rise in Islamic militancy worldwide does not reflect Samuel Huntington's "Clash of Civilizations,"[1] but is instead a violent prelude to the modernization of Islam, and a major step toward the integration of human civilization. In the end, Islam will cease to be a factor in politics and will gain a status akin to that of present Christianity, Hinduism and Buddhism. I will also briefly discuss the collapse of the present model of global trade.

Post-Cold War Theories

After the end of the Cold War in 1991, several American thinkers, including Francis Fukuyama, John Mearsheimer, Robert Kaplan, Thomas Friedman, and Samuel P. Huntington proposed theories of the shape of the future global order. I will discuss these theories.

In his 1992 book, *The End of History and the Last Man,* Francis Fukuyama saw the end of history after the victory of liberal democracies over the Soviet Union. As he saw it, the future fault line in international politics would lie between liberal democracies and non-democratic countries. He derived his view of human history from the works of German philosopher G.W.F. Hegel, from whom Karl Marx also picked up some ideas. According to Hegel, human beings are like animals in so far as they have desires for material objects like food, drink, and shelter. The important difference between the two is that human beings want to be "recognized." According to Hegel, it was the desire for recognition that started bloody wars among human beings and created the two classes—masters and slaves—at the beginning of human history. Hegel saw the American and French revolutions as the end of history because these revolutions gave people universal and reciprocal recognition. According to Fukuyama, the defeat of fascism and communism by the liberal democracies are the completion of this process. Liberal democracy symbolizes the end of history because it seeks to abolish the distinction between masters and slaves by making men masters of themselves. He advises the United States to work with other democratic countries in preserving the sphere of democracy around the world and expanding it wherever possible.

The problem with Fukuyama's theory is that "liberal democracy," especially the American version he praises, has been hijacked by wealthy people and lobbyists for multinational corporations. The two classes—slaves and masters—have not disappeared, but still exist in his "ideal liberal democracy" (Fukuyama, 2006, p. 279). This phenomenon characterizes almost all liberal democracies, in Europe, Asia, Latin America, and Australia. Apart from this, his ideal liberal democracy, the United States, supported dictators and repressive regimes all over the world during the Cold War and then left most of those countries in economic and political chaos. The United States still supports repressive regimes and dictators, especially in the Middle East.

In 1990, John Mearsheimer, one of the co-authors of the provocative 2007 book, *The Israel Lobby and U.S. Foreign Policy* (Mearsheimer & Walt, 2007), wrote an article "Back to The Future: Instability in Europe After the Cold War" (Mearsheimer, 1990), predicting that without the two superpowers, Europe would revert to a multipolar environment similar to that in the first half of the 20th century, and would therefore be more prone to instability and violence than in the past 45 years. He argued that the removal of the superpowers' large nuclear arsenals, which had a pacifying effect in Europe, would affect European politics. One reason why his prediction has failed to materialize is the emergence of the European Union (EU), which has become a strong, binding force for practically all of Europe. The United States took an active part in enlarging both the EU and NATO by accepting Eastern European countries and taking advantage of Russian weakness in the 1990s. In addition, it is now too late to redraw national boundaries by force unless a superpower becomes involved, so violence among the European democracies seems unlikely.

Robert Kaplan devised the theory of "West versus the Rest" in his article, "The Coming Anarchy" in the February 1994 issue of *The Atlantic Monthly*, and later wrote a book with the same title. After his extensive travels to the Third World, Kaplan came to the conclusion that the fault line of the future would center on rich and poor countries' socioeconomic conditions. According to Kaplan:

> Future wars will be those of communal survival, aggravated or, in many cases, caused by environmental scarcity. These wars will be subnational, meaning that it will be hard for states and local governments to protect their own citizens physically. This is how many states will ultimately die. As state power fades—and with it the state's ability to help weaker groups within society, not to mention other states—peoples and cultures around the world will be thrown back upon their own strengths and weaknesses, with fewer equalizing mechanisms to protect them. (Kaplan, 2000, p. 49)

In support of his theory, Kaplan quoted the 1991 paper of Thomas Fraser Homer-Dixon titled "On the Threshold: Environmental Changes as Causes of Acute Conflict"

(Homer-Dixon, 1991). According to Homer-Dixon, future wars and civil violence will often arise from a scarcity of resources such as water, cropland, forests, and fish. Just as there will be environmentally-driven wars and refugee flows, there will be environmentally-induced "praetorian" regimes—or, as he puts it, "hard regimes" (Kaplan, 2000, p. 21).

Kaplan further wrote that democratic systems would collapse because of soaring populations and the shrinking availability of raw materials. Resource depletion, environmental issues, and population growth would cause developing nations to collapse, and this would pose a threat to the developed world. He predicted that Africa in the immediate future would be worst, causing foreign embassies to shut down, states to collapse, and contact with the outside world to take place through dangerous, disease-ridden, coastal trading posts. He wrote:

> Given that in 2025 India's population could be close to 1.5 billion, that much of its economy rests on a shrinking natural-resource base, including dramatically declining water levels, and that communal violence and urbanization are spiraling upward, it is difficult to imagine that the Indian state will survive the next century. (Kaplan, 2000, p. 51)

The countries that Kaplan counted as poor (like China and India) at the time of writing "The Coming Anarchy" are clearly undergoing a radical change in economic terms, as both countries are witnessing a burgeoning middle class with Western corporations eager to satisfy their wants. Contrary to Kaplan's thesis, it is likely that not only economic, but geopolitical power will shift from West to East. Moreover, it is because of rampant corruption, especially at the political level, that the Third World suffers economic hardship, not an innate scarcity of resources or helplessness. Even in the Third World, nature has been kind enough to provide abundant natural resources to employ the population cent-per-cent and to fulfil the minimum requirements of local people.

The *New York Times* columnist Thomas Friedman wrote in his 1999 book, *The Lexus and the Olive Tree,* that the deciding factor in future global fault lines would be the rules of globalization, and that the fault line will lie between countries that follow the rules of globalization and those that do not. States that play by the rules will be rewarded, and states that do not will be punished. Friedman wrote that the world is currently undergoing two struggles: the drive for prosperity and development, symbolized by the Lexus, and the desire to retain identity and traditions, symbolized by the olive tree (Friedman, 1999). According to Friedman, "In the Cold War, the most frequently asked question was: 'How big is your missile?' In globalization, the most frequently asked question is: 'How fast is your modem?'" (Friedman, 1999, p. 9), Economic globalization, controlled by international financiers and corporate executives—the "electronic herd"—will make or break nation states depending on the level of cooperation those states give to those corporations. Financial controllers are fast and ruthless, he wrote, because investors can decide in a moment to vacate a country, plunging it into an economic tailspin.

In his other book *The World is Flat* (2005), Friedman suggests that because of the latest technologies the world is now "flat" in most regards, in the sense that the competitive playing fields between industrial and emerging-market countries have been leveled, and that countries like India and China are becoming part of large global supply chains. He does acknowledge, however, that some three billion people still live in an "unflattened" world in places like rural India, rural China, and Africa.

Because of technological innovations, productivity is increasing at the same time the number of jobs is decreasing, all this in a state of affairs where the number of "players" (countries capable of competing in global markets) is, according to Friedman, increasing. This will lead to chaos. The combined population of China and India is more than 2.4 billion, and in the next couple of decades, 60–70% of them will be wired to the Internet. If the "electronic herd" Friedman writes about has a final say in the international economy, then the Chinese and Indian economies will end up almost nowhere. Only a few hundred million out of their 2.4 billion people will be required to produce electronic gadgets and work in related service sectors for the Chinese and Indian domestic economies and for the rest of the world. The majority will remain unemployed. In addition, most countries, including the United States and possibly India, may also have to declare bankruptcy owing to their massive debts to China, which is now the world's main source of cheap manufactured goods. This recent development has put more than $3.6 trillion in foreign exchange (FOREX) in the Chinese treasury, and its FOREX is increasing at an alarming rate with no end in sight. Regardless of what happens to traditional or globalization-antagonistic nations, the fault line described by Friedman actually lies within the globalization-friendly camp itself. The economies clustered around it will function successfully for only a few decades before it gives rise to an economic tsunami and the collapse of the global economy. As discussed later in this paper, the Great Recession was just a symptom of the impending global economic tsunami.

Samuel P. Huntington proposed his theory in the 1993 *Foreign Affairs* article "A Clash of Civilizations?" He also published a book in 1996 called *The Clash of Civilizations and the Remaking of World Order* based on the article. According to him, the future fault line will center on culture and religion. His theory of the clash of civilizations predicts alignments and wars among various civilizations—Western, Islamic, Chinese, Japanese, Orthodox/Russian, Hindu, African, and Latin. The term "clash of civilizations" was first used by Bernard Lewis in an article in the September 1990 issue of *The Atlantic Monthly* titled "The Roots of Muslim Rage." According to Huntington:

> The great divisions among humankind and the dominating source of conflict will be cultural. Nation states will remain the most powerful

actors in world affairs, but the principal conflicts of global politics will occur between nations and groups of different civilizations. The clash of civilizations will dominate global politics. The fault lines between civilizations will be the battle lines of the future (Huntington, 1993).

Huntington's hypothesis postulates a global conflict in 2020 between two alliances—the United States, Europe, Russia, and India on the one side, and China, Japan, and most of Islamic countries on the other. Because both sides have major nuclear capabilities and these are brought into play, both sides could be substantially destroyed; but if mutual deterrence is effective, mutual exhaustion might lead to a negotiated armistice. The West may be able to defeat China by supporting insurrections against Chinese rule by Tibetans, Uighurs, and Mongolians, and by deploying Western and Russian forces eastward into Siberia for a final assault on Beijing, Manchuria, and the Han heartland. According to Huntington, because the economic, demographic, and military power of the major participants in the war will decline dramatically as a result of the conflict, the center of world politics will move south to nations that avoid it, such as the Latin American nations, New Zealand, Mynamar, Sri Lanka, Vietnam, Indonesia, and India as well if it escapes major devastation despite its participation.

Huntington did not consider Islamic militancy and a rise in Islamic fundamentalists in MENA countries—or in countries like India and many European countries, having large Muslim populations—to be a major factor in his global conflict, whereas the latter has become a major source of conflict worldwide.

Also, China can never join hands with Islamic countries because of its own problem in Xinjiang which has a Muslim majority and also has large deposits of minerals and oil. Since the 1990s, China has faced a bloody separatist movement by local Muslims. In August 2012, *Global Times*, a state-run Chinese daily, published an op-ed article saying, "Pakistani support of the Taliban as well as other militant networks has led to many terrorist attacks in Pakistan and India. In the future, jihadist networks may undertake major attacks in Xinjiang and other parts of China" (Farley, 2012). China blamed Pakistani-trained Islamic militants for a July 2012 terrorist attack in Xinjiang that left 11 people dead.

The 2001 attack on the World Trade Center and subsequent U.S. attacks on Afghanistan and Iraq have led political scientists to believe in Huntington's theory of the clash of civilizations. It was because of economic greed (for oil) and the Israel lobby that the United States attacked Iraq in 2003, however, not because of civilizational fault lines. Moreover, the world has not witnessed any significant increase in conflict along civilizational fault lines for the last century. It is economic greed more than all other factors that creates and maintains fault lines among nations and peoples, and it is that which drives wars.

In addition, Huntington's civilizations are only partly unified in nature, especially Islam. In Islam, Shi'a and Sunnis fight bitterly with each other, and for this reason, Saudi Arabia, which is ruled by Sunnis, is collaborating with its bitter enemy, Israel, to fight Shi'a Iran. Although Muslims in Turkey, Pakistan, Indonesia, North Africa, and the rest of the Arab world are Sunnis, they have different viewpoints among themselves, and several of them have been struggling with secessionist movements and other internal conflicts for decades–for example, the Kurds in Turkey, the Baluchs and Pashtuns in Pakistan, and the Aceh in Indonesia. These factors make a unified Islam at least next to impossible.

Finally, as we saw during the Cold War, and in particular in the Nixon government's theory of Mutually Assured Destruction ("MAD") *vis-à-vis* the Soviet Union, a prolonged conventional war is unlikely to occur between two countries that have sufficient nuclear bombs and missiles to destroy each other. Therefore, Huntington's prediction of a bloody, cataclysmic clash between the Chinese and Western civilizations is not going to happen.

The problem with all these theories, not just Huntington's, is that the people who devise them are entrenched in what can be called "the American box." Most of the world, even the European allies, do not like the United States, not because the United States is the lone superpower, but because of what it does, especially under Republican administrations like those of Reagan and Bush Jr. During his eight-year rule, President Clinton was greeted by tens of thousands of people in foreign countries wherever he went, but foreign governments have had a hard time controlling angry protesters whenever President Bush visits. Huntington has summarized it in the following words:

> Hypocrisy, double standards, and "but nots" are the price of Universalist pretensions. Democracy is promoted, but not if it brings Islamic fundamentalists to power; nonproliferation is preached for Iran and Iraq and not for Israel; free trade is the elixir of economic growth, but not for agriculture; human rights are an issue with China, but not with Saudi Arabia. (Huntington, 1996, p. 184)

Why is Modernization of Islam Required?

Nearly all major religions, except Islam, went through a modernization process in the past. Like the founders of other major world religions, the Prophet Muhammad also was a great person. He united the entire Arab population, which had been divided into several clans. It is wrong to criticize him for his deeds, as whatever he did was relevant at the time. For instance, he provided an eye for an eye judgment in the *Qur'an* as there was no prison system wherein a convict could serve a term at the time. We should blame the present-day people who are following these 7th century practices. Except for the divinity aspects of Muhammad's revelations, the *Qur'an* consists of the social practices of 7th century Arabia.

In pre-Islamic Arabia, the condition of women was terrible. The *Qur'an* elevated the status and rights of women in 17th century Arabia; however, these seem too restrictive now, in the 21st century. In the ancient environment, where women were so devalued that female infanticide was a common and tolerated practice, the *Qur'an* introduced reforms that prohibited this practice; permitted women to inheritances; restricted the practice of polygamy; curbed abuses of divorce by husbands; and gave women the ownership of the dowry, which had previously been paid to the bride's father. As the thrust of the Qur'anic reforms regarding women's status was an ameliorative one, it seems reasonable to conclude, as did Fazlur Rahman, an eminent liberal scholar of Islam, that "the principle aim of the *Qur'an* was the removal of certain abuses to which women were subjected" (Mayer, 1999, pp. 97–98; Rahman, 1983, p. 38).

Today, Islam is the only religion that is being enforced by several countries having a Muslim majority population. Shari'a is Islamic law. It is based mainly on the *Hadith*, or sayings of Muhammad. The *Qur'an* and Shari'a impose *jizya*, a tax, on non-Muslims, which Muslims are not required to pay. The Ottoman Empire (1299–1923), and Muslim rulers in India since the 11th century have imposed jizya on non-Muslims. In Persia, jizya was paid by the Zoroastrian minority until 1884. In North Africa, jizya was collected by Islamic rulers until the late 19th century. Until the early last century, Jews in Yemen were forced to wear clothes and shoes of a particular color. In Afghanistan, fundamentalist Talibans forced Hindus to put a two-meter yellow cloth on their houses. In the Ottoman Empire, Christians and Jews paid personal jizya, while Muslims did not—on a regular basis (Hourani, 1991, p. 217). In the Mughal Empire, fundamentalist Muslim rulers like Aurangzeb forced only Hindus to pay personal taxes.

In several Islamic countries there are numerous cases in which Shari'a courts have forced Muslims who converted to other religions to remain Muslims, and they are given prison terms. In several Islamic countries, a non-Muslim gets only a fraction (ranging from one-half to one-tenth) of what a Muslim gets in a similar legal settlement in courts. In Shari'a courts, non-Muslims cannot even represent themselves because Shari'a does not accept the evidence of a non-Muslim. Saudi Arabia implements the *Qur'an* and *Hadith in toto*. No other religion is allowed in Saudi Arabia. Although American soldiers remain in the country to protect the kingdom from outside threats, soldiers who wear a cross or a Star of David must keep the symbols hidden, and they must worship in private.

The *Qur'an* discusses rules and laws in the House of Islam (*Dar al-Islam*), but is silent on how Muslims should live, where non-Muslim "infidels" rule, or how they should live in the House of War (*Dar al-Harb*). The presumption is that it is the duty of Muslims to continue fighting infidels in the House of War, interrupted only by truces, until the entire world either adopts the Muslim faith or submits to Muslim rule.

In Islamic law, conversion from Islam is apostasy, a capital offense for both the one who is misled and the one who misleads him. On this question, the law is clear and unequivocal. If a Muslim renounces Islam, even if a new convert reverts to his previous faith, the penalty is death. In modern times, the concept and practice of *takfir*, recognizing and denouncing apostasy, has been greatly widened. It is not unusual in extremist and fundamentalist circles to decree that some policy, action, or even utterance by a professing Muslim is tantamount to apostasy, and to pronounce a death sentence on the offender. This was the principle invoked in the *fatwas* (religious decrees) against Salman Rushdie, in the murder of Egypt's President Sadat, and against many others (Lewis, 2003, p. 55–56).

Discrimination against non-Muslims takes place in most Muslim countries. In Malaysia, Shari'a courts can overrule any other court's decision; Shari'a courts' decisions are supreme and final. For example, it so happened that one Maniam Moorty, a national hero in Malaysia and a Hindu, was made a Muslim on questionable authority by a few of his superiors in military and Shari'a court. He had been the first Malaysian to climb Mount Everest in 1997. Despite a plea by his wife, who wanted to give his dead body Hindu rites, he was given a Muslim burial. According to her, she did not know that her husband had embraced Islam before his death on December 20, 2005. Neither his family members nor his close friends saw him participating in any Islamic religious activities. Records of the Malaysian Armed Forces said that he embraced Islam in October 2004 and filed an application with his superiors to be registered as such on March 8, 2005. He died in a coma in a hospital in December 2005 due to complications following a fatal accident. However, his military identity card was never modified to reflect this change of religion or his reported new Muslim name of Mohammad Abdullah. Despite his so-called conversion to Islam, Moorthy remained uncircumcised, continued to take part in Hindu festivals, ate pork, and drank alcohol. He appeared on television on October 31, 2005 (just 11 days before he fell into a coma), being interviewed about his celebration of the Deepavali, a Hindu festival. The Syariah (Shari'a) Court ruled that he was a Muslim. When his wife went to the High Court, against the judgment of the Syariah Court, it ruled that it did not have the jurisdiction to hear her application because the matter had been decided by the Syariah Court, which had the final say in any case (Shanmuga, 2005). According to the Islamic Inheritance Law, Maniam Moorthy's brother, Muhammad Hussein who had earlier converted to Islam and was the immediate family's only practicing Muslim, was given the rights of all of his benefits. But Abdullah agreed to sign a written release, giving up his entire claim to it, so that Moorthy's widow and child could receive the full amount (Bernama, 2006).

Islam is not alone in discrimination against non-Muslims. Nearly every religion has done so throughout history. The Hindu rulers of India, also ruled under discriminating religious terms. Until the first millennium, Buddhism was enforced by several rulers in India. Until the Middle Ages, nearly all Christian rulers in

Europe and the Middle East were enforcing Christianity and imposing restrictions on non-Christians.

Following the Crucifixion of Jesus, Christians were persecuted during the Roman Empire until the 313 Edict of Milan, when Christianity was legalized; Christianity became the state religion of the Roman Empire in 380. On the eve of the Arab–Muslim conquest, the clash of two great empires–Sassanian Persia and Byzantium–spread war throughout Asia Minor, where Christianity–through fire and sword–was emerging from paganism. Under ecclesiastical pressure, a considerable amount of discrimination of Jews was introduced into Byzantine law. Jews were killed periodically, and synagogues were expropriated or burned down (Simon & McKeating, 1986).

In Visigoth Spain, after King Reccared converted from Arianism to Catholicism in 587, the state gave force of law to the anti-Jewish canons of the Councils of Toledo from 613 to 694. In 613 and again in 633 and 638, Jews were subject to expulsion or baptism. The Twelfth Council of Toledo (680) adopted King Erwige's edicts that: Jews renounce Judaism within a year; forced baptism be administered on pain of confiscation of property; and those resisting be punished by head-shaving, accompanied by one hundred strokes of the rod and exile (Juster, 1912; cited in Ye'or, 2002). This anti-Jewish policy, which was opposed by some members of the clergy and the nobility, pushed King Egica (687–702) to impose his authority by hardening his stance. The Sixteenth Council of Toledo (693) ordered that the property of Jews be confiscated and their taxes increased. A proclamation by the Seventeenth Council (694) ordered all Jews to be made slaves and dispersed over the kingdom. Their families were to be broken up and their children from the age of seven taken from them and brought up in the Christian faith (Ye'or, 2002).

The Seljuk Turks defeated the Byzantine army in 1071 and cut-off Christian access to Jerusalem. Owing to the destruction of many Christian sacred places and the persecution of Christians under the Fatimid caliph Al-Hakim, the military units of Roman Catholics from all over Western Europe, along with the Byzantine army fought several wars (called the Crusades) against the Muslim Turkish army from 1095 to 1272 to liberate Jerusalem and also to help the weak Christian Byzantine Empire, also called the Eastern Roman Empire. The Byzantine Empire finally collapsed in 1453, when the Ottoman army, led by Sultan Mehmed, defeated the last Byzantine Emperor, Constantine XI Palaiologos, after a two-month siege.

Pope Gregory IX added the following decrees in 1227: Muslims and Jews must wear distinctive clothing. They must not appear on the streets during Christian festivals or hold public office in Christian countries. And the *muezzin* was forbidden to offend Christian ears by summoning the Muslims to prayer in the traditional way (Armstrong, 1992, p. 28).

Prophet Muhammad thus lived in an era of violent interreligious clashes and forcible conversions. We therefore see similar provisions in the *Qur'an* for how Muslims should treat non-Muslims, and many of these are in effect today.

In non-Muslim countries, especially in the United States and Western Europe, Shari'a is considered to be an evil because it does not provide any rights to non-Muslims. But almost all religions had similar legal codes in the past.

After the killing of Osama bin Laden, newspapers published the photo of President Obama and his national security team huddled around a conference table in the White House Situation Room watching the real-time Navy Seal team attack the bin Laden compound. Two women, including Secretary of State Hillary Clinton, were in the photo. While publishing this photo, an ultraorthodox Hasidic (a branch of Orthodox Judaism) New York newspaper, *Der Tzitung,* edited both women out of the picture, claiming that the photos did not display women, in accordance with their own anachronistic policy. In some Jerusalem bus routes, women are required to ride in the back of the bus. In a December 2011 closed-door meeting of the Saban Forum at the Brookings Institution's Saban Center, U.S. Secretary of State Hillary Clinton said that the attitudes of a growing and increasingly powerful ultra-Orthodox community in Israel, particularly its attitudes toward women, are reminiscent of Iran. She gave the segregated busing on some routes as an example (Murphy, 2011).

In the United States, fundamentalist Christians claim that the country should be run on rules based on the Christian faith, and it should not grant any religious rights to non-Christians. They openly claim that everyone except good Christians are certain to go to hell.

Hindus also used to have their own legal code, *Manu Smriti*, similar to Shari'a. When Manu Smriti was written, the caste of a person was based on occupation and was not hereditary. For example, Krishna was born in a Vaishya family, whereas one of his uncles, Maharishi Garga, who gave him the name Krishna, was a Brahmin, as he was a priest, and his maternal uncle, the tyrannical king Kansa, whom he killed, was a Kshatriya. There are four traditional Hindu castes—Brahmins (scholars, teachers, and fire priests), Kshatriyas (kings, warriors, law enforcers, and administrators), Vaishyas (agriculturists, cattle raisers, traders, and bankers), and Shudras (artisans, craftsmen, and service providers).

Certain people, like foreigners, nomads, forest tribes, and the chandalas (who dealt with disposal of the dead), were excluded altogether and treated as untouchables. According to Manu Smriti, a person could marry only within his own caste, as well as a person below him in the caste system (e.g., Brahmins could marry with any from the other three castes, but not vice versa). Also, the punishment given by a legal court depended on the caste of the convict. For instance, if a Brahmin was found guilty of killing a Shudra, he just had to donate a few animals as punishment, whereas a Shudra was given the death penalty. All non-Hindus were considered as below Shudras. Brahmin means one who knows Brahma (i.e., God), and hence he was considered to be more valuable to society than others. According to the Manu Smriti, doctors/physicians had to live outside the villages, as they were considered filthy because in those days, surgery was considered to be a very dirty job. At present, the majority of Hindus in India and elsewhere do not even know about Manu Smriti, although its unhealthy influence on their society is tremendous.

All major religions, except Islam, went through the modernization process. Gradually, by sociopolitical enlightenment, it was realized that it was wrong to limit religious freedoms, and secularism became the norm. Non-Christians are able to practice their religions freely in the Christian majority United States, not because their forefathers fought for their religious freedoms, but because of the secularization of the majority of Christians. Such a secular majority is missing in nearly all Islamic countries. Even in non-Muslim majority countries such as India, Muslims have separate civil codes, based on their Shari'a.[2]

A person's education has a direct relationship with his religious faith. In the 1970s, NASA launched four spacecrafts, Pioneer 10, Pioneer 11, Voyager 1, and Voyager 2, to study our Solar System and eventually interstellar space. Now, all four of these spacecraft are on the verge of crossing the boundary of the Solar System. They are travelling in different directions to reach four different stars and they will arrive in times ranging from 70,000 years to 2,000,000 years. In our Milky Way galaxy, there are tens of billions of hospitable planets like our Earth and human-like creatures may be there. Also, in our universe, there are tens of billions of galaxies like our Milky Way (Hirschler, 2012). Once one reads these kinds of things, one stops believing that God created the Universe in six days.

Table 1, which shows the educational attainment by the U.S. states as of April 2009, proves this point: The last nine out of ten states (except Nevada) have the least educated majority, and are from the "Bible Belt" region, where socially conservative evangelical Protestantism is a significant part of the culture, and Christian church attendance is generally higher than the rest of the country. On the other hand, the top ten states, having more educated people than the national average, are considered as "progressive states," where the majority embrace concepts such as environmentalism and social justice and are of the opinion that governmental practices ought to be adjusted as society evolves, and the majority does not emphasize religion in their day-to-day lives.

It is worth noting that only about 15% of the MENA countries' adult population have a bachelor's degree or higher in MENA countries (World Bank, 2010). One can give a counter-argument that all 19 hijackers, who deliberately crashed airplanes in New York and Washington, DC on September 11, 2001, were educated people. Some of them had engineering degrees, and hence, it appears that education does not have a bearing on religious faith. Fifteen out of these 19 were from Saudi Arabia; but as we will see later in this paper, the blame lies with the education system of Saudi Arabia that brainwashes Saudis from childhood and produces fighters in the name of Islam.

Table 1. Education Attainment by States as of April 2009 for Persons 25 Years and Over in Percentages

	State	Bachelor's degree or higher	Advanced degree or higher
Mean/Avg.	United States	27.9	10.3
1	Massachusetts	38.2	16.4
2	Colorado	35.9	12.7
3	Maryland	35.7	16.0
4	Connecticut	35.6	15.5
5	New Jersey	34.5	12.9
6	Virginia	34.0	14.1
7	Vermont	33.1	13.3
8	New York	32.4	14.0
9	New Hampshire	32.0	11.2
10	Minnesota	31.5	10.3
41	Tennessee	23.0	7.9
42	Oklahoma	22.7	7.4
43	Indiana	22.5	8.1
44	Alabama	22.0	7.7
45	Nevada	21.8	7.6
46	Louisiana	21.4	6.9
47	Kentucky	21.0	8.5
48	Mississippi	19.6	7.1
49	Arkansas	18.9	6.1
50	West Virginia	17.3	6.7

Source: U.S. Census Bureau (2012). *Statistical Abstract of the United States.*

Islamic Empires and MENA Countries

While Islam was enjoying its golden age from the 7th to the 14th century, Europe was undergoing its dark ages. At the end of this period, in the 14th century, the bubonic plague, or "Black Death," ravaged the entire continent, killing anywhere from one-quarter to one-half of the population. During the 15th and 16th centuries, Islam comprised of three empires: the Ottoman (eastern Europe, western Asia, and most of the Maghrib, the region of North Africa bordering the Mediterranean Sea), the Safavid (Persia, or modern Iran), and the Mughal (the Indian subcontinent). The Ottoman Empire (1299–1923) was far ahead of European countries during its prime years. In several cities in the Ottoman Empire, there were paved and lighted roads and universities with libraries.

As part of the evolution of Islam, special schools, called *madrassas*, began to be established in the 11th century to teach legal studies or a particular madhhab. A madrassa usually consisted of a building for study, residences for teachers and students, and a library. The *Qur'an* and *Hadith* were common subjects in all madrassas. Muhammad ibn Mūsā al-Khwārizmī (780–850 AD), the father of algebra, studied and taught at the madrasas at Bukhara and Khiva in Central Asia, and was also a member of the House of Wisdom in Baghdad during the rule of Caliph al-Ma'mun. His book *Al-Kitab al-Jabr wal-Muqabala* provided symbolic operations for the systematic solution of linear and quadratic equations. The word "algebra" is derived from *al-Jabr*. The word "algorithm" (a definite list of well-defined instructions for completing a task) is a corrupted form of his name, which is derived from algoritmi, the Latinization of his name. The Latin translation of his book on the Indian numerals introduced the decimal and the zero to the Western world in the 12th century. Mathematical techniques like division are very cumbersome using Roman numerals, whereas they are easy to do using Indian numerals. His book on Indian numerals was behind the rise of European mathematicians.

During this period, the Ottomans formed alliances with European nations. For example, they entered into a military alliance with France, England, and the Netherlands against Hapsburg Spain and Hapsburg Austria, and they granted France the right of trade within their empire. In addition, the major European powers established embassies and consulates in the empire; and the Ottomans eventually sent missions to those countries.

Until the middle of the 18th century, the Ottoman army was in a position to defeat any European country in war. But after the rise of European naval power and the introduction of new technology beginning in the 18th century, the empire declined *vis-à-vis* the Europeans. European economies were thriving, and a few Europeans countries, in particular Britain, France, and the Netherlands, had colonized parts of Asia and Africa. The new technology and new wealth from their colonies allowed Europe to surpass the Ottomans, whose military power became weaker in relative terms as well. In 1798, Napoleon occupied Egypt for three years; and although he was ousted thereafter, the Ottomans could accomplish this only through an alliance with the British. This was the first incident in which they had to accept the help of a European power to oust someone from a Muslim state.

The population of Europe increased by about 50%, between 1800 and 1850. By 1850, London had become the world's largest city, with a population of 2.5 million. Other capital cities also grew, and there emerged a new kind of industrial city dominated by offices and factories. By the middle of the century, more than half of the population of England was urban. This concentration in cities provided manpower for industry and the military, as well as a growing domestic market for the products of factories. Between the 1830s and the 1860s, regular steamship lines connected ports of the southern and eastern Mediterranean like Marseille and Trieste with London and Liverpool. Textiles and metal goods found a wide and growing market, and British exports to the eastern Mediterranean increased by 800% in value between 1815 and 1850; by that time even Bedouin nomads in the Syrian Desert were wearing Egyptian cotton shirts made in Lancashire. At the same time, Europe's need for raw materials for the factories and food for the population that worked in them encouraged the production of crops for sale and export. The export of grain continued, although this became less important as Russian grain exports grew. Tunisian olive oil was in demand for the making of soap, Lebanese silk for the factories of Lyon, and above all, Egyptian cotton for the mills of Lancashire (Hourani, 1991, p. 267).

On the other hand, the economies as well as the populations of Arab countries were stagnant. They had not yet entered the railway age, except for small beginnings in Egypt and Algeria. Internal communications were bad, and famine could still occur. Populations changed little in size during the first half of the 19th century, and though Egypt's population increased from 4 million in 1800 to 5.5 million in 1860, in most other countries it remained stationary. In Algeria, it decreased considerably, from 3 million in 1830 to 2.5 million in 1860. Some of the coastal ports grew in size, particularly Alexandria, the main port for the export of Egyptian cotton, which increased from some 10,000 persons in 1800 to 100,000 by 1850. Otherwise, most cities' populations remained roughly the same size. Apart from areas that produced crops for export, agricultural production remained at subsistence level, and was so insufficient as to lead to an accumulation of capital for productive investment (Hourani, 1991, pp. 267–268).

From the 1850s onwards, because of the need for money for the army, the administration, and public works, the Ottoman government started borrowing from European banks, which had come into being as institutions with the purpose of investing accumulated European capital globally. Between 1854 and 1879, the Ottoman government borrowed on a large scale, and on unfavorable terms. Of a nominal amount of 256 million Turkish pounds, it received only 139 million, the remainder being discounted. By 1875, it was unable to carry the burden of interest and repayment. In 1881, a Public Debt Administration was set up to represent foreign creditors. It was given control of a large part of the revenues, and in that way, had virtual control over acts of government that had financial implications. Between 1862 and 1873, Egypt borrowed 68 million British pounds, but received only two-thirds of that, the rest being discounted. In spite of efforts to increase its resources, including the sale of its shares in the Suez Canal–which was built in 1869 mainly with French and Egyptian capital and Egyptian labor,–to the British government, by 1876, it was unable to meet its obligations. A few years later, Anglo-French financial control was imposed. In 1882, the British invaded and occupied Egypt (Hourani, 1991, pp. 281-283).

European occupation of Muslim territories was begun by France, which occupied Algiers in 1830 and made Algeria a French colony. In 1839, the British occupied the port of Aden in the Arab peninsula. During the First World War, the Ottoman Empire fought alongside Germany and Austria and lost to Britain, France, and the United States. After the war, the empire was dissolved on August 10, 1920, under the Treaty of Sèvres. This treaty was rejected, however, by the Turkish National Movement, led by Mustafa Kemal, a military commander. Kemal led the movement to victory over occupying Greek, Italian, and French forces, and signed the Treaty of Lausanne in 1923 for the establishment of the Republic of Turkey, which brought the Ottoman Empire to an end. The sultan was exiled, and the caliphate later abolished.

Following the dissolution of the Islam-centered Ottoman Empire after World War I, the leading colonial powers, Britain and France, carved up the Middle East and North Africa, creating most of the countries we know there today–now about 40 in number–for administrative reasons and installed their lackeys as rulers in these countries. Later on, military generals (such as Nasser in Egypt, al-Qadhafi in Libya, Qasim and then Saddam in Iraq, and al-Assad in Syria) overthrew several of those rulers and established their own dictatorial rules. At the time, these army officers were hailed as heroes in their countries. Over the years, those military dictators began to behave in the same way as the leaders they had overthrown, thus leading to the disenchantment of their masses.[3]

Saudi Arabia and Wahhabism

We need to study the situation in Saudi Arabia in detail, because in most of the Islamic hotspots worldwide, Islamic militants are trying to enforce Wahhabism, the most radical and original form of Islam followed by Saudi Arabia. As noted earlier, 15 out of 19 hijackers in the September 9, 2001 attacks were from Saudi Arabia. The Saudi government did not fund the Afghan mujahedeens directly in their war against the Soviets during 1980s. Instead, Saudi businessmen financed them, considering it to be a struggle against infidel Soviets. Because of the Saudis' involvement, the Pakistani army and its ISI were indoctrinated into Wahhabism. Apart from this, the U.S. administration also funded or trained mujahedeens via Pakistan's ISI and Pakistan's army. After the Soviets left Afghanistan, Pakistan used the training facilities of Afghan mujahedeens for training Kashmir militants.

Madhahib (jurisprudence) or Islamic schools of thought (singular: *madhhab*) are the *sunnah* (Muhammad's practices and way of life) for followers to emulate. There are four madhahib: Hanafi, Maliki, Shafi'i, and Hanbali.

1. *Hanafi*: This is the oldest and the most liberal of the four Sunni schools of legal thought. It was developed in Iraq by Abu Hanifah (699–767) and put more emphasis on *ra'y*—private opinion or human reason. It is dominant in Turkey, Albania, Central Asia, Afghanistan, the Indian subcontinent, and Iraq.

2. *Maliki:* This school is based on the works of a judge of Medina, Malik ibn Anas (715–795). Apart from the *Hadith* and *ijma* (consensus of the scholars), it also used citizens of Medina as a source. It is dominant in North and West Africa.

3. *Shafi'i:* The third important school was that founded by Muhammad ibn Idris ash-Shafi'i (767–820), who was a disciple of Malik, and is more conservative than the Hanafite and Malikite schools. Although it accepts the authority of four sources of jurisprudence (the *Qur'an, Hadith, ijma,* ' and *qiyas,* or analogy), it downgraded provisions for ra'y, private judgment. It is dominant in Egypt, some parts of India, Somalia, Yemen, Indonesia, Thailand, Sri Lanka, Maldives, and Malaysia.

4. *Hanbali:* This school, founded by Ahmad ibn-Hanbal (780–855), is the most conservative of the four. It accepts only those traditions that are in accordance with the *Qur'an* and *Hadith*, and insists on following religious duties and responsibilities as defined by the Shari'a. It was dominant in Iraq and Syria in the 14th century, and was revived again in the 18th century with the rise of Wahhabism in Arabia.

Wahhabism, founded by Muhammad ibn Abd-al-Wahhab (1703–92), is based on the teachings of Ahmad ibn Hanbal, founder of the Hanbalite School, and Ibn Taymiyya (1263–1328). He advocated observance of the original teachings of the *Qur'an* and *Hadith*, and was against any innovations. Because of his views, he was forced out of his birthplace, the ancient oasis town of Uyaynah, now part of Saudi Arabia. He then settled in Dir'iyah, the capital of Najd (present-day Saudi Arabia), ruled by Muhammad ibn Sa'ud, who converted to Wahhabism. Ibn Hanbal opposed worshipping saints and the construction of shrines and mausoleums, and considered these acts worthy of the death penalty. By funding and providing arms to pro-Wahhabi Islamic fundamentalists, Saudi Arabia is trying to export Wahhabism to the rest of the Muslim countries. Some of these countries are also subjected to the rising tide of *Salafism,* mainly based on the teachings of Ibn Taymiyyah (1263–1328), following the first three generations, called Salafi in Arabic, of close companions of Prophet Muhammad. They have significant followings in Libya, Tunisia, and Egypt.

According to Wahhabism, the *Qur'an* is the Constitution, and all laws must follow Islamic law. No other religion is allowed. As mentioned earlier, American troops stationed in Saudi Arabia are there only to protect the kingdom from outside threats, U.S. soldiers who wear a cross or Star of David must keep the symbols hidden, and they must worship in private. In November 2005, a Saudi court sentenced a teacher to 40 months in prison and 750 lashes for "mocking religion"—for discussing the Bible and praising Jews (*Washington Times*, 2005).

Fayhan al-Ghamdi, a "celebrity" Saudi preacher accused of raping, torturing, and killing his five-year-old daughter was released from custody after agreeing to pay "blood money." He was accused of killing his five-year-old daughter Lama, who suffered multiple injuries including a crushed skull, broken back, broken ribs, a broken left arm, and extensive bruising and burns. It was also alleged that she had also been repeatedly raped and burnt. He admitted using a cane and cables to inflict the injuries after doubting her virginity and taking her to a doctor. Rather than getting the death penalty or receiving a long prison sentence for the crime, he served only a few months in jail before a judge ruled the prosecution could seek only "blood money" (Hall, 2013). Al-Ghamdi, who regularly appears on television in Saudi Arabia, paid £31,000 to Lama's mother. The money is considered compensation under Islamic law, although it is only half the amount that would have been paid had Lama been a boy. It is true that this type of crime—the rape of a daughter by her father—occurs in every country. But unlike Saudi Arabia (and a few other Muslim countries), the father gets more than a slap on the wrist from the legal system. Despite Saudi Arabia's famously strict legal system, "Women to Drive," a Saudi campaign group, say fathers cannot be executed for murdering their children in the country. Equally, husbands cannot be executed for murdering their wives (Hall, 2013). Due to world-wide condemnation, the Saudi Royal family intervened, and now Fayhan is not going to be released for a long period of time. In Shari'a, a woman's evidence is given only half the weight of a man's evidence.

In Saudi schools, up to one-third of every child's schooling is on religious topics. In the early years, the curriculum focuses on simple things such as rules for prayer. By the time Saudi students reach high school, they have at least one period in six devoted to the study of religious topics, including interpreting the holy texts and ways of keeping their faith pure. A student cannot move on to the next grade if he fails a religion class, unlike other subjects. Learning is by rote; and questions are discouraged (MacFarquhar, 2001).

Eleventh-graders at the elite Islamic Saudi Academy in northern Virginia study energy and matter in physics, differential equations in pre-calculus, and stories about slavery and the Puritans in English. In their Islamic studies class, however, textbooks tell them that the Day of Judgment cannot come until Jesus Christ returns to Earth, breaks the cross and converts everyone to Islam, and Muslims start attacking Jews (Strauss & Wax, 2002).

King Fahd Academy, a Saudi-run school, was opened in 1995 near Bonn in Germany, with a $20 million donation from Saudi King Fahd bin Abdul Aziz Al Saud. It was established so that Saudi diplomats' children could be educated in conformance with their culture. Later on, conservative German Muslims began sending their children to this school because of its orthodox education and low tuition. The academy came to prominence in 2003 when a television news show secretly taped a teacher's sermon in its mosque. According to a transcript of the sermon, he said children must learn "to throw a spear, swim and ride, to be strong and brave, so they will be willing to join the jihad," (Crawford, 2005, p. A12).

Following this, the local government launched an investigation. It obtained copies of class schedules and found that the Saudi embassy and school routinely understated the time devoted to religion and overstated the time devoted to math, science, and academics. The government also commissioned a study of the school's textbooks. The findings shocked local leaders: Two-thirds of the textbooks taught students to hate non-Muslims, while one in five praised martyrdom, urged violence against non-Muslims, or threatened hell for infractions against Muslim rituals (Crawford, 2004).

Saudi Arabia's religious police, also known as *muttawa'*, are employed by the "Commission for the Propagation of Virtue and the Prevention of Vice" whose police-like forces patrol public places. They ensure that women are covered in black cloaks, that the sexes do not mix in public, that shops close five times a day for prayers, and that men go to the mosque for worship. The Taliban, when they ruled Afghanistan, had a similar governmental office called the Department for the Promotion of Virtue and Prevention of Vice.

In 2001, the Taliban destroyed two ancient, colossal images of the Buddha in Bamiyan Province, about 150 miles from the capital of Kabul, using explosives, tanks, and anti-aircraft weapons, claiming that Islam forbids the construction of images of humans and animals. This was not unique on their part, however. They were only following in the footsteps of the Saudis, who have destroyed almost all of the buildings related to the founder of Islam in order to make room for modern structures. Today, there are fewer than 20 structures remaining in Mecca that date back to the time of the Prophet–1,400 years ago. The litany of this lost history includes the house of Khadijah, the wife of the Prophet, demolished to make way for public lavatories; the house of Abu Bakr, the Prophet's companion, father of 'Aisha (Prophet Muhammad's favorite wife), and the first caliph, now the site of the local Hilton hotel; the house of Ali-Oraid, the grandson of the Prophet, and the mosque of Abu Qubais, now the location of the king's palace in Mecca (Howden, 2006). In October 2012, the Saudi government announced plans to demolish three of the world's oldest mosques in Medina, and to build the world's largest building, a mosque with the capacity for 1.6 million worshippers. These three oldest mosques hold the tombs of Islam's founder and two of his closest companions, Abu Bakr and Umar (Taylor, 2012).

In 2012, al-Qaida-linked militants captured and occupied a large area in Northern Mali, as Mali troops were no match for them. They imposed strict Shari'a rules; forcing women to wear veils, or else face public whippings. A couple accused of adultery was stoned to death. During their occupation, the militants systematically destroyed the ancient tombs of Sufi saints–UNESCO Heritage sites–claiming that the tombs contravened Islam. One of the tombs destroyed was of Sidi Mahmoudou, a saint who died in 955. In January 2013, France had to send its troops to force them out from the captured areas. Before fleeing from Timbuktu, the fabled city, the militants set fire to a library, which held ancient manuscripts.

Global Islamic Militancy and Modernization of Islam

The 2010 self-immolation by Mohamed Bouazizi, a Tunisian street vendor, in protest of the confiscation of his wares and his harassment and humiliation at the hands of a Tunisian police woman became a catalyst for the drastic changes in the entire Middle East and North Africa. A majority of the population in almost all MENA countries is under 30 years old, as shown in Table 2. Because of the advent of the World Wide Web and its accessibility in almost every corner of the globe, these young people have come to know about the tremendous progress being made elsewhere, and they are leading the Arab Spring throughout the region after having watched how their own country lagged far behind others in terms of economic and living standards. They blame their rulers for their backwardness. In their revolutions, they are being helped by technologies such as Facebook and Twitter, which help to sustain the organizing of these movements.

The January 2013 Arab Spring resulted in the overthrow of dictators in Egypt, Tunisia, Yemen, and Libya, and Bashar al-Assad is on the verge of losing power in Syria. One point, which should be emphasized, and which is common to Egypt, Yemen, and Libya, (and also al-Assad of Syria) is that their ex-rulers were not Islamists. Mubarak (Egypt), Ben Ali (Tunisia), al-Qadhafi (Libya), and al-Assad (Syria) were die-hard anti-Islamists. Islamic fundamentalist countries, like Saudi Arabia and Qatar, are funding the anti-al-Assad Islamic fundamentalist opposition groups in Syria, whereas on the other hand, they financially supported the recently deposed Islamist president in Egypt, and also sent its troops to crush the anti-government uprising in Bahrain. Several crates of weapons from a Ukrainian arms manufacturer, intended for the Saudi military (addressed to Saudi Arabia), were found in a base being used by rebel Islamic fighters in the Syrian city of Aleppo (BBC News, 2012).

Qatar was among the first countries to provide warplanes to a NATO-led bombing campaign against al-Qadhafi. It supported Islamic militants against al-Qadhafi, and Somali's al-Shabab, an anti-U.S. Islamic militant group, is currently doing the same in Syria. It is financially helping Egypt's Islamic government and Hamas. In January 2013, it increased its deposits in Egypt's central bank by $2 billion to stem the slide of Egyptian currency.

Before leaving her office in January 2012, Hillary Clinton, the then U.S. Secretary of State, stated the danger of Islamic fundamentalist groups affiliated with al-Qaeda becoming the main opposition group fighting in Syria. She said that the opposition was increasingly being represented by al-Qaeda extremists receiving instructions from the ungoverned areas in Pakistan where some of the al-Qaeda leadership was believed to be hiding (Fisher, 2013). Al-Nusra, an al-Qaeda-affiliated group, was thought to have 10,000 fighters in Syria. Some U.S. intelligence officials said they are gravely concerned that al-Nusra militants, including some who had western passports, might move elsewhere in the Middle East, or into Europe when the rebellion in Syria ended (Fisher, 2013).

Table 2. Median Age and Population Under 30 in Certain Muslim Countries		
Arab Country	**Median Age**	**Population Under Age 30**
Yemen	18	73%
Iraq	21	68%
Syria	22	66%
Jordan	22	65%
Oman	24	64%
Egypt	24	61%
Libya	24	61%
Saudi Arabia	25	61%
Morocco	27	56%
Algeria	27	56%
Kuwait	28	54%
Lebanon	29	51%
Tunisia	30	51%
UAE	30	49%
Bahrain	31	48%
Qatar	31	48%
All Countries	**26**	**63%**

Source: Slackman, M. (2011, 17 March). Arab Spring's youth movement spreads, then hits wall. *New York Times*.

The Muslim Brotherhood grabbed power in post-Mubarak Egypt. After the parliamentary elections in Tunisia in 2012, a coalition of the moderate Islamist Ennahda and two center-left secular parties took over power. After the January 2013 assassination of Shokri Belaid in Tunis, Tunisia was left in turmoil. Mr. Belaid was head of the anti-Islamist Democratic Patriotic party who accused the Ennahda of having an Islamic militia, also known as the League of the Protection of the Revolution, and also of secretly sympathizing with the Salafists (Spencer, 2013).

In Tunisia, the Salafis destroyed several mosques associated with Sufis (Sufism is an Islamic sect, defined by its adherents to mysticism, the principal of tolerance and peace; and it is against any form of violence). The Salafis were also behind the killings of four U.S. officials, which included the U.S. ambassador to Libya in the assault on the U.S. consulate in Benghazi. After three days, they attacked U.S. embassies in Tunis and Cairo. In 2012, the Salafi's Nour Party obtained about 20% of the votes and won a quarter of the seats in the election for Egypt's lower house of parliament, which was subsequently dissolved by The Egyptian High Court. The Nour Party calls for destruction of the Sphinx and Giza Pyramids, as they consider it idolatry.

Since the beginning of the Arab Spring, almost all other rulers have appeared vulnerable and hence, they are trying to mollify their population by giving more powers to elected representatives or by providing monetary bribes. The Moroccan king has unveiled his plan to make his country a constitutional monarchy with a democratic parliament. But the king will still be the head of the powerful army. Saudi Arabia is spending $130 billion in raising salaries and building houses to silence its critics. In nearly all the MENA countries, the main opposition groups are Islamic fundamentalist parties and they are just waiting to capture power as they have done in countries like Egypt and Tunisia.

Recently, there was a sea change in the Islamic militancy in Pakistan, which does not bode well for its own existence. According to Pakistani investigators, despite a crackdown on al-Qaeda's command structure, which has yielded significant arrests, the terrorist organization is finding new recruits in the middle class and is forming smaller cells. Terrorist cells "are multiplying with the crackdown on al-Qaeda," said Tariq Jamil, Karachi ex-chief of police (Hussain & Solomon, 2004). Educated, middle-class Pakistanis run many of these new groups, rather than the madrassa students who were associated with Islamic extremism in Pakistan in the past. Militant groups have regularly recruited from seminaries inside Pakistan's tribal areas, but traditionally have had less success in Pakistani cities (Hussain & Solomon, 2004).

According to Seymour M. Hersh, a veteran journalist, the militancy and the influence of fundamentalist Islam has grown by leaps and bounds. In the past, military officers, politicians, and journalists routinely served whisky during their talks, and drank it themselves. But now, even the most senior retired army generals offer him only juice or tea, even in their own homes. Officials and journalists said that soldiers and middle-level officers are increasingly attracted to the preaching of Zaid Hamid, who joined the mujahedeen and fought for nine years in Afghanistan. On CDs and on television, Hamid exhorts soldiers to think of themselves as Muslims first and Pakistanis second (Hersh, 2009).

In Pakistan, there are two groups of Islamic militants—one is the anti-Pakistan government, who wants to bring strict Shari'a rule to the country, and the second is the pro-Pakistan government group, whom Pakistan's ISI (Inter-services Intelligence) and army are using to fight in India-held Kashmir and elsewhere in India, and also the U.S.-led NATO forces in Afghanistan. The first group of militants regularly attack and kill scores of policemen and armed forces. In early 2012, Pakistani authorities foiled two separate plots by the militants to attack the parliament. The militants had plans to fire rockets at the parliament buildings when President Zardari was addressing the joint session of parliament from mountains overlooking Islamabad, at which point suicide bombers' would begin their attack (*Deccan Herald*, 2012).

Talibanization of Pakistan is currently in the advanced stage, and if the United States does not support Pakistan's civilian government and army financially, the country will fall to Taliban in no time. However, once the United States withdraws the majority of its troops from Afghanistan, it is just a question of time when the Taliban will take it over—similar to what happened to the Najibullah government once the Soviets left the country.

At present, only secular Islamic countries are falling into the hands of Islamic fundamentalists. Fundamentalist countries, like Saudi Arabia and Qatar, are funding Syria and Libya, but Saudi Arabia and Qatar would also fall to Taliban-type groups. Pakistan allowed the Taliban to flourish in the 1990s and now the Taliban may take over Pakistan entirely. Also, in nearly every MENA country, the main opposition group is an Islamic fundamentalist. Hence, in a democratic election, Islamic fundamentalist parties will attempt to attain power in these countries.

Countries like Pakistan, Afghanistan, Yemen, Mali, Sudan, Somalia, Libya, Syria, Egypt, Iraq, and Tunisia are on the verge of falling into the hands of Islamic fundamentalists in the very near future. Once this happens, it will set off a domino effect throughout the Islamic world, particularly in the Middle East and North Africa. In almost all Middle East and North African countries, an Islamic fundamentalist party, being the largest opposition group, could take over.

The evolution of the Arab Spring in various countries has shown that the U.S. and its Western allies are no longer capable of influencing this movement. Instead, the people behind the Arab Spring in a country are using the United States and its allies to help them capture power.

Egypt and Turkey were the two main pillars of the U.S. policy in the region. Until the present Islamist government in Turkey, both the secular military and the government in Turkey were pro-Western. Turkey has the second-largest army in NATO, after the United States. There are signs that Egypt may unilaterally withdraw from the 1978 Camp David accord and form an alliance with Turkey.

Also, due to economic woes (discussed in the next section), the United States will be unable to support its allies in the Middle East and North Africa either economically or militarily. Following the further deepening of the global economic depression, the intensity of Islamic militancy will surge. Economic depression will make it easier for militants to take over Islamic countries, as large-scale unemployment and acute poverty coupled with corruption in high places produce militancy.

The United States and other Western governments will impose economic embargoes against these regimes and isolate them, creating tremendous hardship for the people there. This strategy may be successful. Saddam Hussein's Iraq and Muammar al-Qadhafi's Libya are two recent examples of the success of this approach. It forced al-Qadhafi to give up his two intelligence officers for the 1988 bombing of Pan Am Flight 103, as well as his WMDs. Hamas in Palestine is another example. After the

January 2006 legislative elections, Hamas won a majority of seats and formed a government in March. But after the United States and the European Union boycott of the Hamas-led government and termination of funding, the government was unable to provide salaries to tens of thousands of Palestinian government employees for several months, leading to chaos.

MENA countries will be witnessing a struggle between new and old guards who will try to turn back the clock, but they will not be successful. Outside forces cannot bring long lasting changes because change should come from within.

The present global Islamic militancy may even lead to a temporary establishment of an Islamic empire in the Middle East and North Africa, with fundamentalist Islamic parties taking power in democratic elections. These ruling parties will try to turn back the clock by imposing Shari'a rules, which is nothing but 7th century Arabian culture.

> If oil-rich countries like Saudi Arabia fall to radical Islamic militants, Islamic clerics would try to establish an Islamic empire like the old Ottoman Empire founded during 14th and 15th centuries....[W]hen ordinary people fail to find relief from radical Islamic regimes, they will force a change in leadership and we will see the emergence of a number of Mustafa Kemals. These Kemals will bring drastic social and religious changes, and the West will help them financially. Although fundamentalist Islamic stated and powerful Islamic clerics in those states will be the losers of a (Cold or Third World) War, Islam as a religion will emerge victorious and shed its Seventh Century image, becoming a new 21st Century religion more tolerant to women and non-Muslims. In the same way two world wars changed the socio-economic and political environment of Europe, this War will change the Middle East and North Africa, which resembles late 19th and early 20th Century Europe. (Kumar, 1995)[4]

The Islamic militants may rule for some time, say 10 to 20 years (may be even 40 to 50 years), but they will never be able to turn the clock back in the present digital age (i.e., they cannot impose a 7th century Arabian culture on the 21st century population of Facebook, Twitter, etc). In the end, these militants are bound to be overthrown by homegrown secular "modern-day Kemal Ataturks"; in other words, when ordinary people fail to find relief from radical Islamic regimes they will force a change in leadership. These Kemals will inaugurate drastic social and religious changes, and the West will help them financially.

After watching the First World War defeat and the disintegration of his Ottoman Empire by the Western powers, Mustafa Kemal, an Ottoman army officer, faced a similar situation. Until the advent of the Industrial Revolution in Europe in the 18th century, the Ottoman Empire, founded in 1299, was far ahead of European countries, especially during its prime years. After the disintegration of the Ottoman Empire, Kemal saw no option but to modernize his country, which led him to the establishment of a secular and democratic Turkey in 1923.

It is important to note that Turkey was the seat of the Ottoman Empire for six centuries, with Istanbul as its capital. Beginning in 1517, it also claimed to be the seat of the caliph, the highest Islamic authority. Kemal Ataturk dramatically altered this state of affairs in just two to three years. However, after taking the reins of Turkey under the Treaty of Lausanne in 1923, the dynasty was abolished, and the sultan was banished. The caliphate, the spiritual and political leadership system of the Islamic world, begun after the death of Prophet Muhammad in 632, was abolished in 1924. Kemal introduced several radical political, legal, cultural, social, and economic reforms, and the Islamic courts were closed.

European laws and jurisprudence were adopted in the new constitution; the Turkish administration and educational systems were thoroughly secularized and modernized. The *fez* or *tarboush* (hat) worn by men and introduced by Sultan Mahmud II as part of the empire's dress code in 1826, was banned, and people were encouraged to wear European dress. In a series of speeches delivered in the early 1920s, Kemal argued eloquently for the full emancipation of women in the Turkish state and society. Their most urgent task, he repeatedly told his people, was to catch up with the modern world; they would not catch up if they only modernized half of their population (Lewis, 2002, p. 72). It became illegal for women to wear a veil or headscarf. Women were given the right to vote and own property-rights that women in several Western countries were denied at the time. Even the script was changed, and the old alphabet based on the Arabic script was replaced by one based on the Roman script used in the West.

Out of necessity, Kemal Ataturk had to take drastic steps in modernizing Turkey after watching his country fall behind the Europeans in every aspect, whereas until the emergence of the Industrial Revolution in Europe in the 18th century, the Ottoman Empire was ahead of the Europeans. In the age of rapid communication due to technology and platforms directly available to the people (e.g., Facebook and Twitter), the younger generation will force the new rulers in the Islamic countries—which are right now far behind most countries in every respect—to take drastic steps, such as those taken by Kemal Ataturk. The establishment of modern Turkey was a product of the First World War, the first war that left scars on the entire global population, and in which millions lost their lives. A drastic change in the Islamic countries, especially in the Middle East and North Africa, will not be an easy affair, and this change will take place only after a violent shake-up in these countries. Also, it will leave scars in several non-Muslim countries, especially those having sizeable Muslim populations. This tremendous shake-up will be due to the struggle between the Islamic fundamentalists–especially the old guard, who will try to establish Islamic regimes based on Islamic tenets—and the new generation, who believe that the Islamic regimes are moving backwards.

Although the present Turkish government of the Justice and Development Party, which is an Islamic party, is trying to remove all secular laws, the country will not turn back the clock in this Internet age. Turkey can never become an Islamic country like Saudi Arabia or Pakistan because the majority of its population will not accept it.

If there is no external threat or the administration is not imposed upon, or supported by the United States or others, then people will vote for political parties that will work for their development. In the 2008 Bangladesh elections, the secular Awami League-led Grand Alliance decimated its rivals by huge margins, garnering 261 out of 300 seats in the National Assembly.

The road to modernization for other Muslim nations may be less democratic. During this period of transformation, the United States, Europe, Russia, India, and other countries with sizeable Muslim populations will in fact see increased Islamic terrorism, including suicide bombings. Although the transition may take several decades and be marked with violence, in the end Islam will no longer be the guiding force behind politics in the Middle East or North Africa. It is worth noting that it took almost three and a half decades (from 1914 to 1945) for Europe to make the transition from its remaining monarchies to vibrant democracies.

The worst is yet to come in countries like India, where there is a large Muslim population (140 million) and a lack of modern technology monitoring and street-level intelligence, which are found in countries like the United States. India is going to witness terrorist attacks in major cities similar to the attacks on two prestigious hotels in Mumbai in 2008. The United States has the danger of homegrown terrorists (i.e., converted Muslims, immigrants, and natural born American Muslims).

Islamic terrorists may be able to get hold of nuclear materials for dirty bombs. On 15 occasions since 2005, dozens of people were arrested in Georgia for smuggling radioactive materials from countries around the former Soviet Union for the purpose of making dirty bombs. In January 2012, Georgian police arrested a man in Georgia's capital, Tbilisi, and seized 36 vials with cesium-135, a radioactive isotope that is hard to use for a weapon. In April 2012, the police arrested a group of smugglers from Abkhazia bringing in three glass containers with about 2.2 pounds of yellowcake uranium, a lightly processed substance that can be enriched into bomb-grade material (Butler, 2012).

If Iran is able to produce the nuclear bomb, then it is certain that Saudi Arabia will also attempt to acquire nuclear weapons from somewhere, as Saudi Arabia considers Iran a worse enemy than Israel. Saudi Arabia does not need to develop nuclear bombs. Instead, it will just buy them, either from Pakistan or North Korea, who are ready to sell any technology, nuclear or missile, for hard cash. Egypt may also follow Saudi Arabia in acquiring nuclear bombs. Hence, as soon as some or all of these countries fall to Islamic fundamentalists, it will only be a matter of time before militants take possession of these bombs and they will not hesitate to use them against countries such as Israel and India, or European countries, or even against China. In this case, the ensuing events will dwarf the number of people killed during World War II and can be termed "Armageddon."

Israel and Palestine

The overthrow of Mubarak in Egypt may have been a major blow for Israel, as Mubarak was pro-Israel and solidly behind U.S. policy in that region. Now, post-Mubarak Egypt is taking several measures to display its anti-Israel stance. In February 2011, it allowed the passage of two Iranian warships through the Suez Canal to the Mediterranean for the first time since the 1979 Iranian Revolution, and lifted the blockade of the Gaza Strip. It will be disastrous for Israel if Egypt unilaterally withdraws from the 1978 Camp David Accords. After the killing of Turkish citizens in the 2010 Gaza Strip aid flotilla in a raid by the Israeli navy, the Islamist government in Turkey has hardened its stance on Israel. After the refusal of Israel to apologize for the killing of Turkish citizens, Turkey has suspended all defense ties with Israel, and its prime minister is trying to build a coalition against Israel.

After the fall of Mubarak, anti-Israel Islamic militants have become active in the Sinai Peninsula and are acquiring sophisticated arms and ammunitions supplied by Western countries to militants fighting elsewhere. In May 2012, Egyptian security forces seized heavy weapons near the Libyan border which included 40 surface-to-air-missiles, 17 rocket-propelled grenade launchers, mortar rounds, automatic rifles, and around 10,000 artillery shells. These weapons were bound for the Sinai Peninsula (Michael 2012). In January 2013, Egypt seized six U.S.-made anti-tank and anti-aircraft missiles, smuggled from Libya and bound for the Gaza Strip. During Libya's 2011 uprising, the United States approved these ammunitions for the opposition groups, fighting al-Qadhafi forces. In December 2012, Egypt seized 17 French-made missiles smuggled to the Gaza Strip. Since the 2011 Libyan uprisings, Egypt has confiscated hundreds of weapons smuggled from Libya. Most of the weapons used by al-Qaeda-linked terrorists in the attack on a gas facility in Algeria in January 2013 which killed 39 foreigners came from Libya (*ANI*, 2013). Thus, it is a catch-22 situation for the U.S. and its Western allies in providing arms to the groups fighting in countries like Syria. As a result, the White House overruled the advice of both the U.S. State Department and the Pentagon to provide arms to groups fighting al-Assad forces in Syria.

Since 2012, Hezbollah has been using drones, acquired from Iran, against Israel. By the end of 2012, Pakistan was able to develop more sophisticated drones, but it was having problems arming them because of the inaccuracy of the missiles attached to drones. China has decided to provide the technology for this purpose to Pakistan.

It is certain that one day, Pakistani drones will make their way into places such as the Gaza Strip and lawless Syria and Egypt. Once other neighboring countries like Jordan and Saudi Arabia fall to Islamic militants, whom no one can control, Israel could be attacked by missiles coming from every direction.

The growth of technology is working against Israel. In the pre-Intifada period, the Israeli territory did not suffer direct attacks. During the First Intifada (1987–1993), and the Second Intifada (2000–2005), Palestinians used Molotov cocktails, hand grenades, guns, and explosives. But in the future, Palestinians will have deadlier weapons to use. During the eight days of Israeli attacks on the Gaza Strip in November 2012, Israel did not send its tanks inside the Strip due to the fear of Hamas having anti-tank missiles. Apart from this, in time (meaning decades not years), the range and accuracy of Hamas's (as well as Hezbollah's) missiles will increase and will penetrate deeper and deeper inside Israel, threatening more and more Israelis. They will have multiple war head missiles to blunt anti-missile batteries which were successful in stopping the hundreds of Hamas' missiles fired from the Gaza Strip during the November 2012 Israel–Hamas standoff. During the 2006 Israel–Lebanon War, Hezbollah sent 4,000 missiles over Israeli territory. In 2010, Hezbollah had 40,000 rockets, twice what it had in 2006, and these rockets had a long range plus higher accuracy than previous models. In any future conflict with Israel, these rockets are capable of reaching the entire Israeli territory. Israel does not have any option other than to come up with a political solution at the earliest possible time. The more Israel delays the two-state solution, the more it increases the probability of one state for the entire region, which does not bode well for the present Jewish population in Israel because then most of them will end up migrating to the United States.

The Global Great Depression

In mid-2010, economist Paul Krugman, a Nobel Prize winner in economics and a *New York Times* columnist, claimed that the U.S. economy was in the early stages of a third depression, and it would probably look more like the Long Depression of the 19th century, which followed the Panic of 1873, than the much more severe Great Depression of the 1930s. According to him, the cost to the world economy and, above all, to the millions of lives blighted by the absence of jobs would be immense (Krugman, 2010). Since the 2008 global economic crisis, Britain has been in a slump worse than during the Great Depression. Its recent economic performance is the worst since records began in the pre-Victorian era, apart from the two immediate post-war slumps (Mason, 2013).

This crisis is going to deepen further still and will drag down the entire global economy in another Great Depression, far worse than the Great Depression of the 1930s and is discussed in detail in *Casino Capitalism: The Collapse of the U.S. Economy and the Transition to Secular Democracy in the Middle East* (Kumar, 2012).[4] It is beyond the scope of this paper to analyze in detail the reasons behind the crisis; however, it will be touched upon as it does affect the MENA countries and the modernization of Islam.

The root cause of the present global economic crisis is the collapse of the 1944 Bretton Woods Accord imposed by the United States on the world in the midst of World War II. This accord made the U.S. dollar a global currency and it also gave veto power to the U.S. in the International Monetary Fund (IMF). In the IMF, all the decisions, including the election of its managing director, require an 85% super-majority. The top three countries, having the highest votes, are the United States (16.75%), Japan (6.24%), and Germany (5.81%). Hence, nothing can happen in the IMF without the consent of the United States.

Americans claim that China has been manipulating its currency, yuan (renminbi), by keeping it undervalued. According to Krugman, the United States needs to impose at least a 25% tax on Chinese items if China does not significantly appreciate its currency. While it is true that China does manipulate its currency, the United States has been doing the same since the 1980s.

Since 2010, the United States has proposed limits on "sustainable" trade surpluses and deficits. The proposal has been rebuffed by the BRIC (Brazil, Russia, India, China) countries and also Germany, which currently produces the second-largest trade surplus in the world. The United States proposal is nearly the same as the one proposed by the British economist John M. Keynes and his team (the Keynesian stimulus plan is named after him) during the deliberations that led to the 1944 Bretton Woods Accord.

Toward the end of World War II, there were two competing plans for the future of the global economic order—Britain's Keynes plan and United States' Harry Dexter White plan. Keynes favored a world currency, to be called *bancor*, managed by a global bank and an International Clearing Union. That "neutral" world currency would be exchangeable with national currencies at fixed rates of exchange. Under Keynes's plan, both debtors and creditors would be required to change their policies. A country with a large trade deficit would pay interest on its account and devalue its currency to prevent the export of capital. On the other hand, a country with a large trade surplus would increase the value of its currency to permit the export of capital. A country with a bancor credit balance more than half the size of its overdraft facility would be required to pay interest on it. Keynes went so far as to propose the severe penalty of confiscation of surplus if, at the end of the year, the country's credit balance exceeded the total value of its permitted overdraft (Monbiot, 2008). Under the White plan, the United States was given veto power in the workings of the IMF and the International Bank for Reconstruction and Development (later incorporated into the present World Bank). The IMF was to be based in Washington, DC, and staffed primarily by U.S. economists and U.S. Treasury officials.

When the future of world trade was discussed, and the Bretton Woods conference was planned in the early 1940s, many Third World countries were still under colonial rule and had absolutely no say in those discussions. The main deliberations took place between the United States and Britain exclusively, and at Bretton Woods all other countries were invited simply for the formal signing-in ceremony. At the time of the conference, the U.S. gross domestic product (GDP) amounted to almost half of the world's GDP. The U.S. gold reserves stood at $20 billion, almost two-thirds of the world's total of $33 billion (Rowland and Brittain, 1976, p. 220). Because of the two World Wars, the European countries were deeply in debt and had transferred huge amounts of gold to the United States. They also needed money from the United States for their postwar reconstruction. Thus, the United States was able to impose its will at Bretton Woods.

Under the Bretton Woods agreement, a system of fixed exchange rates was announced using the U.S. dollar as a reserve currency. The United States committed to convert dollars into gold at $35 an ounce. At the conference itself, the IMF and the International Bank for Reconstruction and Development (IBRD) were established. In 1971, the Nixon Administration unilaterally cancelled the direct convertibility of the U.S. dollar to gold and effectively ended the Bretton Woods system of international financial exchange.

Had Germany developed long-range missiles and destroyed U.S. industries like it destroyed the British industries during World War II, the United States might not have emerged as the postwar economic superpower. However, the United States emerged as the right country at the right time. Had the same treaty been signed in the late 1950s or later, the United States would not have had the final say on the treaty, and a global currency and even an International Clearing House as proposed by Keynes may have come into existence.

John Maynard Keynes was a brilliant economist who foresaw a global crisis due to large trade imbalances (discussed next in this section) that would lead to instability in the global economy. His proposals may have been construed as if he represented a country—the United Kingdom—in decline and in huge debt, a country that would be accumulating large trade deficits for the foreseeable future. It is worth mentioning that Keynes resigned from the British Treasury, as he was against the large reparation amount imposed on Germany in the 1919 Versailles Peace Treaty after World War I. The stupendous burden thus imposed on Germany is considered to be a main cause for the rise of Hitler.

Tables 3a, b and 4a, b show the budget surplus/deficit and balance on the current accounts of two groups of EU countries and the United States. The balance on the current account is the sum of the balance of trade (exports minus imports of goods and services), net factor income (interest and dividends), and net transfer payments (such as foreign aid). Euro-Group A countries (Germany, Holland, Belgium, Austria, and Finland) are not affected much by the current economic downturn. On the other hand, Euro-Group B countries have suffered badly. The latter group of countries is now known as PIIGS (Portugal, Ireland, Italy, Greece, and Spain) and economists are predicting that in the very near future, France will also join this group, needing to be bailed out.

Table 3a. Government Fiscal Balances in Euro-Group A Countries (2001–2010) in Percent of GDP

	2001	2002	2003	2004	2005	2006	2007	2008	2009	2010
Germany	-2.8	-3.6	4.0	-3.8	-3.3	-1.6	0.3	0.1	-3.0	-3.3
Holland	-0.3	-2.1	-3.2	-1.8	-0.3	0.5	0.2	0.5	-5.5	-5.3
Belgium	0.4	-0.2	-0.2	-0.4	-2.8	0.1	-0.4	-1.3	-6.0	-4.2
Austria	-0.2	-0.9	-1.7	-4.6	-1.8	1.7	-1.0	-1.0	-4.2	-4.6
Finland	5.0	4.0	2.3	2.1	2.5	3.9	5.2	4.2	-2.9	-2.8

Source: Organization for Economic Co-operation and Development (OECD).

Table 3b. Government Fiscal Balances in Euro-Group B Countries and the United States (2001–2010) in Percent of GDP

	2001	2002	2003	2004	2005	2006	2007	2008	2009	2010
France	-1.6	-3.2	-4.1	-3.6	-3.0	2.3	-2.7	-3.3	-7.5	-7.0
Italy	-3.1	-3.0	-3.5	-3.6	-4.4	3.3	-1.5	-2.7	-5.3	-4.5
Spain	-0.7	-0.5	0.2	-0.4	1.0	2.0	1.9	-4.2	-11.1	-9.2
Greece	-4.4	-4.8	-5.7	-7.4	-5.3	6.0	-6.7	-9.8	-15.6	-10.4
Portugal	-4.3	-2.9	-3.1	-3.4	-5.9	4.1	-3.2	-3.6	-10.1	-9.2
Ireland	1.0	-0.3	0.4	1.4	1.6	2.9	0.1	-7.3	-14.3	-32.4
U.S.A.	-0.6	-4.0	-5.0	-4.4	-3.3	-2.2	-2.9	-6.3	-11.3	-10.6

Source: Organization for Economic Co-operation and Development (OECD).

Table 4a. Balance on Current Account in Euro-Group A Countries (2001–2010) in Percent of GDP

	2001	2002	2003	2004	2005	2006	2007	2008	2009	2010
Germany	0.0	2.1	1.9	4.7	5.1	6.5	7.9	6.7	5.7	5.6
Holland	2.4	2.5	5.5	7.5	7.3	9.3	8.7	4.8	4.9	7.2
Belgium	3.4	4.6	4.1	3.5	2.6	2.0	2.2	-2.5	0.3	1.0
Austria	-0.8	2.7	1.7	2.2	2.2	2.8	3.6	3.2	3.1	2.6
Finland	8.6	8.8	5.2	6.6	3.6	4.5	4.2	3.0	2.3	3.1

Source: Organization for Economic Co-operation and Development (OECD).

Table 4b. Balance on Current Account in Euro Group B Countries and the United States (2001-2010) in Percent of GDP

	2001	2002	2003	2004	2005	2006	2007	2008	2009	2010
France	1.9	1.4	0.8	0.6	0.4	-0.5	-1.0	-2.3	-1.5	-1.8
Italy	-0.1	-0.8	-1.3	-0.9	-1.7	2.6	-2.4	-3.4	-2.1	-3.2
Spain	-3.9	-3.3	3.5	-5.3	-7.4	-9.0	-10.0	-9.6	-5.1	-4.6
Greece	-7.3	-6.8	-6.6	-5.9	-7.4	11.3	-14.5	-14.5	-11.0	-10.4
Portugal	-9.9	-8.1	-6.1	-7.6	-9.5	10.0	-9.4	-12.1	-10.9	-9.9
Ireland	-0.7	-0.9	0.0	-0.6	-3.5	-3.5	-5.3	-5.3	-3.0	0.5
U.S.A.	-3.9	-4.3	-4.7	-5.3	-6.0	-6.0	-5.2	-4.9	-2.7	-3.2

Source: Organization for Economic Co-operation and Development (OECD)

Until the start of the present economic downturn in 2008, the government fiscal balances, which denote the budget surplus/deficit, of both groups, except Greece, were nearly the same. But there is a stark difference between these two groups in their current account balances. Euro-Group B countries had recurring negative balances during the 2000s, whereas Euro-Group A countries had positive balances during the same period. Within the Eurozone, France's share of exports fell to 13.4% in 2009, from 17% in 2000; Italy's share fell to 10.1% from 11.9%. The German share increased during the period (Norris, 2010). Since the economic downturn started, the budget deficits of Euro-Group B countries have worsened.

Major European economies, such as Germany and France, are trying to save the Euro-Group B countries by giving them billions of Euros for support. Apart from redeeming the Euro, they would like to save their own banks as well, as these banks would lose large sums of money should the countries in trouble default on their loans. These are the same banks that funded the spending binge in the troubled countries.

One remarkable point we observe from the tables below is that the U. S. economy resembles the economies of Euro-Group B but is still surviving, as it can print its currency to fund its deficits, whereas the Euro-Group B countries can do no such thing, as the Euro is managed by the European Central Bank (ECB).

With a debt-to-revenue ratio of 312%, Greece is in dire straits at present. However, the debt-to-revenue ratio of the United States is 358%, according to Morgan Stanley. The Congressional Budget Office estimates that interest payments on the federal debt will rise from 9% of federal tax revenues to 20% in 2020, 36% in 2030, and 58% in 2040. Only America's "exorbitant privilege" of being able to print the world's premier reserve currency gives it breathing space. But this very privilege is under mounting attack from the Chinese government (Ferguson, 2010).

Table 5 shows the balance on the current account of the BRIC countries, as well as South Africa and Vietnam. Except for China and Russia, they all have sizeable negative balances on their current accounts. The positive balance on Russia's current account is due to an increase in oil prices and other minerals, which are its main exports. During the late 1980s and 1990s, Wal-Mart divested itself of family-owned stores in American cities. Similarly, since the 2000s, China has been forcing the closing of manufacturing plants for mass consumption items in other countries. It has resulted in trade imbalances in several countries.

Table 5. Balance on the Current Account in Selected Countries (2003-2010) in Percent of GDP								
	2003	2004	2005	2006	2007	2008	2009	2010
China	2.8	3.6	7.1	9.3	10.6	9.6	6.0	5.2
Russia	8.2	10.1	11.1	9.5	5.9	6.2	4.1	4.9
Brazil	0.8	1.8	1.6	1.2	0.1	-1.7	-1.5	-2.3
India	1.5	0.1	-1.3	-1.0	0.7	-2.0	-2.8	-3.2
South Africa	-1.0	-3.0	3.5	-5.3	-7.0	-7.1	-4.1	-2.8
Vietnam	-4.9	-3.5	-1.1	-0.3	-9.8	11.9	-6.6	-3.8

Source: World Economic Outlook, IMF.

In 2008, Vietnam's export to China was $4.5 billion, whereas imports from China were $15.7 billion. In February 2011, Vietnam devalued its currency by 6.7%, the fourth devaluation of the *dong* in 15 months. In 2010, India imported $40.8 billion worth of items, mainly finished products, from China, whereas its export to China was only $20.9 billion worth of items, mainly minerals. Countries like India are surviving due to remittances from people living overseas and from foreign investments.

The trade deficit of India is increasing every year. In just seven years, the trade deficit of India increased by six-fold, from $28 billion in the 2004–2005 (April through March) financial year to $185 billion in the 2011–2012 (April through March) financial year. With an increase in the number of consumers, the trade deficit of India has the potential to surpass the U.S. trade deficit level ($600–$700 billion a year), which is unsustainable for India as, unlike the United States, it cannot print its currency to fund it.

In 1991, India approached the IMF for a loan because its foreign exchange (FOREX) was worth only three weeks of essential imports, and India was on the verge of default. India had to airlift 67 tons of its gold reserves to London as collateral in order to get $2.2 billion from the IMF. In addition, it had to liberalize its economy and sell several of its profit-making public firms at throwaway prices to U.S. firms such as Enron.

Brazil has followed in India's footsteps. That country's previous U. S. positive balance on its current account is going deep into the red, due to its increasing trade deficit. Brazil's exports, mainly minerals, are not increasing at the rate of its imports due to the increase in the number of consumers in the country.

Nearly every global financial crisis–such as the present Euro Crisis; the 1994 Peso Crisis; and the 1997 East Asian Financial Crisis–occurs due to the country's not having sufficient FOREX to fund its trade deficit. Right now, only countries that have significant current account deficits are facing a severe economic downturn, but it is going to bring down other countries like China and Germany who also have an export-based economy. Thus, the world does not have any option but to implement the Keynes' plan of a global currency managed by a global bank and an International Clearing Union to keep tabs on the exports and imports of various countries.

The U. S. economy is exceptional in that it may print its currency as much as it wants to fund its twin deficits—budget and trade deficits. On the other hand, countries like India and Vietnam have to "earn" dollars to pay for their imports. Because of trade deficits, the latter countries have to devalue their currencies so that their exports will become cheaper. In the late 1980s, the conversion rate of Indian currency was 1:15, whereas in late 2012 it was 1:55 (about 250% in the last 22–23 years). In February 2011, Vietnam devalued its currency by 6.7%, the fourth devaluation of the Dong in 15 months.

> 'We [U.S.] get cheap goods in exchange for pieces of paper, which we can print at a great rate,' said Allan H. Meltzer, an economist at Carnegie Mellon University. However, the mountain of U.S. bonds that foreigners are accumulating means the United States is going deeper into debt to fund its import binge, to the tune of about $3 trillion as of this year. 'Sooner or later, the rest of the world will decide that the United States is no longer a safe bet for lending more money,' said William R. Cline, a scholar at the Institute for International Economics and author of a new book titled *The United States as a Debtor Nation*. (Blustein, 2005)

According to Lou Crandall, chief economist at Wrightson ICAP, who analyzes Treasury financing trends, "While the current market for [U.S.] Treasuries is booming, it's unclear whether demand for debt can be sustained…There's a time bomb somewhere …but we don't know exactly where on the calendar it's planted" (Montgomery, 2009).

By the end of 2012, the economy seemed to have stabilized due to the $1.5 trillion stimulus money provided by the Bush and Obama administrations. During the Great Depression, too, the economy had temporarily improved because of two stimulus packages provided by the Roosevelt Administration. U.S. unemployment was 25% in 1933 and 15% in 1940 measured by the fact that in those days only one person in the family would work. The real numbers were actually much higher reckoned by present standards. Mass unemployment in the United States ended only after the outbreak of World War II, when its economy started to churn out arms and armaments initially for the European allies and later for itself.

There is a major difference between the Great Depression of the 1930s and the forthcoming Great Depression. During the former, the Keynesian stimulus (generating employment by government spending) worked. Unlike today, during the 1930s Great Depression, both consumer debt and government debts were not high. At present, the Keynesian stimulus alone is not going to solve the problem because the U.S. is completely dependent on the import of consumer items.

Table 6 shows the major holders of U.S. Treasury securities. By the end of 2008, China had surpassed Japan as the largest holder of U.S. Treasury securities. At the end of 2012, the oil-exporting countries and Brazil were the third and the fourth largest holders of U.S. Treasury securities. Caribbean Banking Centers (Bahamas, Bermuda, Cayman Islands, Netherlands Antilles, and Panama) and Taiwan are the fifth and the sixth largest holders of U.S. Treasury securities and are not shown in Table 6. Russia, the United Kingdom, and Hong Kong are the eighth, the tenth and the eleventh largest holders of U.S. Treasury securities. The holding of significant amounts of its Treasury securities by China, Russia, and the oil-exporting countries does not bode well for the United States because if those countries start to dump the treasuries, U.S. interest rates will increase drastically.

Figure 1 and Table 7 show the FOREX of selected countries. Apart from the U.S. Treasury bonds, most of the Chinese $3.6 trillion FOREX are invested in the United States. China and Japan had as much as $400 billion and $74.5 billion investments, respectively in Fannie Mae and Freddie Mac when the U.S. government bailed out these two agencies. As U.S. officials were deciding in August 2008 whether to take over Fannie Mae and Freddie Mac, the Treasury Department held informal talks with officials from the People's Bank of China (China's central bank). The Chinese representatives told them that they expected the U.S. government to "do whatever is necessary to protect the investments" (Harden & Cha, 2008). Russia also cut its investments in these two mortgage giants from $100 billion in early 2008 to $20 billion in November 2008. China is also reducing its stakes in these two after their rescue by the U.S. government.

The massive amount of China's FOREX and its U.S. investments has given China an immense hold over the American economy. In March 2009, the Pentagon, for the first time held a series of economic war games exercises. The Wall Street bankers, economists, and academics—about 80 in total—were flown to a bunker at the Applied Physics Laboratory in Maryland for a two-day event in 2009. The weapons were stocks, bonds, and currencies. The participants were divided into teams: the United States, China, Russia, Japan, the European Union, and so on. Then, the teams were presented with different scenarios—North Korea is imploding, a major global economy is melting down—and told to do what was in their best interests. Uniformed officers from the highest levels of the Pentagon watched as the economic conflicts played out (Rumbelow, 2011; Weiner, 2010).

Table 6. Major Holders of U.S. Treasury Securities in Billions of U.S. Dollars							
(At the end of year)	Japan	China	UK	Oil Exporting Countries*	Russia	Hong Kong	Grand Total
2000	317.7	60.3	50.2	47.7	N/A	38.6	1015.2
2001	317.9	78.6	45.0	46.8	N/A	47.7	1040.1
2002	378.1	118.4	80.8	49.6	N/A	47.5	1235.6
2003	550.8	159.0	82.2	42.6	N/A	50.0	1523.1
2004	289.9	222.9	95.8	62.1	N/A	45.1	1849.3
2005	670.0	310.0	146.0	78.2	N/A	40.3	2033.9
2006	622.9	396.9	92.3	110.2	N/A	54.0	2103.1
2007	581.2	477.6	158.1	137.9	32.7	51.2	2353.2
2008	626.0	727.4	130.9	186.2	116.4	77.2	3076.9
2009	765.7	894.8	180.3	201.1	141.8	148.7	3685.1
2010	882.3	1160.1	271.6	211.9	151.0	134.2	4437.9
2011	1058.4	1151.9	114.3	261.1	149.5	121.7	5007.4
2012	1120.2	1202.8	142.0	262.5	157.6	141.8	5555.4

* Oil exporters include Ecuador, Venezuela, Indonesia, Bahrain, Iran, Iraq, Kuwait, Oman, Qatar, Saudi Arabia, the United Arab Emirates, Algeria, Gabon, Libya, and Nigeria. Source: U.S. Department of Treasury

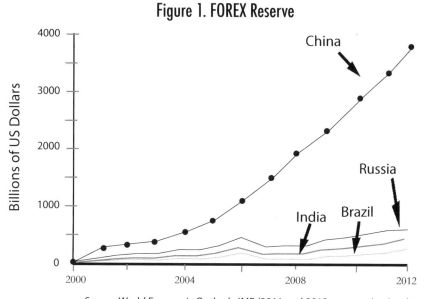

Figure 1. FOREX Reserve

Source: World Economic Outlook, IMF (2011 and 2012 were projections).

Table 7. Foreign Exchange Reserves in December 2012 in Billions of Dollars	
Country	**FOREX**
China	3,549
Japan	1,351
Saudi Arabia	627
Russia	561
Switzerland	530
Taiwan	391
Brazil	371
South Korea	319
Hong Kong	300
India	287

Source: The U.S. Central Intelligence Agency's *The World Factbook* at the CIA website, February 2013; Switzerland data is from Swiss National Bank for October 2012.

What the exercises showed was that the United States consistently lost to China in economic warfare. China won without so much as reaching for a gun. Part of the reason was that the United States could be easily distracted by expensive side conflicts that sapped its economic strength. But the more important reason was that China could inflict real pain on the United States without feeling it at home. For instance, by simply moving the maturities of some of its $850 billion in Treasury holdings from 90 days to 60 days, it could cause chaos in the U.S. stock markets. Or China could sell just a trickle of its U.S. financial assets and signal that it did not have confidence in the American economy, setting off a panic. According to Paul Bracken, "In the 1970s the West feared that its enemies had their fingers on a nuclear button. The modern equivalent may be China's ability to press button on U.S. Treasury bills" (Rumbelow, 2011). Bracken is professor and expert in private equity at the Yale School of Management who serves on government advisory committees at the U.S. Department of Defense. He was one of the key players behind the 2009 economic war games (Rumbelow, 2011; Weiner, 2010).

According to the president of the Council on Foreign Relations, Richard Haass, China may bring down the United States in the same way the Eisenhower administration brought down its close ally Britain during the 1956 Suez crisis. Haass said:

> Essentially the US took advantage of Britain's sterling problem to exercise some economic leverage over the British government, and that led to a

hasty retreat. So one can imagine a situation nowadays, where say there is a crisis over Taiwan between the US and China—which holds a significant number of dollars—and one can imagine the Chinese might be prepared to threaten the dollar, make some comments to weaken it unless the US backs off some of its support of Taiwan. (Webb, 2011)

World Union

In spite of the outbreak of military conflicts every few years, much of the world is heading toward unity. Most Islamic countries are going through crises of a similarly violent nature–meaning Islamic militancy. On the other hand, the rest of the world is witnessing a macro trend toward unification in the form of the EU (European Union), ASEAN (Association of Southeast Asian Nations), SAARC (South Asian Association for Regional Cooperation), AU (African Union), and UNASUR (Union of South American Nations).

It took a couple of centuries to form the nation that is the present superpower: the United States of America. Until the mid-1700s, the United States was just a collection of villages and towns, but over time it evolved. Similarly with the EU, which has now united most of Europe; this is something beyond the imagination at the onset of the last century. The origin of the EU lies in the establishment of the European Coal and Steel Community (ECSC) by the Schuman Declaration of 1950. France, Italy, Belgium, Netherlands, and Luxembourg were its founding members, and signed the Treaty of Paris in 1951. Then in 1957, two new communities—the European Economic Community (EEC, a customs union) and the European Atomic Energy Community (Euratom, for cooperation in the field of nuclear energy)—were established by the Treaties of Rome. In 1967, these three bodies were merged to form the European Community.

During the next 25 years, several treaties were signed and several new countries were admitted into the European Community, and then finally the EU was created under the Maastricht Treaty in 1992. In 1999, a common currency, the Euro, was introduced. The first direct elections to the European Parliament were held in 1979, and in 1986, the European flag was adopted. The EU now consists of a Commission, a Council, and a Parliament. The European Commission is the executive branch, the Council of the European Union consists of the ministers of member countries, and the European Parliament is composed of representatives directly elected by the citizens of EU member countries with elections held every five years. The European Court of Justice is composed of 27 judges, one from each member country. The European Central Bank (ECB) headquartered in Frankfurt, Germany, controls monetary policy within the Eurozone. In 2004, an agreement was signed to create a European Union Rapid Reaction Force (EURRF), which will have 60,000 soldiers.

In September 2012, five of the six biggest countries in the EU, excluding Britain, have called for a radical overhaul of European foreign and defense policies to create a powerful new pan-European foreign ministry, a possible European army, and a single market for EU defense industries. They support a directly elected European president, a new European police organization to guard the union's external borders, and a single European visa (Traynor, 2012).

Over the next several decades, the European Union will become the United States of Europe: It will control its members' military forces, and member states will have uniform constitutions, uniform laws, etc. Only a century ago, an organization like the EU and a common currency like the Euro were beyond anybody's imagination. With two world wars as catalysts, however, a multi-polar and strife-ridden Europe has been transformed into a unified and peaceful Europe within a century. Only a few trouble spots like Kosovo and Cyprus remain, though after the lost decade of the 1990s, Russia is trying to regain some of her lost power by exerting it economically (especially via its huge gas reserves) on its neighbors. This is natural, since Russia is going to play an important role in the international arena on account of its military and economic capabilities. Fifteen of the EU's 25 nations receive as much as 90% of their natural gas from Russia. As the United States and the EU have evolved, so can other collections of states.

ASEAN (the Association of Southeast Asian Nations) consists of all Southeast Asian countries. Its origin lies in the foundation of the Association of Southeast Asia (ASA) in 1961, which consisted of the Philippines, Malaysia, and Thailand. In 1967, Indonesia, Malaysia, the Philippines, Singapore, and Thailand signed the Bangkok Declaration establishing ASEAN for economic cooperation among its members. In 1984, Brunei Darussalam became its sixth member, Vietnam joined in 1995, Laos and Myanmar joined in 1997, and Cambodia joined in 1999. Every year, the heads of ASEAN member countries meet to discuss and resolve regional issues. In 1994, a regional forum was founded to foster constructive dialog and consultation on political and security issues, and confidence-building and preventive diplomacy in the Asia-Pacific region. It now has 26 member countries—the ASEAN nations, Australia, Bangladesh, Canada, the People's Republic of China, the European Union, India, Japan, North Korea, South Korea, Mongolia, New Zealand, Pakistan, Papua New Guinea, Russia, Timor-Leste, and the United States. In the next several decades, ASEAN will also follow the path of the EU; it will become a political, economic, and military organization with a common currency like the Euro integrating the entire Southeast Asia. Although there are several trouble spots near this part of this world, only two—China-Taiwan and North Korea—are the major ones that might result in full-scale war involving several nations.

The South Asian Association for Regional Cooperation (SAARC) is an economic and political organization in Southern Asia. It was established in 1985 by Pakistan, India, Bangladesh, Sri Lanka, Maldives, Nepal, and Bhutan. Afghanistan joined in 2007. Unlike the ASEAN's role in the integration of Southeast Asia, SAARC is unable to play a crucial role in the integration of South Asia due to rivalry between India and Pakistan.

But once the differences between these two neighbors are solved, SAARC will play an important role in integration, as the two nations' cultures are more or less similar.

Africa's slave trade, which caused Africa to lose a large number of its working population, adversely affected the African economy. Table 8 shows how severely the size of the population leveled off during the slave-trade years.

Table 8. Distribution of World Population in Various Continents from 1650 to 1900 in Millions				
	1650	1750	1850	1900
Africa	100	100	100	120
Europe	103	144	274	423
Asia	257	437	656	857

Source: Rodney, W. 1982. *How Europe Underdeveloped Africa*, Washington, DC: Howard University Press, 97.

But slowly and steadily African countries are also moving toward the EU type organization. The African Union (AU) is an organization of 53 countries formed in 2001 after the merger of the African Economic Community (AEC) and the Organization of African Unity (OAU). The aims of the AU are to have a single currency and a single, integrated army. Its organs (parliament, judiciary, etc.) are more or less similar to those of the EU. During the mid-1990s, close to one million people were killed in the Rwandan genocide. Since 2003, more than 450,000 people have been killed in the Darfur region of Sudan. Seven thousand African Union troops were sent to Sudan in mid-2005 on a peace mission under United Nations Security Council Resolution 1564, but they were ill-equipped and too few to stop the genocide there. In hotspots, like Somalia (since 2007) and Mali (2013), AU troops have been deployed for peacekeeping.

UNASUR, the Union of South American Nations, is going to merge two existing free-trade organizations, MERCOSUR and the Andean Community. It will eventually also integrate South American countries on the pattern of the EU, with a common currency and parliament, with its capital in Quito, Ecuador. The target date for complete union along EU lines is 2019. Its members will be Bolivia, Colombia, Ecuador, Peru, Venezuela, Brazil, Argentina, Uruguay, Paraguay, Chile, Guyana, and Suriname. Panama and Mexico have observer status.

In the next several decades, all three organizations—SAARC, the AU, and UNASUR—will follow the path of the EU and become political, economic, and military organizations with common currencies integrating their respective regions. Subsequent to this, we will see a global umbrella organization integrating these organizations, which we may call the World Union or Global Union. It will be formed according to a bottom-up approach, unlike the United Nations, which was formed after the Second World War on top-down lines, with five nations having veto powers. This can be seen as a unification of human civilization.

Conclusion

Two factors, the ongoing global economic depression and global Islamic fundamentalism, are going to redefine human civilization in the same way as the Great Depression and the two World Wars redefined human civilization. The Great Depression of the 1930s resulted in the rise of Hitler, who tried to establish the Third Reich, an awesome colonial power like Britain's, which would rule over the world for a thousand years. In the first half of the last century, the independence movements in the European colonies were on the rise, which would have eventually ended colonialism. Hitler was simply trying to turn back the clock. Instead of achieving his goal, he helped pave the way for thriving democracies in most of Europe and decolonization in Asia and Europe. Similarly, the present global rise in Islamic militancy is going to work as a catalyst for the modernization of Islam.

The collapse of the U. S. economy will lead to radical political changes in the world, not the least in the Islamic world, which will open up for the modernization of Islam. During the period of modernization of Islam, the world may be experiencing turmoil while it moves toward stability. Europe, India, the United States, Israel, and perhaps even China will constitute war fronts, particularly for homegrown terrorists. If Pakistan's nuclear arsenal falls into the hands of Islamic militants, we may witness large-scale nuclear attacks on these countries. In the end, the modernization of Islam will be a major step toward the integration of human civilization.

It is very difficult to predict the exact sequence of events that will lead to the modernization of Islam in these Islamic countries. In 1900, nobody would have been able to predict the exact sequence of events that would lead to the collapse of kingdoms in Europe, leading to the vibrant democracy in Western Europe, with most Asian and African countries gaining independence from their colonial masters within five to six decades. Right now we are witnessing a rise of Islamic militancy globally, and with the collapse of U.S. economy, Islamists are going to take over in a number of countries. As suggested earlier, if one discards the divinity aspects of Muhammad's revelations, the *Qur'an* is just the social practices of 7th century Arabia, and it cannot be imposed on the 21st century population for a long period of time. Hitler also tried to create a thousand years of the Third Reich, but it lasted only a decade or so. Although these types of events result in the deaths of a large number of innocent people, they speed up the process of changes in human civilization. Changes that would have taken several centuries to occur take but a few decades.

Notes

1. The theory of the clash of civilizations predicts alignments and wars among various civilizations—Western, Islamic, Chinese, Japanese, Orthodox/Russian, Hindu, African, and Latin. The term "clash of civilizations" was first used by Bernard Lewis in an article in the September 1990 issue of *Atlantic Monthly* titled, "The Roots of Muslim Rage."

2. Once, a Muslim of India criticized an article on my blog that proposed provisions for a uniform civil code in a country's constitution. I asked him, "Why do you want only the civil code of Shari'a (for example, a man to have up to four wives, denying alimony to divorced women, and divorcing the wife by just uttering the word 'divorce' three times) and not the criminal code of Shari'a? Why does the government not implement the criminal code of Shari'a on Muslims, i.e., if the court convicts a non-Muslim, then he shall have to go to jail, whereas if the convicted person is a Muslim, his limbs (hand/leg) will be cut off, an eye may be taken out, or death by stoning may be administered according to Shari'a?"

3. In 1995, I wrote a piece for the *Global Times* (Denmark) based on the analysis of the social, political, and religion environments in MENA countries: "The United States has sowed the seeds of the next Cold War by employing the low-cost war strategy in Afghanistan. Although a rise in Islamic fundamentalist movements worldwide was inevitable, United States involvement in Afghanistan only hastened the process. Iraq only delayed this growth by its war with Iran. Large-scale unemployment and acute poverty, coupled with corruption in high places, produce the militancy, and are not stopped by war. Previously, these conditions were responsible for the rise of communist movements in countries like India, Vietnam, Yemen, Chile, and Nicaragua. Nowadays, the unemployed and poor masses are swayed to militancy in the name of religion: Hindu parties Shiva Sena and Bajrang Dal in India, the Islamic Salvation Front in Algeria, Hamas in Palestine, the Islamic Group in Egypt, and An-Nahda (Renaissance) in Tunisia among others exemplify this trend. Bal Thackeray, head and founder of Shiva Sena, the fundamentalist Hindu party controlling Bombay, the financial capital of India, says that he would like to be India's Hitler. Thackeray has threatened to prevent Muslim pilgrimages to Mecca if Hindu pilgrims to the Amarnath Cave in heavily Muslim Kashmir are injured (all Indian Muslims going to Hajj in Mecca fly from Bombay). The trend of religious militancy is especially dangerous in Islamic states because Islam and its holy book the *Qur'an* do not differentiate between state and mosque or between politics and theology. It is a general feature even in India (12% Muslim) for clergy to give a political lecture after Friday prayer" (Kumar, 1995).

4. My book, *Casino Capitalism: The Collapse of the US Economy and the Transition to Secular Democracy in the Middle East* (iUniverse, 2012) was an extension of Chapter 6 "The Collapse of the American Economy" of my book, *The Modernization of Islam and the Creation of a Multipolar World Order* (Booksurge, 2008).

PART TWO

Policy and Economic Challenges

A major factor in the recent Arab Awakening throughout the MENA (Middle East and North Africa) region is the economy. While some progress was made by President Anwar El-Sadat after the Camp David Accord and the influx of financial, economic, and military support of the U.S. and European countries, the Mubarak era was more hesitant in following Sadat's footsteps and adopting a free market economy for Egypt. The Mubarak regime was also plagued with corruption, cronyism, and favoritism spearheaded by his two sons and their wealthy friends who exerted an influence on the Egyptian economy. Economic stagnation and hardship for the less fortunate and massive unemployment among an exploding young population are in contrast to the amassed wealth of the Egyptian ruling and influential class, their families and surrogates. The short stints of some economic growth and open market (*infitah*) during Sadat's post-Camp David era quickly vanished, along with the trickle down economic benefits for most Egyptians, which was very minimal and short-lived. The situation in the Arab Spring countries like Tunisia, Yemen, and Libya was no different. In every MENA country, unemployment among the youth—including college graduates—is among the highest in the world and hovers in most of these MENA countries around 30%, and in some like Egypt and Jordan around 40%. This time bomb is ticking faster and louder as the Arab economies in general are not creating enough jobs for the unemployed young nationals.

In the Gulf Cooperation Council (GCC) countries, the private sector is dominated by and primarily dependent on a more skilled work force of expatriates. Past efforts of Saudization, Kuwaitization, Emiratization, and other government plans to implant nationals in jobs filled by expatriates have not been as successful as governments had expected. Government jobs have been used as dumping grounds for many functionally ill-suited college graduates with a growing sense of entitlement that has taken hold among them. Calls for education reforms have gone unheeded; food and housing subsidies and salary increases have been given to citizens of oil-rich Arab countries, along with the introduction of and/or promise of some resemblance of a democracy where none existed before. Attempts at privatization and expansion of the private sector have been mired in corruption, as was the case of Tunisia under Ben Ali and Egypt under Mubarak.

In addressing the topic of economic "relative deprivation" felt by the Arab masses, Dr. Bessma Momani points out that such deprivation was a contributing factor to the reason that the Arab people chose to rise against their autocratic governments. Dr. Momani addressed economic development in Arab countries, and the increased investments the Arab Gulf States have made in the economies of their poor neighbors such as Egypt, Jordan, Morocco, and Tunisia since 2000. Momani uses the argument of "built environments"—case-study and primary data collected from Jordan—to examine how this neoliberal urban change has negatively affected people and is considered a partial precursor to the Arab Spring. Momani highlights the discontent of these poor masses as many Arabs remain disconnected from the rapid economic growth taking place in their countries. According to her findings, "these disconnections were also mal urban landscape investments (high-rise mixed-use towers, western-inspired residential villas, grandiose tourist resorts, and entertainment complexes) that were, in part a contributing factor to the sense of relative deprivation felt by poorer Arabs. Thus, the Arab Spring was in part due to some of these social and economic frustrations with non-inclusive urban development.

While democracy has been a common rallying cry, it was certainly the economy that failed people—especially in the poorer MENA countries—who also look with envy at their small oil-rich neighbors around the Gulf. States, such as the UAE are following a different model referred to sometimes as UAE, Inc. Such economic renaissance in the UAE has made some believe that the experience of economic development in the UAE, and running the country as a corporation may be the answer. Dr. Kenneth Wise describes this economic phenomenon as it relates to the UAE, its policies, politics, and future. According to Dr. Wise, several theories about the future of Arab Gulf States in general and the United Arab Emirates in particular rest on givens that may be accurate in some ways but inadequate in most others. These theories, Wise contends, "are variations of a theme of "fragility"—that mounting pressures, both internal and external along with lack of democracy will soon push the UAE (along with the rest of the Gulf monarchies) into becoming democracies. To make the UAE more understandable, he suggests adding a cultural variable and the concept of "UAE, Inc." This culture, he writes, "will show why the sentiment of loyalty runs deep." The image of the UAE as a single company will outline the modern basis of association and the possible cohesion of the country when it faces challenges and opportunities such as finding ways to cope with a growing pool of second-generation expatriates. To date, the UAE has been remarkably cohesive and appears resilient enough to avoid or withstand what has brought down neighboring Arab governments.

Could a union or federation of Arab countries help solve their current political, economic, and security problems? The ideas and dreams of a Pan Arab Union, Arab Federation, or their equivalent became popular among Arab nationalists in the 1950s and were written about by intellectuals like Satiʿ al-Hosari and acted upon by political figures like Gamal Abdel Nasser who formed with Syria the short-lived United Arab Republic in 1956. In addressing the long sought-after aspiration of some Arab intellectuals, Dr. Alan L. Moss presents a far-sighted proposal to establish a Middle East Union (MEU) similar in scope to the European Union (EU) but "customized to meet the specific needs and aspirations of the people of the Middle East." Moss' paper evokes memories of the most recent proposal by King Abdullah of Saudi Arabia in 2012 to establish a union of the Arab Gulf States to replace the existing Gulf Cooperation Council (GCC), much to the chagrin of most GCC members, with the exception of the King of Bahrain. A previous attempt—also advanced by Saudi Arabia during the height of the Arab Spring—to extend to the kingdoms of Morocco and Jordan some form of GCC membership in order to preserve the remaining MENA monarchies, has not produced any tangible results. A previous federation was formed from January 1, 1972 to November 19, 1977 that involved Libya, Egypt, and Syria, and was known as The Federation of Arab Republics (*Ittiḥād Al-Jumhūriyyāt Al-ʿArabiyya*), which also failed. In spite of its long history and its founders' aspirations in the 1940s, the League of Arab States remains dysfunctional and ineffective.

American foreign policy in the Middle East is examined by Dr. Lawrence Davidson, specifically on how certain organized lobbyists have managed to falsely convince the American public that their lobbying interests are in America's national interests. After examining the role of media and pro-Israel lobbies in shaping America's public opinion, Davidson goes on to recommend a thorough and transparent review of past and present U.S. foreign policy in the Middle East and what America's national interests in the region are, or should be. The harsh and unjustified attacks by the 2012 Republican candidates on Islam, Muslims, and Arabs underscore Dr. Davidson's observations. He writes "with very few exceptions these candidates repeated their canned scripted attacks and wanted to outdo one another in their unconditional support for Israel, condemnation of the Palestinians and sweeping attacks on Muslims as well as American Muslims." The recent events in Egypt and attempts to dismantle and discredit the Muslim Brotherhood and political Islamists with support from the conservative Gulf States led by Saudi Arabia will shape future global debates on this and related subjects.

Arab Gulf Investments into Non-Inclusive Urban Development in the Middle East: A Partial Precursor to the Arab Spring

Bessma Momani

Abstract

Despite rapid development of the Arab Middle East's urban landscape resulting from Gulf Arab investments, the Arab masses became increasingly disenchanted with the so-called macroeconomic success of the region. The Arab Spring was in part due to some of this social frustration with non-inclusive urban development. Using the argument of "built environments" and based on a case-study of Jordan and primary data collected from Jordan, this paper will examine how this neoliberal urban change had negatively affected people, and will argue that this is a partial precursor to the Arab Spring.

Introduction

The Arab Gulf states were rapidly increasing their investments into the Middle East, and the type of investments should be of interest. The Arab Gulf was investing in particular classes of assets: real estate, banking, construction, and tourism projects (Smith, 2007). In Jordan alone, there have been nearly 20 real estate developers from the Gulf who have initiated over 80 real estate projects throughout the small kingdom in the mid-2000s. Many of these projects are high-rise mixed-use towers that combine retail outlets, offices, and residential condominiums in addition to Western-inspired residential villas, grandiose tourist resorts, and entertainment complexes.

With the influx of billions of dollars in direct foreign investments coming from oil-rich Arab Gulf states that have experienced large capital surpluses, several Middle Eastern cities have become replete with high-rise towers and mega-development projects. The urban landscape of many Middle Eastern cities has changed dramatically. While Middle Eastern governments and many of their socioeconomic elite publicize the rapid "modernization" of their countries, many of the Arab people remained disconnected from the rapid urban development growth happening in their countries. While we cannot yet know the causes and determinants of the Arab Spring, this paper argues that the non-inclusive urban development experienced throughout the Middle East was a contributing factor to a social sense of exclusion leading to frustration that partially led to the Arab Spring.

Leading up to the Arab Spring, the Middle East experienced macroeconomic growth that was impressive and high, but yet it was *non-inclusive.* There is overwhelming academic and anecdotal evidence to believe that economic factors are a key part of the puzzle in searching for determinants of the Arab Spring. Ironically, the Arab Spring started in countries that actually had macroeconomic growth: in 2009 and 2010, Tunisia had 3% and 4% GDP) growth; Egypt, 4.7% and 5%; Libya, 1.8% and 5.2%; Yemen, 3.9% and 7.8%; and even Syria, 4% and 5%. These countries were also leading economic reformers, "successfully liberalizing" their economies. If the Arab world was prospering and growing economically, why then did a number of countries experience political revolution?

Again, the challenge facing many Arab countries is that growth has been non-inclusive. Inclusive growth, as defined and explained by the World Bank, is when growth is long-term, sustained, and reaches a broad spectrum of the population and across sectors. Here, economic growth is viewed as successful when it is diversified across sectors, inclusive of various groups in the labor force, attributable to productive employment (not rents), and where the market takes a lead role (World Bank, 2009). The Arab Middle East appeared to have economic growth, but it was non-inclusive (Shafik, 2012). The Arab Spring was in part due to some of this social exclusion and then frustration with non-inclusive urban development. This paper argues that despite macroeconomic growth in the Arab world, the revolutions hit the region because economic growth was not distributed to the masses in a pace that met rising expectations. Using the argument of "built environments" and based on a case-study of Jordan and primary data collected from Jordan in 2010, this paper examines how this neoliberal urban change had negatively affected people, and will argue that this is a partial precursor to the Arab Spring. Indeed, it has been argued that the Arab Spring was an attempt to reclaim many public places as a result of social exclusion and alienation felt by the Arab masses (Aly, 2011; Tripp, 2012).

Theoretical Framework: The Neoliberal City, Social Exclusion, and Frustration

With increased globalization, urbanization, and industrialization, cities are competing against one another to attract capital accumulation and investment—creating a race to the bottom of urban standards and planning (Kantor, 1987). As central states devolve their authority through diminishing regulatory standards at the national level, city and regional authorities become more vital to economic policy-making (Clarke et al., 2004). To attract capital into a competitive environment among cities, urban governments are offering more inducements and incentives to bring more capital into cities, generating public costs offset by increased residents' taxes (Boyle & Rogerson, 2001). As globalized cities continue to compete with one another for scarce capital and foreign investment, some urban sectors have increased in wealth and connections to the globalized world, while others remain detached from increased poverty and urban neglect in poorer neighborhoods (Keyder, 2005).

Increasingly, Middle East cities are bifurcated by a glamorous, shiny, and modern city with clear official and private investment, while poorer areas are neglected, ignored, and dilapidated. The latter is also on the rise as governments rely on private capital to fund and finance former public works projects and developments. Private investors gravitate toward the affluent areas, increasing the discrepancy of services and development in the bifurcated areas. The Middle East, throughout the 2000s, experienced a competition for regional and international real-estate companies, consulting firms, and urban consultancies to create neoliberal and large-scale urban developments (Daher, 2008). Finally, as cities are forced to compete for private and foreign investment, land and business taxes need to remain low and competitive. This decreases the potential revenue earnings and creates incentives to direct limited tax revenue into urban areas where investors predominate.

Megaprojects throughout the Middle East attempted to reshape the urban cores, such as Solidere in Beirut, Lebanon; Dreamland and CityStars in Cairo, Egypt; and Jabal Omar in Mecca, Saudi Arabia (Daher, 2008). This "regeneration" of urban development in Western, neoliberal fashion is what Adham (2005) refers to as "Oriental vision of Occident." Similarly, the creation of exclusive resort towns along Egypt's coastline—such as Marabella and Marina—were fantasy resorts that were disassociated from the reality of most Egyptians (Adham, 2005). These neoliberal urban transformations are emblematic of class inequalities. As Mona Abaza (as cited in Adham, 2005) noted about Egypt: "…walled off, protected areas, gated communities, condominiums, private beach resorts, leisure islands of peace, snow cities in the desert and amusement parks, monitored by private security forces and advanced technology to protect them against the 'barbarians' outside, are no longer just futuristic fantasies." This class-based analysis of urban development also fits with similar views about urban governance or local politics in urban planning literature. Referred to as "regime theory" in urban studies, local politics is captured by economic and financial interests and therefore pursues a maximization of profits (Logan & Molotch, 1987). The competition among cities to capture capital can then fail to serve the needs of a large segment of the city's residents (Lauria, 1997).

In academic studies of the "built environment"—which refers to a multidimensional concept involving local and regional characteristics, such as density, land use, street connectivity, and regional structures—there has been an anthropological turn in better understanding the cross-cultural and symbiotic meaning of buildings and their spatial organization (Lawrence & Low, 1990). Researchers in these "environment-behaviour" traditions have argued that the built environment can have an affect or influence, directly or indirectly, on the behavior and feelings of people (Lawrence & Low, 1990). Some neuro-scientific studies have even tried to examine how the built environment can influence brain processes (Eberhard, 2007). The research is scattered among a number of unrelated disciplines, but the core argument is that the built environment is rarely just about physical structures; there are also social, political, and cultural implications. Clearly, urban developments can have a social and political effect that goes beyond just changes to the built environment.

The bifurcated Middle East cities also reflect the widening gap between the globalized affluent and the poorer segments of the city. The widening income inequality also perpetuates social exclusion of poorer people into city life. As Keyder (2005) explains: "Social exclusion refers to a failure of social integration at economic, political and cultural levels—a market phenomenon reinforced by failures in the welfare regime and by the lack of cultural integration" (p. 128). What is important to note is that social exclusion is done by the act of one group, the globalized affluent, to another poorer group of city inhabitants (Byrne, 1999, p. 2). This us-versus-them concept is both physical in terms of the spatial layout and character of the built environment, and also in promoting networks, social circles, and status. Identifying one's neighborhood is less about the physical placement than the positive or negative connotation about one's perceived success. This carries forward into political participation, decision-making power, and job opportunities. To elaborate then:

Social exclusion is defined as a multi-dimensional process, in which various forms of exclusion are combined: participation in decision-making and political processes, access to employment and material resources, and integration into common cultural processes. When combined they create acute forms of exclusion that find a spatial representation in particular neighbourhoods. (Madanipour, 1998, p. 22).

Regional Dynamics of Arab Gulf Investments

Many Arab Middle Eastern countries underwent extensive economic and institutional reforms throughout the 1990s in order to pursue greater integration with the world economy (Eid & Paua, 2003, pp. 108–109; Mohamed & Sidiropoulos, 2010, pp. 76–77; Sadik & Bolbol, 2001). Countries such as Tunisia, Jordan, Egypt, Syria, Algeria, and Lebanon became more hospitable to foreign investment and proceeded to privatize state-owned assets as well as revitalize their domestic stock exchanges. In an attempt to render Arab Middle East markets more friendly to international trade and foreign investments, these countries streamlined and lowered tariffs and deregulated their economies over the past two decades, often building from already established trade and investment agreements with the European Union and the United States.

During the economic liberalization of the past decade, these Middle East countries were generally hungry for capital investment, had a growing consumer base of young people, and a highly educated and yet relatively inexpensive workforce; simultaneously, however, they also had a difficult time attracting international investors because of the negative "neighbourhood effect" of regional insecurity (Onyeiwu, 2008). However, one class of investors who increased their investments in the Middle East region was Arab Gulf investors.

Arab Gulf investments have increasingly moved into Asia and the broader Middle East, throughout the 2000s, with notable capital flows to the Mashreq region in recent years. This can be explained by both push and pull factors. On the pull side, Arab Middle East governments have initiated a series of incentives, including economic liberalization policies that encourage foreign investment, protect investors' interests, and facilitate Gulf real estate developments. This marks a real change in these Middle Eastern governments' economic policies. Gulf investors are less spooked by geopolitical instability in the region, are more familiar with the political and bureaucratic constraints of these countries, and view the Arab Middle East as having relatively safe investment climates.

A major push factor driving a shift in the composition of Gulf Arab investment includes the deterioration in U.S.–Gulf relations after September 11, 2001. The oil price boom years of 2003 to 2008 had prompted Gulf investors and sovereign wealth funds to seek investment into fixed, tangible assets, specifically, real estate in liberalized Middle East economies. With the added scrutiny of Arab Gulf investments in the United States, as seen in the Dubai Ports Controversy, shifts in Gulf petrodollar recycling beyond the United States began to occur (Momani, 2010). Based on estimates from June 2003 to June 2008, 13% of Gulf foreign assets—or $120 billion (which more than doubled nominally from 2001 to 2006)—went to the Middle East and North Africa, predominantly to Jordan, Egypt, and Lebanon (Samba, 2008). This represents a significant increase from previous years and a shift away from U.S.-based assets. It was estimated, for example, that 50% to 75% of Egyptian and Jordanian stock exchanges were Gulf owned (Siddiqi, 2009), and 47% of direct foreign investment in Egypt (Khalaf & England, 2008), 60% in Lebanon, and 70% to 80% in Jordan (IMF, 2009), were Gulf owned.

Gulf investors have also chosen to invest in assets that they are most familiar with at home: urban development in real estate. The "dubization" of urban areas has become a growing phenomenon in many Gulf cities. The attraction to high rise towers, resort towns, and malls is part of the Gulf vision of modernization. For better or worse, the cultural trend toward mass consumption in Gulf society, the appreciation for glistening towers erected out of deserts, and the luxurious lifestyle they wish to portray, are cemented among Gulf society and encouraged by the Gulf political and economic elite. As Gulf investors have ventured into the neighboring Middle East, they have brought the kind of investment knowledge they know well at home: investment in real estate.

These push factors, however, do not explain why we have seen a shift in Gulf Arab investments toward the Middle East specifically. Those same economic forces that induce states to liberalize their economy (in particular, the need to move away from oil dependence in the Gulf, and a corresponding need to attract foreign investment in the Mashreq) cause the structure of trade and investment to take on a more regionalized form, as states seek regional arrangements to participate in globalization rather than to avoid it. This "new regionalism" approach suggests that states voluntarily choose to deepen integration, not because of top-down structural pressure, but because within the state there are bottom-up distributional coalitions pushing for regionalism. This is further evidenced in an emboldened Arab Gulf business class as it divorces itself away from rentier politics (Hertog, 2011; Hvidt, 2011).

Three key political economy variables also explain the increasing investment ties between the Arab Gulf and the Arab Middle East. These variables include economic reforms in the Arab Middle East described above; the drive to diversify Gulf Arab investments, driven by various factors not limited to economic welfare-driven incentives to prolong the state bargain between Gulf monarchies and its citizens; and the existence of "horizontal networks" that bind the citizens of both regions closer together, and economic diplomacy prompted by an abundance of skilled Arab labor in the Gulf (Momani, 2011). All three factors can be understood within the context of increasing economic liberalization, and the role of regionalization in minimizing its costs and maximizing its benefits. So while the economic pull and push factors created a ripe environment for Arab Gulf investments into the Middle East, the sense on the ground was that these urban developments were not benefiting the masses and were non-inclusive.

Case Study: Investment and Urban Development in Jordan

Despite common misperceptions that the Arab Spring did not affect Jordan, the revolutions sweeping the Middle East did affect this tiny kingdom. Calls for economic and political reforms were present from the beginning of the Arab Spring and continue to this time. Demonstrations, political protests, boycotts, labor protests, strikes, and other non-violent actions have been noted throughout the country (Adely, 2012). Like much of the Arab Middle East, but with some factors peculiar to Jordan itself, there were a number of factors to explain how the real estate sector was similarly ripe for Gulf investment.

After 2003, Jordan had an influx of Iraqi migrants fleeing the U.S. occupation of Iraq. Numbers reported have ranged from 160,000 to 750,000. These migrants, nevertheless, brought significant amounts of capital with them to Jordan. A good portion of this capital went into purchasing Jordanian real estate. At the same time, as oil prices continued to rise from 2003 to 2008, Arab Gulf purchased Jordanian real estate remained cheaper than real estate in the Gulf. As a country that is viewed as one of the most politically stable in the region, Jordan continued to attract capital and real estate investment throughout the 2000s. This investment into real estate, as opposed to other economic sectors including manufacturing, stems from the impression of many that Jordanian real estate represents a long-term, risk-free investment in a troubled region.

Jordanian policymakers have not tried to implement strategies that move away from investment into real estate. According to interviews with government officials, much of the Jordanian elite have been rather impressed by the 'modern' urban development of Amman. They have been culturally and socially predisposed to appreciate this type of urban development. At the same time, many Jordanian elites partnered or benefited directly or indirectly by the boom in real estate development. This was compounded by the fact that the underdeveloped Jordanian stock exchange does not soak in much of the capital inflow from abroad, or from generated capital surplus at home. According to one analyst interviewed, 30% of central Amman stands empty because of investment concentrated on property holdings. Real estate is a lucrative sector for domestic and foreign investors alike.

It can be difficult to give precise data on how much capital is invested into Jordanian real estate, particularly since there is no accurate means of determining Jordanian national wealth, when 25% of the economy is in the informal sector. That said, according to a 2006 and 2008 Jordanian survey, national expenditures or consumption is higher than national income. This is in part due to the return of Jordanian expatriates who, upon return, typically want to purchase land. According to a Jordanian economist interviewed, there are many landowning Jordanians who may have assets that make them millionaires, but have little fluid or disposable capital to spend in everyday life. This creates a tight land market and inherent price distortion. For instance, it is hard to explain why in Amman a single *dunom* costs approximately $3 million in a country where the average GDP per capita is approximately $4000/annum. There is a strong local and regional preference to acquire and collect landholdings. In many respects, it is difficult to find landowners who are willing to sell their land holdings, for both cultural and utilitarian reasons.

Historically, landowners have held on to land for long tenures, which in turn, constrict land supply and driving prices upward, which furthers inflation. Indeed, in the 1970s, it was possible for Jordanians to use land inheritances to start a factory that became profitable and served as a basis for household income. But these types of success stories are no longer happening in Jordan. Today, Jordanians are less apt to sell their land to start a business; rather, they start a business to buy land. This has led to the freezing of savings in land, which employs no one, provides little value-added production to the economy, and diverts capital away from stock markets or bank savings. Land is perceived to be an easy and safe investment.

The International Finance Corporation (IFC) *Doing Business* report traced how many steps it takes to establish a business in Jordan; and it was found that the easiest sector to invest in was real estate, easier than setting up a factory. Foreign investors consequently face few obstacles to purchasing real estate in Jordan. In addition, not only it is easy to buy land, but there is also no penalty for having idle and vacant land. Once land is sold, there is no capital dividend tax, but a 10% registration fee for transferring land ownership that is commonly shared between the buyer and the seller. Despite being an extremely lucrative asset, however, it is this type of business that is harmful, not only for the reasons already discussed, but perhaps most importantly, because it thrives on the misery of others (i.e., landless Jordanians, conflict in surrounding Gulf countries). Indeed, people who have diversified from that rule have regretted it as they end up losing their money in the stock market.

Jordanian policy does not facilitate Greenfield investment. One measure of country success is whether businesses come in to buy existing businesses, go into partnership with local businesses, or establish their own companies—in other words, whether the country can attract Greenfield investments. If a country can attract Greenfield investments it implies that a country's business environment is developed: you can easily buy land, set up a manufacturing firm, and get all your proper licenses. Jordanian policies do not facilitate this. Real estate remains the most attractive form of foreign investment, given the low profitability of investing in other things such as establishing manufacturing firms. To be sure, the factories that have succeeded are cement factories, which incidentally are classified as mining. Moreover, another factor for the small growth potential and low profitability ratios of Jordan's business environment is that there is no bankruptcy law.

Since the mid-2000s, the urban landscape of Jordan's capital Amman has changed dramatically. For some observers, the rapid urban development in Amman represents a form of 'modernization' for the city and its small kingdom. But how is this rapid urban development perceived by Jordanians? Do these real estate investments in Amman have any unintended social or political consequences? To answer these questions, this study undertook a multi-layered and interdisciplinary research design in December 2010, preceding the Arab Spring that swept the Middle East.

Findings: Urban Development and Social Frustration in Amman

To investigate how the built environment affects people is to ask them directly about their experiences and their views using structured questions, standardized data collection, and triangulation (Vischer, 2008). Using this triangulation method, urbanites in Jordan were interviewed, surveyed, and participated in structured focus groups which asked about their experiences and feelings toward their city of Amman. Content-analysis of local media and archived web postings were also conducted to determine public attitudes toward Amman's real estate development. Finally, focus groups were carefully designed to include diverse groups representing an array of socioeconomic, age, gender, and professional group identities. Each focus group was comprised of approximately 10 participants; the aim of the groups was to assess their perspective on their participation in the planning process. Research benefits from the impacts of group synergy, stimulation, spontaneity, and reflection, as well as from the ability to document non-verbal responses in such contexts. Accordingly, data from focus groups transcend mere assessment of group reactions to stimuli (mega-scale urban development) and document more complex issues, attitudes, and normative understandings.

First, an online survey of Ammanites was used to gather their perceptions of urban development in late 2010. Online survey questionnaires guarantee anonymity for participants and allow them to express their opinions without reservation—something that may be hard to achieve otherwise. Surveys in general possess three properties that collectively put them ahead of other data collection methods. First, probability sampling allows precise data from a non-biased sample of respondents with well-defined characteristics (particularly, demographic and geographic boundaries) that are representative of the general public. Second, surveys offer the consistency of a standardized measure across all respondents and hence ensure comparability of data through statistical analyses. Finally, the design of a special-purpose survey questionnaire will ensure that data are complete and inclusive of all variables, which will inherently ensure the ability to conduct various analyses and link them to each other. To make this as inclusive as possible, an array of socioeconomic backgrounds in the urban areas affected, and several types of websites were used to target two predominant urban groups in Jordan: elite, English-speaking Jordanians with high Internet connectivity, and middle working-class, Arabic-speaking Jordanians. The former were reached via Google ads and social networking sites such as Facebook and Twitter, while the latter were reached through Arabic media websites, such as Jordan-based Khaberni and Ammon, that cater to the mass public with lower educational levels and that appeal to socioeconomically disadvantaged groups.

The survey was implemented, using 2,118 citizens of Amman, with 533 complete responses. The respondents were 75% male and 25% female, but there were no visible voting preferences among males or females on any issue. While every age group was represented in the survey, most of the 533 respondents were young people. Seventy-one percent of the respondents were between 18 and 29 years of age (which actually account for 20% of the national Jordanian population), which marks a significant (3.5 times) overrepresentation of young people in the survey. The majority of respondents, 56%, had a bachelor's degree and an additional 12% had a post-graduate degree. Moreover, a majority of respondents were employed (54%), or were students (37%), and the remaining were unemployed (9%). Respondents were from a wide distribution of income levels. There was a wide distribution of respondents from throughout Amman, although a slight increase of respondents from the Tila Al Ali area (18%). Of those from the Tila Al Ali area, 30% of respondents were between 18 and 29 years of age. Hence, we cannot fully explain why Tila Al Ali respondents were mainly students or young people.

Survey findings show that the citizens of Amman are deeply passionate about their city and have a keen interest in getting involved in the future of their city. For many of the survey respondents and focus group participants, Amman was described or characterized by visual images of its homogeneous hills and old (or East) Amman. Most of the 485 respondents thought Amman was best described or characterized by pictures of homogeneous hills and old (or East) Amman; an overwhelming number would not describe Amman by its towers or malls.

Many individuals who participated in focus groups talked about their feelings about the high rise towers and explosion of malls throughout the city in very negative terms. Many described them as "depressing," "alienating," or "visual reminders of my poverty." There was greater hostility toward the towers in poorer neighbourhoods than in more affluent ones. Out of 461 respondents, the majority (63%) believed that the future of Amman in 2020 would be an image of high rise towers as depicted by the Jordan Gate Towers. Despite the rapid urban development occurring, an overwhelming number of study participants would not describe Amman by its towers or malls. Indeed, the overwhelming number of respondents to the survey and the focus group questions felt that high rise towers in the city were not indigenous and were "out of place." When asked about how often they visited malls and other regenerated urban areas, the responses were often lower in poorer areas. Their reasoning was that they could not afford to enjoy such spaces and that they felt out of place. That said, the majority (63%) of online individuals believed that the future of Amman in 2020 would be an image of high rise towers as depicted by the Jordan Gate Towers. There is a great gap between the idealized image of Amman according to its inhabitants and the perceived future course of the city.

When 467 respondents were asked what would you prefer city authorities to prioritize in its planning initiatives, both public parks/recreation and road enhancements reported the highest interest. After these items, respondents wanted city officials to prioritize public transportation facilities and schools. Putting this response into the context of previously asked question of what do you think city officials are prioritizing, one could infer that there is general dissatisfaction with city officials in the prioritizing of public parks and places of recreation, as this was perceived to be very low on municipal government priorities. Similarly, schools were not highlighted as an official priority, and yet were the fourth largest concern of respondents. In focus groups, individuals repeatedly noted their frustration with transportation issues. Women and young women of university age were most upset with the inaccessibility to public transportation and the perceived humiliation in using public transport when pushing, shoving, and other tight quarters were met with intimidation.

While many remained concerned about divisions in Amman, particularly what has been commonly reflected as an East–West divide, a preponderance of online respondents believed that these were socioeconomic divisions and not socio-cultural divisions. In other words, the East–West divide is not considered to be a question of being of Palestinian or Jordanian origin. Out of the 501 respondents, 68% thought the East–West divide in Amman was based on social class and not on income or social affiliation. Moreover, there is no clear response to whether people thought integration between East and West was increasing or diminishing, irrespective of age, income, or gender.

Analysis and Conclusion

This paper sought to begin discussions on how the urban development of many Middle East cities had a negative effect on the Arab masses. With the influx of billions of Gulf investments into the Arab Middle East, the urban landscape has changed dramatically throughout the regions. While academics are in early phases of understanding the root causes of the Arab Spring, the preliminary evidence gathered in Jordan in 2010, at the cusp of the Arab uprisings sweeping the region, was a sense of social exclusion and alienation from the urban development occurring throughout the Kingdom. People had expressed this frustration stemming from non-inclusive economic growth in both political and social terms. There is strong evidence of similar Gulf investments throughout the Arab Middle East. While determining the causes of the Arab

Spring a priori was not conducted in many of the countries with regime change, this paper argues that some of these same trends were evident beyond Jordan. Indeed, the initial research design of a larger research project was interrupted by the events of the Arab Spring, but had included Egypt as a key case study as well. Nevertheless, future research on the causes and determinants of the Arab Spring will continue for many years to come: This paper seeks to contextualize and start academic research into the question of non-inclusive urban development and social exclusion that was initiated by years of promoting neoliberal policies and creating a welcoming investment climate for Gulf investors in the Arab Middle East's real estate sectors.

The Arab Spring has increased the geopolitical profile of Arab Gulf countries' involvement in the Arab Middle East. Most noticeably, Saudi Arabia, Qatar, and the UAE have played leadership roles. With Gulf countries actively involved in geopolitical support for the overthrow of Libya's al-Qhadafi, the negotiation and eventual transition from Yemen's Saleh, and the continued international and Arab League pressure on Syria's al-Assad, there is a greater likelihood that the Gulf has the incentive and capacity to get increasingly involved in Middle East reconstruction and development. Consequently, in the light of the Arab Spring, will Arab Gulf investments be more targeted in their investments toward key countries and sectors? Will Gulf investment shift toward sectors that aim to absorb more of the labor market, taking advantage of high unemployed and educated youth? Using the terms of international economic history and as called for by a number of Arab policymakers in the 2011 World Economic Forum meetings, will the Arab Gulf initiate a bolder "Marshall Plan" with its investments and capital in the Arab world? These questions are vitally important at a time of great change in the region; gaining a better sense of understanding the constraints and opportunities before the Arab Gulf in taking the lead is extremely important. The past trajectory of Gulf investments in the Arab Middle East has not, however, been productive.

Notes

1. Retrieved from http://www.dos.gov.jo/sdb_pop/sdb_pop_e/ehsaat/alsokan/2010/2-5.pdf.

Citizenship, National Identity, and the Future of "UAE, Inc.": Confronting the Fragility Thesis

Kenneth L. Wise

Abstract

Several theories about the future of Arabian Gulf States in general, and the United Arab Emirates (UAE) in particular rest on givens that may be accurate in some ways, but also inadequate. These theories are variations of a theme of "fragility"—that mounting pressures both internal and external in the UAE because of its lack of democracy will soon push it and the rest of the Gulf monarchies into becoming democracies, whether or not the countries are prepared. To make the UAE more understandable, we should try adding a cultural variable and the concept of "UAE, Inc." The culture will show why the sentiment of loyalty runs deep. The image of the UAE as a single company will outline the modern bases of association and possible cohesion of the country when it faces challenges and opportunities, internal and external, such as finding ways to cope with a growing pool of second generation expatriates. To date, the UAE has been remarkably cohesive and appears resilient enough to avoid or withstand what has brought down nearby neighbors.

Introduction

Theories old and new predict the collapse—perhaps imminent but certainly inevitable—of the current governments of the Arabian Gulf. They assume, and sometimes presume to prove, that unless the region builds certain institutions that undertake specified policies, the existing forms of government and authority cannot endure the many pressures building against them. Contemporary external challenges added to demands emanating from their public will bring them down, these propositions say. In short, the Gulf monarchies are "fragile."

This paper contends that at least one Gulf country is not, in these terms, fragile: the United Arab Emirates (UAE). The demonstrable legitimacy, stability, and resilience in governance in the UAE raises questions about the propriety of applying some of the analytical tools social scientists and policymakers have been using to describe and predict the future of this modernizing social experiment on the north-eastern edge of the Arabian Peninsula. A useful addition to the tool kit would be the "corporation thesis" and an analytical scheme that focuses more on function and less on structure.

Confronting the Fragility Thesis

Conventional academic and public policy approaches to explaining the UAE often open with givens that deserve re-examination; they may be accurate in limited ways, but they are insufficient, even if taken all together. Here, in short form, are two examples of such givens that we will unpack.

First, traditional society and patriarchal ruling elites will inevitably give way to a modern state with the proper array of branches of government and the political pluralism of competing sources of authority in a diverse civil society that includes private enterprise. Because the Gulf States share a culture and important current conditions, when one traditional ruling elite goes, they all will go. This view appears not to understand the democracy and accountability inherent in UAE culture or the special circumstances of the country's economic growth, demography, and governance. The view also fails to clinch its prediction of a cascade of change.

Second, unless the UAE and its Gulf Arab neighbors commit to serious and sustained programs to "Democratize Now," they will go into Arab-Spring-like receivership or become certified failed states.

This view mistakes institutional formalism such as "the republic" for effective governance, and thus leaves UAE prosperity and effective rule unexplained. It assumes that, because an entity is a state in name, the rules of causality applying to it are the same as in European history. Though one can view these givens as two sides of the same coin, their origins differ. Further, the routes that theorists and policymakers take starting from them also differ. And both routes can fail, unnecessarily.

The Gulf Cascade

One form of the fragility of the Arabian Gulf thesis popular at the moment is "The Myth of the Cascade." It says that when one government in the region goes, all will go. International news media find this image captivating, especially in Britain. In his book, *After the Sheikhs: The Coming Collapse of the Gulf Monarchies*, Christopher Davidson predicts the wholesale overnight disappearance one after another of the Gulf Cooperation Council (GCC) members ruled by royal families (Davidson, 2012, pp. 191–228). The GCC includes the UAE. And after the cascade, democracy will spring forth (Clinton, 2011).

Well-known older academic theories feed this myth: dependency, rentierism, and pluralism. This paper will give special attention to pluralism since it appears to be the major battlefield between Western advocacy and Emirati values (Dahl, 1961; Lipset, 1960).

Dependency Theory

Dependency theory extracts a single frame from a motion picture of global interaction, primarily in the economic sphere. Then, it examines that frame to heap "blame" for "underdevelopment" of the "peripheral" states onto the shoulders of the "rapacious central managers" of the world, or their minions at the centers of the individual states that are trying to develop in commerce and trade (Chase-Dunn, 1975).

In most of its variations, this theory has harboured a flaw: reality does not show up in a single frame or scene. In our interconnected world, dependency is always two-way; every transaction has a systemic consequence that manifests itself again in the original arena. For example, the United States continues to depend upon Gulf petroleum, and the vagaries of the markets for oil and natural gas will extend that dependence well into the fracking era. These countries remain critical in geostrategic position for the United States for more than petroleum—soft power, Israel, and sway in south-west Asia and the heartland of Eurasia as well. Meanwhile, the UAE, in particular, depends on a healthy global economy to strengthen its role as a hub for logistics, trade, tourism, and finance.

Those who chose to use a snapshot view of the exchange relatedness of the economic world can conclude, as do those who often comment in Gulf News, that the GCC monarchies remain so dependent on the protective U.S. geostrategic posture in the Arabian Gulf that a U.S. move to fold its umbrella and decamp from the region could be enough to topple one or more of them. Davidson, in a contrary but similarly dependency-driven illustration, finds that the continuing presence of U.S. military installations, including in the UAE, constitutes a social pressure on the regime because it thrusts western values into UAE society in a way that upsets local conservatives (Davidson, 2012, pp. 156–163).

The Rentier Thesis

Another older tool of analysis is "the rentier thesis" (el-Beblawi & Luciani, 1987). In Davidson's application of this theory, the kings and sheikhs of the Gulf use their oil profits to buy their citizens' loyalty in a "ruling bargain." They reward their citizens' loyalty with cushy salaries, housing support, utilities, health care and other subsidies, turn after turn. Gulf governments do this in a belief that a sated public is a quiescent public. Satisfied with their rulers' largess, the citizens feel no need to participate in making the decisions that will importantly affect their lives (Davidson, 2012, p. 49). They trust their leaders will continue to provide "the good life" that their grandparents did not enjoy. When pollsters ask these citizens about their future material concerns and safety, the answer they receive is: "The Sheikh will provide…Our government is concerned about our welfare" (B'huth Dubai, 2013).

That Emiratis profess strong loyalty to their families and leaders and receive abundant shares of their country's wealth lends the weight of correlation to the rentier thesis: the sheikhs share the collective wealth, and the populace continues to grant them authority to rule. Yet, the thesis at the same time ignores other conditions that have endured for centuries. For example, sheikhs are well aware that they need to ensure their peoples' security and prosperity. They must care for their peoples' welfare or they will lose their right to rule. Both the leader and the led know that the leaders who use petroleum profits today will find ways to deliver what they can under any circumstances.

Yes, Emiratis feel looked after. But should the wealth of this era disappear, the Emiratis would not necessarily blame the leader, and would be likely to accept the need to accommodate the new reality. Of course, this generalization assumes continued good governance by sensible leaders and fortune's keeping a tight leash on potential demagogues.

The rentier thesis, in the case of the UAE, also ignores the identity issue which the demographic makeup of the UAE exacerbates. While no reliable official statistics on the population of the UAE are publicly available, consensus in news media and scholars' estimates puts its February 2013 total at 8.8 million—with 2.1 million in Dubai. Nationals (or "citizens") now comprise less than the 2011 UAE National Statistics Bureau estimate of 11.5% (9% in Dubai) and the percentage is projected to continue to decrease steadily. The country's net migration rate—its churning—is about 22% and the world's highest. Its gender imbalance is the world's greatest: 75% male (United States CIA, 2010, 2011, 2012). Of the expatriates, at least two million are from India; another million from the Asian subcontinent; nearly one million from the Philippines; and other large contingents hail from China and Iran. Britons tally about 100,000.

The Emiratis, who, though they are a minority, constitute the official body of citizens, and determine the parameters for the interaction of all the country's minorities. For historical and cultural reasons, the UAE has not extended citizenship beyond descendants of the 1971 core who met tribal membership standards at the time of the country's formation (Abdullah, 1978; Al-Abed and Hellyer, 2001; Ali, 2010; Crystal, 1990; Zahlan, 1979).

Because the citizenship principle in the UAE Constitution is *jus sanguinis*, enlarging this pool of citizens, let alone turning it into a majority, would be possible only at unacceptable cost: by deporting the expatriates on whom Emiratis depend, or spreading the wealth so thin that it would lose its ability to capitalize over persons whose culture and expectations regarding living respectfully could diverge markedly from those of today's Emiratis. This raises some anxiety for Emiratis about their identity—that in unifying the country, they might go the way of Native Americans in North America.

The UAE's economic growth policy has required that it import millions of skilled and unskilled labor. These imported laborers sign in from nearly 200 countries, but for the short term. The ruling Emirati minority depend on the expertise of talented expatriates to run Emirates and Etihad Airlines, for example. They have depended on the sweat labor of Asians to raise the cloud-piercing Burj Khalifa and 100 other skyscrapers, to construct the roads, and to drive the taxis and trucks.

Political Pluralism versus UAE Nationality

The UAE's demographic realities bear heavily on how UAE leaders and their people respond to outside advice and advocacy about political pluralism. For all its normative persuasiveness in Western society, any policy prescription that would lead to the creation of disparate socio-political authority-wielding entities, such as political parties, labor unions, or free-standing pillars of alternate propriety, raise hackles for leader and led alike. Their anxiety over, and apparent resistance to, the check and balance character of pluralism rises from what local politicians term "demographic imbalance" and from the Emiratis' perception of who they are and what they value.

The Emiratis have become a "minority in their own country" in the short span of one generation and have not fully developed yet the concepts of political sharing, compromise, identifying the common good or long-term goals with their expatriate neighbors and co-workers. As a decreasing minority in their own country, they now tend to resent any pressure from outside to accommodate the UAE's "temporary" residents.

At the same time, their culture calls them to show hospitality and tolerance; and their economy insists that they shall value diversity to survive. Yet, the economic downturn of the late 2000s, the unease spilling into their society from the Arab Awakening, the sometimes numbing speed of existential change swirling around them, their perception of risk to their lifestyle and position in society have all strengthened conservative sentiment and willingness to grant credibility to appeals made in the name of UAE "national identity." Only with the increasing evidence of economic recovery have Emiratis generally opened again to leaders' attempts to appoint and reward based on merit, for example.

The UAE may illustrate, in some respects, a new way to meld social, economic, and political development and stand as a striking model for other Gulf societies—and perhaps beyond. And it may yet prove that some Western presumptions about political pluralism as a requirement for democracy and capitalism to work effectively may be in error. Certainly, the hyper-partisanship of contemporary political contention in the United States offers little evidence that the UAE is on a wrong path.

The UAE Constitution provides for separation of powers—an Executive comprised of the rulers of the seven emirates seated in the Supreme Council, a Cabinet with quasi-legislative prerogatives, an advisory proto-legislature named Federal National Council, and a titular independent judiciary. However, the latter two entities depend heavily on the Supreme Council for their authority. While the requisite institutions of formal government exist, Emiratis seem to be emotionally detached from them and generally obeisant to higher authority.

At the same time, taking literally any contention among UAE nationals that democracy or capitalism are not Islamic, or that Arab culture imposes unique requirements on governance would be a mistake. (Hudson, 1979, p. 148). Rhetoric on this latter point can be less a product of informed thought than leaders' and intellectuals' jostling for position and recognition in international politics and appealing to emotions of nationals at home (Kubálková, Onuf, & Kowert, 1998; Rosenau, 1990).

This is a lesson of the UAE for all development theorists. Rather than uniqueness, we need to weigh elements differently and allow that the UAE may meet the requisites of good governance in ways we do not expect. Decades ago, the UAE pioneered home-grown blended public-private-government-associated ownership and management of companies and financial mechanisms. This was an early version of what recent economic disturbances have caused so-called more mature countries to contemplate. At the time of the Dubai Ports World (DPW) controversy in the United States, that company, being semi-government, implied that it could be a tool of the owning government's political interests. The U.S. opposition understood neither DPW's independence nor "UAE, Inc.'s" expectation that such a company exists to make a profit. Both became more apparent in November 2009, when DPW could not meet its loan payment on time.

Transparency and accountability may be less than in more financially mature countries at this stage, but no country meets the ideal. The UAE model displays its resilience and adaptability every day.

UAE's Democratic Voice Versus Political Pluralism

The UAE's democratic voice may be hard to hear over the din of "revolution" elsewhere in the Middle East and North Africa (MENA) region. But the sense of direct democracy lives in the core of the UAE's social being. It helps to mark a source of UAE's resistance to political pluralism.

This description of the importance of Emirati kinship may make the UAE sound as if ethnicity or sectionalism dominates political life, as if its citizens do not know their own national interests. Yet compared to most of the rest of the MENA region, the UAE is free of the negative causes of Arab Awakening: brutal authoritarianism, intolerance of minority identity, a history of coups, a predisposition against constructive dialog and compromise, geographical divisions tied to identity, and using Islam as a legitimizing factor to implement unpopular policies.

Even more relevant for understanding the political environment is the reality that any leader other than an Emirati in the UAE would represent the interests of a group that identifies with peoples elsewhere in the world—India, Egypt, or Iran, for example. Thus, Emiratis throw up defensive psychological and social walls to protect political authority as well as citizenship and identity. Laws about the sanctity of symbols such as the flag or religious belief essentially dare desecration, but their enforcement tends to be moderate, dependent on social pressure of a personal complaint than on rigorous official policing.

The theory of political pluralism says that having diverse, competing centers of active influence in society to create and manage the marketplace of ideas portends stability because it reins in leaders. It denotes continuous bargaining among self-aware, relatively stable groups that voice their interests and mobilize to pursue them. Pluralist faith says that the contending of such multiple groups will result in the best possible formulation of the nation's interest because it will hold leaders and dominant actors in check (Dahl, 1961).

By contrast, UAE political culture perceives multiple sources for mobilizing opinion and any intermediary "representation" through a dark lens of patriarchy for at least two reasons. First, in the UAE cultural narrative, the family's spokesperson speaks directly to the ruling sheikh and receives grants of resources directly from the sheikh, no intermediary necessary. Transparency and accountability are givens. If a sheikh refuses to listen, or fails to deliver the resources and services that the heads of respected families expect, or cannot persuade them to patience, then through direct democracy or other acts of expediency, those families can move authority to a new sheikh. Alternatively, the disgruntled family or clan can leave to pledge their loyalty to a different sheikh (Lienhardt, 2001).

Second, having the family as the magnet of loyalty relieves Emirati society—citizens—and its leaders from having to acknowledge the unresolved and probably irresolvable divisions of four schools of Sunni thought on law and jurisprudence—Hanafi, Shafi'i, Maliki, & Hanbali—as well as multiple Shi'a schools (Hunter & Malik, 2005). Instead, leaving this to the family and submerging the larger society in unity through ritual religious practice minimizes having to confront diversity. The sectarianism that political leaders elsewhere stoke for partisan or legitimizing purposes does not occur in the UAE.

Similarly, the UAE citizen, family and tribe experience leads to invoking "Islamic values" without having to itemize them. Relations of citizens with anyone outside the citizenry are covered by the national values of tolerance and hospitality. The real, but often ignored progress in this regard, has been the secular international law with its *jus cogens* counsel of reciprocity (golden rule) and peaceful settlement of disputes—with the law bearing the authority in the absence of a sheikh. Inside the UAE, the sheikhs—higher authorities—practice the same rule, frequently overturning court sentences such as death. The most common sentence for expatriates is time served followed by deportation.

The UAE's traditional culture approximated pluralism in that only a fraction of the population—heads of extended families—exercised influence. The bystanders in the community considered these leaders capable of representing their interests. "Everyone knew everyone" who spoke and made decisions. They knew which families to trust. This social circle could function as an effective authority because the agenda of public concerns traditionally were minimal in number, and manageable in complexity.

Today, however, the population of the UAE—an amalgam of dozens of tribes of the former Trucial States, plus expatriate minorities—has grown and its problems have multiplied. Tribalism still appears in family, clan, and tribe members voting for their own; we will note this again later in this paper. The elites come largely from business; the growing importance of professionals hints of the existence of social classes; government runs short of technocrats and engineers; royal and merchant families collaborate to minimize effective political change that might erode their privilege; and laws of media ownership and a practice of self-censorship tend to restrict public policy commentary to "regime-loyal intellectuals" (Al-Qassemi, 2012). These restrictions and laws agitate both leaders and the led and threaten to raise constitutional questions.

The Constitution: Citizenship Only for Emiratis?

UAE culture is wrestling with the constitutional question of whether an individual human being has the autonomy to have rights and duties apart from a group, regardless of the source of this autonomy—whether state or religion or other social designation (Lévinas, 1999). The answer will bear on the issue of citizenship—who can be and who ought to be a citizen; who can and should have full rights in, and bear full duties to—the community.

Constitutions formalize rules about who has access to certain kinds of resources for what purposes. They express a community's long-term desires and sometimes codify the ways the community has learned to help to resolve certain questions about appropriateness and substitutability of resources and goals (Reisman & McDougal, 1981). But not all constitutions are written. Moreover, not all written constitutions carry the weight of legitimacy more than do less visible principles residing in the peoples' minds. To find that constitution and its citizenship provisions, we ask: 1) what does being a citizen of the UAE mean? 2) what values and rituals stir such a consciousness? and 3) what do such values and rituals say about who has sovereign authority? (Wise, 1997)

The informal constitution of the UAE explains the country's stability more than does its formal one, but closing the gap between the two presents as much challenge to the UAE as does the existence of the global constitution to a state such as the United States whose political culture blinds it to the binding character of custom. Custom in the UAE creates the family–clan–tribe social order that remains morally compelling and at the same time, potentially threatening to the economic reality upon which the UAE's prosperity and growth plans rely.

Thus, the UAE faces questions of citizenship both as a formal, positive legal status in a community and as normative obligation based on custom. To what extent does the citizenship attach to members who consciously share goals and resources? How well does the citizenship status protect autonomy and promote cooperation through communication? Does it place authority and empower authorities sufficiently that citizens will comply sufficiently to have maximum effect and efficiency in both protecting autonomy and promoting cooperation (Ruggie, 1998)? And how do answers to these questions weigh in a discussion of the fragility of the UAE?

Western contemporary concepts of citizenship on the state level rest on at least three values: liberty, community, and obligation (Fain, 1987). First, liberty, a personal status, expresses the ancient moral philosophy and medieval rights regarding latitude in the pursuit of goals; it builds its abstract and cosmopolitan rights—civil and social— on natural law. Such a liberty requires tangible conditions of a permanent attachment such as residency as well as the opportunity to make a living. A sense of personal security is its actual operational test. The UAE could pass this test while offering a status of less than full citizenship, provided that status assures liberty.

Second, a right to membership in a community assures one has access to a common decision-making unit and a home for ritual and sentiment. Political community is a logical consequence of Enlightenment. Participant citizens choose leaders and hold them accountable; hence, franchise is this value's operational test. The operational question in the UAE is whether participating in choosing leaders—now through electors or in a few years, through full suffrage—is sufficient and whether the route to the top is open for would-be leaders or the system has effective ways to co-opt them.

Third, whether from the patrician root, pragmatism, or a hidden tyranny, a citizen has duties to: live by the rules; pay taxes; be accountable to help preserve the group—serving in the military, for example— and, by reciprocity, to honor others' rights. Testing value three in the UAE, in isolation from the others, is straightforwardly empirical. While the UAE passes this test at this time, its commitment to do so for another generation remains unsure.

These values do not rest easily with one another. The content of "citizenship" in one state or time no more serves one state or time than does one constitution serve another. The territorially-based abstract state is obviously no longer the sole mint of the coin of citizenship than it is automatically a legitimate coercer. The constituting action of governance now has to occur in many new places, from village to globe, from professional to domestic. Every constitution has to help citizens define and manage the inevitable tension between membership and burdensome obligations (Reus-Smit, 1997).

For example, assertions of rights to material equality emerged from this tension and from nationalist rationalizations for war and consumed politics in the 20th century. A variant of the second value causes tension over whether self-determination is a universal or only a right of a territorially integral group. The second value runs afoul of the first by threatening the territorial integrity of the state that is to provide security. Resolving this tension on behalf of the citizen is the role of the holder of legitimate authority, the sovereign. The Constitution says who this is, how the community fills that position, and who holds the sovereign accountable—how and when.

Perhaps the transition that global political society made from cities to states is now occurring in the UAE in the movement from smaller tribes to alliances of tribes. Perhaps these transitions will effectively express the three values of citizenship. Nevertheless, the UAE, though transitioning from tribe to community, seems immune to being a "state" in any form other than name. Loyalty is tied to the patriarchal leaders of tribes. The concept of secular "state" as a sphere of legal competence eludes most UAE citizens, though the leadership is trying to introduce it. The idea is foreign, honored in word, but not in heart, understanding, or deed.

Emiratis are uncomfortable with civil society organizations; they see these as potential threats to their leaders' authority and ability to protect them. They show little appreciation for how institutions of representation could improve cooperation of national and non-national-resident communities (Khalaf & Luciani, 2006).

The UAE has spent more than 40 years trying to meld tribal identities into a single nation, but only recently has committed to gradual increase in citizen participation in governing. Universal suffrage is set tentatively for 2019. Hoping to avoid mistakes of neighboring "republics," the UAE intends to develop its own institutional character and political processes rather than importing the trappings of "democracy" or framing the shell of a "republic."

At their core, UAE citizens understand the transparency and accountability aspects of democracy. In this understanding, and their strong cultural value of hospitality, they show promise of tolerance and inclusion of non-national residents. But the citizens also agree they shall not be ruled by others, by members of other minorities. Further, they have yet to show that they are ready to trust the intermediary institutions required by todays much larger and diverse populations and complex policy problems in the UAE.

For the UAE, taking the next step—to a constitution that embodies all citizens and non-citizen residents in law and equality—seems impossible. Perhaps the UAE needs to consider intermediate steps. For the UAE to pursue a demographic majority by targeting particular expatriate communities or expatriates in general for expulsion would lead to the collapse of the country's economic and social development. Thus, the UAE may consider opening a revolving door to "contributing membership" for those expatriates who accept the duties of citizenship—including the obligation to stay during hardship and to sacrifice to preserve as well as to share in the greater good. A cosmopolitan outlook would best comprehend this shift and provide policy guidance in current issues of sovereignty (legitimate authority to strike the balance between autonomy of the individual and the community's need for physical and social survival and security), self-determination (autonomy of persons and groups), and citizenship (an individual's obligation to community to preserve the group's capability to protect and improve life) (Wise, 1998).

As a step toward a more inclusive identity for the UAE, enlarging the ranks of "citizen"—or giving "national" it's more common international denotation—can be positive. A study of policy options for such enlargement would assume that the policy-makers' primary goal is to retain and improve social cohesion. In their history, Muslim peoples can point to eras in which non-citizens (that is, non-Muslims) had essentially equal but separate status (Lyons, 2009, pp. 61–77). The citizens of the UAE have leaned toward openness in religious practice while remaining nearly closed as a society. Perhaps organizing expatriates and Emiratis by professional association or guild across their cultural boundaries is an option. Failure of early UAE experiments moving in this direction—teachers, lawyers—has posted a flag of caution, of course.

Social cohesion requires that the members of society share purpose—a sense of destiny and reward, an identity that says, "We are all in this together." Achieving this sense of common fate usually focuses first on what already exists: living in the same territory, working interdependently, that is, experiencing important parts of reality together. Sharing a common history, culture, and language will help. Living together over the years can produce mutual reliance, respect, and affection provided leaders wrap these elements into a narrative of unity and promulgate it. Though unity as the outcome is not guaranteed, its prospect is higher to the extent that the population is aware that this is possible and that the civic culture and the economy support it.

The UAE government needs to consider the financial implications of any enlargement of course—the impact on its habit of awarding subsidies and social blessings to "citizens." But its best choice may be to enlarge citizenship and reduce subsidies and raise revenues to the point that it can accept the needed new members.

Davidson's Cascade

In effect, Davidson argues that time is not on the UAE sheikhs' side, which internal pressures akin to those that erupted into public demonstrations in the Arab Awakening will merge with external pressures, such as Iran and U.S. sanctions to rob the sheikhs of their ability to provide the security and "good life" that citizens expect (Davidson, 2008). These pressures include reaching the peak oil mark; excessive promises that leaders made in 2011 to stifle formation of any opposition, such as the costly and inefficient public sector make-work jobs; withdrawal of the U.S. geostrategic shield; or the continued foreign presence which disturbs the moral universe for conservatives; and growing alienation among the expatriate groups upon whom the UAE relies to run the economy, staff hospitals, provide commercial and trade services, and look after Emirati children.

Thus, while the rentierism and pluralism theses lay open certain facts, they give insufficient weight to others, such as social history, political culture, and economic prosperity that both drive and stabilize the UAE. Some risks remain for the UAE, of course, and this paper will weigh them. But Davidson's projected cascade remains an assertion not convincingly supported.

"Democratize Now or Fail"

The fragility crowd's low-pixel picture of the UAE leads U.S. policymaking regarding the oil-rich UAE toward potential for disserving error. This is especially evident in the wake of the 2000's campaign to bring the blessings of "democracy" to the members of the Gulf Cooperation Council (GCC), along with the rest of MENA in order to "win the war on terror." Unchastened by the thermal blast raging from Tunis to Cairo to Sanaa to Damascus—not to mention the sad embers of Iraq and Afghanistan and soon Syria—some former democracy champions remain true believers and advocates.

The "Democratize now or fail" policy advocates say, mythically, that Aristotle planted a seed that Machiavelli nurtured and the Congress of Vienna brought to blossom. This Euro-centric conviction that every polity will eventually be re-born as a nation-state has energized missionaries, foreign aid managers, and U.S. marines—all the believers in development. Their normative and prescriptive impulses to "develop the undeveloped" sometimes fail, however. A plant may die before bearing fruit.

A prime exemplar of this faith in "progress"—the United States—tends to consider itself the model for all "less developed" polities. Its secular religion roots deeply in this soil of "natural history" in which the country grew and prospered. At the same time, though, its seed-stock of peoples who survived the storm-covered oceans on their way to the modern "promised land" or fled oppressive regimes and poverty in neighboring lands, are genetic links that trouble U.S. society. The United States' perpetually adolescent psyche seeks continually for ratification of its worthiness by trying to plant and propagate itself wherever in the world it thinks it has found fertile ideological soil.

In the UAE, for example, the United States has tried to tap into a surviving root of a tree of democratic institutions that Great Britain planted in the late 1930s. This was the *majlis* experiment by which Britain sought to rationalize a leadership change in Dubai by importing political mechanisms from Kuwait and attaching them to the emir's traditional council. That British experiment failed, and the foliage died quickly. In recitative, the U.S. political missions of the Republican and Democratic Parties encamped in Abu Dhabi until 2012 were sent home unceremoniously by the UAE government. The British had a good idea, but, like the United States in the 2000s, their timing was off. To their credit, the British returned to the status quo ante in a matter of weeks (Zahlan, 1979).

The fervor with which some U.S. policymakers continue to pitch the "Democratize Now" line today suggests that they are still in therapy for having failed to anticipate the Arab uprisings of 2011 that wafted the scent of jasmine from Tunis to the likes of Sanaa and Damascus. They keep insisting that the scent arises from the blossom of democracy. Careful observation shows, however, that it is instead the perspiration of energetic youth seeking jobs and identity and places in the social sun. The "republic" with its promising foliage of participation failed them; why should they give it much heed?

A bit of reflection on the words "third world" or "developing world" is in order. Policymakers often use such language to justify actions that have little connection to the realities they want to change. If "development" is facility in assimilation of modern technological advances, ease of communication among the social groupings within a state's territorial boundaries, access to public services of education and healthcare, and utilities, then the UAE—with about four smart phones per capita, traffic-jammed highways 24 hours a day, and the world's largest carbon footprint per capita—then the UAE is fully developed. To say that the UAE political processes differ from those common in the West is only to say that the two countries are "differently developed."

A Complementary Added Thesis: UAE, Inc.

The relevant questions to ask of the UAE polity pertain to legitimacy of ruler and ruling, loyalty and enterprise, and a sense of communal identity that enables subgroups to adapt to changing circumstances and suffer the trials of and seizes the opportunities brought by change. The UAE answers these questions and passes their implied tests.

While the UAE is not a "liberal democracy" of European derivation, it is not despotic or repressively authoritarian. Rather, it is benevolent and paternalistic; importantly, it is consensual. Its cultural anchor is loyalty to family and tribe. In this context it is socially liberal. In its initiative and enterprise, it is the finest of corporations. In our polling at B'huth, the citizens are not yet noticeably disrupted by the appeal of Western abstract artifacts of political participation. The large majority of UAE citizens are not aspiring to have quadrennial circuses to elect a new president and parliament. The mechanisms of participation that make sense to them are those of their historic democracy: the majlis, talking directly with the sheikhs. As a model, "talking directly with the sheikhs" in order to ensure effective governance of the UAE fits the felt requirements of UAE nationals and, in general, causes expatriates little frustration.

From nearly nine years of personal observation, the author of this paper suggests that to understand how "one of these things—members of the GCC—is not like the others," one should look at the UAE through a lens marked "UAE, Inc." The blended private–public–government-sponsored entity view of the polity in which the entire country constitutes an integrated commercial enterprise captures the essential institutions and operations of the UAE that enable it to command loyalty for its efficient and effective governance.

The UAE "business polity" population divides into three categories:

First, at the top is an elite group of visionary entrepreneurs, the "senior corporate executives." These are almost exclusively members of the ruling families and their close associates. They built and continue to build the organization and reap personal and collective wealth from the polity's growth.

Though one might expect corruption to be rife in such a closely-held "family" stratum, it is not. Of course, special access and proprietary information serve to enrich this group and motivate the group to want to continue to run the corporation untrammelled by regulation that greater transparency would bring. For this reason, the Prime Minister, His Highness Sheikh Mohammed bin Rashid al-Maktoum fostered legislation to prevent persons in government from being able, in any way, to steer the awarding of government contracts to firms in which they have financial interest. But the ambiguity of affiliations and of tight though large extended families can neutralize such attempts at regulation. How the UAE's modern commercial economy grew—through exclusive enterprise grants and free zones operating outside the normal laws and beyond the reach of most regulators—and because of the requirement that any company outside the free zones must be majority-owned by a local Emirati—preventing corruption or easily achieved enrichment has become an on-going test of transparency and accountability. But expression of disapproval among our poll-takers is minimal.

Members of the next group one might call shareholders; some of these are also managers or employees. They provide the start-up resources for the enterprise sectors of "UAE, Inc." which remunerates them based on the corporation's success. These shareholders are UAE nationals—the Emirati citizens who hold this position by right of birth. They contribute their loyalty, energy, and confidence. Not only do they draw very high salaries if they are in the public sector, they also receive bonuses in the form of multiple subsidies and fringe benefits equal to, or in excess of salaries provided in other wealthy Gulf States.

Lest these middle management personnel become too comfortable in their positions, the UAE Prime Minister has a stable of "secret shoppers" who pose as regular customers seeking Ministry services and who report back to the Prime Minister on the quality of government performance. The Prime Minister himself may show up unannounced in any office he chooses and become a fully visible shopper. With the help of persons knowledgeable in modern quality assurance, he hands out awards annually, including to the best gardener on the royal estate.

The third group are the non-Emirati, the expatriates who join "UAE, Inc." with a goal of greater income or trying out a career in a less fettered environment than back wherever home is. These expatriates comprise essentially 90% of the UAE population and thoroughly dominate the private sector. They either plan to return home, some day, or know that the corporation expects them to return.

Each group—the ruling top management, shareholding Emirati, and expatriate workers—gets sufficient return from its investment. So long as they are happy, the polity prospers. "UAE, Inc." enjoys rising stock prices and pays large dividends in job satisfaction and proffers "the good life"—even to the Asian laborer and the Filipina nanny. So far, they also live respectfully, generally. This "UAE, Inc." model explains why UAE nationals have little concern with political participation in the instrumental and institutional manner of the West. Many a treatise on "corporate politics" line the shelves of a bookstore's business section (Jay, 1996); but none will speak of the size of the corporation's electorate or the existence or periodicity of corporation-wide contested elections, or whether the electorate can at the next election turn out those just elected. Instead, the Board of Directors will vote on the principal officers. Everyone else picks up his/her paycheck and profit-shares so long as he or she is on the human resources role.

The UAE Constitution grants the "UAE Board of Directors" power to the rulers of the seven emirates sitting as the Supreme Council. They select the President, and the Vice President and Prime Minister. They guide the Cabinet's policymaking, though the final operating authority is the President. "Constituent" employees in corporations do not vote to retain or dismiss a boss. They vote with their feet, not at a ballot box. In the UAE, expatriates come and go. Similarly, citizens inherit a tradition of the Arabian Peninsula in which one's family supports the sheikh who rules well. If and when the sheikh fails to fulfill his role, one's family leaves to join a different sheikh—unless the sheikh's family removes the ruler and gives another a chance to lead.

In the corporation and "UAE, Inc." the bottom line is the final test. The UAE has some of the largest sovereign wealth funds on the planet and leaders manage them with the future of the citizens in mind— their education, healthcare, and retirement—in much the way of well-run major corporations. Our B'huth[1] polling shows the UAE citizens generally to be "happy campers." Barrett Values Center studies reinforce this. Further, nominal GDP (gross domestic product) rose from $46 billion in 1995 to a forecast for 2013 of $412.01 billion with a growth of 3.7% while much of the world remains flat lined (Business Monitor International, 2013).

A UAE, Inc. "Annual Meeting"

The norms and social traits that guide the operations of "UAE, Inc." were visible in a debut event in Dubai in February of 2013: the region's first Government Summit. (It should be noted that the number of persons reaching for translation headsets when the next speaker was either English or Arabic was about the same: six. "UAE, Inc." is fully bi-lingual.) As Prime Minister of the UAE (while also UAE Vice President and Ruler of Dubai), His Highness Sheikh Mohammed bin Rashid al-Maktoum assembled 2,500 of the UAE government's top officials and mid-level managers for two days of plenary and workshop sessions. Here, Sheikh Mohammed sought through his forceful personality (George, 2003; Mameli, 2013; Terry, 1993) to instil in his federal chiefs the spirit of "Dubai, Inc." about which many have written exuberantly (Krane, 2009). He has for years been imposing his leadership and management style on what a U.S. observer would consider the executive branch of the UAE government. His success was fully on display at this conference.

For two and one half hours in an early plenary session, Prime Minister Mohammed interacted on stage with these government invitees. He answered questions sent to him in two ways: 1) via brand new Hewlett Packard tablet devices given to each Summit registrant, and 2) pre-taped videos from UAE citizens, residents, and tourists. Following him on stage in a later plenary, and adopting the same openness were the deputy Prime Minister, the Ministers of Interior and Education, and several other Cabinet members.

Overall, the extravaganza was worthy of an annual meeting by Apple, Microsoft, First Data Resources, or General Motors and very much the same in flash and "go sell those products" motivational speeches. Sheikh Mohammed opened, for example, by saying, "Our job is to serve, not to control." Locals noted that he proclaimed that the main function of the government is to make sure that the people, all the people, are happy. U.S. President Thomas Jefferson would have felt at home.

Risks of Corporate Failure

Of course, corporations may fail. The cost and consequences of corporate failure for a dynastic polity with a tribal social core producing for the markets of a loose international community and powered by a business engine can become "an Afghanistan" or a Bahrain or an Egypt. The prospect of such a collapse is rife in the minds of the leaders of "UAE, Inc." It would devastate all persons associated with it and would reverberate across the globalized planet.

Thus, while "UAE, Inc." is capitalizing today, producing the happiness the Prime Minister stipulates, its managers wait impatiently for the equivalent of the next quarter-end report. They anxiously attend the daily indices marking their international reputation, for upon this depend the corporation's ability to attract foreign direct investment, to sell bonds to finance "UAE, Inc." projects, to draw upon the world personnel pool to keep its engines running and children cared for. They also monitor the loyalty of their constituents. They know they lead and prosper only with the cooperation of all.

The UAE's fiscal health depends on the international financial community's willingness to restructure the country's debts and roll over the country's bow wave of borrowing that individual emirates and semi-government businesses took on during the 21st century boom years up to 2008. To date, these negotiations are proceeding normally and successfully. "UAE, Inc." borrowing that emphasized short-term repayment is converting into more rational longer-term arrangements it should have used in the first place. It is also promoting itself as the future center of the world's Islamic financing.

Weighing the Variables Differently

It should be apparent, then, that the variables that "UAE, Inc." takes into account and the weights it gives these do not comport with those of the "Fragility Thesis." In addition to the question of fiscal and monetary health addressed just above, the following concerns that UAE nationals and their leaders share, and outsiders may also see as "risks"—elections and the Federal National Council, protecting domestic workers, and human rights—will further illustrate this proposition.

First, the UAE decided in 2005 to respond to entreaties from the United States and EU to hold the country's first election the next year. We at B'huth designed and ran workshops for candidates, introducing them to concepts such as "national interest," public policy, and issue platform with the intention of moving candidates away from basing their appeals to the electors on family, tribe, and "what my father did for us." In this, we had some success.

In keeping with the UAE government's intent to introduce political participation gradually, the first election's voters, the so-called "electoral college," numbered fewer than 7,000. The ruler of each emirate appointed these proportionately. Candidates self-nominated from this pool and campaigned in their emirates for several weeks. Turn-out on election day was more than 70%.

The country's second election was to be in December, 2010, but stirrings of what became the Arab Awakening stimulated extended internal discussion of what should come next in political evolution and led to the postponing of the election. The National Election Commission (NEC) pushed the election off a couple months and events of February and March in 2011 across the Middle East and North Africa stretched the wait for the next election into the fall. The Electoral College this time was more than 129,000—an increase of about 19 times in the size of the pool. However, because the NEC organized the election and announced its date less than three weeks ahead, interest in the election had no time to build, and turn-out dropped from about 70% to less than 30%. Election planners were too distracted by the Arab Awakening events to do their job fully. No candidate workshops took place. Electors practiced using the electronic voting machines. As a result, electoral conduct slid backward. The keys of family and tribe turned the locks of candidacy and voting—a backward step. Tribalism appeared in family, clan, and tribe members voting for their own.

These elections were for half of the members of the proto-legislature, the Federal National Council (FNC). This body has begun to grapple with issues with increasing competence and vigor. In February, the FNC sank its teeth into a Ministry-prepared draft law on companies by debating whether foreign ownership of companies outside the free zones can exceed 49%, and whether the same law should bind foreign ownership and trade laws and whether professions such as law and medicine should be covered by the same law, have separate statutes, or be left unregulated.

An FNC member discussing the Jasmine Scent Uprising in March 2011 said: "We want to increase citizen participation in governance but certainly not by imitating the chaos in Kuwait." Other regional experiments with being "democratic republics" have not gone well in Lebanon, Iraq, Bahrain, or Palestine, so UAE leaders are reluctant to grant the enlarged legislative competence that some activists have demanded.

Second, another risk is that, in the name of internal order, elaborate police and security forces have evolved from being the only major institution unifying the tribe and country. These entities can be amazingly efficient. Note the cases of the Dubai Police capture of the Pink Panther gang that had hit 200 times in Europe but met capture after its first try in the UAE; or the case of the "man with the golden gun," whose murderers police caught almost immediately; or the Palestinian arms buyer's assassination, apparently by Mossad, in which Dubai Police quickly turned up almost 40 false passports plus a videotape of the murderers' movements near the scene.

After 9-11-2001, these forces assisted the United States in its "war on terror" hunt for Islamists. But in an apparent over-reaction to political activism, UAE authorities have detained and put on trial more than 100 of its citizens, accusing them of trying to form a foreign-funded organization for the purpose of mobilizing sufficient support to overthrow the government of the UAE. Security apparatus targets potentially disruptive elements that the government accuses of being tied to Egypt's Muslim Brotherhood (Rashid, 2013).

A risk in this crackdown is that the royal and merchant families, collaborating to minimize political change that might erode their privilege and trying to prevent disruptive political demonstrations may put in the hands of demagogues, the hounds of "national identity." Locking up friends and neighbors and intimidating their families, though fully legal and done with good intent, may create the conditions for a self-fulfilling prophecy about dissent that would not have been there but for their attempt to prevent it. Twitter chatter in 2013 suggests that this is happening (B'huth Dubai, 2013).

However, the EurAsia Group has given the UAE a fat tail risk rating of only 10%, meaning that the country is quite stable compared to the region (Bremmer & Keat, 2010). And the UAE enjoys an escalator of prosperity despite the continuing repercussions of the global downturn. The UAE is socially tolerant, marking a path in Gulf diplomacy for others to join and adapting to strategic and environmental realities.

Third, a major stimulus to the Arab Awakening was youth unemployment and general underemployment in an environment that had promised jobs and dignity (Cincotta, 2012). In the UAE, the government professes that its top priority in 2013 is "emiratization"—absorbing into the workforce the (officially) 14% unemployed youth, many of whom find living on welfare more to their liking than taking low-paying, demanding jobs in the private sector (United Nations Development Program, 2012).

Fourth, like its Gulf neighbors, the UAE risks overbuilding its logistics capability, especially ports and airports in the longer term. All the Gulf States simultaneously are trying to imitate "UAE, Inc.'s" successes in transportation, logistics, tourism, and non-oil trade. To date, development misadventures have resulted in a few empty, sometimes low-quality buildings and unsustainable multiple airlines and airports. These heighten the weak infrastructure investment in the five emirates other than Abu Dhabi and Dubai.

Fifth, UAE public policymaking often has a "see—shoot—aim" character. On the one hand, this phenomenon could be evidence of its being responsive to public opinion. On the other, it sometimes confuses the majority of residents. For example, recently the Central Bank, normally a source of well-considered moves to serve the financial interests of the UAE for the long term, apparently sought to prevent the UAE's recovering real estate market against returning to its run-away bubble behavior by announcing sharp increases in required down payments and limits on loan lids. However, it had done this without consulting the industries. This action would affect or even show evidence of having taken international best practices into account. The resulting public backlash caused it to retract its actions.

Sixth, that the UAE may have "artificial borders" does not make it automatically vulnerable to collapsing in the face of either internal or external challenges. The UAE's borders fit as well the population's "native" or "historical" lands as do borders of almost any Western country. Though the contention with Iran over three islands in the Strait of Hormuz often reaches high decibels, the UAE also continually professes its willingness to accept an International Court of Justice judgment on the competing claims of sovereignty if Iran refuses direct negotiations. As for the prospect of Iran's having nuclear weapons, Prime Minister Mohammed in 2011 asked, Why would Iran want nuclear weapons; they cannot use them (CNN, 2011).

Seventh, competing corporations can form alliances and even mergers. For cultural reasons, if not normal geopolitical reasons, the Gulf States, including the UAE, resist both of these forms of collaboration. They will occasionally, but temporarily attempt to secure protection from an outside threat, to divvy up the market, to improve competitive advantage, or to appeal for policy that will level the playing field of trade. They may ally to learn what other GCC members are thinking, not to standardize policy toward the United States or the United Kingdom, not to cooperate on defensive strategy against anyone, not to share or integrate weapons inventory or management of operations, and not to rehearse contingency plans. Rather, they ally to plot their independent courses forward with the benefit of better intelligence about their neighbors' thinking. While theorists of "fragility" may find this behaviour evidence of "UAE, Inc.'s" vulnerability, it also limits the likelihood of the predicted cascade of collapse. The UAE can stand on its own feet—one in the Arabian Gulf, the other in the Gulf of Oman.

Conclusion: Lessons and Way Forward

In sum, "UAE, Inc.'s" strengths and demanding circumstances are these:

The UAE is free of the need to emancipate itself from outside powers. It was not a colony, and nearly all of its minorities are invitees. In their first generation in the UAE, the expatriates are linked emotionally to their home countries and, for the most part, hoping or expecting to return to them. They have refugee or temporary worker attitudes.

The UAE tolerates difference in culture, even in religion and religious practice, providing it does not promote conflict or thrust into the public space. "UAE, Inc." even celebrates cultural difference and identity. After all, it enhances the country's cosmopolitan attractiveness for tourism and comforts expatriates who may be considering taking up residence to add themselves to the collective corporate enterprise.

The UAE was born of a consensual assembling of disparate but historically related groups that found common interest under inspired leadership to conjoin. The UAE's federal structure mitigates the propensity of the wider region that "winner should take all."

"UAE, Inc." operates alongside a federal structure not unlike that which the United States experienced under The Articles of Confederation. The corporate energy is gradually but persistently building a political culture of federation and union. This is because the formal federal structure and the needs of "UAE, Inc." conduce to the culturally strong mechanism of consensus-building. Sheikhs listen to their people and lead, informed by that knowledge.

Challenging the status quo is not a form of subversion, provided it respects a certain line. The UAE holds nearly sacred the name and person of its top leaders. Crossing this line can provoke official retaliation backed by family and tribal shaming and even intimidation. But the interests of "UAE, Inc." are mitigating even this cultural knee-jerk. Social order in hand with the high value of productivity and prosperity promote living respectfully.

The temptation for leaders anywhere to mix religious identity into political identity to justify rule and manufacture exclusivism is strong. So far the UAE and "UAE, Inc." have avoided this. However, the current centrality of emiratization—getting Emiratis employed, especially in the private sector—is necessary for cohesion, but will have to give way somehow in the coming decade to a higher priority of engaging second generation expatriates who are now barred from citizenship. They are growing in their attachment to place and raising the volume level of difference. Thus, the ruling group's temptation to resort to that volatile mix will also grow in the UAE.

The rationale for compromise—justification for sacrificing individual preference to group good—is, as yet, too weak in the UAE to sustain the privileged political status of Emiratis going forward. The UAE will have to find ways to adjust, perhaps by inventing degrees of citizenship such as some kind of "contributing membership" for those who accept the duties of citizenship. Muslim peoples can reach back to eras in which non-citizens had essentially equal but separate status. (Lyons, 2009) Organizing by guild or profession is an option. The Western notion of conventional egalitarianism is not the only model for building social cohesion and active cooperation.

Social cohesion requires that the members of society share purpose, a sense of destiny and fair reward. This identity has to say, "We are all in this together." Achieving this sense of common fate best focuses first on what already exists: living in the same territory, working interdependently—sharing a common history and important cultural rituals and language. Living together over decades can produce mutual reliance and respect and even affection. Though this outcome is not guaranteed, its prospect is higher to the extent that the population is aware that this is possible and that the civic culture and economy support it. This "UAE, Inc." appears to understand.

To prevent deadlock or the rise of any group's compulsion to dominate, "UAE, Inc." will want to have in place by 2020, a sufficiently persuasive ideological rationale embodying shared values that will grease the wheels of federalism and social unity. This challenge, not the cascade posited on lesser current risks, is the UAE's greatest.

Notes

1. B'huth, the Arabic word for Research, is short for Dubai Consultancy Research and Media Centre, a leading independent guide to Public Policy, Geostrategic Analysis, Natural Security, Development Studies as well as a dedicated outfit for Strategic Communication. B'huth also conducts proprietary public opinion polls in the United Arab Emirates, some are cited in this paper. (www.bhuth.ae)

Middle East Union (MEU): A Futuristic Approach for Democratic Transition and Economic Development

Alan L Moss

Abstract

The Arab Spring has seen many thousands sacrifice their lives fighting for democracy, prosperity, and integrity. In spite of their brave efforts and initial successes in toppling authoritarian regimes, lack of experience in democratic nation building and entrenched forces with a stake in the status quo has limited the fulfillment of the ideals sought. What if there was an organization dedicated to the realization of Middle East democracy and development, a regional coalition aided by international experts and funding to guide national transformation? This paper describes how such a resource, a Middle East Union (MEU), might be formed, its agency content, and operations. It assumes that the drive to freedom and economic advancement could convince the region's nations to put the old grudges and divergent interests aside and work together. While this may be a contentious supposition, it should not divert efforts to explore the means that might lead to better lives for Middle East populations.

The MEU would be open to all nations of the Middle East and North Africa (MENA), including the Gaza Strip and West Bank unified into a new Palestinian state. The organization's administrative structure would consist of an Agency for Democratic Transition, Economic Development Agency, Union Educational Institute, MEU Rights Council, Office of Economic Opportunity, Legislature, Office of Management and Budget, and Security Center. Enabling negotiations would act as a stimulant to MEU membership and operations, establishing a non-aggression pact, open access to all religious and historic sites, and forming a Palestinian State and Jerusalem settlement. For most MENA nations, the MEU could offer restoration of dignity through accomplishments that would take advantage of Arab Spring reforms and earn the respect of the family of nations worldwide. For Israel, the MEU could offer peace among its neighbors and an opportunity to establish trade and working relationships with regional powers.

Introduction

The Arab Spring has created a new environment for political study of the Middle East (Bellin, 2012; Lynch, 2012). Brave youth have toppled autocratic administrations thought to be invincible. Rather than accepting the promise of security in place of modernity, the region's populations have taken to the streets to demand the benefits of democracy, prosperity, and integrity.

In spite of these successes, lack of experience in democratic nation building and entrenched forces with a stake in the status quo has limited the fulfillment of Arab Spring ideals. What if the drive to freedom and economic development opened the door to formation of a Middle East Union (MEU), a regional coalition aided by international experts, and funding dedicated to establish democratic institutions and promote economic development? If nations were able to put the old grudges and divergent interests aside, they might work together under an MEU umbrella to record unprecedented progress. While cooperation among Middle East nations may be a contentious supposition, this should not divert efforts to explore means that might better the lives of the region's population.

The MEU proposal recognizes the serious problems faced by many of its potential members: poverty; corruption; religious prejudice; the absence or unsettled emergence of basic human rights and democratic institutions; over-dependence on oil and natural gas; unprecedented numbers of uneducated and unemployed youth; uneven distribution of income; uncertain borders; fear of aggression; high expenditures for military equipment; and high costs of living relative to average incomes.

The Union could face these difficulties by focusing on positive change initiated through new concepts and ideas that would offer a practical path to freedom, human rights, economic development, and political maturity. Rather than dwelling on roadblocks of the past, the proposal would rely on thinking out of the box to build ladders over and pathways around barriers to a better future.

The central idea would be to stop talking about problems and past injustices and to start implementing innovative steps that promise a better life for today's citizens of the MENA region, their children, and grandchildren. Of course, there are areas of reconciliation that would require negotiations. Under the MEU strategy, they would be conducted in the context of a comprehensive drive to realize the dreams that gave birth to the Arab Spring.

The MEU would invite all Middle East nations, including Israel, to support one another in an historic transformation. The proposal rests on the assumption that conflict resolution may be obtained through efforts to achieve positive and mutually beneficial goals that eclipse fundamental disagreements.

Determining who is right has not been a productive use of time and energy. Solving the Middle East puzzle one nation or issue at a time has drained resources yielding few significant results. With the promise ushered in by the Arab Spring and majorities seeking ways to establish democratic institutions, the MEU could offer an overarching strategy and administrative mechanism to unite the region into a force for democracy, development, mutual respect, and peace.

Once democratic institutions and human rights guarantees negate historical prejudices and competitions based upon different religious beliefs and practices, all persuasions would be free to practice their beliefs and honor their traditions. Democracy would trump race, religion, and culture as the political system of choice.

MEU in the Context of Middle East Coalitions

The proposed Middle East Union (MEU) would enter a region with much experience in intra-regional confederations. For example, the League of Arab States, founded in 1945, is intended to improve coordination among its members while preserving the sovereignty of its 22 Arab states, including Palestine (Masters 2012). Early objectives were to prevent the emergence of a Jewish state in Palestine and to limit further colonial influences.

The Gulf Cooperation Council (GCC), formed in 1981 by six oil rich Gulf States, intends to increase economic cooperation, enhance security, and counter threats from Islamic extremism (BBC News, 2012). It was precipitated by the Islamic revolution in Iran and the Iran–Iraq War. Its members (Saudi Arabia, Kuwait, the United Arab Emirates, Oman, Qatar, and Bahrain) are led by autocratic monarchies or Sheikdoms that allow limited or non-existent political freedom.

In December 2011, Saudi Arabia proposed taking the GCC a step further to form a Gulf Union (Hammond, 2012). Its purpose would be to limit the Arab Spring contagion, spreading Iranian influence, and Shi'a Muslim dissent in Bahrain.

While these initiatives demonstrate the capability of Middle East nations to join together to advance their national aims, overall, they have little in common with the Middle East Union. For example, the MEU focuses on national transformation to democratic institutions, universal provision of human and civil rights, the full engagement of Israel in a multi-nation effort to obtain regional advancement, and the attainment of specific, region-wide economic objectives, such as a Union-Wide Tourism Network. The MEU would call for no compromise of sovereignty, just a shared commitment to mutual freedoms and development. Its nonaggression pact, open access to all religious sites, and Israeli–Palestinian settlement would be designed to mute national competitions and free each nation to focus on it own path to progress.

The Middle East organizations cited above, on the other hand, mostly aim to protect political systems that often deny democratic practices, human, and civil rights; oppose Israel's existence; and prescribe economic objectives in loose terms. Furthermore, based upon bylaws and record of accomplishment, one may legitimately question their effectiveness. For example, decisions made by members of the Arab League are only binding on those who vote for them, undermining the League's uniformity and impact. In terms of specifics, the Arab League was unable to halt Israel's march to statehood, take uniform positions during the cold war, make a united stand concerning the U.S. invasion of Iraq, halt the killing in Syria's civil war, or turn Iran from the development of a nuclear capability.

Similarly, the GCC made no attempt to counter the 1990 Iraqi invasion of Kuwait while it deployed troops to Bahrain in 2011 to increase security during antigovernment protests by the nation's Shi'a majority. Independent free-trade deals between Bahrain and Oman with the United States also threaten efforts to unify GCC economies. At the same time, the Saudi Gulf Union plan has been met with skepticism from nations who fear domination from Saudi Arabia and difficulties in integrating distinct social and political systems.

Advancing communications technology, large numbers of unemployed youth, and Arab Spring ideals combine to motivate downtrodden Middle East populations to rise up and demand the freedoms and benefits guaranteed by democracies around the world. The application of MEU administrative tools could offer one way for democratic institutions, rights, and economic development to be obtained by these populations in an orderly and comprehensive manner, avoiding the conflict and missteps that often accompany open rebellion and military action.

MEU Composition and Objectives

The MEU's administrative structure could be designed to support eight distinct objectives:

1. An Agency for Democratic Transition (ADT) could facilitate passage of the region's governments into functioning democracies.

Taking advantage of already democratic regional governments and political/academic experts from around the world, nations that join the MEU could be assisted by the ADT through the provision of technical assistance for the development of democratic constitutions and the formation of basic legislative, executive, and judicial branches of government. Significant progress could be required during the first year to maintain MEU membership.

Many regional populations have little or no experience with democracy. At the same time, entrenched political, military, police, and religious power bases may have a stake in delaying or defeating democratic initiatives. The MEU could help to ensure that democratic goals are met through an orderly and effective process.

2. An Economic Development Agency (EDA) could diversify and develop national economies.

The EDA could work with national and international experts to design and launch initiatives to free selected economies from their over-dependence on the extraction and sale of oil and natural gas and to promote a high growth regional environment. Economies with relatively low per capita Group Domestic Product (GDP) could be assisted through grants and planning for the birth and expansion of new industries and further development of established industries attuned to the global demands of the 21st century. Similar initiatives could modernize agricultural techniques and equipment and launch natural resource management and rural development projects, providing for a huge increase in the availability of clean water and required foodstuffs.

A Union-wide Tourism Network (UTN) composed of new and/or renovated hotels and innovative means of transportation could be created to provide a vast increase in regional visitors with a seamless path from one historic site to the next, regardless of location.

Eventually, a Union-wide Free Trade Zone could be established to multiply the intra-regional exchange of goods, enhance intra-regional dependence, and strengthen individual economies through new nation-to-nation trade.

3. A Union Education Institute (UEI) could provide MENA youth, who have doubled in numbers between 1980 and 2010, with education and training to significantly increase labor force participation (currently the lowest regional rate in the world) and reduce unemployment (the highest regional rate) (Roudi, 2011).

The UEI could offer world class education and training units and teacher instruction to be applied at the pre-school, elementary school, preparatory school, and university levels. The emphasis could be on developing knowledge and skills to allow for the smooth transition from school to work.

Concurrently, the EUI could plan and carry out initiatives to gain employment for currently unemployed youth and young people out of the labor force. Coordination with EDA initiatives, including new public works projects, could provide youth with income and valuable work experience. These programs could enhance the social and economic prospects of the region's youth while increasing demand for the goods they would be empowered to purchase.

4. A MEU Rights Council (RC) could provide each nation with means to guarantee basic human and civil rights and imbue Middle East populations with respect for diversity of religious beliefs, race, gender, and differences in sexual orientation.

Through such organizations as Amnesty International, the RC could sponsor studies of each member nation to determine its human and civil rights status and to form the basis for remedial action. Human rights, inalienable rights of all members of the human family, include the right to life, freedom from torture, freedom from slavery, the right to a fair trial, freedom of speech, and freedom of thought, conscience, and religion (United Nations, 1948).

Civil rights, those guaranteed through citizenship, include the right to a free press, assembly, and vote; freedom from discrimination in public places based on race, color, religion, or national origin; and due process/equal protection under the law (Legal Information Institute, 2010).

Especially relevant to Middle East rights initiatives is the age-old competition and prejudice among Sunni and Shi'a populations. While this schism originated in religious differences, since the 1970s, sectarian tensions have escalated and expressed themselves in terms of politics and competition for power, influence, and privilege (Hunter, 2012). MEU rights actions could help to create a sense of nation above tribal and sectarian affiliations while encouraging the equal treatment of individual citizens and reducing discrimination and retaliation as democratic institutions become established. Significant progress in assuring rights could be required during the first year to maintain MEU membership.

5. An Office of Economic Opportunity (OEO) could work to reduce poverty and income inequality, raising the standard of living of the region's population currently below the poverty line.

National data indicate that a majority of MENA nations have at least 20% of their populations subsisting below the $2.00 per day poverty line (Naggar, 2006). The OEO could focus its efforts on rural areas, city slums, and female populations where poverty in the region is concentrated. The OEO could provide food, medical care, literacy instruction, and vocational training to individuals in need.

6. A MEU Legislature could provide a unique forum for Intra-Union negotiations and deliberations.

Members of the MEU could utilize this forum to introduce new initiatives, debate questions concerning operations, and vote to approve or disapprove the budgets and plans of MEU administrative components.

7. A MEU Office of Management and Budget (OMB) could assess annual dues to be paid by member states, seek international funding and grants for MEU projects, obtain private sector capital to support commercially viable initiatives such as the Union-Wide Tourism Network (UTN), and channel funding received to component agencies. Establishing democratic institutions and providing expanded rights could free additional funding from the West and international economic organizations. At the same time, private capital available could be multiplied as political stability and consumer markets grow.

In addition to collecting and providing funding for MEU operations and programs, the OMB could execute a continuous program of audits to ensure that resources are allocated appropriately while modern, efficient, and corruption-free procedures are followed.

8. The MEU Security Center (SC), staffed by United Nations forces, could be charged with maintaining the integrity of member borders and enforcing agreements reached.

The SC could ensure that non-aggression and disarmament pacts are strictly enforced. The establishment of demilitarized zones, the guarantee of free access to religious and historic sites, and protection of Palestinian state borders could also be the responsibility of Center forces.

Enabling Negotiations

Agreements regarding three key issues could facilitate MEU launch. Negotiations could be led by neutral experts skilled in the development of mutually beneficial treaties. Settlement of these questions could act as a stimulant to MEU membership and operations: 1) a non-aggression pact; 2) open access to all religious and historic sites; and 3) formation of a Palestinian State and Jerusalem resolution.

Context

How do you negotiate agreements when the context is one of continued conflict? Iran and Syria fund terrorist activities. Hamas fires rockets into Israeli civilian areas. Iran builds long-range rockets and a nuclear capability while its leaders make outlandish charges regarding Israel's legitimacy. Hezbollah rockets threaten Israel across the Lebanese border. While the West Bank is in the hands of Fatah, trying to build the institutions of future statehood, Gaza is governed by Hamas, trying to destroy the State of Israel by any means available, and Israel expands its holdings in the West Bank and East Jerusalem.

This is not a context in which accords may be reached. These irritations continually build until one side or the other goes ballistic, creates massive violence and casualties, and produces more resentment, unrest, and retaliation.

Prospects of the MEU could change the Middle East context to one in which lasting peace may be achieved. During its first year, after the Union's basic charter has been finalized, the MEU's members could become a force to lower the rhetoric of violence and territorial expansion and raise the calls for agreements. Membership in the MEU could encourage states to end the cycle of violence so they might get on with the business of rebuilding their own nations.

With regard to Israel and the Palestinians, former combatants, in lock-step, could accept a deal in which the cessation of terrorist activities is matched by the suspension of settlement expansion in the West Bank and East Jerusalem.

Negotiated Agreements

1. Signature on a membership non-aggression pact, enforced by the MEU Security Center, could be a prerequisite to joining the organization. Freed from the fear of regional conflict, MEU members could be empowered to focus on positive outcomes, rather than continue the nonproductive work of acquiring the instruments of war and securing military objectives.

Recent Middle East threats and aggression have provided short-term gains at a high price. Israel endures terrorism and Hamas rockets from Gaza, while the Palestinians must live with an aggravating network of barriers, tight restrictions on materials allowed to enter, military outposts, and the fear of surgical strikes and invasion. While Hezbollah's activities have, for the time being been marginalized, 30,000 Hezbollah rockets remain ready to assault Israel if that nation should follow through on its threats to attack Iran's nuclear facilities.

When one takes a broader view, it is evident that an aggressive mindset has maintained the conditions for enduring conflict, not a lasting peace. Furthermore, aggression cannot solve the social and economic problems that plague the Middle East. Conflict does not address an over-dependence on oil and natural gas; huge uneducated, unemployed, and underemployed youth populations; uneven distribution of income; and egregious human rights violations. At the same time, military strikes do not assuage disrespect and hatred among neighbors, but intensify barriers to understanding and peace.

The non-aggression pact between MEU members could be an elixir to allow the Union's members to focus on positive outcomes, rather than continue the nonproductive work of acquiring the instruments of war and securing military objectives. Signing that pact could be a mutual concession that alone may justify MEU membership for many of those involved.

Under this framework, nations working together under the MEU umbrella could turn away from aggression and violence. Not in spite of the limited successes of past conflicts, but because they recognize that conflict cannot provide solutions to their most serious problems. Ideally, Middle East nations joining the MEU could renounce aggression as a viable foreign policy and instead work together for their mutual benefit.

2. MEU Security Center staff, including archeological experts, could provide protection and open access to all religious/historic sites within Israel and the new Palestinian State, as well as in all other MEU nations. Open access could contribute to the shared sense of the region's religious history and add to the attraction of the Union-wide Tourism Network (UTN).

3. Another prerequisite to a MEU launch could be formation of an independent Palestinian State, a homeland for Palestinian refugees and other Palestinians seeking to live in their own nation. One design could have the Gaza and West Bank joined by a secure corridor to form a demilitarized Palestinian State, with borders protected by the MEU Security Center.

Survivors who fled their homes during 1946–1948 could be offered new homes within the borders of the new Palestinian homeland. Also, they could be provided with reparations that compensate for lost income. If some of these refugees prefer to remain in their current homes, reparations could represent what the cost of a new home would have been.

Two levels of compensation could be provided to refugee descendents. For those currently living within the borders of what would become the Palestinian state, and for those who wish to return to that new nation, reparations, in the form of a lump sum payment, tuition free education, and/or training in a marketable skill could be provided. For those who wish to stay in their current locations, outside the new state's borders, including many of the two million refugees who are citizens of Jordan, a lower level of reparations could be provided. These costs could be shared by Israel and those nations who formerly supported establishment of the Jewish state.

As part of this treaty, East Jerusalem could serve as the Palestinian state's religious capital while the city's Jewish Quarter could become Israel's religious capital. Reconciling this piece of the Middle East puzzle could provide four valuable advantages to creating a peaceful and prosperous region:

First, it could eliminate the refugee camps and undermine the hatred of Israel, Jews, and the West that they engender. With the promise of widespread construction and reparations funded by international sources, the momentum for reconciliation and prosperity could overtake the forces of violence and revenge.

Second, it could provide a huge economic stimulus to the Palestinian state, through new construction, education and training, and income provided to its residents. To a lesser but still significant extent, it could provide economic stimulus to nations such as Jordan where refugees may choose to remain.

Third, it could provide a strong incentive for unification of Hamas and Fatah and the building of institutions to establish and then promote growth of the Palestinian state.

Fourth, and most importantly, it could allow the parties to get past perceived injustice and move on to positive objectives.

MEU Opposition

If the MEU were to take hold in advancing countries, neighboring leaders with a stake in maintaining the status quo, supported by military police and religious hardliners, could be presented with a choice. They could shepherd their nations into the union, its reforms and economic benefits, seek to keep things as they are, or attempt to set a unique course. In any case, successful implementation of MEU initiatives could cast a shadow of opportunity on those in authority who fail to provide comparable rights and economic opportunity. Such resistance could invite the organization of domestic movements to change course.

Another kind of MEU opposition could be posed by terrorists who seek to continue their acts of destruction. Those groups who attempt to undo MEU progress could attack its structure with explosions from suicide and car bombs and other instruments of violence. Unable to adjust to a new more positive Middle East environment, they could claim that the MEU represents an unholy alliance that betrays religious and political obligations.

In spite of such threats, the long-term impact of the union could be to reduce terrorism. According to recent psychological studies (DeAngelis, 2009), terrorism flows from:

- Extremist beliefs taught early in life;
- A strong sense of victimization and alienation;
- A belief that the other side has committed serious moral violations, justifying violence against the enemy;
- A fear that one's ethnic, religious, or nationalist group is being threatened;
- The absence of political power to affect positive change without violence;
- Membership in a group that encourages risk-taking through social pressure; and
- A strong motivation to achieve a meaningful national life that may be reached only through one's own death and related violence and destruction.

The MEU could impact these motivators through obtaining positive results:

- With regard to extremist beliefs taught early, there is no way to go back and undo what has already been done. However, eliminating refugee camps and the hatred they implant in their populations, especially youth, and encouraging nonsectarian education could begin to reduce extremist beliefs accepted by the young.
- For members of the MEU, as economic life improves and peace is maintained, the sense of victimization and alienation could decline;
- As MEU nations work together toward mutual gains, moral violations of the past could fade while understanding expands;
- By removing the fear of aggression and by encouraging more democratic beliefs, ethnic, religious, and nationalist threats could be reduced;
- Steps taken for the mutual benefit of MEU members and their people could show that there are peaceful, political avenues to affect positive change without violence; and
- Finally, by increasing opportunities, the MEU could convince covered populations that their national lives can have real meaning without having to sacrifice life and limb.

While terrorist groups are sure to remain for a while, MEU agencies could act as a powerful countervailing force. Once the MEU begins to make real progress, groups that offer nothing but violence and death would not be able to compete.

Would terrorist groups attack MEU units to try to break the Union before it is established? Of course they would. They would know that if the MEU survives and prospers, the days of al-Qaeda and the like would be numbered. Given the promise of benefits to MEU member populations, the Union should be able to withstand the terrorist challenge.

National Benefits

For many of the region's nations, the MEU could offer restoration of dignity through enhanced rights, democratic institutions, and economic gains that would take advantage of recent revolutions to earn the respect of the family of nations worldwide. For Israel, the MEU could offer peace among its neighbors and an opportunity to establish trade and working relationships with regional powers.

The Israelis and their neighbors have been captive to their own demons. Many of the region's nations have been burdened by inefficient, antiquated, and often corrupt governments that have failed to raise the standard of living of large segments of their populations. To stay in power, their leaders have exploited a hatred of Israel and the West as enemies responsible for their social and economic hardships. They have kept their people in line by rallying them against a common enemy.

Some of these despots have been removed by those fighting for democracy and economic equity, while those who remain in power are being threatened by the growing tide of reform. This creates a real opportunity for reconciliation between Israel and its neighbors (Foxman, 2011).

By working together to take advantage of MEU initiatives, the MENA states could have an opportunity to establish democratic institutions in an orderly manner, diversify and develop their economies, obtain access to MEU member technological know-how, lift their people out of poverty, and guarantee the human and civil rights typical of developed nations.

Pressure created by the MEU Human Rights Council could allow perceptive political leaders to solidify their peaceful transitions into democracy. In other cases, where resistance is encountered, citizens may demand the change that will lead to membership.

What about Israel? What does that nation have to gain? Why would Israel join with surrounding nations who regularly threaten its very existence?

The Israeli demon is being the outsider, threatened by terrorism and extinction. Defending the nation has required the maintenance of a huge and expensive military force that has raised the cost of living, alienating those Israelis of modest income.

Fear created by missile strikes and violent border incursions encourages Israel's expanding settlements and intervention in occupied territories. This feeds the resentment that leads to more violence and the need for additional military capabilities. Without reconciliation, there can be no peace, no devotion of resources to raise up its own citizens, and no normal relations with its neighbors.

Israel's pathway to peace could be accelerated through MENA advances in the level of education, income, democratic institutions, and human rights. What better way to achieve this end than by joining with their neighbors in a union that has as its principal objective the mutual advancement of member populations?

One could hypothesize that MEU proceedings would be unbalanced with many MENA states automatically voting against Israeli interests. But Israel would have two powerful advantages. First, it has superior experience dealing in a democratic environment, knowing how to advance its interests through democratic processes and institutions. Second, many of the issues debated by MEU members would involve positive initiatives to which Israel would contribute, increasing the promise of mutual benefits.

Unless the parties learn to work together, the union's potential could not be realized. Through MEU participation, Middle East nations could emerge from ancient mindsets and their harvest of pain and into modern times and the dignity that progress would engender.

The Path to a Middle East Union

Establishment of the MEU could proceed in four distinct steps:

1. The proposal could be circulated among potential members and their populations and interested parties around the world. This could be achieved through academic journals such as the *Digest of Middle East Studies* and *The Middle East Journal*, popular websites, and daily newspapers and TV broadcasts that could cover the initiative, provide the public with summaries, and direct those interested to where they might obtain more detailed information.

2. If adequate support for the MEU concept became evident, academic and political experts could convene a working session to put more meat on the bones of the proposal. Taking advantage of extensive experience with Middle East nations and similar initiatives of transition, more detailed descriptions of proposed MEU components, their goals, and operation could be developed. Volunteers from this group could assume the administrative responsibilities required to advance MEU objectives.

3. At the conclusion of the above work, an international MEU conference could be organized. All Middle East nations could be invited to participate in work group sessions whose aim would be to refine and amend the product of the expert session. Proceedings could be restricted to the realm of problem solving and the design, content, and operation of MEU components. Specific issues would not be viewed individually but treated in the context of an organization designed to promote the Middle East as a region of nations working together to establish democracy, peace and prosperity. Changes and additions could be approved through a majority vote of those in attendance.

4. The final product of the above sessions could be consolidated into a formal treaty and transmitted to each Middle East nation for consideration and signature. Operations of the MEU could begin as soon as three countries signed and returned the treaty to a designated administrative unit.

Policy or Pipedream

There are those who will view the MEU proposal as a pipedream. They will place the ideas advanced against the backdrop of thousands of years of conflict and authoritarian rule. They will conclude that Middle East nations will never be free to put the old hatreds and oppressive ways aside and focus on bettering their own people through cooperation and mutual action.

On the other hand, students of history may look to the success of the European Union and recall how its earliest rendering helped to move member states away from extreme nationalism and towards democracy and economic recovery, eventually emerging from the rubble of World War II.

Certainly, Arab youth and other concerned citizens sacrificing their lives to finally turn the page is a powerful symbol that times are changing. They have been willing to pay the ultimate price to transform their nations into democracies that value the individual and promote prosperity for all. They seek the dignity developed democracies guarantee and are ready to dive head first into new frontiers of Middle East development.

However, once freedom fighters dethrone authoritarian leaders, will they be able to establish functioning democracies, given their lack of experience in democratization and the means to form an equitable economic system? Recent experience testifies to the difficult challenges they must overcome. Construction of a Middle East Union, as described, could provide the tools, expertise, and funding required for successful transformation.

Ignorance, Lobby Power, and the Formulation of U.S. Foreign Policy

Lawrence Davidson

Abstract

Opinion polls often indicate that most Americans pay little attention to foreign policy and consider it of low importance when deciding how to vote in national elections. The long list of dictatorships that Washington has seen fit to subsidize and arm, the coups and right wing revolutions that the CIA has been involved in (sometimes aimed against democratically elected governments), the subordination of whole economies to the interests of United States' business concerns, the collusion of multiple United States' administrations in the destruction of Palestinian people, all go largely unnoticed. It would seem that most Americans, like many others in the world, are too engrossed in their own domestic affairs (what we might call "natural localism") to take notice of foreign affairs.

A major consequence of this disregard is that actual foreign policy formulation has come under the influence of well organized and financed lobby groups which do have interests in matters abroad. This is certainly the case as regards U. S. policy formulation for much of the Middle East. Here both Jewish Zionists and Christian fundamentalist Zionists have achieved ascendant influence over policy formulation toward Israel and the Palestinian territories and much of the rest of the region as well. Likewise, a neo-conservative interest group with strong ties to Israel achieved command positions in the Defense and State Departments under the administration of George W. Bush. And, they now constitute the major advisers to the [then] Republican presidential candidate, Mitt Romney. Relative to these lobbies, the influence of oil companies is secondary. One can argue that as a result of this situation, there is no foreign policy reflecting genuine U.S. national interests for this important part of the world. There has been, and continues to be, only the parochial goals of special interests which present their own aims to the public as "national interests."

The public's inattention has inevitably led to a deep and persisting ignorance of the consequences of U.S. foreign policy. The mainstream mass media, whose editors and reporters are themselves often biased in their perspectives and ignorant of the "facts on the ground," have helped fill the void of ignorance with a myth that American foreign policy is mainly an altruistic effort to export our domestic ideals: democracy, modernity, development, etc. Thus, when those abroad who resist United States' policies do damage to American lives and property, the vast majority of American citizens have no context to understand their behavior. They are easily convinced that they are terrorists who simply "hate our values."

Yet, the truth of the matter is that America's policies in the Middle East have been lobby driven for at least the last 60 years. And, unbeknownst to the general public, they helped create the historical context for the September 11, 2001 attacks. Then, the response of the Bush administration to that tragedy went on to make things much worse for the United States. There are more than a billion Muslims in the world and a growing number of them are now seriously angry at the United States. There are over 300 million Arabs and many of them are willing to materially support those who stand up against the United States and its ally Israel. The United States has neither the manpower, the intelligence capacity, nor the staying power to fight and defeat all the various organizations that have and will arise to confront it. Keeping in mind that these will not be regular armies, but will be guerrilla operations and clandestine groups who, as we have seen, are already capable of doing us great damage both in their own part of the world and in the U.S.' homeland. Under the circumstances, it is in the interest of all Americans that there is a thorough review of past and present foreign policy efforts in the Middle East. This should be done with transparency and include a national public debate on just what are U.S. national interests in that part of the world. Is Israel really a country that is important to the United States, or just important to certain powerful but parochial special interests? And, what has truly been the result of Israel's U. S. subsidized policies toward the Palestinians? If oil is a national interest, is it necessary to use force to control that resource at its source? Finally, is it an offense warranting impeachment when the president lies, misleads, distorts information, and then sends American troops to their deaths based on that presentation? These issues are important to all Americans. They deserve to be publicly aired. Progressives should demand that these subjects be taken up at all levels of government from town and county councils on up. Media outlets should be picketed with demands for open debate on foreign policy. Americans should insist that future administrations promote the necessary public debate on national interests and foreign policy formulation. If we ignore this, and allow things to go on as they are, then we can expect nothing but continuing disaster.

Introduction

In 1977, George Kennan, the country's most respected foreign policy expert, made the following observation, "our actions in the field of foreign affairs are the convulsive reactions of politicians to an internal political life dominated by vocal minorities" (Kennan, 1977, p. 4ff). It was an observation that deserves widespread public attention because, particularly since the end of the Cold War, making foreign policy by "convulsive reaction…to an internal political life" has had increasingly dangerous consequences for the United States (Kennan, 1977). This paper will explain why and how U.S. foreign policy has indeed been captured by "vocal minorities" and just why this is so dangerous (Kennan, 1967, p. 85).

Foreign Policy and Public Awareness

Most Americans do not pay attention to foreign policy except at times of crises. For instance, Gallup polls taken every presidential election year since 1976 show that, with the exception of 2004 (the first post 9/11 election year), foreign affairs was of little concern to most American citizens (Granitsas, 2005).[1] As to how foreign policy is made, it is safe to conclude that the great majority of Americans do not know and probably do not care.

None of this is unusual. Under normal conditions, most people will naturally focus on their local environment because, on a day to day basis, it is our immediate surroundings that are most important to all of us. These surroundings supply the vast majority with their place of work, and are where one finds friends, peer groups, and one's immediate family circle. One can even speak of this in evolutionary terms for it is the local environment that supplies the majority with the knowledge necessary to make useful and successful choices relevant to their lives. Therefore, a concentration on this arena has survival value. This means that, even in this day and age of great mobility, worldwide communications, and economic globalization we are still, as individuals and in our daily practice, village oriented.

Nonetheless, while there are rational reasons for the people to concentrate their attention on their immediate environment there are also, in our modern age, serious drawbacks to this provincialism. "Tuning out the rest of the globe" as Alkman Granitsas (2005) puts it, and concentrating exclusively on one's locality means that most of us live in ignorance about what is going on beyond the local sphere. This can result in a false sense of security right up till the moment of crisis when, suddenly, something threatening looms on the horizon. At that point a greater number of citizens than usual will suddenly pay attention to this foreign threat. They quickly discover their own ignorance and, out of necessity for information, turn to others assuming that they know what is going on abroad. These others, government officials, news "pundits," and other "reliable experts," may or may not present a biased picture of events from afar. In either case, it is this limited category of "opinion makers" that are almost automatically sought out by the mainstream media to produce the interpretations upon which citizens rely in order to make sense of foreign issues. Thus, a general ignorance of outside events leads to the public's dependence on media edited news and "establishment" experts (Holsti, 2004).[2]

Powerless Individuals and Engaged Interest Groups

To this state of general ignorance of and indifference to the world abroad, we can add the average citizen's sense of domestic political powerlessness. After all, most ordinary people do not believe that they can influence government policy beyond their local sphere. That is one reason why so many of them do not bother to vote in national elections.[3] Once more, this feeling of political powerlessness is not unusual in a country with a large and complex political system where there is little or no room for votes of no confidence, third parties, and doable recall efforts. To take advantage of the structures of power one must be motivated to master the bureaucratic maze and numerous rules of the system.

Over time, the relatively small number of motivated Americans understanding the power inherent in the political system have developed ways around the problem of the powerless citizen. In doing so, *they have transformed American society from a democracy of individual citizens into a democracy of competing interest groups*. How does this work? Individuals with similar interests and goals come together and form an interest group that pools their financial resources and voting numbers. Then, as lobbies, they use these resources to influence politicians and government officials to shape legislation and policy to their liking. This happens all the time on the domestic political scene. It also happens when it comes to foreign policy where the effectiveness of special interests is helped along by the normal indifference the general public shows in events abroad. Simply put, the interest group nature or our politics combined with popular indifference maximizes the influence over foreign policy formulation of those lobbies (Kennan's "vocal minorities") that do have interests abroad.

Consequences for Foreign Policy

A) The Doubtful Status of "National Interest"

The central role of interest groups in foreign policy formulation calls into question the notion of national interest. American citizens assume that such a thing as national interest exists and, in some formal way, guides the government in the making of foreign policies. Also, just about three quarters of citizens seem to believe that "moral principles" play a "guiding" role in the pursuit of national interests (Lindsay & Boot, 2004). However, can these assumptions be true when foreign policy is often the product of the desires of dominant lobbies pursuing their "special" interests?

Of course, in the abstract, one can always come up with a list of ends that *should* constitute national interests—for instance, maintaining a military posture adequate to national defense, or ensuring access to sufficient resources. But who has the influence to sway politicians on such questions as what is adequate and sufficient? Who helps decide the parameters and policies that shape the pursuit of these ends? Given its record of indifference to foreign policy, it cannot be the public at large. And if the public is not engaged in a discussion of these matters, some other group(s) must be the guiding force when it comes to the making of policy.

B) The Triumph of Parochialism

How is foreign policy actually made? In theory, foreign policy is made by the executive branch of government with financing and "advice and consent" coming from Congress. The president receives the assistance and guidance of the State Department, the National Security Council, and various intelligence agencies. He and they are supposedly guided by national interests. However, the president and the members of Congress are politicians. They, and their appointed staffs, are "informed by their political ambitions" and their fates are tied to an electoral cycle (Trubowitz, 2000). Politicians work within a system in which powerful interest groups supply much of the money that makes campaigning possible and/or help rally the votes that make elections successful. Under these circumstances, how are politicians, confronted by supportive lobbies with vested interests abroad, likely to define "national interest"? The answer to this question is that, more often than not, national interest becomes what suits the interests and ambitions of the nation's political leaders *and their most influential supporters*. They will, in fact, often be more responsive to these groups than to conflicting advice given to them by the diplomatic corp.[4]

It should be noted that the more sophisticated interest groups often make an effort to solidify public opinion behind their position by framing their parochial interests as national ones. Not only does this make it easier to gain the help of the Congress and political parties, but also helps obstruct any challenge that might be launched by competing interest groups. Thus, we often find various lobbies taking the "What is good for General Motors is good for America" propaganda approach. On the foreign policy level, the repeated assertion that Zionist interests in Israel somehow reflect an American national interest is an example of this gambit. Such assertions are, however, propaganda exercises. By their very nature, interest groups are bound to promote the "special" interests of their membership. They do not exist to sacrifice those interests to some amorphous greater national good.

Thus, when it comes to places such as the Middle East, the State Department will have no more capacity to shape final policy than the Department of Interior's petroleum engineers can command policy on Alaska oil, or the Department of Agriculture's horticulturists can set farm subsidy policy. In such cases, policy is intricately tied to politics.

Creating a "Closed Information Environment"

The United States has an uncensored press. We might then ask, can that press be relied upon to give objective information that will allow Americans to see through the trick of presenting special interests as national interests? The answer, most of the time, is no. As it turns out, the press is not exactly uncensored. It is in fact self-censoring. Remember, the U.S. information outlets automatically rely on government officials and "reliable experts." In the vast majority of cases this produces a one-sided presentation. It must also be kept in mind that American media is made up of for-profit market components owned by individuals and corporations supportive of (or at least responsive to) the very interest groups that maintain controlling influence over aspects of American foreign policy.[5] And, all private news outlets have financial reasons not to frighten off advertisers by becoming associated with unpopular positions. Thus, America's mainstream media outlets are not ones that will usually give the public all sides of a story.

Therefore, unless one takes the trouble to look for a small number of information outlets that provide a skeptical analysis of government policy and lobby influence, one is condemned to a "closed information environment." However, it is yet another aspect of the provincial nature of the citizenry that most, even when confronted with important events, will feel no need to go searching for alternative sources of information. Most will feel comfortable with their traditional sources: local newspapers, the better known news magazines, radio talk shows, and especially television (Pew Research Center, 2004).[6] Brand loyalty is the best term for this behavior.

A major consequence of this information dependency is that it becomes relatively easy to, as Herman and Chomsky (1988) put it, "manufacture consent" by creating pictures of events and situations that are biased to favor particular points of view. This can be done by consistently presenting and interpreting the news in a certain skewed way and/or by simply leaving out important information judged by media editors, owners, and financial backers to be undesirable.

By presenting such skewed and incomplete pictures, the mainstream media creates a public mind set which some scholars have called "low information rationality" (Holsti, 2004, p. 322), while others wonder at just what point "low information rationality becomes no information irrationality" (Holsti, 2004, p. 323). However you want to characterize it, it is a condition wherein most of the American public cannot accurately understand the behavior of either alleged enemies, or that of their own government. This is, of course, an ideal environment for those lobby groups which wish to have their parochial interests thought of as national interests. It allows the lobbies, in the name of national interest, to encourage the media to demonize those who may stand in the way of their economic or ideological ambitions, or those states (such as Iran) which are the enemies of their friends (such as Israel).

But what happens when there are unexpected results—when millions of foreigners across the globe start criticizing American behavior, when most Arabs scorn the notion that the United States is an "honest broker" promoting a "peace process" between Israelis and Palestinians, when Fidel Castro and Hugo Chavez condemn Yankee imperialism to the delight of multitudes? And finally, what happens when someone flies a jet liner into the World Trade Center? When such events take place, Americans with their skewed news, have no hope of placing these events within an accurate historical context. The resulting bewilderment and resentment, further fed by yet more manipulated information, is then a major cost of an otherwise natural indifference to things that lay beyond the next hill.

Over The Next Hill is Israel and the Middle East

If there is a national interest in the Middle East that should determine U.S. foreign policy, it is the continuous *trade based* access to energy resources. Policies adopted by the government which unnecessarily complicate or endanger this access would seem to be illogical or, at the very least, ill advised. Yet, given the nature of our competitive interest group manner of formulating policy, there is no guarantee that what is best for the nation as a whole will actually determine government behavior. And, indeed, for over 60 years, the United States has pursued policies in the Middle East that have systematically alienated nearly the entire Muslim, and most of the Christian, population of the region.[7]

Among these policies is not only consistent support for Israel, but also Washington's support of cooperative Middle Eastern dictatorships. Such support (which identifies the United States with anti-democratic behaviors) trades weapons, loans, and other "assistance" for economic, political, and military cooperation. Washington has seen this policy approach as a way of maintaining "stability" in the region. However, this policy requires regional "allies," such as, King Abdullah of Jordan, the recently deposed Hosni Mubarak in Egypt, and the Shah in pre-1979 Iran to, among other things, cooperate with Israel and disregard their own citizens' views on the horrid fate of the Palestinians. As recent events have shown, in the long run, this is a policy approach that has helped condemn many of these regimes to rebellion.

That this is a short sighted approach that contributes to a predictable build up of discontent not only with the dictators but their American supporters is, apparently, of no concern to the interest groups that influence U.S. policy. No one, beyond a few insightful members of the diplomatic and intelligence corps, seems to understand (or perhaps care) that these policies have produced another candidate for a national interest—the growing need to protect U. S. citizens from those who would express their alienation through acts of violence and terror.

Under the circumstances, U.S. presidents and other politicians can talk about democracy all they want, but unless they are completely out of touch with reality (which is always a possibility) they are merely spouting propaganda for an American audience.[8] Thanks to the 60 plus years of America's special interest driven policies, if you give many nations in the Middle East real democracy, the people will give you back an anti-American government. Some of the consequences of the on-going Arab Spring demonstrate this fact.

The policy of supporting dictatorships and avoiding popular governments in the Middle East has not, of course, produced perfect results. On occasion, some dictators have slipped their leashes (such as Saddam Hussein after 1988) and taken independent stands against Israel and other U.S. interests. The Shah of Iran, America's dictator, was easily overthrown once an opposition movement was able to organize itself. The new Islamic Republic replaced the Shah's embrace of Israel with an energetic pro-Palestine policy. Unrest in Pakistan reflects growing discontent with that country's close alliance with the United States. The present Iraqi government, if it can be called that, is dominated by Shi'a with strong ties to Iran. And, whatever the end product of the current civil war in Syria, the likelihood that it will produce a pro-American government is small.

Despite the increasing probability of more and more anti-American regimes coming into existence, U.S. policy has held firm to the position that support for Israel and cooperative dictators (increasingly focused in the Persian Gulf area) is foundational and thus non-negotiable. The skewed outcome of this position has led various administrations and Congresses to pursue punitive policies against countries that take a stand against Israel—even when they have been otherwise helpful to the United States. Let us take a look at one such example of this counter-productive policy.

The Case of Iran

In September of 2005, this author was among a group of U.S. academics that paid a visit to the outgoing Iranian president, Mohammad Khatami. Khatami laid out his efforts to improve relations with the United States. These took place during the Clinton presidency and paralleled Khatami's reform efforts in Iran. Khatami was encouraged to approach the United States following a March 2000 talk by Secretary of State Madeline Albright in which she stated that the 1953 CIA supported coup against the democratically appointed Prime Minister Mohammed Mossadegh "was clearly a setback for Iran's political development." She also admitted that the United States' backed regime of the Shah had "brutally suppressed political dissent," and that the U. S. support for Iraq during its war with Iran was "regrettably shortsighted" (Sanger, 2000). Soon after Albright's speech, the Iranian president reciprocated with an announcement that if the United States followed its words with deeds indicating friendship, "we can expect our two countries to enjoy good relations" (Amirahmadi, 2000). Bill Clinton seemed to agree that this was an important goal when he told CNN that "one of the best things we could do for the long term peace and health of the Middle East and, indeed, much of the rest of the world is to have a constructive partnership with Iran" (Sanger, 2000).

Khatami explained to the author's group that the United States and Iran have many mutual interests that go beyond oil. Both countries want stability, particularly in Iraq and Afghanistan and, according to the outgoing president, both have a long-term interest in minimizing the influence of religious fanatics (Khatami was referring to Christian and Jewish fanatics as well as Islamic ones). He pointed out that Iran had cooperated with the United States in its efforts against the Taliban regime in Afghanistan, and still was interested in better relations with America.

Yet, nothing came of the year 2000's mutual statements that good relations were to be desired. Prior to 2000, the U.S. Congress, working under the assumption that Iran was involved in the June 1996 Khobar truck bombing, and also at the urging of special interest groups that included the Zionist and expatriate Iranian lobbies, had passed an array of anti-Iranian bills. The most notable of these was the August 1996 Iran–Libya Sanctions Act. In the same March talk in which Albright admitted mistakes in past U.S. policy toward Iran, she explained that this sanctions bill had two objectives. One was a desire to prevent Iran from developing nuclear technology. It is to be noted that during Khatami's tenure the Iranian government had worked hard to improve transparency in its effort to develop nuclear energy. The other U.S. goal was to get Iran to stop financing and supporting terrorist groups, including those violently opposed to the Middle East peace process. This latter goal was a long-standing United States' demand and referred specifically to Iran's support for Israel's enemies, Hezbollah and Hamas.

In other words, Iranian cooperation on issues that an objective observer might see as reflecting American national interest—i.e., cooperation in Afghanistan, keeping the Shi'a population of Iraq from open rebellion, mutual agreement on the price and dispersal of oil supplies, and even some incremental movement in terms of the nuclear issue—was not sufficient for the establishment of normal relations with the United States. Indeed, shortly after Iran helped the United States expel the Taliban regime in Afghanistan, the Bush administration labeled Iran a member of the "Axis of Evil." The behavior that seems to have earned Iran its place on this "axis" was its failure to satisfy the needs of a powerful lobby within the United States, which had managed to make its special interest (support of Israel) the cornerstone of national interest in the Middle East.

Subsequently, Congress and the executive branch have strengthened sanctions against Iran so that it has become quite clear that the goal of Washington is regime change in Teheran. Now, surrounded by countries that host the troops and bases of a nation (the United States) that openly seeks to overthrow their government, the Iranian authorities are most likely working to obtain nuclear weapons capability as quickly as possible. From their perspective, the ability to possess such weapons must seem to be the best way of preventing an eventual American invasion.

The pro-Israel lobby has, of course, latched on to the issue of Iranian nuclear weapons as a major unsettling factor in today's Middle East. Both the lobby and the administration ignore Israel's own possession of over 100 nuclear warheads. These constitute weapons of mass destruction in the hands of a state that is inherently racist in its domestic treatment of non-Jews and is illegally colonizing Palestinian lands—both policies which an objective observer might well recognize as significant destabilizing behavior in the region. Nonetheless, on February 17, 2006, Secretary of State Condoleezza Rice declared that Iran, along with its "sidekick Syria," were the ones "destabilizing the Middle East."[9] Such a statement coming from a high ranking member of the executive branch does not reflect reality so much as the point of view of "special" interests of powerful lobbies.

After President Bush's 2002 "Axis of Evil" State of the Union speech, President Khatami came to the conclusion that American foreign policy had somehow been captured by a "radical warmonger" element that included America's pro-Israel lobby (Agence France Presse 2007; Fitchett, 2002). This element was willing to risk war in the Middle East to achieve American military control of parts of the region and also protect Israeli interests (Agence France Presse 2007; Fitchett, 2002). Today, it is hard to disagree with him.

Conclusion

The fact that important aspects of American foreign policy have essentially been turned over to lobbies, and has led the United States to pursue increasingly disastrous policies reflecting parochial interests, should be called to public attention. Indeed, it should be made the subject of a national debate. How is foreign policy presently constructed? Whose interests does the process presently serve? What should "national interest" really mean? Is there some obligation that it be tied to "national values"? What are our "national values"? Are they reflected in or contradicted by the influential special interests that now shape much of foreign policy? The list of questions that need answers goes on and on.

Unfortunately, for such a debate to take place the population must leave off its natural inclination both to localism and to reliance on mass media sources of news. At present most of the traditional information outlets are indifferent to undertaking any systematic examination of the role special interests play in U.S. foreign policy dilemmas. Nor does the average citizen yet look beyond his or her traditional sources of information.

But conditions might change so as to allow a successful demand for a broad review of foreign policy. Unfortunately, that means conditions changing for the worse (for instance, the country finding itself bogged down in multiple wars leading to public outrage over the rapid increase in American casualties), for it seems to be one of the tragedies of the human condition that only disaster produces serious questioning of long standing government policies by the general population. And, even if things deteriorate in this fashion, the special interest lobbies which now have such a negative influence on policy can be expected to defend their vested interests with misinformation and obfuscation. Within a "closed information environment" such tactics have worked well for them and may continue to do so.

It also should be noted that there are quite possible disasters that might act to further entrench the powers that be, rather than call their policies into question. For instance, the longer present policies are adhered to the more likely it is that the United States will suffer another 9/11 style attack. That is the sort of disaster that will certainly magnify present anti-Islamic paranoia and allow the government to shut down all criticism as if it were high treason, while simultaneously mobilizing the nation for further war in the Middle East.

Thus, the United States appears to be caught between Scylla and Charybdis. We are in a race to see what sort of disaster will befall us first—the type that will likely entrench the powers that be, or the type that may stimulate questioning and possible change. Either way, more foreign policy misfortunes are in the forecast.

Notes

Note: an earlier and longer version of this paper first appeared in 2006 in the journal *Middle East Policy*, XIII(2), 134-147.

1. For a more positive assessment of American attitudes toward foreign affairs, see the Chicago Council on Foreign Affairs 2012 survey of U.S. popular opinion entitled, "Foreign Policy in the New Millennium" on line at http://www.thechicagocouncil.org/UserFiles/File/ Task%20Force%20Reports/2012_CCS_Report.pdf

2. As the political scientist Ole Holsti put it "...elite political beliefs are in fact more highly structured than those of the general public." This contributes to the assumption that "the general public will have little or no influence [in shaping foreign policy] and will play a role primarily as the target of elite manipulation." (see Ole Holsti, 2004, pp. 127 and 160. For a similar, but far more detailed, interpretation of this process see Edward S. Herman and Noam Chomsky, *Manufacturing Consent: The Political Economy of the Mass Media*, p. 2. They put forth a "propaganda model" to describe that function of the mass media that "filters" the news and relies on "information provided by government, business and 'experts' funded and approved by these sources and agents of power."

3. In the hotly contested 2004 presidential election, 59.6% of eligible voters turned out at the polls. Historically, this was a relatively high percentage for Americans. The U.S. ranks 139th out of 172 democratic countries in voter turnout according to the Federal Election Commission. Winning politicians tend not to bother too much about the percentages of eligible voters voting. As Tom Stoppard once put it, "it's not voting that's democracy, it's the counting" (1972, "Act 1").

4. The standard studies of American foreign policy tend to see "domestic political conflict" as but one of an array of inputs into the foreign policy process. And, some of them assert that the result is a debate that "can facilitate a more thorough consideration of the issues." See Bruce W. Jentleson, *American Foreign Policy: The Dynamics of Choice in the 21st Century* (New York, NY: W.W. Norton, 2000, p. 27). The problem with this assessment is that it assumes a decision maker, standing independent of the interest

groups, and capable of objectively assessing conflicting arguments. It also fails to take into consideration the fact that, for all practicable purposes, the debates end when, and if one interest group achieves political dominance.

5. See "Who Owns the Media?" at http://www.freepress.net/content/ownership. The most notorious example is the extensive media and publishing empire of Keith Rupert Murdoch. His News Corporation owns newspapers on three continents and all of them uniformly support the Israeli and neo-conservative interpretation of events in the Middle East.

6. Another important source of information for people is informal personal communication with peer groups. See "Where do people get their information?" ACE Project Encyclopaedia Version 1.0. Retrieved from http://aceproject.org/main/english/me/meb01.htm

7. See the Zogby International poll report, "How Arabs View America" (June, 2004). Speculative talk by some U.S. leaders about developing a pro-American "third way" for Middle East politics (a way leading to something other than oppressive secular dictatorship and Islamic governments) is really beyond America's ability to manufacture. See Shibley Telhami, "In the Middle East, the Third Way is a Myth" in *The Washington Post*, February 17, 2006.

8. Part of the Zogby poll cited in footnote 7 shows that a majority of the Arabs do not believe that the U.S. government is really pushing for democracy in their region. They also feel that, since the United States invaded Iraq, the Middle East has become less democratic rather than more so.

9. Testimony given before the Senate Foreign Relations Committee.

PART THREE

Civilizational and Sectarian Cooperation and Conflict

Just when Egyptians were hoping that their uprising and the downfall of the Mubarak autocratic regime would unify their country, religious and sectarian strife began to rear its ugly head. Church burnings, the killing of fellow Egyptians who happen to be the minority Copts or Shi'a, and disputes over the use of certain phrases in the new constitution brought to surface long suppressed hostilities between some of the religious extremists on all sides. The removal of Saddam Hussein by the American forces brought about the domination of the Shi'a majority over the once ruling Sunni minority and what amounted to a civil war and ethnic cleansing in certain Iraqi towns and neighborhoods. In Bahrain, the majority Shi'a population is controlled and mistreated by the Sunni minority ruling class. The Shi'a uprising in Bahrain was quickly put down by the GCC's Peninsula Shield forces spearheaded by the Saudi monarchy to prevent a similar uprising from spreading to neighboring GCC sheikhdoms and kingdoms, some with relatively large Shi'a population.

While there are predictions that there will be an inevitable "clash of civilizations" between the Muslim world and the West, Dr. Amitai Etzione contends that there are many opportunities for constructive dialog between the two that can bridge the cultural divide. As an advocate of constructive inter-faith dialog, particularly on social justice, he suggests that the West "is more likely to be able to move from a position of exhortation to one of genuine dialogue—and from a position of assumed moral superiority to one closer to moral parity—if it would pay much more attention to socioeconomic rights." Dr. Etzione attempts to show the intense support in several well-founded interpretations of Islam and in the programs of key Islamic movements and political parties (although they much more often referred to as elements of social justice rather than as rights). He concludes that the West—and in particular the United States—has much more to *learn* and less to *teach* in this socioeconomic realm, as compared to the political/civil one. Etzione proposes a cross-cultural dialog on social justice as a promising starting point for productive intercultural dialog.

Dr. Andrew Wender explores the role of sectarianism, especially in locations sensitive to previous historical conditions (like Lebanon) and whether it is a particularly modern phenomenon, or a more universal human historical experience. He inquires whether religious sectarianism is a real, distorted, or purely imagined dimension of the historical and contemporary Middle East, utilizing an analysis of how Sunni-Shi'a sectarianism is conceived in opposing ways. Wender concludes that inflammatory caricatures of sectarianism should be eschewed, as sectarianism may in fact reflect basic differences in human identity that command respect.

Dr. Paul S. Rowe investigates Egyptian Christian–Muslim relations in the wake of the Arab Spring. Dr. Rowe asserts that while Egyptian Copts participated in large numbers in the protests that brought about regime change in February 2011, the broader implications of the revolution to Egyptian Copts were then unclear, but the recent events of August 2013 revealed a tragic twist that threatens the shaky relations between the minority Copts and majority Muslims in Egypt. Rowe addresses the changes in Christian–Muslim relations that attended the development of a new republican regime in Egypt. While the former regime of President Hosni Mubarak had formed a stable elite partnership with the hierarchy of the Coptic Orthodox Church (a "neo-millet" system), the 2011 revolution contributed to the erosion of this partnership in favor of a republican and pluralist model of citizenship in which individual Copts represent their own interests. Rowe is in agreement with Davidson's statement in which he declared that "…the increasingly assertive public role of lay movements among Copts, coupled with the death of the Coptic Patriarch (pope) and his replacement by a younger successor, points to the continued erosion of the elite partnership in favor of the new model." Time will tell whether or not pluralist representation or a retrenched corporatism that favors the church will dominate Christian–Muslim relations in Egypt in the future.

In their study of violent conflict in tribal areas of Pakistan Drs. Zia and Hameed argue the difficulty in reducing the vulnerability of vulnerable populations in complex adaptive systems that for decades have been marred by violent conflict. They present findings from their field research and interviews in Pakistan's tribal areas afflicted with intense conflicts since 1979. They present a conflict map depicting different stakeholder groups in the tribal areas from the perspective of indigenous tribes, and demonstrate the complex politics of conflict that indigenous tribesmen have endured while transitioning from one conflict (1980s war against Russia) to another (2000s war against the Taliban).

The historical analysis of the Iranian Euro-American relations, as presented by Maysam Behravesh examines the relations between Iran and Britain during the reigns of Margaret Thatcher and Ayatollah Khomeini, and how these relations are impacting present day foreign policy for both Iran and the UK. Behravesh tries to offer an in-depth political analysis of the salient factors and developments that informed the bilateral relationship in a span of over 10 years since Iran's 1979 revolution. The main issues he explores consist of the American hostage crisis and its impact upon Anglo-Iranian relations, the Iran–Iraq War and its implications for Tehran's relations with London, and finally Khomeini's execution *fatwa* against Salman Rushdie and its political impact at home and abroad. Behravesh's paper demonstrates that a fundamental conflict of interests and ideologies as well as consequential mis-perceptions of one type or another served to deeply bedevil Anglo-Iranian relations during the period, creating a chill ground of tensions whose legacy lasts to date.

Socioeconomic Rights: A Dialogue with Islam

Amitai Etzioni

Abstract

There are some who believe that there will be an inevitable "clash of civilizations" between the Muslim world and the West. By contrast, this paper contends that there are many opportunities for constructive dialogue between the two that can bridge the cultural divide. Specifically, the paper proposes a cross-cultural dialogue on social justice as a promising starting point for productive intercultural exchanges. The paper discusses the rich tradition of social justice in the Muslim world, and the ways in which these Islamic tenets are by a range of Islamist political parties, including Turkey's Justice and Development Party (AKP), Morocco's Justice and Development Party (PJD), and Tunisia's Ennahda Movement. Given the West's relative dearth of mainstream social justice parties, the paper proposes that, on this count, it has much to learn from the Muslim world.

Introduction

The West has urged the Muslim world to adopt democratic norms and institutions, and to protect human rights with new intensity since the Arab Awakening. In this context, it has focused exclusively upon political and civil rights. This chapter suggests that the West can move from a position of exhortation to one of genuine dialogue—and from a position of assumed moral superiority to one closer to moral parity—if it pays much more attention to socioeconomic rights. These rights (although they much more often referred to as elements of social justice rather than as rights) I will try to show in the following pages, find intense support in several well-established interpretations of Islam and in the programs of key Islamic movements and political parties. Moreover, the West—and in particular the United States—has much more to *learn* and less to *teach* in this socioeconomic realm, as compared to the political/civil one. In these transnational moral dialogues, the West often grounds its defense of rights in the UN Universal Declaration of Human Rights (UNDHR), a document endorsed by both Western and Muslim nations. It should be noted, however, that the UNDHR includes both kinds of rights and does not grant one particular category of rights a higher standing than another.

One may argue that the very concept of human rights (of any kind) is alien to Islam because the faith is centered on God as opposed to the individual, which is the focus of liberalism. Islam's fundamental claim is that "there is No God but God." However, many other religions center around God, yet still allow and even promote the notion of individual human rights. Several scholars, for example, have pointed out that the modern concept of universal human rights has deep roots in the Judeo-Christian tradition (Pryor, 2011). In both Judaism and Christianity the idea that humans possess inherent dignity comes from the Biblical claim that men and women were "created in the image of God" (Genesis 1:27). Human equality before God is reinforced by the New Testament, in which St. Paul tells the Galatians, "There is neither Jew nor Greek, there is neither bond nor free, there is neither male nor female: for ye are all one in Christ Jesus" (Galatians 3:28; Bielefeldt, 2000). These humanitarian motifs were developed in the European tradition of natural law, which found expression in the United States' founding documents. That men are "endowed by their Creator with certain unalienable Rights" assumes a source of human dignity that belongs to the individual prior to any man-made legislation and regardless of religious or political association.

Islam, Edward Said (1979) held, is open to the same interpretation.[1] "In Islam, as in the other religious traditions, human rights are concerned with the dignity of the individual, the level of self-esteem that secures personal identity and promotes human community. The religion of Islam establishes a social order designed to enlarge freedom, justice and opportunity for the perfectibility of human beings. It also defines political, economic and cultural processes designed to promote these goals" (p. 63).

Social Justice in Muslim Texts

All religious texts (and most secular ones) are open to a variety of interpretations. Hence, any statements such as "…according to Islam" or "the Koran states…" are subject to challenges. Therefore, the following observations should be read as if each were preceded with the statement, "According to some highly-regarded interpretations of Islam…"

With that disclaimer aside, it is first worth noting that Islam puts a strong emphasis on the religious importance of redistribution of wealth to the poor. One of the five "pillars" of Islam is a religious obligation to help those in need, an obligation that takes the form of an alms tax called *zakat* (Dean & Khan, 1997).[2] A communitarian may argue that zakat is a communal responsibility and not a matter of individual rights. A person is obligated to attend to the poor as part of his commitments to God, as both a true believer and as a religious person in good standing (Said, 1979).

However, Muslim scholars directly counter such an understanding by pointing out that "*Zakat* is not only the duty of those with disposable wealth, it is the right of those in need. The *Qur'an* itself (51:19) says 'And in their wealth is the right of him who asks, and him who is needy.' It is argued that *Zakat* is the right of the community on the wealth of individuals, just as prayer is the right of God on all Muslims" (Said, 1979, p. 198).

Defining zakat as a right as opposed to an expression of charity is highly consequential in that it empowers the underprivileged and allows them to accept its benefits without a loss of dignity or pride, according to Timur Kuran (Bonner, Ener, & Singer, 2003). However, the *Qur'an* also points out that according to the doctrine of zakat, there are groups other than the poor who are its designated recipients, including those who collect zakat, recent converts, and people fighting for God. Moreover, zakat is not generally held to require egalitarian outcomes; indeed, the *Qur'an* does not specify how zakat is to be allocated among these various groups (Bonner, Ener, & Singer, 2003, p. 278). Other scholars report that this vagueness has historically been used by the leaders of Islamic states to grant more to the poor than to other groups by assigning them a greater share (Ahmad & Mohamad, 2012, p. 198). It should also be noted that the same holds for Western secular interpretations of socioeconomic rights: all are entitled to them; yet respecting those rights is generally not viewed as requiring equality (which is advocated on different grounds). However, in practice, the poor tend to be privileged here as well.

The spiritual significance of zakat is reflected in the *Qur'an*'s depiction of this act as a method for purifying the self. The *Qur'an* contains multiple examples, wherein feeding the poor is mentioned as a method for expiating a sin and for purifying one's possessions and wealth (Bonner, 2005). For example, "When they ask you what they should expend, say: Whatever you expend in charity [*ma anfaqtum min khayr*] should be for your parents [*waldayn*], your kinfolk [*al-aqrabun*], the orphans [*al-yatama*], the poor [*al-masakin*] and the traveler [*dhawi el-sabeel*]. God is all-knowing regarding what you give in charity" (Bonner, 2005, p. 400).

In addition to zakat, there is a further mandate for charitable giving under Islam called *sadaqa*. While zakat is obligatory and required of all Muslims, sadaqa is an additional, supererogatory form of giving that, while not qualifying as a duty, is expected of the virtuous Muslim (Said, Abu-Nimer, & Sharify-Funk, 2006). Thus, the *Qur'an* "repeatedly recommends the giving of sadaqa, understood as charity in a broad sense," to the same groups who are eligible to receive zakat, as well as one's close family members (Singer, 2006).

The *Qur'an* also has much to say about procedural questions of fairness and non-exploitation. These economic prescriptions have been explored in depth by Qur'anic scholars who, over the past 50 years, have attempted to integrate these Islamic economic principles with modern economic scholarship (Kuran, 1989, p. 171). In "Economic Justice in Contemporary Islamic Thought," Timur Kuran extensively catalogues their conclusions. He stresses that the Islamic precept of economic justice rests upon the twin principles of fairness and equality (Kuran, 1989, p. 172). With respect to the latter, he emphasizes that the principle of equality forbids gross inequalities in the distribution of goods:

> … 'moderate' inequality is acceptable, but 'extreme' inequality is ruled out. A society would not be considered properly Islamic if it allowed some of its members to live in luxury while others eked out an impoverished existence. (Kuran, 1989, p. 172)

Kuran further explores this commitment to limit inequality by pointing to a number of Islamic injunctions about which there is widespread consensus in contemporary scholarly work on Islamic economics. These include not merely zakat, but also "the Islamic law of inheritance, which spreads a deceased person's wealth among all his immediate relatives"—a law that "serves the principle of equality by interrupting the growth of family estates" (Kuran, 1989, p. 173). Further, Kuran lists a series of injunctions mandating private charity and discouraging the sort of wanton accumulation of wealth that might lead to greater inequality. Admittedly, the language is not strictly one of socioeconomic rights, but the moral injunctions are similar enough in kind to be relevant to this paper's thesis.

With respect to questions of procedural fairness and moral economic behavior, Kuran finds consensus in the literature regarding an "obligation to behave altruistically—that is, to demonstrate an unselfish concern for others' welfare" (Kuran, 1989, p. 174). This obligation is manifested in a number of procedural requirements, including the assurance that consumers are fully informed about the nature of what they are buying and, most importantly, a prohibition on charging interest on loans and profiting from selling insurance (Kuran, 1989, p. 174).

Some scholars note that Islam is not alone in its commitment to social justice, as all major religions emphasize social justice and the related concerns of charity and welfare (Harrigan, 2009). However, Jane Harrigan and Hamed el-Said point out that Islam stands out among other religious belief systems, with over 1,000 mentions of "justice" in the *Qur'an* alone (Harrigan & el-Said, 2009, p. 18). Moreover, there is no question that social justice is accorded much more weight than civil and political rights, given the few meager references that can be interpreted as supportive of the latter.

In contrast, civil and political rights are granted primacy in the West—and especially in the United States. Unlike many European countries, the U.S. has no major socialist, social democratic, or labor-oriented party pressing for the recognition of such rights. In addition, the U.S. is one of only six UN member states to have failed to ratify the International Covenant on Economic, Social and Cultural Rights and, in 2010 had "one of the poorest records of economic and social rights achievement of all high-income countries" according to the Center for Economic and Social Rights (Center for Social and Economic Rights, 2013; Piccard, 2010). In fact, some prominent Western rights advocates such as Aryeh Neier, former Executive Director of Human Rights Watch and National Director of the ACLU (American Civil Liberties Union), deny that socioeconomic rights should be considered human "rights" at all (Nathan, 2012). Rather, these rights are often cast as "positive rights" whose corresponding duties might infringe upon individuals' liberty—as opposed to less-demanding "negative" political rights that merely require that individuals to refrain from certain actions (Narveson, 2001).

Although the United States and Western Europe do have fairly expansive welfare-state programs in place, it is not clear that such programs represent a recognition of socioeconomic rights. For example, the move from "welfare" to "workfare" across the Western world renders many economic benefits conditional; even a basic standard of living is not guaranteed by virtue of inherent rights, but, rather, is conceded only insofar as individuals fulfill some obligation of labor—an arrangement that is much closer to a private contract than state-sponsored entitlement (Handler, 2004, p. 2).

Such reluctance in the West to take socioeconomic rights seriously provides an additional reason why social justice would make a good starting point for a dialogue between Islam and the West. In addition, by engaging the Muslim world in dialogue, we might bring a new perspective to the long-standing quarrel between the communitarian left and the neoliberal right. For, as Hartley Dean and Zafar Khan note, "To the left it is the market which corrodes freedom and altruism; to the right it is the state; for Islam it is not a question of freedom or altruism but of faith" (Dean & Khan, 1997, p. 207).

Social Justice in Action

The texts here discussed speak volumes about values and norms, but also raise questions about the extent to which such religious mandates translate into actual actions on the part of adherents (Pepinsky & Welbourne, 2011). To examine the intersection between Islam's emphasis on social justice and political life in the Arab world, it is useful to consider the prominent role of "Islamism" (defined by political scientist Sheri Berman as "the belief that Islam should guide social and political as well as personal life") and the place of social justice in politicized Islam (Berman, 2003).

Islamism is reported to have emerged as a way to contest the decline of historically Islamic communities and the perceived depravity of secularism and the West that seemed to be taking its place (Adib-Moghaddam, 2012). Major Islamist figures view Islam, not as a private spiritual endeavor, but as "a revolutionary concept and a way of life, which seeks to change the prevalent social order and remold it according to its own vision" (Adib-Moghaddam, 2012). This Islamist commitment to transform the tenets of Islam into social practice is evidenced in the extensive network of charitable organizations run by both mosques and political parties, in particular the various offshoots of the Muslim Brotherhood, including Hamas and Hezbullah. As Harrigan and el-Said (2009, p. 15) report:

> Faith-based, particularly Islamic, social welfare programmes and provisions in the Arab World have outdone, outperformed, and, in some cases run by far the size of official safety nets provided by their states. Over the past two decades, there has been an exponential growth in the size and extent of voluntary, charitable and other 'acts of mercy' by Islamic associations in the Arab World.

They note that while mosques have long been deeply involved in the provision of charitable redistribution and social services, the past decades have witnessed a dramatic expansion of these activities (Harrigan & el-Said, 2009, p. 21).

The Muslim Brotherhood serves as an umbrella organization with subsidiaries throughout the Arab world dedicated to charitable distribution of social services (Harrigan & el-Said, 2009, p. 21). In Egypt for instance, the Muslim Brotherhood has long been "particularly active in the area of healthcare and education, running schools, hospitals, day care centres, job training centers, after school programmes, Koranic instruction and other services" (Harrigan & el-Said, 2009, p. 104). In addition to this wide network of hospitals, schools and social networks, the Muslim Brotherhood also has a large collection of professional syndicates in Egypt through which it distributes goods and services to a broad swath of the population (Harrigan & el-Said, 2009, p. 104).

The extensive welfare provisioning by the Muslim Brotherhood and its affiliates in Jordan, Gaza, and elsewhere in the Arab world are—at least in areas where private giving is not heavily suppressed—comparable to what the Muslim Brotherhood provides in Egypt (Harrigan & el-Said, 2009, p. 56).

Some have argued that providing social services is a powerful organizational device used to gain the support of the faithful for the Muslim Brotherhood's political agenda.[3] Representatives of the Muslim Brotherhood themselves have pointed out that although they are motivated by compassion and the *Qur'an*, providing social services is a very effective way to win votes.[4] Whatever the motivation, the fact is that charity is not merely preached, but practiced on a very considerable scale. Thus, socioeconomic rights—though sometimes cast more in the language of social justice—are honored to a significant extent, even in places where political and civil rights are shortchanged.

As Philip Nel reports, in areas where Islam is prevalent, there has been greater historical effort to curb economic inequality with tangible results (Shogimen & Nederman, 2009). He finds that between 1950 and 2000 (once one controls for income level), countries where Islam was the dominant religion were 50% less likely to be characterized by high income inequality than similarly-situated non-Muslim-majority nations (Shogimen & Nederman, 2009). Additionally, further evidence suggests that these relatively high levels of equality were likely the direct result of Islamic social welfare initiatives. For example, Jane Harrigan (2009) reports that in Tunisia, Egypt, Jordan, and Morocco strong "social contract arrangements" such as the "free provision of health and education and extensive subsidies on food and utilities" helped to keep poverty levels low—as low as 3% in Jordan and, by 2000, 4% in Tunisia.

Social Justice and Muslim Political Parties

Several political parties in the Muslim world reflect their supporters' commitment to social justice in both the names they choose to characterize themselves and in the platforms they develop. Like other political parties, their motives are mixed and there is a considerable gap between their exhortations and their actual agendas. Nevertheless, the difference between their public face and the ones presented by American political parties is itself revealing. Thus, while several major Muslim parties chose to define themselves as parties of Justice and Development, no major democratic party in the West defines itself in this way, i.e., leading with a commitment to economic development and social justice.

Among the parties in the Muslim world that follow the above-stated pattern is Turkey's Justice and Development Party (AKP). According to the party's founder, Recep Tayyip Erdoğan, the mention of "development" in the title of the party reflected the need to address the unemployment that was plaguing the country (Heper & Sule,

2003). Thus, according to scholars Ziya Öniş and E. Fuat Keyman, the AKP's commitment to development rejects neoliberal beliefs in favor of reaffirming the importance and centrality of social justice to development:

> The AKP does not see the question of social justice as an indirect problem that will be solved when the primary challenge of economic growth has been met. To bolster its case, the AKP adopts its own version of the logic of indirectness by arguing that promoting fairness and equal respect is an oblique but effective way to foster the widespread social trust that every sophisticated modern economy requires. (Öniş & Keyman, 2003, p. 101)

The party endorses a commitment to social justice in its manifesto, wherein it states that, "It is unavoidable to introduce a concept of a Social State, which cares for unemployed, poor, needy, ill and handicapped people and which allows them to live in a way that [is] commensurate with human honor" (Justice and Development Party, 2013). It is an ethos of social justice that is directly tied to faith, as underlined by Erdoğan's claim that "service to people is service to God" (Akan, 2011, p. 373).

Moreover, the party has taken a number of concrete steps towards helping the poor via the provision of government services (Öniş & Keyman, 2003, p. 24). Unlike other parties that tend to ratchet up the provision of social services prior to elections in order to win votes, the AKP has continuously provided and encouraged assistance for the poor (Öniş & Keyman, 2003, p. 24). Under AKP governance, poverty rates declined by 9.2% from 2002 to 2007, social expenditures steadily increased, and the difference between the lowest and highest income groups decreased by 0.6% (Akan, 2011, p. 373). The party also worked to expand private charity, providing tax cuts to companies that contributed to poverty alleviation efforts, and facilitated expanded social service provisioning by civil society organizations (Akan, 2011, p. 374). Admittedly, the party's ideology is more mixed than the above might lead one to believe (Taşpınar, 2012). As Taner Akan notes, "rather than being clear-cut, [the AKP's approach to welfare] has a changeable character that drifts between egalitarianism and pragmatism" (Akan, 2011, p. 379).

Another example of politicized Islam can be found in Morocco's Justice and Development Party (PJD). Much like the Turkish Justice and Development Party which the PJD takes as its inspiration, the name of the PJD reflects the economic and social values of Islam—a move intended to distinguish the party from its modern secular rivals who tend to emphasize "freedom" and "progress" in their titles (Haqqani & Fradkin, 2008; Knickmeyer, 2007). Also, much like the AKP, the PJD has a platform favoring economically moderate policies, with a specific focus on improving welfare and reducing poverty through growth-conducive policies coupled with employment and anti-poverty programs (Saif & Abu Rumman, 2012). This orientation towards social justice is further revealed by the fact that the PJD has campaigned repeatedly on the promise of better addressing poverty in the country (Willis, 2004, p. 66). For example, in the 2007 elections, it put social justice at the forefront of its campaign with its slogan "Together Build a Just Morocco" (Hamzawy, 2007).

When it comes to actual governance, the PJD has passed a number of initiatives intended to help the poor and unemployed, including subsidies, hiring initiatives, and wage increases for the public sector (Arieff, 2012). The PJD has also taken principled stands against economic policies that come into conflict with Islamic prohibitions on exploitative economic practices. For example, the PJD opposed a micro-credit scheme on the grounds that it would have charged interest on the money it loaned out (Willis, 2004, p. 56). In addition, reports suggest that a considerable number of party members are involved in charitable work (Harrigan & el-Said, 2009, p. 140). However, the high level of government price subsidies is cited as a reason the PJD has found it difficult to significantly expand social services (Arieff, 2012, p. 11; Harrigan & el-Said, 2009).

The guiding document of Tunisia's Islamist *Ennahda* Party's guiding document affirms that while "every person is entitled to the fruits of his own labor …he is also entitled to have his basic needs met under all conditions" (Saif and Abu Rumman, 2012). It is a pro-social justice sentiment reiterated by its leader, Rachid Al-Ghannouchi, who has stated: "I believe that we must adopt the form of social democracy practiced in Sweden and the other Scandinavian states. Economics must be dominated by social values and not simply the aggressive forces of the free market" (Saif & Abu Rumman, 2012). Observers report that these principled stances are reflected in the party's promise to help the unemployed by providing free medical insurance and a 50% discount on public transportation for all those seeking employment (Saif & Abu Rumman, 2012). In addition, Ennahda is currently drafting a bill to promote the creation of Islamic banks—institutions which operate in accordance with the principles laid out in the *Qur'an* and Islamic economics (Amara, 2012).[5] The high regard Islam accords to social justice relative to political rights is illustrated by a description of the revolution that ushered the Ennahda Party to power in Tunisia during the Arab Spring uprisings in 2011. In an interview with the Council on Foreign Relation's co-founder, Rachid Al-Ghannouchi denied that there was any ideological motivation beyond a demand for basic human rights. However, he described these rights as follows:

> These revolutions did not have a leader, so there were no picture [sic] of any leader during these revolutions, nor did they carry any ideological slogans. The only slogans were slogans that were asking for human dignity and human rights, basic rights: employment, dignity and democracy. (Council on Foreign Relations, 2011)

This list, which leads with employment—a socioeconomic right—and lists democracy last, sharply contrasts with similar promulgations that appear in the West, especially in the United States, where civil and political rights are treated as "self-evident" while socioeconomic rights are the subject of a great deal of controversy.

The purpose of the preceding lines is not to assess the extent to which these parties truly live up to their public statements and platforms—few do. At the same time, clearly something more than lip service is found. Moreover, what parties choose to present as their public face reveals what they take their current and potential followers to hold dear. Clearly, social justice ranks high from this viewpoint among Muslims, akin to the role of liberty and democracy, and the attending political and civil rights, in the West, and in particular in the United States.

Dialogue vs. Clash of Civilizations

Several scholars—most famously Samuel Huntington in his *Clash of Civilizations*—have argued that the modern concept of universal human rights is essentially the heritage of the West, with deep roots in the Judeo-Christian tradition.

Moreover, Huntington gained widespread notoriety with his argument that Western civilization is superior to all others, and that it is bound to clash with all other belief systems, in particular with that of Islam. In contrast, the reformers in Iran founded a center deliberately named the *Dialogue Among Civilizations*, in whose meetings the author participated and which led to this inquiry in addition to a previous major work. In this preceding work (Etzioni, 2007), the author sought to show that there is a dividing line that cuts across all civilizations rather than among them, separating those who advocate and legitimize violence and those who reject it. The author showed that terrorists and crusaders who legitimize violence can be found in all civilizations—and not just in the Islamic one—just as there are those who reject the use of force and favor non-violent advocacy (Etzioni, 2007, p. 87). For example, Christians have a history of both pacifism (as exemplified by the Quakers) and violence, ranging from the crusades to the harsh punishments inflicted upon heretics and blasphemers (Etzioni, 2007, p. 103). It is a divide that reflects the dual portrayal of Christ in the New Testament as a shepherd sacrificing his life for his sheep (John 10:11), and as a wrathful conqueror striking down sinners with his sword and ruling with an iron rod (Revelation 19:15). Jews have been similarly divided, with some interpreting "an eye for an eye, a tooth for a tooth" (Exodus 21:24) as an exhortation for violent revenge, while others interpret it as a requirement to provide monetary compensation to victims of violence (Etzioni, 2007, p. 114).[6] Moreover, he showed that the majority of Muslims favor nonviolence and hence, argued that if the West would approach the Muslim world along these lines—focusing initially on the individual right to live—it would find numerous reliable partners in peace (Etzioni, 2007, p. 89). However, if the focus of such Western engagement was on promoting the full array of political and civil rights, the support in the Muslim world will be much thinner (Etzioni, 2007, p. 140).

This article suggests another focal point for constructive dialogue with Muslim civilization: socioeconomic rights. Islam seems much more open to these than to political and civil rights—and the West has much more ground to cover before it properly sorts out the status of these rights in its own belief systems and, above all, in public policies. That is, the dialogue on socioeconomic rights is, on the face of it, less prone to one side casting itself as superior—a balanced arrangement much more conducive to the initiation of fruitful dialogue.

Conclusion

While parties that assert the importance of socio-economic rights have largely been marginalized in the West—and particularly in the United States—the Muslim world has granted the tenets of social justice on a high standing in public life. Grounded in Islamic texts and scholarship, socioeconomic rights have been codified in the platforms of major parties in several nations in the Middle East, and some have been transformed into practice.

Notes

1. This is perhaps to be expected given the significant overlap between the tenets of Islam and those of Judaism and Christianity. F. E. Peters discusses the commonalities of the three faiths in detail in his book: Peters, F. E. (2004). *The Children of Abraham: Judaism, Christianity, Islam*. Princeton, NJ: Princeton University Press.

2. As Timur Kuran has noted in an email exchange, *zakat* was not originally an alms tax, but funded all government programs and was the primary source of revenue for Islamic states. However, today it is understood as a tax that exists to fund charity.

3. Timur Kuran, for example, argues that the "Muslim Brotherhood combined charity with politics from the start," and that its "political and charitable activities have fed on each other." Timur Kuran, email message to the author, January 7, 2013.

4. Frederick Kunkle has also commented on the Muslim Brotherhood's charitable work and its impact on public political support for the Brotherhood (published in the *Washington Post*, 4 July, 2011).

5. However, as Timur Kuran has noted in an email exchange, although Islamic banks theoretically act in accordance with the tenets of Islamic Economics, no Islamic bank has found a way to do interest-free financing. It is not clear that this necessarily amounts to more than mere lip service.

6. With respect to the latter interpretation, see the Babylonian *Talmud*, Baba Kam 83b: "Does the Divine Law not say 'Eye for eye'? Why not take this literally to mean [putting out] the eye [of the offender]?—Let not this enter your mind, since it has been taught: You might think that where he put out his eye, the offender's eye should be put out, or where he cut off his arm, the offender's arm should be cut off, or again where he broke his leg, the offender's leg should be broken. [Not so; for] it is laid down, 'He that smiteth any man…' 'And he that smiteth a beast…' just as in the case of smiting a beast compensation is to be paid, so also in the case of smiting a man compensation is to be paid."

Re-approaching-Not Merely Reproaching-Religious Sectarianism within a Tumultuous Middle East

Andrew M. Wender

Abstract

Especially following the post-2010 Arab uprisings, today's Middle East is frequently represented by depicters—ranging from journalists, to scholars, to political actors—involved in regional struggles, as well as outside policymakers, as the site of bloody sectarian contestations. Beginning with a detailed illustration of how sectarianism in the Syrian conflict is framed in ways that signify complex and varied competing interests, perspectives, and identities, this paper then analyzes the contested idea of sectarianism, together with the root term from which it derives, "sect," in Middle East studies generally, and especially within the sub-discipline, sociology of religion. The paper explores usages and critiques of the concepts that both underscore their dark connotations of deviant as opposed to normative religious beliefs and practices, and encourage their being employed only in non-reductive fashions that are sensitive to historically specific conditions in locations like Lebanon; also, it asks whether sectarianism is a peculiarly modern phenomenon, or more universal human historical experience. Thereafter, this paper inquires whether religious sectarianism is a real, distorted, or purely imagined dimension of the historical and contemporary Middle East, utilizing an analysis of how Sunni–Shi'a sectarianism is conceived in opposing ways. Ultimately, it is concluded that inflammatory caricatures of sectarianism should be eschewed, as sectarianism may in fact reflect basic differences in human identity that command respect.

Introduction

For the sake of clarity, we begin with the need to re-examine the discursive specter of Middle Eastern sectarianism. The concept of "sectarianism," together with the root term from which it derives, "sect," looms as a dark, threatening motif pervading a multitude of media, scholarly, and political discourses that frame today's Middle East, both from within and outside the region. As such, these discourses act to perpetuate the notion that, especially in the wake of the post-2010 Arab uprisings, states and societies from Syria, to Egypt, to Iraq, and even beyond the Arab world itself, such as Pakistan, are marked by a new, acute inflammation of age-old, essential inter-communal hatreds in which Sunni and Shi'a, Muslim and Christian, Alawi and non-"heterodox" Muslim (van Dam, 2011, p. 17) regard one another as dangerous deviants. This paper seeks to re-examine the seeming ubiquitous specter of Middle Eastern sectarianism, asking, for one, whether the ways in which it is depicted—indeed, caricatured—might not exacerbate bloodshed in the service of contending political interests; moreover, does the reproachful representation of sectarianism legitimately capture the phenomenon's driving influences on the shaping of human history and identity, within the Middle East and beyond?

As a scholar like Ussama Makdisi (Makdisi, 2000, 2008) has illustrated with respect to Lebanon, the specific forms of sectarianism that have emerged in the modern Middle East attest to the pivotal roles played by colonial powers and local, post-colonial aspirants to political power in constructing communal identities that were positioned in rivalry with one another. Beyond this, such an analysis helps open a door to reveal the falsity of the modernist pretense that religious sectarianism within the Middle East embodies the atavistic "Other," so to speak, of enlightened modern, "Western" rationalism. If anything—as Shmuel Eisenstadt (1993; 1999; 2012) has helped exemplify with his analyses of sectarianism as a basic historical force that is, to no small degree, constitutive of human civilizations—modernity is as prone to sectarian impulses as any historical epoch—perhaps more so, given modernity's yearning quest for meaning. Ultimately, this paper suggests that the religious sectarianism now marking the Middle East may constitute neither a uniquely modern construct, nor a timeless essence, but rather, a natural manifestation of dynamic, ever-shifting human identities during a period of singular historical tumult.

A Closer Look at the Seeming Ubiquity of Sectarianism in Today's Middle East: The Telling Example of Syria

Amidst the churning fluidity of emerging, unforeseeable history, and violent contestations for power and identity that are today flowing from the Arab uprisings, an observer who tracks current news reporting and commentary, expert analysis, and policymakers' proclamations concerning the Middle East is bound to be struck by the message that "sectarianism" is a ubiquitous scourge across the region. Major media outlets embodying a broad spectrum of ideological orientations and political sympathies, based both within (e.g., *Al-Ahram,* Al-Jazeera, and Press TV), and outside the Middle East (e.g., *The New York Times, The Economist,* and *The Financial Times*), participate alongside an international organization like the United Nations (UN), a state actor like the Syrian government, and a myriad of individual analysts—from authors working within academe to independent bloggers (see, for instance, the website "Inside Sectarianism")—in constructing and propelling a train of discourse that depicts an expanse of territory from North Africa to south-central Asia as being fissured with sectarian divides and their bitter, typically bloody consequences. Certainly, this discourse has profound internal variability, in terms of the sheer diversity of locales and actors that are regularly referenced. For instance, among relevant states are countries at the epicenter of the Arab uprisings, such as Syria, Egypt, and Bahrain; others, Arab and non-Arab, whose geographic boundaries, internal dynamics, and geo-strategic interests are pivotally interlinked with the uprisings (e.g. Iraq, Saudi Arabia, Lebanon, Qatar, Turkey, and Iran); and states that are somewhat further removed, spatially, from the Arab world, yet inseparable from its constituent phenomena like Sunni–Shi'a relations. The latter includes countries such as Pakistan, or even Nigeria and Myanmar, where inter-religious and inter-ethnic animosities between Muslims and Christians, and Arakan Buddhists and Rohingya Muslims, respectively, are of keen significance for communities and governments that are more directly situated within the Middle East. Also evoked is a non-state entity like al-Qaeda, which the iconic British journalist Robert Fisk suggested to be—during November 2010, in an apt instance of timing immediately preceding the initial upheavals in Tunisia and Egypt—"one of the most sectarian organizations ever invented" (Fisk, 2010).

Continuing in this vein, the interpretive standpoints and motivating rationales informing differing actors' invocations of the concept of sectarianism can be vastly divergent; at the same time, there is a general shared tendency to treat the term, in one fashion or another, as a pejorative label. As an opening example—but one displaying qualities so singularly telling that they are useful to explore in detail at this point—consider the case of Syria. That country's extraordinarily complex, brutal, and thus far interminable civil conflict has crystallized, in many distinct manifestations of the local, regional, and global imaginations, as practically the quintessence of sectarianism. On the view of the UN, specifically its Human Rights Council, as expressed in a December 2012 update on the "unrelenting violence in Syria": "the Syrian conflict['s] devol[ution] from peaceful protests seeking political reform to a confrontation between ethnic and religious groups" indicates that "the conflict has become overtly sectarian in nature" (United Nations High Commissioner for Human Rights, 2012, pp. 1, 3). This state of affairs, asserted Chairman Paulo Pinheiro of the UN's Independent International Commission of Inquiry on Syria, owes to "human rights and humanitarian law violations" committed both by troops representing President Bashar al-Assad's government, and by al-Assad's diverse opponents. The Commission cited evidence of "Government forces and supporting militias attacking Sunni civilians, and reports of anti-Government armed groups attacking Alawites and other pro-Government minority communities [e.g., the 'Armenian Orthodox, other Christian, and Druze communities']" (United Nations Regional Information Centre for Western Europe, 2012; United Nations High Commissioner for Human Rights, 2012, p. 5). As the UN report further explains:

> …the sectarian lines fall most sharply between Syria's Alawite community, from which most of the Government's senior political and military figures hail, and the country's majority Sunni community who are broadly (but not uniformly) in support of the anti-Government armed groups. (United Nations High Commissioner for Human Rights, 2012, p. 4)

By comparison, around the time that the UN was completing its report, *The New York Times* (a journalistic source that some readers would describe as a newspaper of record) related in grave if evocative tones that the Syrian situation had emerged as the "unraveling of a society whose mix of sects, identities and traditions were held together by the yoke of a dictator" (Arango, 2012). As such, *The Times*'s cited "[a]nalysts fear this combustible environment could presage a bloody ethnic and sectarian conflict that will resonate far beyond Syria's borders…" (Arango, 2012). Subsequently, the often-maligned (in the view of Middle East affairs analysts like Fisk, Zackary Lockman, and Belén Fernández, who are critical of what they broadly regard as his reductive and establishmentarian apologias for neo-colonial power), but influential and much-quoted *Times* columnist Thomas Friedman has called for an internationally brokered "multisectarianism" to supersede what he implies as being the more perilous, existing sectarianism in Syria (Fisk, 2009, pp. 410, 418; Lockman, 2010, pp. 219–220; Fernandez, 2011; Friedman, 2013).

In contrast to the UN and *The Times*'s reportage, the Syrian state itself invokes the specter of sectarianism to lambaste those whom President al-Assad, in January 2013, derided as "'murderous criminals' and 'terrorists' financed by [states like] Qatar and Saudi Arabia with American blessing" (Barnard, 2013). As SANA (Syrian Arab News Agency) more recently attributed the country's Deputy Prime Minister for Economic Affairs as observing, "terrorist organizations, including [the 'Al-Qaida affiliated'] Jabhat al-Nusra, in Syria, [together with their supporters,]…want to stoke the sectarian conflict in Syria and the region" (Raslan & Sabbagh, 2013; Chulov, 2013). And from a pro-opposition point on the observational spectrum, in November 2012, a commentator for the Egyptian-based *Al-Ahram* was contemptuous of the al-Assad regime's "attempts to incite one group or sect against another," together with the government's "official rhetoric" "[h]urling accusations about the sectarian nature of the uprising" (Oudat, 2012). In fact, he argued:

> The Syrian people raised the torch of liberty because they believed the battle for freedom would be a social, political and economic one rather than a battle to make one sect dominate the others or create a religious state. Sectarianism in Syria, although seemingly linked to the ongoing crisis, is not a widespread phenomenon, and it does not undermine the unity of the Syrian people. When it rears its ugly head, it is based on local and circumstantial reasons that do not go beyond these specific incidents. (Oudat, 2012)

How is one to assess the relative meanings and significances conveyed by these contending applications of the idea, sectarianism, to the Syrian scenario? Is it true that the actions of either the Syrian regime, or others among the regime's arrayed opponents (or both) are responsible for causing or exacerbating inter-communal divides and conflicts in that country which might be accurately designated as sectarian? Connected with this, is it valid or appropriate to imply that some forms of religious belief, practice, and identity represented in Syria are normative, while others are somehow deviant and dangerous?

It would indeed be difficult to argue that sectarianism (which, paralleling Ussama Makdisi's important studies on the phenomenon's history in adjoining Lebanon, Nikolaos van Dam equates to the Arabic *ta'ifiyya* (translated as "acting or causing action on the basis of membership of a specific religious community")) is a new intrusion upon the Syrian state, society, or national consciousness (Makdisi, 2000; 2002; van Dam, 2011, p. 181). Historical inquiry amply demonstrates that, extending back to the period of Ottoman rule, and perhaps vastly earlier, to the intersecting genealogies of faiths, including Judaism, Zoroastrianism, Christianity, Islam, and Gnostic traditions, a juxtaposition and competition among "various religious communities" has been integral to the landscape (in every sense, from geographic to socio-cultural) in what is today Syria (Masters, 2004; Crone, 2012, p. 437; van Dam, 2011, p. 3). This being said, a watershed appears to have occurred during the 19th and early 20th centuries, when the Ottomans' millet system—which accorded a measure of autonomous political identity to Christians and Jews within the Sunni-dominated Ottoman Empire—met with the pressures of "political interference …by France, England and Russia, acting as self-appointed protectors of religious minorities" (van Dam, 2011, p. 3). When France's post-World War I colonial Mandate in Syria saw that particular empire decide to "deliberately [incite]" "sectarian loyalties… in order to prevent or suppress the rise of Arab nationalism," a chief consequence became the improbable, rising political fortunes of the Alawi community which is now so prominent in the country (van Dam, 2011, p. 4).

As for Alawi religious doctrine, it stems from the community's founder Ibn Nusayr (hence, the Alawis' having usually been referred to, prior to the 1900s, as Nusayris), who, hailing greater than a millennium ago from the area of present-day Iraq, initiated "a highly secretive syncretistic theology containing an amalgam of Neoplatonic, Gnostic, Christian, Muslim, and Zoroastrian elements" that found "refuge" in northwestern Syria (Ruthven, 2011a, p. 18). As such, the "Nusayri-'Alawi faith is an excellent example of a syncretistic esoteric religion with self-conscious elite who zealously guarded its sectarian literature…it fuses elements of cults and creeds…in a syncretistic system that is clothed in heterodox Shi'a garb" (Bar-Asher & Kofsky, 2012). Thus, it stands to reason that the Alawis ultimately transmuted their modern political authority into the secular socialist ideological form of Ba'thism, whose central role in conjuring contemporary Syrian nationhood is predicated, in significant measure, on preventing "political and socio-economic discrimination against non-Sunnis or, more particularly, against members of heterodox Islamic communities" (van Dam, 2011, p. 17). In turn, the ongoing regime of Bashar al-Assad and, previously, his father Hafiz, has long been viewed by some of its Sunni opponents as a "[sectarian]…pawn of neo-colonialist foreign interests that underwrite [the regime]" (Abd-Allah, 1983, p. 138). These opponents (particularly the Muslim Brotherhood lineage brutalized by Hafiz al-Assad at Hama in 1982) have a history of representing themselves as seeking "an Islamic state that will preserve the rights of all religious and ethnic minorities, prevent domination by any sect or ethnic division, and guarantee equal opportunity for all" (Abd-Allah, 1983, p. 138). However, within the practical setting of the current uprising, militant Sunni activism against the regime and its communal allies can assuredly be read as feeding "a horrid cycle of sectarian violence and hostility" (Dabashi, 2013b).

Ultimately, the Syrian scenario—invoking the notion of sectarianism as if it denotes an aberrant, recently occurring, or at least worsening condition that rational, well-intentioned actors would seek to treat—risks superimposing a problematic caricature of human motivations, and conceptions of identity; as a result, the term acts to hinder the nuanced understanding of multiple, contending perspectives on what is at stake in Syria, and, with this, the effective policy development that are necessary to help ameliorate conflict. Instead, if one allowed for the possibility that "passionate sectarian differences" (Akhtar, 2008, p. 331) over how humans engage with ultimate reality are not so much inherently abnormal, as they are a genuine, organic dimension of religious experience and organization, this allowance might better reflect deeply situated, inextricably intertwined, and profoundly held historical elements of human identity formation that can no more be reconceived as solvable problems than can other fundamentally existential quandaries. Alternatively, suppose one were to grant that "the idea of the [Syrian] nation itself is disappearing amid cycles of sectarian bloodshed" (Fahim & Saad, 2013, p. A1), and that new forms of socio-political consciousness may need to be imagined for where Syria had previously lain—which may prove to be the situation that is presently faced. This would merely renew the challenge of how such a re-imagining can be achieved without falling prey to the antagonizing notion that some among the collapsing country's diverse plurality of believers are pure, whereas others are heretical. In Syria, and elsewhere in today's tumultuous Middle East, it may be crucial to re-approach—not merely reproach—religious sectarianism. What ideas and further historical and contemporary illustrations might it be productive to explore for advancing this endeavor?

Contested Conceptualizations of Sectarianism, and its Root Term, Sect, in Middle East Studies

There exists a substantial body of literature describing and critiquing the idea of sectarianism, as well as the concept of sect from which it derives, that I draw on and allude to, rather than exhaustively cite or replicate in this paper. With respect to the applicability (or, as some analysts emphasize, the limited or dubious utility) of sectarianism to the historical and contemporary Middle East, examples of useful entry point into this literature include the following: a 2011 report and annotated bibliography prepared by the Governance and Social Development Resource Centre in the United Kingdom (Governance and Social Development Resource Centre, 2011); a series of articles in the *International Journal of Middle East Studies* responding to the question, "How Useful Has the Concept of Sectarianism Been for Understanding the History, Society, and Politics of the Middle East?" (Davis, 2008; Joseph, 2008; Makdisi, 2008; Peteet, 2008); and the country-specific research of scholars like Makdisi (2000, 2002) on Lebanon, van Dam (2011) on Syria, and Fanar Haddad (2011) on Iraq. On the whole, these sources underscore the dark connotations of sectarianism, whether it is evoked within the Middle East, or outside, yet with reference to the region. Thus, as Haddad explains:

> In Iraq, as elsewhere in the Middle East, the term 'sectarianism' is an irrevocably negative term. 'Sectarian', 'sectarianism', indeed even 'sect' often conjures images of repression, discrimination, division, treachery and weakness. As one Middle Eastern analyst lamented, sectarianism is so sensitive an issue that merely discussing it is, in itself, considered evidence of sectarian attitudes. (Haddad, 2011, p. 31)

In addition, authors caution against imprecise usages of the term, not least by academic and policy-oriented analysts, who would impute essential, religion-based societal fissures to a Middle East viewed, inferentially, through an Orientalist lens. Consistent with this, Haddad and others go on to elaborate how sectarianism must be viewed, on a case-by-case basis, as a varying embodiment of specific, historically constituted local conditions involving unique interplays among religion, ethnicity, language, geography, class, nationalisms, and further elements of "political climate" (Haddad, 2011, p. 31). Only in such a vein, Makdisi argues, can analysts surmount "the traditional Orientalist paradigm of sectarianism, which began crystallizing in the 19th century and has quite literally exploded following the events of 9/11":

> The Orientalist paradigm of sectarianism…is suffused with assumptions not only about Islam, the East, the Ottomans, Lebanon, and Iraq, but also with a core assumption about the liberalism of the West. To criticize the Orientalist paradigm of sectarianism—to question the notion of religious violence as an expression of immutable and atavistic religious solidarities in the East—we must take issue with not only what it says about the East but also what it assumes about the putatively "tolerant" West. (Makdisi, 2008, p. 560)

Makdisi's well-placed suspicion of those who would imagine sectarianism to be an ingredient timelessly planted in the soil of the Middle East, ready to spring forth in ever-appearing outgrowths from age-old holy wars, fits with his particular understanding of sectarianism in Lebanon as the modern product, during the mid to late 19th century and subsequently, of intersecting political ambitions on the part of imperial as well as local actors (Makdisi, 2000, 2008). In other words, in Makdisi's view, "sectarianism refers to the deployment of religious heritage as a primary marker of modern political identity" (Makdisi, 2000, p. 7). Moreover, Makdisi's analysis serves to underscore the inherent hypocrisy of the notion that the modern West somehow stands antithetical to sectarianism; as writers like John Gray have intimated, Western modernity is a category marked by nothing so much as its amalgamation of competing visions for worldly salvation, which amount to sects rendered in such ideological forms as communism and neo-liberalism (Gray, 2007).

Yet, ponder the implications of the idea that the modern, "Western" civilizational milieu associated with propagating Orientalism seems eminently prone to the very sorts of overlapping fissures of belief and socio-political identity that Orientalists ascribe to the civilizational milieus of the "East"; and the notion that these "Western" and "Eastern" sectarian fissures are in no small part constitutive of one another. Might this realization lend credence to the possibility that, within the context of modernity no less than other historical settings, sectarianism does in fact refer to a basic, variable human force linking the development and eventual splintering of worldviews with the transformational restructuring of politics, society, and other facets of civilization (see Eisenstadt, 1993; 1999)? This is Shmuel Eisenstadt's understanding of how—extending from the epoch of modernity, back into the first millennium BCE and early first millennium CE "Axial" civilizations (e.g., Judaism, Zoroastrianism, ancient Greece, and Christianity) in which modernity is genealogically grounded—sectarian tensions between "orthodoxy and heterodoxy" have acted as one of the most influential drivers of "revolutionary changes and transformations" in human history (Eisenstadt, 2012, p. 282). Eisenstadt's insights are revealing, especially, within the context of the scholarly sub-discipline that is most closely associated with the study of sects and sectarianism, the sociology of religion, and, as such, help to surmount the "pejorative coloring" that the Latin root *secta* (meaning "to follow") "did not [actually] acquire . . . for a long time" (Dubuisson, 2003, p. 73; Oliver, 2012, p. 12).

The now-classic—although quite distinctly modern, peculiarly Christian in its orientation, and by no means uncontested, or unrevised—sociological notion of sect traces to the early 20th century (pre-World War I) theorizing of figures including Max Weber and Ernst Troeltsch. This usage of the term rests on the idea of a dichotomy between church and sect, in which the former denotes a religious organization into which members are born, whereas the latter, arising from "schisms within churches," indicates a movement voluntarily joined by adults who have committed to an exclusive new path towards salvation (Dawson, 2009, p. 527; Weber, 1958 [1904–1905]). By the late 1920s, the ambiguities of the sect designation had begun to be suggested by the work of someone like H. Richard Niebuhr, who (albeit in the service of a passionate call for Christian unity) postulated a rapid, "second-generation" process by which "the sect [itself] becomes a church"; and, as well, began "popularizing the term 'denomination' to denote the more pluralistic realities of [specifically] religious life in America" (Niebuhr, 1987 [1929], p. 20; Dawson, 2009, p. 528). Soon thereafter, the word "cult" emerged to join church, sect, and denomination as a theoretical tool; the newest term served, above all, as a means for sociology of religion to signify religious groups that moved ever-further away from an established church, and towards a distinct "personal [form]" of religion (Dawson, 2009, pp. 528, 531). However, as cult and sect have become conflated, and imbued with shared normative content in the popular mind, if not in the minds of those who initially invoked the terms (in the case of "cult," the American sociologist Howard Becker) (Dawson, 2009, p. 528), the problematic implications for fair and accurate use of the idea, sectarianism, are made apparent.

Increasingly, the drawbacks associated with "church-sect-cult typologizing," from the inaptness of this paradigm to settings other than the predominantly Christian contexts that inspired it, to its manifest tendency towards differentiating between religious communities that are presumed to be normative and those that are not, have led contemporary religious studies scholars to be exceedingly cautious with, in particular, the terms sect and cult (Dawson, 2009, pp. 530–533). One approach has become to favor the phrase, New Religious Movements (NRMs), when one refers to the marked proliferation, in various locations around the world, of emerging religious communities and organizations since the 18th and 19th centuries (Oliver, 2012). Several among these NRMs show especial significance, with respect to contested applications of the idea, sect, in discourses surrounding the contemporary Middle East. One thinks, for instance, of the Baha'i Faith, which, having arguably stemmed from a messianic sect in 1800s Persian Shi'ism, continues to be referred to as an illegitimate sect and political adversary by its nemesis, the Islamic Republic of Iran; this, even as the Faith's development into a widespread world religion would seem to exemplify a sect-to-church growth pattern, along with political quietism (Dabashi, 2011, p. 266; Press TV, 2009; Sanasarian, 2006). Consider, as well, devout Jewish movements like the Lubavitch Hasidim, and the very recent (originating during the 1970s) but, socio-culturally, ideologically, and politically, highly influential *Gush Emunim* (Bloc of the Faithful) (Partridge, 2004, pp. 103–122). Each of these movements points to profound struggles within Israel, to say nothing of between Israel and Palestine, concerning the question of what versions of Judaism confer sovereign legitimacy—with sovereignty being envisioned, here, in the full, relevant range of complex and intersecting forms, from the theological, to the modern state sphere.

Is Religious Sectarianism a Real, Distorted, or Purely Imagined Dimension of the Historical and Contemporary Middle East?

The modern intellectual setting giving rise to sociology of religion, when read together with this paper's preceding discussions, could give the disorienting impression that we are addressing a phenomenon of relatively recent origins. It does seem to be the case that a panoply of modern historical factors may help to create exceptionally fertile ground for the growth of competing sectarian identities; this is underscored by studies of sectarianism ranging from overall scholarly analyses of the phenomenon, to Makdisi's account of its 1800s emergence amidst the landscape of Mount Lebanon, as Druzes and Maronites forged new embodiments of political consciousness against the backdrop of Ottoman-European colonial contestation (Makdisi, 2000). Indeed, in 1990, Bryan Wilson advanced the still-compelling, broadly-relevant argument that sectarianism's "growing…importance in contemporary society" may reflect the expression of humans' timeless quest for individual and communal meaning, in a modern epoch where such meaning has undergone, and continues to be subjected to, profound dislocation and transformation:

> The search for meaning, for fulfilling relationships, and for a distinctive mode of living which confers a sense both of belonging and of identity, has become a significant reaction to the encompassing impersonality of the often abrasive rationalization of modern life. (Wilson, 1990, p. v)

Notwithstanding the modern world's arguable propensity towards the cultivation of sectarianism, it is vital to call to mind the notion that sects may constitute an integral facet of humankind's religious life that cannot be ascribed, *a priori,* a good or bad normative value; and that sects may comprise a natural element of civilizations' historical development. Thus, in one possible view, that of a writer reflecting from the standpoint of comparative religion, rather than sociology of religion:

> A sect can be a dissenting group which has broken away from the main body of a religion, in the sense that the Puritans, say, were a rigorist sect of the Anglican Church, which is itself a branch of Protestant Christianity. But more generally, *sect* is synonymous with *denomination,* meaning any viable subset of a major religion that differs from other sects in interpreting the revelation of that religion. Roman Catholicism and Lutheranism are both sects of Christianity, just as Shi'ites and Sunnis belong to differing sects of Islam…. [As such, the author] uses the term *sect* in its broadest sense, with no pejorative connotations. (Occhiogrosso, 1996, p. xxix)

This set of observations raises, in turn, the delicate question of whether sectarianism is a phenomenon basic to the historical and contemporary Middle East—in the form of, perhaps above all, the seminal, 7th century Sunni-Shi'a divide, together with subsequent "sectarian splits among the Shi'a" giving rise to such branches of Shi'ism as the Zaydis, Isma'ilis, and *Ithna Asharis* (Twelvers) (Zubaida, 2009, p. 551). For that matter, as John Esposito underscores, "[a]lthough the *Qur'an* warns against sectarianism (e.g., 30:31–32), divisions and sects emerged within the Muslim community as early as the first civil war (656–661)" (Esposito, 2003, p. 282). As these Qur'anic passages read, in Marmaduke Pickthall's translation:

> 31. Turning unto Him (only); and be careful of your duty unto Him, and establish worship, and be not of those who ascribe partners (unto Him);
> 32. Of those who split up their religion and become schismatics, each sect exulting in its tenets. (*Qur'an*, 1992 [1909], p. 415)

Taken on its face, there would appear to be plentiful evidence indicating that animosities between Sunni and Shi'a course through the heart of the collective sectarian dynamics affecting the Middle East today. Examples abound: inter-communal violence in countries like Iraq, Afghanistan, and Pakistan; tensions between Iran and the Gulf Cooperation Council (GCC) states, hinging on GCC fears (exemplified at present in Bahrain) that Iran acts to incite "sectarian conflict…, especially a Shi'a revolt against the Sunni GCC rulers" (Kostiner, 2011, p. 101); and Iranian assertions, in turn, that Sunni militancy, backed by states spanning from Turkey to the Persian Gulf, "is responsible for a wave of sectarian terrorist attacks" in countries such as Iraq and Syria (Fernandez, 2013). However, as these examples illustrate, it is crucial to parse the ways in which Sunni-Shi'a sectarianism is represented, to help reveal the interests and presuppositions underlying depictions of ostensible, intra-Islamic religious conflict.

Following the 2003 fall of Saddam Hussein in Iraq, and the 2004 intensification of Sunni vs. Shi'a "sectarian strife" (Juergensmeyer, 2008, p. 75) in that country, King Abdullah of Jordan, in late 2004, advanced the now well-known thesis—or infamous, if one concurs with those who find it a "weak" claim colored by Abdullah's own interests, and those of other United States-backed "conservative" "Sunni Arab leaders"—that an Iranian-dominated "'Shiite Crescent' [now stretches] from Iran into Iraq, Syria, and Lebanon" (Hassan-Yari, 2012, pp. 75–76; Ruthven, 2011b, p. 89). Subsequently, a scholar like Vali Nasr, who has been influential in U.S. academic, as well as policymaking circles, helped to propagate the idea that the Sunni-Shi'a conflict, and "the Shi'a revival's" "challenge" to "Sunni ascendancy" seems fated to exacerbate the "Middle East's sectarian pains" (Nasr, 2007, pp. 21, 28) into the foreseeable future. Nasr's analysis—underscored by his more recent claim that, "coinciding with the destabilizing force of the Arab Spring", the re-intensifying of civil strife in Iraq "[signals] that sectarianism is ascendant" (Nasr, 2013, p. 152)—supports the finding that sectarianism is an undeniable presence within the Middle East, and within the world as a whole; this, when some might have presumed, in a spirit of modernist triumphalism, that sectarianism is bound to be vanquished by post–Enlightenment liberalism. As David Rieff recently argued in criticism of such modernist self-delusion, "What Nasr said about Iraq is, in reality, overwhelmingly the global rule, not some atavistic Middle Eastern exception" (Rieff, 2012, p. 36). Yet, in a contrary assessment, Nasr's argument has been met with powerful opposition by, for one, Hamid Dabashi, who sees it as embodying a distortion of Islam, in which "the existing and evident syncretic cosmopolitanism of a world religion [has been shrunken] to one sectarian aspect" (Dabashi, 2011, pp. 277–282; see also Dabashi, 2013a, *passim*). This distortion, Dabashi maintains, materializes largely as a political favor to the United States: in his view, Nasr's analysis serves to bolster the U.S.'s anti-Iran ideological and geopolitical stance, as well as the American self-defense which holds that essential religious divides, rather than that country's own malfeasance, bore responsibility for the carnage ravaging post-Saddam Iraq (Dabashi, 2011, pp. 277–282).

Closer still to the present day, one encounters predominating journalistic accounts which, like a fluctuating temperature gauge, seem to have now pinpointed "Hotheaded Sunnis" from North Africa to Pakistan, "targeting Shi'a Muslims whom they consider heretics", as the foremost impediment blocking the "sad and slender hope… for intra-Muslim accord" (*The Economist*, 2012, p. 67; Saigol, 2013). Further, this current emphasis on Sunni-perpetrated sectarianism fits with a distinct suspicion that is now being leveled against actors like the Muslim Brotherhood in post-Hosni Mubarak Egypt—namely, a concern for the fate of Christians living under governments that, amidst the Arab uprisings, are seeing an overtly Islamic orientation supplant the secular authoritarianism that had previously offered them a modicum of protection (Tadros, 2012). Therefore, the question remains: is there a concrete reality to sectarianism in today's Middle East that lies beyond competing political appropriations and manipulations of, and impassioned interpretive divergences over this incendiary concept?

Conclusion:
Is Sectarianism Aberrant, or Is It Basic to Human History and Identity?

There is a great deal of potency to a number of the critiques—and to some of the scorn—directed against both the varying practices and representations of sectarianism in the contemporary Middle East. Whether in the wake of the Arab uprisings, or at the confluence between those recent events and prior historical processes, numerous episodes of searing violence and hostility do seem to involve inter-communal struggles over intertwined, religious and political power and identity. Within these contexts, the term sectarianism emerges as a weapon as well as a signifier, through which actors across the ideological spectrum accuse one another of heinous crimes and a suspect level of humanity. However, reductive caricatures of sectarianism, undertaken by those involved in the struggles, as well as by those depicting the phenomenon from outside, do not help matters; if anything, these depictions may distort and inflame in ways that occlude meaningful recognition of the power with which differences among religious and ideological worldviews do in fact shape persons' perceptions of reality.

In his recent book, *The Tribal Imagination,* the anthropologist Robin Fox suggests that human beings are very much sectarian creatures, whose "ethnographic dazzle of differences, for example in religious and political sects," answers to the "low and persistent [mammalian Drumbeats]" that impel "the dispersal and migration of ideas" (Fox, 2011, pp. 83–113). While the specific "cultural and historical factors" that render "the formation of sects [at some points] relatively quiescent, whereas at other times sectarianism seems to explode"… "are not well understood," the singular tumult in today's Middle East may exemplify the "eruption" of "vast social changes" that act as such factors (Fox, 2011, pp. 105–107). Whether or not one concurs, in whole or in part, with Fox's disciplinary frame of reference, with its orientation towards unearthing biological seeds of sectarianism, his overall point resonates in the light of human religious history. Perhaps considering today's tumultuous Middle East as a setting for unique manifestations of an ongoing human historical experience, rather than as a peculiarly atavistic time and place, is a useful step towards re-imagining forms of political recognition that can honor and respect, rather than seek to parody and conceal profoundly held, yet shared differences in identity.

Christian–Muslim Relations in Egypt in the Wake of the Arab Spring

Paul S. Rowe

Abstract

The Arab Spring protests which brought massive and largely unforeseen political change to Egypt comprised all sectors of society, including the Egyptian Christian population, known as Copts. Copts participated in large numbers in the protests that brought about regime change in February 2011, but the broader implications of the revolution to Copts are unclear. In this essay, I address the changes in Christian–Muslim relations that attended the development of a new republican regime in Egypt as a result of the Arab Spring. While the former regime of President Hosni Mubarak had formed a stable elite partnership with the hierarchy of the Coptic Orthodox Church (a "neo-millet" system), the 2011 revolution contributed to the erosion of this partnership in favor of a republican and pluralist model of citizenship in which individual Copts represent their own interests. The increasingly assertive public role of lay movements among Copts, coupled with the death of the Coptic Patriarch (pope) and his replacement by a younger successor, points to the continued erosion of the elite partnership in favor of the new model. Time will tell whether or not pluralist representation or a retrenched corporatism that favors the church will dominate Christian–Muslim relations in Egypt into the future.

Introduction

Justice alone will protect the Copts. They cannot demand justice for themselves to the exclusion of others, and they cannot obtain it alone at the expense of the Muslims. Justice must be achieved for all and justice comes about only through democracy, for democracy is the solution.
—Alaa al-Aswany, *On the State of Egypt*, 2011, p. 98

The words of famed Egyptian author and dissident Alaa al-Aswany, delivered in 2009, were a call for Copts (Egyptian Christians) to support regime change and stand with the majority against the authoritarian policies of Hosni Mubarak and the rule of his National Democratic Party (NDP). Al-Aswany's complaint was that Copts needed to respect the democratic project instead of the partnership that had arisen between the Coptic Orthodox Church and the regime. They had compromised democratic governance in favor of sectarian autonomy, a Faustian bargain that ultimately strengthened the injustices of the authoritarian regime. The Coptic Orthodox leadership had pursued a *neo-millet* relationship with the regime that gave it pre-eminence in Coptic minority affairs (Rowe, 2007). Lay movements, diaspora activists, and rank and file Copts sometimes challenged the neo-millet system, but they remained deferential to the Church leadership which remained the primary interlocutor with the regime and Egyptian society (Hasan, 2003). However, to secular liberals like el-Aswany, Coptic Church autonomy threatened the emerging concept of national citizenship represented by the revolutionary movement, and promised only to ghettoize and marginalize Copts into the future.

When revolutionary movements overthrew the Mubarak regime in February 2011, Copts were anxious and divided. The Coptic Orthodox Church hierarchy remained committed to its relationship with the regime while ordinary Copts joined the protests in large numbers. The Church gradually accepted the necessity of contributing its support to the demonstrations, hosting open-air masses in Cairo's Tahrir Square and allowing lower-level clergy to participate. However, the overthrow of the regime ushered in a period of high tension among Copts. Widespread fear of the electoral success of the Muslim Brotherhood's affiliate Freedom and Justice Party (FJP) and the rising influence of the Salafist movement in Egypt appeared to be justified amid the acceleration of attacks on churches in middle Egypt and Cairo over the following months of mid-2011. The sense of fear deepened in October when public demonstrations led by Copts were put down with violence, and more than two dozen Coptic citizens were killed. Islamist victories in the legislative and presidential elections of 2011–2012 and the death of Coptic Patriarch Shenouda III added to the malaise. The consolidation of power under President Mohamed Morsi has ushered in a period of Islamist dominance that presents a challenge for Egyptian Christians and belies the merits of the liberal alternative presented by el-Aswany and the secular opposition.

What are the prospects for the future of Christian–Muslim relations and the status of Copts in Egypt?

Under the regime of Mubarak, Copts were able to take advantage of relative pluralism to strengthen their own status through the expansion of their own civil society organizations (Makari, 2007). They have also formed partnerships with the Islamist movement (Scott, 2010, pp. 147–165). Lay Copt activism has typically taken a back seat to the influence of the Coptic Orthodox Church hierarchy in the past, but with the death of the former pope amid a new constitutional regime, will the Church remain the strongest intermediary for Coptic interests? The future of Coptic interests in Egyptian politics could be understood in terms of two general models. First is the perpetuation of the neo-millet partnership between the Coptic Orthodox Church, perhaps restructured under a military or Islamist-dominated regime. The second is the choice of Copts to embrace a republican alternative where their interests are represented within a sectarian political party or parties, or, as is more likely, under the banner of the liberal opposition. The authority of the Church as the key representative of Coptic interests is unlikely to disappear. But in this paper, I will argue that the neo-millet partnership between church and state is gradually eroding in the face of Coptic participation in the broader scope of Egyptian politics, even with the ascendance of the Islamist movements. The erosion of the neo-millet system is a largely positive development for Copts, though the sectarian vision of most Islamists will pose a barrier to the consolidation of full equal rights for the Christian community.

Copts and the Arab Spring

The Arab Spring had its start with the eruption of persistent and widespread protests in Tunisia in response to the self-immolation of street vendor Mohammad Bouazizi on December 17, 2013. These protests gained steam in late December 2010 and led to the ouster of Tunisian President Zine el-Abidine Ben Ali on January 10, 2011. The growth of the protests almost overshadowed a dramatic bomb attack that took place in Egypt on New Year's Day, 2011. Just as a Coptic Orthodox service was concluding, a massive bomb was detonated outside the *Qadiseen* (Two Saints) Church in Alexandria. The blast proved to be one of the most deadly attacks against Egyptian Christians in modern history, eventually claiming the lives of at least 23 people (*Reuters*, January 4, 2011). The event sparked protests in Cairo's Shubra suburbs and poured fuel on the fire of global news stories that highlighted the precarious position of Middle Eastern Christians. The Egyptian government of Hosni Mubarak publicly denounced the attack and insisted that evidence pointed to an otherwise unknown al-Qaeda affiliate based out of the Gaza Strip.

The timing of the attack, coming just before the celebration of Coptic Christmas, fell into a recurring pattern. Sectarian incidents against Copts often arose in the period prior to

Christmas. On New Year's Day, 2000, simmering tensions boiled over in the small town of al-Kosheh in Upper Egypt, leading to the deaths of at least 21 Copts in sectarian violence. In the run-up to legislative and presidential elections in October, 2005, news reports in the Egyptian press about a play performed at St. George's Coptic Orthodox Church sparked riots in Alexandria that led to the death of three Copts (BBC News, October 22, 2005). In January, 2010, eight Copts were killed in an attack on a church on Christmas day. In each case, the Mubarak regime responded with public remorse and promises to prosecute the perpetrators, while strengthening security cordons around churches throughout Egypt. The violence was used implicitly to underline the seriousness of the sectarian threat in Egypt and to bolster the case for authoritarian limitations on the participation of the Islamist movement. Riots that turned deadly in election years served only to increase the anxiety of Copts and foreign observers and to pillory the intentions of Islamists in Egypt.

Under the Mubarak regime, relations between Copts and the Egyptian state had been increasingly cemented through an understanding between the patriarch of the Coptic Orthodox Church and the regime.

This arrangement gave a special place to the head of the church as the singular representative of Coptic concerns, among other things recognizing the Church's authority in the realm of personal status law and its rights over church properties throughout Egypt (many of which had been expropriated at the time of the 1952 Free Officer's Revolt). In return, the Coptic Orthodox Church maintained an implicit stance of support for the regime and sought to defuse tensions stemming from sectarian violence or widespread discrimination against the Copts. In this way, the Coptic Orthodox Church and the state maintained a partnership that mirrored the autonomy provided to religious minority communities under the Ottoman Empire known as the millet system. Even the construction of churches remained governed under a law that dated back to the late Ottoman period, reinforcing a neo-millet relationship between the Egyptian regime and the church (Rowe 2007). According to Fiona McCallum (2007), "the political role of the patriarch is defined as acting as the civil representative of the community and liaising between the community and the ruling authorities." (p. 923)

This understanding emerged out of the intense political crisis of the late 1970s and early 1980s. During those years, the introduction of President Anwar Sadat's *infitah* policies and the rise of radical Islamist opposition to the Egyptian government's conclusion of a peace treaty with Israel led to mounting street demonstrations and intersectarian violence (Farah, 1986). The President's attempt to co-opt the Islamist movement and his introduction of constitutional changes to enshrine *Shari'a* as the principal source of Egyptian law moved Coptic Pope Shenouda III to engage in vocal opposition to the government. Shenouda's agitation and opposition to the regime led to his internal exile to a monastery in the northwestern desert in September, 1981. The action was combined with an attempt to promote an alternative leadership within the Church. Only a month later, President Sadat was assassinated and was succeeded by his vice-president, Hosni Mubarak. Over the following four years, Mubarak reassessed his relationship with the Church authorities, even as Shenouda pursued a rapprochement with the new regime. The patriarch was released from exile in 1985 and rehabilitated as the head of the Coptic Orthodox Church. Over the following two decades, Shenouda turned away from his earlier agitation and agreed to support the government so long as it respected his role as representative of the Church, according to McCallum (2007) returning "to the *millet* systems of supporting the government in return for enjoying autonomy over the community" (p. 933). At the same time, he sought to consolidate his control over the Coptic community, such as while "laity participation remains an important tradition in the Coptic Orthodox Church, such activities cannot be described as effective constraints on patriarchal authority" (p. 927).

Although Mubarak had garnered the tacit support of the Coptic Orthodox Church under Pope Shenouda, his determination to continue Sadat's pursuit of neoliberal reforms and peace with Israel quickly damaged his reputation with the Islamist movement, in spite of his moves to restore elections following 1985. The expansion of terrorist activities led by the *Gama'a al Islamiya* (Islamic Group) throughout the 1990s included numerous attacks against Copts in Upper Egypt in addition to those that targeted government and military installations. In addition to the low-level Islamist insurgency that gathered steam in the mid-1990s, sectarian incidents involving Copts and Muslims also gained particular notoriety. Perhaps most notable was the case of the al-Kosheh incident of autumn 1998, in which a large number of Copts were subjected to torture and severe mistreatment at the hands of police in the midst of a murder investigation. Tensions in the town remained until the New Year's incidents of the year 2000.

In response to these incidents, Pope Shenouda came under considerable pressure to respond.   Pressure on the patriarchate came from a new generation of Coptic activists. Since the 1980s, an activist movement in the diaspora had become significant in agitating that the United States and other western governments to put pressure on the Egyptian regime (Rowe, 2001). They lobbied their governments to influence Egyptian authorities to redress Coptic concerns, such as the inability of Egyptians to convert to Christianity on their official identity cards, restrictions on church construction, protection of places of worship, or investigation of alleged cases of abduction for the purposes of marriage or conversion. These groups of civil society activists posed a significant challenge to the church. In Egypt, the activity of the diaspora Coptic movement emboldened the growth of Coptic activism in the years prior to the 2011 revolution. Copts also began to become involved in secular opposition groups. For example, Coptic politician George Ishak was a key organizer of the *Kefaya* (enough) movement that sought to oust Hosni Mubarak. Another lay Copt, Rafiq Habib, joined the *Wasatiya* movement of moderate Islamists who sought to create an alternative to the Muslim Brotherhood in the early 2000s.

Although Habib articulated his continued support for the regime, he did demonstrate an increasing proclivity to voice Coptic complaints about the second-class status of Copts under Egyptian law and the stultifying centuries-old laws that governed church construction in Egypt. In response, the Mubarak regime engaged in public assertions of support for the Coptic Orthodox Church's demands. The government sponsored the refurbishment of several churches and celebrations on the eve of the millennial celebrations of the Holy Family's sojourn in Egypt. It declared Coptic Christmas to be a national holiday in 2002. It also engaged in devolving authority for church repair permits to the local governorates in the early 2000s (Rowe, 2007, p. 342). However, low-level discrimination against Copts and the occasional outbreak of intersectarian violence stoked international concern for the status of Egypt's Christians.

Toward Maspero: The Revolution and its Aftermath

The outbreak of persistent street demonstrations against the Mubarak regime in late January, 2011 quickly came to involve Egyptians of all stripes. Islamist leaders of the Muslim Brotherhood did not take public leadership of the demonstrations until they began to mobilize followers a few days into the demonstrations. Instead, the primary leadership of the movement came from a wide variety of young activists and liberals such as former IAEA (International Atomic Energy Agency) Chief Muhammad Elbaradei or Internet activist and Google executive Wael Ghonim. They had been emboldened by the success of the revolution in Tunisia less than two weeks previous (Brynen, Rex, Moore, Salloukh, & Zahar, 2012, p. 24). The revelation of allegations that the Mubarak regime may have been involved in the bombing of the Alexandria church in early January fueled Coptic anger toward the regime (*Al-Arabiya News*, February, 7, 2011). Coptic activists among the demonstrators came to be known as the "Coptic Youth Movement." It is common for the Arabic term for youth, *shabab*, to be used in an elastic way to describe young generations of political activists, but the term had rarely been so applied among Copts, whose clerical leaders are often conspicuous by their age. The liberal spirit of the street protests cultivated a new air of interreligious unity in Egyptian politics. Soon after a tent city developed in Tahrir Square where the protestors remained encamped, religious services became a fixture of the gathering, including both Muslim prayers based out of the neighboring mosque and open-air Christian liturgies and prayer meetings led by the Coptic Orthodox and Evangelical Churches in Egypt. A common slogan of the street protests was the litany that affirmed "Christians and Muslims, one hand."

Though individual Copts participated in the demonstrations in large numbers, the Coptic Orthodox Church demonstrated its unease with the revolutionary movement by restating its commitment to a peaceful relationship with the regime. Amid the protests, Pope Shenouda counseled Copts to avoid the demonstrations, communicating his concern for the deteriorating security situation (*Egypt Independent*, February 5, 2011). Many priests and other leaders of the church were publicly sympathetic to the demonstrations, but the Coptic patriarch did not pronounce his support of the demonstrations until he issued a terse commendation to the "honest youth" of Egypt who had led the revolution and the army for its role in protecting Egypt after the fall of Mubarak (*Arab West Report*, February 23, 2011).

The patriarch's concern for public order appeared well founded in the weeks and months following the revolution. The breakdown in interreligious relations demonstrated the increasing limitations of the Church hierarchy in controlling Coptic political participation. Some Copts saw the revolution and the ensuing breakdown of authority as an opportunity to engage in building projects and to enjoy their new found freedoms of association and free speech. The development of a new sense of civil freedom became an impetus for the assertion of greater and greater autonomy among the Copts. For decades, church construction in Egypt had been limited by the modern reiteration of an Ottoman-era code drawn up in 1856, the *hatt i-humayun*. In effect, the code made it impossible for Christians to construct or refurbish new churches except with the permission of the president. Though changes were made to the administration of this code in 2003, it has remained next to impossible for church members to obtain building permits for their churches due to the bureaucratic and political hurdles that Copts face.

In some cases, this contributed to violent incidents that pit local Muslims against Christians in Upper Egypt and Cairo. When a church was destroyed by a group of vigilantes in the southern environs of Cairo in early March, Copts protested that the armed forces were not keeping their commitment to defending Christian places of worship (*Reuters*, March 7, 2011). That weekend, another group of Islamist vigilantes associated with the Salafist movement attacked and burned a church in Imbaba where they alleged that a Christian convert to Islam was being held against her will, leaving 15 dead in their wake (el-Rashidi, 2011).

The attack galvanized Christian efforts to demand protection and human rights in the new Egypt and led to ongoing organized protests led by Coptic youth throughout the spring and summer of 2011. These protests focused on the State Television headquarters in the Cairo suburb of Maspero. The demonstrators sought to develop a Coptic opposition movement that would parallel the January 25th movement and bring about results for the Coptic community. In this sense, there was a feeling that while the revolution had achieved the end of the Mubarak regime, a new revolution was necessary to extend this success toward liberation of Copts from discrimination and sectarian abuse. Tamer Wagdy, one of the demonstrators, put it this way: "We want to be treated as equals. This is our revolution, the Coptic one" (el-Rashidi, 2011).

The largest organization of demonstrators styled themselves the Maspero Youth Union. The group sought to extend the Coptic youth movement that had gained influence during the revolution and took a deliberate stand as a rival to the political representation offered by the Coptic Orthodox Church. They were joined in their efforts by two Coptic priests, Father Philopater and Father Mattias, who participated despite the disapproval of the Coptic patriarch. During an interview in May 2011, Fadi Philip, a veterinarian who served as media spokesman for the movement, explained that the movement was seeking to provide an outlet for Coptic grievances outside the Church:

> We aim to be a political face for Egyptian Christians, doing so away from the church. We are not trying to be leaders in place of the church, but rather to show people they do not need to run to the church when they meet with difficulties… The problem is that the Christians do not have leaders in any significant way. We must have these leaders, but we must have them outside the church. (Casper, 2011, para 2)

By mid-autumn, the Maspero movement had been gaining steam and numbers, as Copts responded to the Union's call to demonstrate amid growing numbers of incidents where Copts were targeted for harassment and violence. Copts also reacted to the increasing sense of suspicion surrounding the relationship between the military government led by the Supreme Council of the Armed Forces (SCAF) and the Islamist movement.

Numerous intersectarian incidents arose throughout 2011 in situations in which Christians sought to build or refurbish their churches without official permission. In the wake of the revolution, Copts throughout Egypt had seized the opportunity to perform work on old and derelict church properties. In late October, one such effort raised the ire of local citizens in the city of Edfu in the southern governorate of Aswan. Locals took the law into their own hands and burned two houses belonging to Copts, as well as setting the Marinab Mar Gerges church on fire. The Awan governor, Mustafa El-Sayed, essentially came to the defense of the vigilantes, stating publicly that the location was not a licensed church and that "[i]f there were any prayers taking place in it, it's against the law," much to the horror of the community bishop, Marcos, who refuted the governor's assertion (Leila, 2011, para. 4). In an attempt to mollify Coptic sentiment, the military government promised to reconstruct the building, but the incident deepened the sense among Copts that Mubarak-era protection of church property was no longer being respected.

The incident sparked some of the largest protests among the Copts demonstrating weekly in front of the Maspero state television headquarters. Hundreds converged on the site on October 4, 2011. Their continuing protests set the stage for the outbreak of violence five days later. During the evening of Sunday, October 9th, shots rang out at the protest. Several explanations emerged that implicated either the military officers providing security at the site, the Coptic protestors, or unknown agitators aligned with the Islamist movement or the former regime seeking to undermine the SCAF military government (Casper, 2011b). In the midst of an evening of violence, at least 26 people were killed, most of them Copts. In later pronouncements, the military disciplined three soldiers, who were given sentences of two and three years in prison for "involuntary manslaughter." Coptic protestors present at the incident contend that many more were involved (Ibrahim, 2012). The evening's events brought an end to the demonstrations and a chill to the Coptic community, but agitation over the massacre has persisted. A funeral for the victims united Copts in indignation, and rallies brought Egyptian Christians together over the next few months in a movement of prayer and solidarity.

After Shenouda: New Forms of Representation

Legislative elections followed soon after the "Maspero Massacre." The People's Assembly elections of November 2011 to January 2012 ushered in a new legislature dominated by the Islamist Freedom and Justice Party as well as the Salafist Nour Party. These results discomfited many Copts, notwithstanding the efforts of many Islamist candidates to minimize their hostility toward Christians. Though many predicted that Copts could not win election, in fact eight Copts were elected, all of them in opposition or marginal parties (Carnegie Endowment 2012). To these were added five Copts appointed by the SCAF, echoing the usual practice of appointing Coptic representatives followed by the former NDP regime. Copts participated in the elections of May and June 2011 with great apprehension over the results. Coptic support broke between the major candidates, their support appearing to fall in larger numbers behind the socialist Hamdeen Sabbahi and the former regime stalwart Ahmed Shafiq.

The death of patriarch Shenouda III in March 2012 raised the open question as to who would represent Coptic interests in the new Egypt. It remained a question without an answer. Though the revolution had clearly undermined the authority of the Coptic Orthodox Church and had created new opportunities for individual Copts to participate in electoral and elite politics, there was no one with the stature or authority to speak directly to Coptic interests in a way that would be heard and respected. Interviewed for *Al-Ahram Weekly*, journalist Youssef Sidhom observed that:

> The relationship between Church and state has changed drastically in the interim period. Before, there was an unspoken pact between ex-president Hosni Mubarak and Pope Shenouda III that the championing of Coptic Christian interests would be delegated exclusively to the Coptic Orthodox Church…. That is no longer the case. Today, the Church is not the primary defender of Coptic Christian interests any more, and the late Pope Shenouda III encouraged Coptic Christian laypersons to participate fully in the Egyptian political process…. (Nkrumah, 2012, paras.10-11)

Shenouda's death came at a crisis moment in the development of the post-revolutionary government, just three months prior to a promised presidential election.

The victory of the Freedom and Justice Party candidate Mohamed Morsi in the presidential election was viewed by most Copts as a major setback in their efforts to construct a liberal regime. Individual Copts—perhaps most notably Rafiq Habib, a Coptic Evangelical who was part of the Wasatiya branch of the Islamist movement—built relationships with the Muslim Brotherhood and other Islamist groups over the years. Habib was appointed deputy chairman of the Freedom and Justice Party in July, 2011 in an attempt to demonstrate the group's interest in cultivating cross-sectarian alliances. However, Copts continued to be concerned that an administration led by President Morsi would gradually move the country toward stricter adherence to Islamic law via a stealth campaign to undermine liberal institutions.

In response, President Morsi sought to bolster his non-sectarian credentials. He publicly suspended his membership in the Muslim Brotherhood. In August, Morsi delivered on an election promise when he appointed four assistant presidents, including a prominent Coptic lay leader and former deputy governor of Cairo, Samir Marcos. The role of the assistant presidents was unclear, but Copts cautiously approved of the choice, many affirming Marcos's role as a bellwether of the President's good intentions toward the Coptic minority. Marcos reflected this perspective himself when appointed to the position. Responding to the news of his appointment, Marcos pointedly responded, "Either I make a difference or I leave" (Casper, 2012, para.4). Early indications were that the appointment was primarily a token of good intentions, but that little authority would be given over to the assistant president. His words would come to haunt the administration in just a few months.

Developments in late 2012 undermined the efforts of Copts seeking to pursue normalization of a non-sectarian and liberal approach to their own interest representation. For several months during mid-2012, the Coptic Orthodox Church remained in limbo as preparations were made for a ceremony in which the new Patriarch was to be chosen. In November, preparations culminated with the selection of three candidates for the papacy, from whom one name would be chosen using an ancient ritual in which a blindfolded child drew a name from a chalice. On November 4th, Tawadros II was enthroned as the new Coptic patriarch. The absence of President Morsi at the ceremony raised complaints from Copts who feared that it indicated an increasingly disdainful attitude for Christians within the regime.

Tawadros was a studious monk from the Egyptian delta governorate of Behera who had been appointed a general bishop under the former patriarch in 1997. He had studied pharmacology—a common occupation among Copts—prior to entering into the monastic life in 1986. Over the next several years, he worked as a minister to youth in the city of Damanhour. Tawadros was largely unknown among parishioners in the Coptic Orthodox Church at large, but was introduced to the nation during a televised interview conducted by Bishop Bula of Tanta and aired on several Coptic television channels among the five leading candidates for the position in early October 2012.

The interview showcased Tawadros's personal warmth and preparation for the ministry and generally steered clear of detailed discussion of church policy. However, toward the end, Bula pressed Tawadros for his plans for relationships with other religious groups within the state of Egypt. "First of all, as Egyptians we are living with our brothers the Muslims, and for us it is a priority that we maintain a life together," he stated. He commended the work of former Pope Shenouda in offering himself as a "safety valve" for the Church, and concluded his discussion of interreligious relations by affirming the lay activity of Copts within their own communities. "Involvement in the community is a true Biblical Christian characteristic, just as in the example of salt and light. They must participate." (*Coptic Youth Channel 2012*, translation by the author)

Tawadros's words were few, but they formed the basis upon which judgments were made about the new pope's attitude toward social and political action on behalf of the Church. His comments at a news conference the following day reinforced news reports that indicated that the new pope would eschew a political role for the patriarchy. "The most important thing is for the church to go back and live consistently within the spiritual boundaries because this is its main work, spiritual work," he told reporters, according to the *New York Times* (Kirkpatrick, 2012, para 3). The article went on to quote Coptic journalist Youssef Sidhom, who asserted that "It is not in the interests of the Copts, if they are trying to speak for themselves as full and equal citizens, to have an intermediary speaking for them, and especially if he is a religious authority. I think the church has gotten this message loud and clear" (Kirkpatrick, 2012, para 6). While the assertion was that Pope Tawadros was adamantly against taking a political role as a representative of Coptic interests, the implication of his comments was slightly more nuanced. They indicated, according to Sidhom and to others, that Tawadros intended to depart from the elite consensus neo-millet model of interest representation followed by Shenouda III. The early months of Tawadros's papacy were to demonstrate his commitment to this course of action.

On November 22, President Morsi promulgated a declaration that had the effect of annulling judicial oversight of government actions. He sought to justify the declaration by asserting that it was an attempt to safeguard the ongoing work of the constituent assembly then drafting the words of the new Egyptian constitution and to sideline entrenched opponents from the former regime. However, Morsi's declaration came under immediate condemnation by the opposition and liberal activists, who were concerned that it represented an attempt by the Muslim Brotherhood to subvert democratic institutions and reinstitute a form of dictatorship. Large protests began again in Tahrir Square and before the Ittihadiya Presidential Palace in Heliopolis, with calls for the President to resign and against the process of the constituent assembly.

The November protests deepened the descent in Coptic support for the President. On November 23, Assistant President Samir Marcos resigned his post (Shalaby, 2012). Two days later, 23 members of the Constituent Assembly stepped down and disavowed their involvement in the process, including prominent members of the opposition as well as Coptic appointee George Massiha. In early December, Rafiq Habib, the longtime Christian ally of the moderate Islamist current, also decided to step down from his position in the Freedom and Justice Party (el-Gundy, 2012). Faced with a wholesale list of defections, in particular among more liberal and Christian allies of the regime, the President's response was to reinforce the constituent assembly with members of the Freedom and Justice Party and to hurry toward affirmation of the constitution as worded by the assembly in a referendum on December 15 and 22, 2012. Many liberals and Copts deliberately boycotted the constitutional vote, which passed the constitution with approximately 64% support. Despite this high level of support the fact that only 32% of eligible voters participated reinforced opposition claims that the constitution was essentially illegitimate. The nadir in tensions over Christian–Muslim relations came in late December, when prominent Salafist sheikhs counseled against the interreligious celebration of Christmas, much to the chagrin of many ordinary Muslims.

President Morsi attempted to mollify opposition criticism of the constitutional vote by promising a national dialogue in January 2013, which did not garner support. An increasingly disillusioned public believed the initiative to be little more than window dressing to sell the constitution. This was reinforced when the new Coptic patriarch made a celebrated trip to the ancient Deir al-Moharraq monastery in Upper Egypt in February, 2013 for a monastic conference. For three decades, the Coptic patriarch had heeded regime warnings against travel to the monastery for security reasons, making Pope Tawadros's trip a groundbreaking event. Responding to reporter's questions about the controversy surrounding the constitution, Tawadros made pointed remarks: "We must and will actively take part in any national dialogue in which we see a benefit for the nation. But when we find that a dialogue ends before it starts and none of its results are implemented then we realize that it is not in the interest of the nation (Ahram Online 2013 para 12). He went on to criticize the work of the constitutional assembly that completed its work three months previously, insisting that it needed to include all of Egypt's citizens. That the pope had taken to speaking out on Coptic interests might be interpreted as a return to the usual role of the patriarch in voicing concerns to the regime—but the nature of his remarks challenged not so much the status of Copts themselves as the way in which citizenship is articulated under the new constitution. In this way, they may mark a crucial juncture in the way the patriarchate sees its role in the nation.

Conclusion

The cumulative effect of the Arab Spring, the growth of Coptic political initiatives among the laity, and the death of Pope Shenouda and enthronement of Pope Tawadros is a growing tectonic shift in the landscape of Christian–Muslim relations in the state of Egypt. In response to the sectarian crisis that had arisen amid constitutional debates in the late 1970s and early 1980s, the Coptic patriarch had emerged from exile willing to do business with the Mubarak regime in 1985. He had constructed an elite compromise with the regime in the form of a stable neo-millet partnership where the regime reinforced the internal authority of the Coptic Patriarch among Christians, while the Coptic Patriarch sought to defuse sectarian conflict and support the regime. This partnership came under considerable strain after the outbreak of massive demonstrations in Egypt in January, 2011, demonstrations that came to involve both Muslim and Christian Egyptians in the demand for justice, a form of justice guaranteed by a non-sectarian citizenship championed by liberal leaders such as Alaa al-Aswany, quoted at the outset of this paper.

What is the future of Coptic representation in the Egyptian state? Though the Coptic Orthodox Church has remained primarily responsible for representing Coptic interests, the assertiveness of Coptic lay movements, protest groups, and civil society that has emerged over the past two decades and accelerated with the outcome of the February, 2011 revolution indicates the growing strength of a republican alternative where Copts represent their own interests in a pluralist manner. The creation of self-constituting movements of Copts, liberal political parties (as well as Islamist ones) that include Coptic representatives and the participation of individual Copts as important spokespeople for Coptic concerns will all continue to rival the political role of the patriarch. As a result, lay Copts have risen to some level of prominence as spokespeople for the community: Youssef Sidhom, Rafiq Habib, Mona Makram Ebeid, George Massiha, and George Ishak are a few examples of prominent lay Copts who have gained influence since the revolution in voicing the concerns of Copts. In such a pluralist environment, the maintenance of a separate Coptic community will be more difficult: separate personal status laws, ongoing deliberation over the use of religion on identity cards, and the development of legislation concerning church properties would all fall to the secular state. It also remains to be seen whether or not such a model of interest representation would serve to improve the status of Copts as individual citizens, particularly under the apparatus of an Islamist state.

Politics of Conflict in Pakistan's Tribal Areas Vulnerability Reduction in Violence-Prone Complex Adaptive Systems

Asim Zia & Kashif Hameed

Abstract

Vulnerability, defined as the degree to which complex adaptive systems are likely to experience harm due to a perturbation or stress, has in recent years become a central focus of global change and sustainability science research communities. This system-level framework for vulnerability has been applied in a range of empirical assessments and socio-political contexts. In this study, we extend this knowledge by expostulating the complexity of reducing the vulnerability of vulnerable populations in complex adaptive systems that have been marred with violent conflict for decades. We present findings from our field research and interviews in Pakistan's tribal areas, as they have been afflicted with violent conflicts since 1979. We present a conflict map among different stakeholder groups in the tribal areas from the perspective of indigenous tribes, one of the most vulnerable populations, and demonstrate the complex politics of conflict that indigenous tribesmen have endured during transitioning from one conflict (1980s war against Russia) to another (2000s war against Taliban). The political analysis of conflict in Pakistani tribal areas is aimed at illuminating the complexity of vulnerability reduction prevalent in the socio-political and economic environment of this region for the indigenous populations. We argue for the establishment of democratically anchored governance networks with active tribal participation to stabilize the region in a "post-conflict" context.

Introduction

While different conceptual notions and theories of vulnerability and resilience have been explored in multiple disciplines (e.g., political ecology, human ecology, disaster management, climatic impacts, and human dimensions of global change), and reviewed by Berkes and Folke (1998), Fussel and Klein (2006), Adger (2006), and Janssen et al. (2006), we focus here on conceptualizing vulnerability and resilience as properties of a complex adaptive system, in which highly vulnerable populations cope with violent conflicts on a routine basis. Vulnerability, defined as the degree to which complex adaptive systems are likely to experience harm due to a perturbation or stress, has in recent years become a central focus of the global change and sustainability science research communities (Kates et al., 2001; Kasperson & Kasperson, 2001). Resilience of a system can also be conceptualized in terms of vulnerability: Ecological resilience, defined as the ability of a set of mutually reinforcing structures and processes to persist in the presence of disturbance and stresses (Gunderson, 2000; Holling, 1973), is particularly prominent within the discourse of the global change vulnerability community (Folke, 2006). This system-level framework for vulnerability (and resilience, by implication) has been applied in a range of empirical assessments and socio-political contexts, but typically these applications do not directly address the political violence and conflict that is observed in some complex social ecological systems. In this study, we first extend the knowledge-base by expostulating the complexity of reducing vulnerability of vulnerable populations in complex adaptive systems marred by violent conflict. We present findings from both our field research and from interviews with indigenous tribes in the Pakistan "tribal" areas afflicted with political violence and conflict since 1979. The socio-economic and political systems prevalent in Pakistan's tribal areas are conceptualized as complex adaptive systems. In the next section, we present a brief history and impact of the violent conflicts in Pakistan's tribal areas. Then, we present an analysis of governance structures in the tribal area, subsequently showing a conflict map derived from the perspective of indigenous tribes and illuminating the complexity of reducing vulnerability of these indigenous tribes in conflict-prone complex adaptive systems. And finally, we conclude the paper by discussing the potential of democratically anchored governance networks in reducing vulnerability of vulnerable populations in complex adaptive systems.

The History and Impact of Violent Conflicts in Pakistan's Tribal Areas

Since the "9/11" terrorist attacks in the United States, the tribal areas of Pakistan and adjoining parts of Afghanistan have been categorized as a "dangerous" region threatening regional and global security. During the last 30 years, continuous warfare in this region has adversely affected the indigenous socio-cultural fabric of "tribal" society on both sides of the Durand line. Consequently, a peaceful non-violent tribal society in the past (e.g., Bachha Khan movement aligned with Gandhian principles of non-violence during the 1930s and 1940s) has transformed into a highly violent and extremist society, perpetually existing in a state of violence and conflict.

There are different manifestations of violent conflicts in the tribal regions that range from direct and explicit violence to structural violence and from the destruction of regions' eco-systems to becoming the active proxy war zone among international powers and regional countries. Indigenous tribes (*Qaba'il*) have been vulnerable to these conflicts, as they have lost thousands of precious lives and faced the displacement of millions. This research paper aims at providing a summary of our findings from more than 30 interviews with indigenous tribesmen and numerous field visits conducted in the tribal areas between 2003 and 2010. In particular, we present a conflict map among different stakeholder groups in the tribal areas from the perspective of indigenous tribes, and demonstrate the complex politics of conflict that indigenous tribesmen have endured during transitioning from one conflict (1980s war against Russia) to another conflict (2000s war against Taliban) and, in the process, expostulate the complexity of reducing vulnerability of vulnerable populations in conflict-ridden tribal areas.

In 1979, Russia invaded Afghanistan and, subsequently, a U.S.-sponsored jihad was waged against the Russians. Religious fighters were recruited, trained, and transported to Afghanistan from all over the Islamic world. Pakistan became a frontline state, and the tribal areas of Pakistan became a hub of training and recruitment of the religious fighters. The Russian invasion and U.S.-led fight marked the end of the peaceful tribal culture as religious extremism, in combination with weapons and drug businesses, flourished in the entire region. A huge influx of three to four million Afghan refugees in tribal areas, North West Frontier Province (NWFP), and Baluchistan further complicated the situation. The last 30 years of political violence has, so far, resulted in the loss of millions of human lives on both sides of the Durand line, along with widespread physical devastation, lawlessness, insecurity, religious intolerance, and increased terrorist activities both in Afghanistan and Pakistan.

After the withdrawal of Soviet forces from Afghanistan and disintegration of Soviet Union in 1989, many international actors, especially the United States and NATO, hastily evacuated from Afghanistan. A subsequent power vacuum resulted in a power struggle between various warlords in Afghanistan, lasting until the emergence of the Taliban in 1996 as the ruling elite in Afghanistan. During that period, many interviewees reported that various intelligence agencies like the Inter-Services Intelligence (ISI) agency of Pakistan; Central Intelligence Agency (CIA) of the U.S.; Research Analysis Wing (RAW) of India; Mossad of Israel; and Russian and Saudi intelligence agencies were actively involved in supporting and promoting specific warlords and their ascendancy to the political leadership of Kabul.

After the "9/11" terrorism attacks on the United States, Afghanistan once again became a battleground between U.S. NATO forces and the Taliban. After 9/11, the so-called war against jihadi terrorism spilled over to the adjoining tribal areas of Pakistan, as the Taliban turned to these areas for refuge after the U.S. invasion. For the first time in the history of the country, the Pakistan army entered the tribal areas. Many interviewees argued that the local tribes were not taken into confidence, but the Pakistan army entered into short-term peace agreements with the local Taliban. These peace agreements provided opportunities for the Taliban to consolidate their position and to establish their control throughout the Federally Administered Tribal Area (FATA) of Pakistan, as well as the adjoining regions of the Swat and Malakand districts.

Those tribal people who supported army actions against the terrorists or raised tribal volunteer fighters (*lashkars*) to help and assist the army efforts were brutally eliminated in target killings and suicide attacks. Since 2004, Pakistan has experienced hundreds of suicide and terrorist attacks, including bomb blasts which killed and injured thousands of innocent civilians. Finally, in 2009, with the change of power in Pakistan, from General (retired) Pervaiz Musharraf to a democratically elected government, a massive military action was launched against the terrorists in the Swat, Malakand, and Dir areas. After hard battles, the area was cleared of the terrorists; Internally Displaced Persons (IDPs) are currently rehabilitating in these areas. A massive military operation—the so-called *Rah-e-Nijaat*—has been launched against the leadership of *Tehrik-e-Taliban Pakistan* (TTP), based in South Waziristan.

Fierce fighting is in progress at the moment in South Waziristan, while U. S. led drone strikes are taking place in North Waziristan in the FATA regions. Some of the areas in the conflict zone were initially flooded during the monsoon season in 2010, leading to widespread evacuation and displacement of the indigenous tribes from these areas, as well as loss of their property and assets. The coupling of political violence with natural disasters in Pakistan's tribal areas provides a unique insight in understanding the nature of vulnerability to which highly vulnerable people in complex social–ecological systems are exposed.

The tribal areas of Pakistan have been marred with political violence due to the prolonged Afghan jihad against Russia, battles between various warlords, the *de facto* Taliban rule, and the post-9/11 spillover from the global "war against terror" in Pakistan's tribal and its adjoining parts. The last eight years of war in that region physically devastated not only the area, but also the indigenous social fabric of the tribal population. The indigenous tribes have been "sandwiched" between the terrorists and the Pakistan army. If the people side with the Pakistan army, they become targets of the wrath of the inhuman Taliban terrorists; if the local people support the terrorists under a state of fear, then they are termed as terrorists by the Pakistan army. Thousands of tribal elite *maliks*, elders, journalists, writers and civil society activists, and their family members have been brutally killed through target killings, kidnappings, and beheadings. Anyone who has raised a voice against violence or the terrorists or their movement, or anyone who has supported and promoted peace and non-violence, social development, or education has been systematically eliminated from the scene. Against the will of their parents, local children are forcefully recruited, trained as suicide bombers, and used for suicide attacks in both Afghanistan and Pakistan. Many tribes also settled their own personal scores under the cover of on-going war.

Owing to a rather ineffective local government and indecisive military strategy, the tribal and semi-tribal areas in Pakistan along the Durand line fell under the *de facto* control of the Taliban and religious parties. Local business and economic opportunities virtually diminished with the passage of time. The indigenous population has been forced to leave their houses, migrate to other areas of the country, and live as IDPs. Yet, inside mainland Pakistan, the indigenous tribal people face problems of free movement, accommodation, employment, and registration as citizens of Pakistan. The tribal people are generally discriminated against and looked down upon as either terrorists or supporters of terrorists.

The last three decades of massive destruction in Afghanistan and adjacent tribal areas of Pakistan can be categorized as one of the most violent conflicts since the Second World War. During the 1980s Afghan war, over one million Afghans were killed, and five million Afghans fled to Pakistan and Iran. Another two million Afghans were displaced within the country. In the 1980s, one out of two refugees in the world was an Afghan. According to some estimates, approximately 1.2 million Afghans were disabled (including jihadi fighters—the *Mujahideen*), government soldiers, and non-combatants) and another three million maimed or wounded (primarily non-combatants).

After the withdrawal of USSR forces, war continued among different ethnic tribes, jihadi factions, and warlords. The Taliban takeover of Kabul, followed by the 9/11 attacks led toward another war against terrorism in Afghanistan and adjacent tribal areas of Pakistan. Day-by-day, the increase in the suicide bombing rates in NWFP and the rest of Pakistan has created a widespread sense of insecurity and fear. It has also shaken the security and economy of the entire region. Continuous military operations in the tribal region of Pakistan have resulted in the loss of thousands of human lives and the displacement of millions of the tribal population.

Table 1 shows the trend in the sharp increase in suicide attacks, bomb blasts, and human losses, presumably caused by the terrorists operating from the tribal areas. Further, Table 2 shows spatial details of more than six million tribal populations that were displaced in 2009 in reaction to the military operations to fight the terrorists.

Table 1. Annual Fatalities in Terrorist Attacks/Military Operations in Pakistan (2003-2009)					
Year	Suicide Attacks	Bomb Blasts	Civilian Fatalities	Security Personnel Fatalities	Terrorists/ Insurgents Fatalities	Total Fatalities
2003	02	41	140	24	25	189
2004	07	137	435	184	244	863
2005	04	245	430	81	137	648
2006	07	300	608	325	538	1,471
2007	56	678	1,523	597	1,479	3,599
2008	59	599	2,155	654	3,906	6,715
2009	65	438	2,004	896	7,223	10,123
Total	200	2,438	7,295	2,761	13,552	23,608

Source: South Asia Terrorism Portal.

Table 2. Total Number of Families Displaced by Violence in 2009			
Jurisdiction	Agency/District	Total Families Displaced	Population in the last census
FATA	Bajaur	97,842	733,815
	Mohmand	44,821	336,157
	South Waziristan	60,753	455,647
NWFP	Buner	73,359	550,192
	Malakand	51,630	387,225
	Shangla	68,675	515,062
	Swat	298,201	2,236,507
	Dir	146,953	1,102,147
Total		842,234	6,316,752

Source: Pakistan Index: Tracking Variables of Reconstruction and Security.

Pakistan's economy has so far suffered a loss of $68 billion directly and indirectly due to turmoil in Afghanistan and adjacent tribal areas. On the other hand, the cost of American military operations (Operation Enduring Freedom 2001–2009) in Afghanistan has reached $226.7 billion. In addition, U.S. counter terrorism funding to Pakistan (2001–2008) was approximately $11 billion.

This introductory contextual/historical analysis from the Afghan War to the War against Terrorism reflects the state of vulnerability of indigenous tribes that has afflicted the tribal region in the violent form of a three decades' long war that has killed thousands of indigenous tribesmen and displaced millions of tribesmen in the region. During this conflict, the tribal regions have been governed through colonial age administrative structures and inhumane laws, as briefly explained in the next section.

Governance Structures in Pakistan's Tribal Areas

Tribal areas in Pakistan, which include both Federally Administered Tribal Area (FATA) and Provincially Administered Tribal Area (PATA), are mainly governed under the colonial age Frontier Crimes Regulations (FCR) of 1906. Under the FCR, the tribal people are deprived of basic human rights, political activities, freedom of movement, and freedom of trade and business. The political administration works under the provisions of FCR only to tame the local people. The "political agent" is the most powerful authority in the tribal areas. The tribal areas of Pakistan are governed by the president of Pakistan through his delegations, the Governor of NWFP, whose representatives are the "political agents." Although the current democratic government has announced an abolishment of discriminatory and inhumane FCR, this decree has not yet been implemented.

Internally, the tribal people are free and autonomous in their day-to-day life. The tribal society is governed by centuries old tribal culture and traditions that are not in written form; however, these values and customs are handed down, from one generation to another. This tribal culture is known as *Pashtoonwali*, which is based on human social equality, self-respect, hospitality, fair play, *jirga* (local judicial system), and revenge. The institution of tribal cultural jirga had maintained relative peace throughout the history of tribal areas until the arrival of the Taliban in FATA; since then, the institution of jirga and the tribal elders has been systematically eliminated. The only jirga that exists now is the "Official Jirga" constituted by the political agent, which is not an independent jirga, but its decisions are made at the whim of the political agent.

Owing to the lack of state institutions and security infrastructure, the tribal people are on their own to protect their lives, properties, and other interests. This is the reason that there is no restriction on the purchase, exhibition, or use of any kind of conventional weapons in the tribal areas. Although tribal areas of Pakistan are part and parcel of Pakistan, the 1973 constitution of Pakistan is not applicable to the tribal areas. The political agent is the sole authority working simultaneously as executive, judicial, and implementing agency. The decisions made by the official jirgas (i.e., by the political agent in the current situation) cannot be challenged in any court of law in Pakistan. There are restrictions and great difficulties encountered in the working of NGOs (nongovernmental organizations) and media organizations under the FCR in tribal areas. Thus, in the absence of free media and fair and transparent judicial institutions in the tribal areas, the political agents, local elite maliks, and religious leaders effectively and concurrently rule the tribal areas to attain their narrowly defined aims and objectives.

On the other hand, indigenous people have a virtually limited role in the decision making and development process of the tribal areas.

One of the main social factors behind prevailing multi-dimensional conflict in the tribal society is the negative tribal tradition of *Payghore*. This tradition typically implies to incite the feelings of one's honor in front of society in such a way that peaceful settlement of the issue by the victim's family is considered a sign of weakness and dishonor. In a tribal society, such traditions of "revenge" generally lead to long-term violent cycles of tribal conflicts that last for multiple generations and over centuries.

Conflict Mapping: The Complexity of Reducing Vulnerability in Conflict-Prone Tribal Areas

FATA is one of the most inaccessible areas of Pakistan and, therefore, makes any empirical analysis of its conflicts only approximate. The topographic conflict map, shown in Figure 1, is to be understood as a complex adaptive system, representing the complexity of the conflict in the region from the perspective of a small sample of 30+ tribal interviewees. Various districts of FATA and PATA have been classified into three categories: primary, secondary, and tertiary conflict zones, as described next.

Figure 1. Conflict map

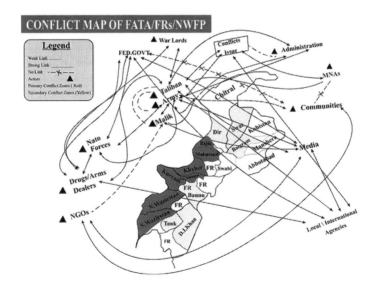

Primary Conflict Zones

These zones are the most volatile in the region. Conflicts affecting these zones are either generated from within or exposed to highly volatile zones, which makes them more vulnerable to conflicts. The following areas in FATA have been identified by interviewees as primary zones of conflict, as shown in Figure 1: South Waziristan, North Waziristan, Bajur, Aurakzai, Khyber, Mohmand, and Kurram.

Secondary Conflict Zones

These zones either experience spillovers from primary zones or internally conflict-triggered from within to a lower extent than primary zones in frequency and level of escalation. The following areas are typically identified as secondary conflict zones, as shown in Figure 1: Swat, Dir, Buneer, Tank, Dera Ismail Khan, Bannu, Karak, FR Kohat, FR Tank, FR Jandola, FR Dera Ismail Khan, and FR Peshawar.

Tertiary Conflict Zones

These zones are relatively calm zones that do not experience frequent escalation of conflicts; however, they do experience perturbations more frequently than other surrounding regions. These include Charsada, Mardan, Manshera, Abbotabad, and Attock.

Based on more than 30 interviews with indigenous tribesmen and numerous field visits conducted in the tribal areas between 2003 and 2010, we have identified important actors and stakeholders engaged in the conflict in those regions. These actors and stakeholders are networked with each other, as shown in the Figure 1 networked lines, through a complex web of inter-dependent relationships. Further, almost all the network actors, with the exception of indigenous tribes, are non-local and more powerful than the typical tribal folks. Further, any intervention in this system with respect to reducing social, ecological, or political vulnerability of vulnerable populations leads to potentially unpredictable (and mostly volatile) consequences, thus giving it a property of complex adaptive systems.

Network Actors

- Tehrik-e-Taliban Pakistan (Hakimullah Group)
- Taliban (Molvi Nazir Group)
- Taliban (Molvi Gul Bahadar Group)
- Taliban (Asmatullah Shaheen Group)
- Taliban (Abdullah Mahsud Group)
- Taliban (Turkistan Baitani Group)
- Religious leaders (Deobandi School)
- Al-Qaida
- Ansar-ul-Islam Group (Khyber)
- Lashkar-e-islam Group (Khyber)
- Taliban-e-Swat (Maulana Fazal-ullah Group)
- Khasadar force
- Para-military forces
- Pakistan Army
- Local lashkars (In army's support)
- Local political administration
- Local outlaws Gangs (Criminal Group)
- Drug Smugglers
- Arms Dealers
- Business Community (For Supplies of food and other logistics)
- Local, national, and international intelligence agencies
- Various tribal groups (those who settle scores with their opponents in the disguise of the Taliban and terrorists

Other Stakeholders

- Communities (Civilian populations)
- Internally Displaced Persons (IDPs) and other trapped/vulnerable populations
- Politicians (JUI-F, ANP, JI, PLM-N, PPP, and PTI)
- Traditional/religious leaders
- Media (Local/National)
- Economic power brokers (business interest)
- Local Political Administration
- Spoilers
- Non-Governmental Organizations (NGOs)/International Non-Governmental Organizations (INGOs)/International Organizations (IOs)

Complexity

All of these network actors and stakeholders are interacting in a very complex and chaotic process of material and non-material transactions, as shown in the conflict map of Figure 1. While Pakistan's federal government is strongly linked with NATO forces, there are serious communication gaps between the tribal elders in FATA and the political agent representing the state of Pakistan. In the mix are drug dealers and war-lords, smugglers, and other hoarders. From the perspective of indigenous tribes, this violent conflict appears to be hoisted upon them by foreign invaders, whether they are Taliban, trained by Pakistani military, or Al-Qaida militants who were initially trained by the CIA and the ISI, but who are now fighting against the CIA and the ISI! There are numerous splinter groups of the Taliban and Al-Qaida, as listed in the network actors above. Further, all of this is complicated by the international interest groups represented by international aid agencies, militaries, intelligence agencies, and corporations that have been operational in the area in the last three decades.

The conflict map shown in Figure 1 depicts the complexity of relationships among network actors and various stakeholder groups who are present in FATA. While different interest groups and actors are maneuvering their tactics and strategies based upon their specific interests, the indigenous tribes are suffering from the continuous violence and conflict engineered and foisted upon them by these external actors. This political and social violence is taking place in the middle of global climatic change-induced natural hazard. Any discussion about reducing the ecological vulnerability of these indigenous tribes cannot be divorced from the political and social realities of violent conflict that has been described above. Yet, the complexity of unraveling political and social violence in FATA precludes any meaningful action on the part of civil society activists and global change researchers in terms of vulnerability reduction and resilience enhancement of indigenous populations in the face of momentous changes expected from global climate change in the medium to long run.

Toward Democratic Anchorage in Tribal Governance Networks

A long-term peaceful resolution of prevailing conflicts in the tribal areas could be potentially improved, and tribal vulnerability could be significantly reduced through changing the governance regime in FATA that explicitly provides a strong voice to the indigenous populations and wrests away the power from the hands of external/non-local network actors. According to the interviews with the indigenous tribes, local tribal governance *Qabail Swaraj* based on truth, purity, and non-violence must be re-institutionalized among the entire tribal population. Others argue that mass scale awareness building and sensitization is required.

Further, many interviewees suggested that non-violent peace activism under the concepts of "Qabail Swaraj" could be promoted among the indigenous tribes of FATA and PATA regions. Inter-positioning, commitment, and consistent efforts through dialogue and diplomacy with the element of trust and selflessness could be the key elements of vulnerability reduction efforts in such complex systems.

A long-term peace program led by the tribal civil society could also be supported and backed by the external support structures. Similarly, in line with aspirations of local tribes, political and administrative reforms could be accelerated on a priority basis. In general, tribal interviewees have identified the following fundamental institutions and principles of tribal governance that could be reconstructed in a post-conflict phase as U.S. and NATO forces pull out in 2014:

- Social equality and decentralization at grassroot levels;
- A principle of social justice and fair play;
- Hospitality, honor, and self-respect;
- The institution of "Jirga" and its sacredness;
- Public participation in decision making;
- Social and religious tolerance;
- Individual freedom and liberty to deal with local issues by the tribes themselves;
- Promotion of pro-active non-violence and purity;
- Less state intervention in personal and social issues relating to the tribes;
- A free, open, and liberal tribal society;
- Respect to tribal culture and to positive and constructive traditions and values;
- Rule of law and absence of FCR 1906;
- Institutionalization of the tribal Jirga institution;
- Freedom of movement, expression, and property;
- Grassroot level democracy from individual to the tribe level; and
- Protection of Indigenous Tribal Culture.

International civil society networks could increase their efforts and mobilize resources for launching a broad vulnerability reduction program for the entire tribal belt of Pakistan and adjacent parts of Afghanistan. External support and resources could be provided to the tribal civil society for the organization of regional peace conventions inside the tribal areas. After the organization of peace conventions, a democratically-anchored "governance network" (e.g., Koliba, Meek, & Zia, 2010) led by tribal civil society could be established and activated in the entire tribal region. Such governance networks could include members from community levels, peace councils at district levels, and peace assembly at regional levels, as shown in Figure 2. These governance networks could work on establishing civil rights, democracy, social dialogue, and conflict resolution. Democratically-anchored governance networks could also facilitate government and civil society coordination in planning and implementing reforms and development programs in the tribal areas of Pakistan.

Public opinion could be mobilized particularly in South Asia and the rest of the world for the promotion and adoption of a regional approach in resolving the conflict generated by Talibanization, terrorism, and cross-border insurgencies. Civil societies in India, Pakistan, and Afghanistan could come up with an action plan to mobilize public opinion in favor of peace and non-violence and encourage better coordination and formation of joint strategies at government levels and security institutions. Increased roles of external international powers must be curtailed, and regional countries could come forward on a single platform to formulate an action plan to reduce and eliminate the forces of war and destruction. Reducing vulnerability in complex adaptive systems is a challenging task; yet democratically-anchored governance networks could provide potential pathways to mitigate politics of conflict and reduce vulnerability for highly vulnerable populations.

Figure 2. Proposed Governance Network in FATA Human Security, Early Warning and Rapid Response System in FATA

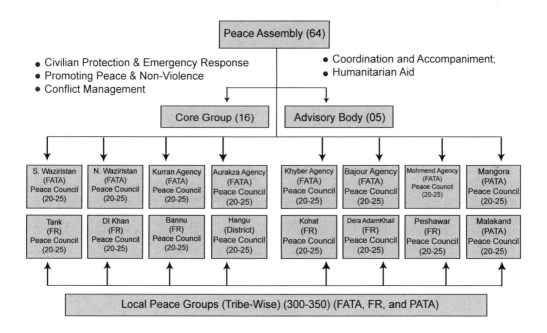

Conclusion

This study focuses on conceptualizing vulnerability and resilience as properties of a complex adaptive system, in which highly vulnerable populations cope with violent conflicts on a routine basis. Pakistan's "tribal" areas, which have been afflicted with political violence and conflict since 1979, are presented as an in-depth case study of a violence-prone region in the greater Middle East. The historical context of this regional case study analysis reveals the highly adverse impact of violent conflicts on vulnerable indigenous populations in Pakistan's tribal area. The persistence of these violent conflicts is assessed to be linked with poor governance structures in the tribal areas, most of which are inherited and preserved from British colonial times of late 19th and early 20th centuries. In particular, we find that the lack of transparency and democratic anchorage in the governance networks of the tribal areas exacerbates the vulnerability of indigenous populations. In the post-9/11-world, explicit and implicit intervention by global and regional powers further complicated the relationship of indigenous populations with the state authorities and international clandestine agencies. Based upon interview and field research data, a conflict map has been developed that presents the perspective of indigenous populations on the persistent war-like situation in Pakistan's tribal areas for the last 35 years. Instead of designing and implementing foreign solutions to resolve this conflict, it is recommended that the governance networks inside the tribal areas could be democratically anchored with broad representation of indigenous representatives and civil society actors. Further, local traditions, cultural norms, and indigenous institutions could be empowered to bring lasting peace. Mitigating the vulnerability of indigenous populations in violence-prone complex adaptive systems requires explicit acknowledgement and support of an indigenous population's right to self-govern.

Chill Ground: Iranian–British Relations during Khomeini–Thatcher Years

Maysam Behravesh

Abstract

While seeking to historically contextualize Iranian–British relations during the almost coincident years of Ayatollah Khomeini and Margaret Thatcher in power in the Islamic Republic of Iran and the United Kingdom, respectively, this article offers a thick political analysis of the salient factors and the developments that informed the bilateral relationship that has spanned more than 10 years since Iran's 1979 revolution. The principal issues explored are the American hostage crisis and its impact upon Anglo-Iranian ties, the Iran–Iraq War and its implications for Tehran's relations with London, and Khomeini's execution *fatwa* (edict) against Salman Rushdie and its political effect at home and abroad. The paper demonstrates a fundamental conflict of interest and ideologies as well as consequential misperceptions of one type or another served to deeply bedevil Anglo-Iranian relations during the period, creating a chill ground of tensions whose legacy lasts to date.

Introduction

The Iranian Revolution of 1979 marked the beginning of an era of radical transformation in Iran's internal socio-cultural and political dynamics as well as its foreign relations. It unleashed an unprecedented powerful desire for fundamental change that had been suppressed in the popular psyche for decades. Influenced by the revolutionary zeal of those days and inspired by Ayatollah Khomeini's impassioned ideological postures, the makers of a new Iran set out to revolutionize everything they came across—from individual dressing style, to the educational system, to the relations of the nascent Islamic Republic (IRI) with other actors in the international community, and even the global order of things. Arguably an ally of the dismantled Pahlavi Monarchy, the United Kingdom (UK) was soon to come into focus as a principal pillar of the "infidel" Western civilization and a close partner of the United States—the revolutionaries' most convenient "other" that soon became their "Great Satan." Remarkably, the 1979 revolution roughly coincided with the rise to power of a hard-headed conservative on the British side, who was as paradoxically revolutionary as she was in other ways. Aspiring to put the "Great" back in Great Britain, Margaret Thatcher was almost as uncompromising as the new Iranian leaders when it came to matters of political prestige, fundamental principles, and also national interests; hence the well-known label, "Iron Lady" of the West (Nunn, 2002, p. 70). She was effectively the first British prime minister to face the stiff challenge posed to the outside world by the new ideological and political atmosphere in Iran. During her premiership, the IRI–UK relationship saw one of the tensest phases in its history, marked by severance of relations, closure of embassies, isolation, and rejectionism.

In fact, one can safely claim that relations between the Islamic Republic and Great Britain—between 1979, when the revolution took place, until 1989 when its founding father Ayatollah Khomeini passed away—were more characterized by their formal absence and informal tension than their existence. A number of factors dramatically affected the IRI's relations with the UK from the very outset, including Iranians' bitter memories of the past Western intervention in their country:[1] Britain's more or less solid support for the monarchical regime of Mohammad Reza Shah until the end of its life, the predominance of obdurate idealists and conservatives within both Iranian and British corridors of power during the time, and finally the resonant strength of the "special relationship" between Britain and America. Notably, most of these elements still serve as the very undercurrents that have continued to disrupt the continuity and stall the improvement of bilateral relations between the two governments. The judicious admission in 1990 of Sir Anthony Parsons, the British ambassador to Tehran from 1974 to 1979, that "all Britain's efforts over the previous quarter century to bury the past and construct a normal relationship with Iran" had drawn a blank and still holds, to a considerable extent (Parsons, 1990, p. 72). Against this backdrop, and perhaps because of it, a number of incidents arose on the ground after 1979 and drew the mutual ties into an all-time low, culminating in Iran's international isolation on the one hand, and the destabilization of Western interests in the region on the other.

Thus, while trying to contextualize Iran–Britain relations during the first decade of the IRI's life (or Thatcher's premiership), this article investigates the key occurrences that shaped the bilateral relationship during the period: the American hostage crisis of November 1979, and its impact upon the IRI–UK ties; the outbreak of Iran–Iraq War (1980–1989) and the Western treatment of it; and finally the publication of *The Satanic Verses* in 1988 and Ayatollah Khomeini's death fatwa on its British author, Salman Rushdie.

The Hostage Crisis, Special Relationship, and Iran–UK Relations

In February 1979, the same month the revolution took place, Britain recognized the Provisional Government of Mehdi Bazargan in the hope of constructing normal and working relations with the new Iranian state, and in spite of the well-founded fears this instilled in its Arab allies in the Persian Gulf. The new diplomatic enterprise, however, did not survive the controversial and unsavory incidents in Iran's revolutionary atmosphere and was curtailed with the formal closure of the British Embassy in Tehran in September 1980. Indeed, during this span of around one and a half years the bilateral relations were marred by charges of espionage against British citizens, hardliner attacks on Anglican churches, and closures of Christian hospitals in Iran's major cities (Parsons, 1989, pp. 221–222).

However, the hostage crisis of 1979 transformed the whole face and fabric of Iranian post-revolutionary politics, casting the IRI's relationship with the outside world, not least the Western powers, in a totally different mould that was hardly conceivable earlier. On November 4, 1979, a crowd of revolutionary students calling themselves "Students Following the Line of Imam" [Khomeini] stormed the U. S. embassy in Tehran dubbing it the "nest of espionage" and took 66 Americans hostage on charges of trying to stage a coup or counter-revolution and undermine the Islamic Republic. The British embassy was attacked a day later on November 5. However, the seizure drew to a quick end after the Islamic Revolution Guards Corps (IRGC) forces intervened. The students demanded that Washington extradite the deposed Mohammad Reza Shah (who had taken refuge there for medical reasons) for trial. Though carried out with apparently "no master plan" (Ansari, 2007, p. 8), the occupation was a self-promoting preemptive action by a group of revolutionaries who feared a 1953-like Central Intelligence Agency (CIA) plot to restore the Shah to power; its continuation was a seemingly concerted attempt by hardliners to further radicalize Iran's political scene and thus marginalize liberal moderates within Bazargan's nationalist government, which stood down in its aftermath (Herring, 2008; Freedman, 2008). The crisis that lasted for 444 days, namely, until January 20, 1981, cost President Jimmy Carter any chances of re-election and caused national humiliation for the United States. In the words of Freedman (2008), "Carter's presidency was marked more than anything else by his failure to cope with the Iranian revolution" (p. 62). For some Americans this was America's, and by extension, the West's "first encounter with radical Islam" (Farber, 2005). Many in Iran engulfed in the revolutionary fervor hailed it as a great victory, with Ayatollah Khomeini throwing his weight behind the venture and defending it as the "Second Revolution" (as cited in Naji, 2008, p. 19; see also Matin-Asgari, 2004, p. 47).

The Carter administration tried a number of formally peaceful punitive measures to secure the release of hostages by the spring of 1980, including stopping the dispatch of military equipment to Iran, prohibiting the import of Iranian petroleum, freezing Iran's official assets in the U.S. banks, demanding United Nations mediation and seeking diplomatic support of its allies; however to no avail (Houghton, 2001; Jones, 2008). With the crisis not yet resolved, and the next presidential elections drawing closer, he decided on April 24, 1980, to embark on "Operation Eagle Claw" to rescue the hostages. That decision led to the death of eight American servicemen as a result of a collision between rescue aircraft in the *Tabas* desert in east-central Iran. This forced Carter to make a live statement on national television acknowledging responsibility:

> I ordered this rescue mission prepared to safeguard American lives, to protect America's national interests, and to reduce the tensions in the world that have been caused among many nations as this crisis has continued. It was my decision to attempt the rescue operation. It was my decision to cancel it when problems developed in the placement of our rescue team for a future rescue operation. The responsibility is fully my own …The United States remains determined to bring about their safe release at the earliest date possible. (Houghton, 2001, p. 3)

And it did, but too late for Carter to stand his electoral ground and win a second term in office.

Among the three circles of the Atlantic Alliance, Europe, and the Commonwealth at the intersection of which Winston Churchill had anticipated Britain to play out its post-imperial role, "Atlanticism" had taken the highest priority for Thatcher (Fry, 2008, p. 182). According to Fry, the common "Soviet menace" to the capitalist West had provided a fertile context for Britain to work towards reinvigoration as well as reinvention of the special relationship that seemed by then to have lapsed into a "one-sided love affair" much adhered to by the British. Thatcher maintained that the Soviet invasion of Afghanistan in 1979 and hostage-taking of American diplomats by Iranian revolutionaries in the same year was a consequence of Carter's being "over-influenced" by the erroneous impression that "the threat from Communism had been exaggerated." This made her government identify quite closely with the ensuing Republican administration of Ronald Reagan (1981–1988) whose head-on confrontation with the growing Eastern threat "made 1981" as Thatcher enthused, "the last year of the West's retreat before the axis of convenience between the Soviet Union and the Third World" (as cited in Fry, 2008, p. 181).

As mentioned, the hostage crisis ushered in a new era of heightened tension between Iran and the Western powers. The North Atlantic Treaty Organization (NATO) soon convened a meeting on December 13 and condemned the measure, calling for an immediate end to the takeover, and release of all hostages. Britain under Thatcher was among the first European countries that lent robust public support to levying economic sanctions against Iran. The prevalent perception in the Iranian elite opinion was that by virtue of their special friendship, Britain acted in the European community as the key promoter and facilitator of America's penal policies against the Islamic Republic. Despite the lack of a close, personal relationship between Democratic Carter and Conservative Thatcher, Carter (1982) acknowledges in his memoir that the British prime minister was Washington's most reliable ally during the hostage crisis. Approving of economic penalties in a statement in December, she assured the United States' administration: "you would expect nothing less and you would get nothing less than our full support," while other European Community (EC) members had not yet arrived at a definite decision by that time (Smith, 1990, p. 18).

With the severance of U.S. diplomatic relations with Iran on April 7, 1980, and in the face of EC restricting itself to vocal condemnation of hostage-taking and its refusal to impose economic sanctions, an indignant Carter expected Britain to provide its promised backing in practice. The UK Foreign and Commonwealth Office headed by Lord Carrington helped devise a detailed pressure plan which included: staff reduction in EC embassies in Tehran and Iranian missions in Europe; placing a halt to oil purchases from Iran; introducing stringent visa requirements for Iranian travelers to the European countries; banning arms sales to the Islamic Republic; denying permission for new exports; and, if the measures did not lead to a meaningful change for the better in the crisis by May 17, 1980, devising a comprehensive trade and economic sanction scheme to follow (Saidabadi, 1998). The collective character of the effort initiated by the British government appeared partly because of its reluctance to sacrifice its national interests individually for the sake of Americans, and at the same time, a desire to keep the "special relationship" up and running at a time when the United States desperately needed its activation.

The Iran (Temporary Powers) Bill was passed in the British parliament. It required the government to reconsider its contracts with Iran and to levy due sanctions against it. However, it fell short of having those agreements signed before the specified deadline of May 17, nor did it cover banking or other financial contracts. Strikingly, on May 19 in Naples, when EC foreign ministers agreed that the imposed penalties would apply to the deals concluded after November 4, 1979 (the day of the hostage-taking), both Tory and Labour parliamentarians inveighed against it, accusing Thatcher's government of duplicity and double standards. "[S]trong British words and weak actions" as the West German Minister of Economy, Count Otto Lambsdorff, put it (as cited in Saidabadi, 1998, p. 90), did little to secure American interests, but much to antagonize Iran's ideological leaders whose position had been further reinforced after the head of the liberally oriented nationalist Provisional Government, Mehdi Bazargan, decided to resign in protest to the takeover. Yet, the British support for the Carter administration during the crisis has been described as one of the principal developments in 1979–1980 that brought "the two countries closer" rather than distancing them from each other (Dobson, 1995, p. 147).

To further inflame the adverse situation of Iran–UK ties, the Iranian embassy in London was, in the meantime, forcefully occupied by an anti-IRI pan-Arabist's group led by Fouzi Badavinejad who kidnapped its working staff, demanded Iran release 91 Arab prisoners, and also proclaimed the independence of Khuzestan (a mostly Arab-populated province in southern Iran). The incident was finally terminated violently through a Special Air Service (SAS) rescue operation leaving some of the Iranian hostages dead. This was interpreted by many on the Iranian side as a British conspiracy to force Tehran to free the American captives. Speculations of this kind gained ground when it was realized that the British embassy staff in Tehran had been significantly reduced before the seizure (Shokrani, 1993). The prevailing perception was that the deadly Iranian embassy affair in London was, in fact a Carter–Thatcher collusion executed by Iraqi hands. Though some Iranian officials, including Foreign Minister Sadeq Qotbzadeh refuted this, it helped push bilateral relations further to the brink of rupture.

Detention of Iranian students demonstrating before the United States' embassy in London followed by the arrest of British missionaries in Iran and the growing threats to "blow up" the UK embassy in Tehran were other occurrences which exacerbated existing tensions and induced Britain to shut its embassy in August 1980. The formal closure and the consequential reduction of ties to the level of holding an interests section in both capitals came around a month later, in September 1980, when Iran's new Prime Minister, Mohammad Ali Rajaee, warned London about his government's "appropriate reaction" if Britain continued to keep Iranian students in custody (Saidabadi, 1998, pp. 93-95). The move endorsed Iranian leaders' preconceptions that the "Little Satan" was indeed a follower of the "Great Satan" and would not hesitate to step into its shoes. The British embassy closure was doomed to last for eight years, until the end of Iran–Iraq war when revolutionary passion would subside in Iranian politics. For all its length, however, the period was by no means a political hiatus.

Iranian-British Relations in the Shadow of Iran-Iraq War

With the Iraqi invasion of Iran on September 22, 1980, political stakes escalated in the Islamic Republic's relationship with the international community, not least the Western powers. Iranian leaders viewed Saddam Hussein a Western puppet, and his war against Iran originally a Western conspiracy to dismantle its newly founded revolutionary state (Mesbahi, 1993). Sensitivities were heightened following the refusal of US- and UK-dominated United Nations Security Council (UNSC) to condemn the attack unequivocally and call for the withdrawal of the aggressor. The war was, *inter alia*, "a reaction to the revived Islamic revolutionary ideology" (Rajaee, 1993, p. 1),[2] and with respect to the power-void created by the fall of the Pahlavi regime, was deemed by Iraqi Ba'ath nationalists a good means to restructure the geopolitical order of the region (McLachlan, 1993; Tehrani, 1993). In a somewhat similar vein, the aggression has also been broadly ascribed to the fierce rivalry between Iran and Iraq for ascendency over the Persian Gulf in the wake of the security vacuum left by the British retreat in the early 1970s and following the overthrow of Mohammad Reza Shah (Pelletiere, 1992). The shock waves the Islamic revolution sent throughout the region, and the far-reaching deleterious effects it exerted on the great power interests in the Middle East, coupled with the notorious hostage crisis and the ensuing prevalent perception of Iran as a "rogue state" and an "outlaw regime" did a lot to alienate otherwise sympathetic intermediaries, and was evidently working to the IRI's disadvantage at a time when it was urgently in need of outside support (Parsons, 1990).

Not only the UK government, which cherished its enhanced bond with the U.S. more than any other time, but also all the other major European actors, including France and Germany, tended to adopt policies that did not conform with the United States' position on the conflict (Naghibzadeh, 1993). In tune with the United States, whose diplomats were still captive in Iran, the British declined to demand Iraqi withdrawal from the Iranian territories which had fallen at the outset of war, and preferred to maintain an uneasy silence over the conflict. Even the first UNSC resolution (479), which came approximately a week after Iraq's military aggression, was in terms more palatable to Iraq than Iran as it appealed for an end to hostilities irrespective, however, of the violation of Iranian territorial integrity by Saddam's forces. Finally, Iranian leaders moved to release the American hostages in January 1981 and, along with that, made compromises to free four British citizens who had been detained on charges of espionage.

The Thatcher government regarded the release of British detainees a constrictive measure by Iranians that could pave the way for normalization of bilateral relations and the reopening of the UK embassy in Tehran. This was largely a non-starter though, as powerful idealists still dominant in Iran's decision-making circles feared that the restoration of normal ties, and the diplomatic latitude and maneuverability it would allow the British might jeopardize the revolutionary establishment; thus, making security matters worse for the government by raising the likelihood of foreign espionage, and subsequently undermining their embattled position. Recognizing this problem, Douglas Hurd, then UK Minister of Europe, declared the official stance of Britain in a parliamentary address in the same month. Echoing his government's desire for a rapprochement:

> We have no quarrel with the Iranian revolution and no desire to interfere in their affairs or influence how they run their affairs or who they choose to govern them. Whatever may have happened in the past, whatever may have been the past nature of our involvement with Iran, its present nature is clear: we have no desire to interfere in the matters which the Iranians rightly regard as entirely their own affairs. Iran is an important country in the Middle East, an important country in our eyes, and we would wish to return to our traditional relationship with it. (as cited in Saidabadi, 1998, p. 99)

As indicated, another chief factor that stood as an impediment to the improvement of relations was the British failure to meet the IRI leaders' growing expectations about foreign attitude towards the raging Iran–Iraq war. While Iranians expected Britain to reciprocate their conciliatory measure (releasing British subjects) by condemning the Iraqi invasion of Iran, the Thatcher government's conservative foreign policy required it to stay in the rival camp, in alignment with the United States' and Britain's regional Arab allies who were, in one way or another, backing Saddam Hussein. The Western connivance at, but also support for, the Iraqi aggression (Karsh, 2002) served to convince the IRI leaders that they had been drawn into a war they had to fight alone and single-handedly. The political indignation against Britain had soared to such a level that an influential Iranian cleric, Ayatollah Meshkini, raised the Northern Irish question in a Friday prayer sermon for the first time after the revolution. He also voiced Iran's support for the "oppressed and deprived people of Northern Ireland" who were engaged in a violent conflict with what he called the "old fox of British colonialism" and prayed for their emancipation (as cited in Saidabadi, 1998, p. 100). Accordingly, the street next to the British embassy in central Tehran was renamed after the separatist Irish Republican Army combatant Bobby Sands, who was imprisoned by British forces and later died in 1981.

Two years into the war, Iran was gradually managing to turn the tide in its favor. By late 1982, it had restored the bulk of its lost territory, and encouraged by significant victories on the battleground, was determined to make bold advancements towards Baghdad and realize its much-vaunted objective of replacing Hussein's Ba'athist regime with a like-minded Shi'ite government (Mesbahi, 1993). This escalated Western, especially American and British, fears that the conflict might spread throughout the Persian Gulf and threaten their political and economic interests in the vulnerable oil-rich sheikdoms of the region. The increasing threat of an attack on oil shipments heading from the Arab ports for Western destinations was another cause for concern. The British realization that

Iraq was no longer on the winning side and unlikely to regain the previous upper hand prompted an implicit shift of policy in the Thatcher government towards the war whereby it strived to persuade the conflicting sides into a negotiated settlement of animosities.[3] Such a policy was also underlined by the understanding that persistence of Iran–Iraq conflict could provide ample opportunity for the Soviet Union to consolidate its position in the Middle East, as it had started developing a working military relationship with Iraq in spite of its declared policy of neutrality once "the pendulum had swung in Iran's favour" (Karsh, 2002, pp. 42–43; Mesbahi, 1993; Sajjadpour, 1997).

Security issues aside, there appears to have been an ideational tension at work that impacted strongly upon the Western powers' double standard treatment of the Iran–Iraq war. As Naghibzadeh (1993) contends, the ideological clash between the liberal West and Islamic Iran disposed the former to keep a "meaningful silence" when Iraq had a superior position, "waiting and hoping that [it] would close the book on Islamic fundamentalism," but to struggle for an end to the conflict when Iranian forces managed to reverse its course (p. 40). Thus when Iran's war machine started moving speedily ahead, clinching victories on the Iraqi territory, Britain and its allies in the UN Security Council worked to adopt a second resolution (UNSC 514) that demanded both sides to respect each other's territorial integrity and insisted on their withdrawal to internationally recognized borders. For Iranians, this stood in sharp contrast to the first UNSC resolution, which had failed to heed their territorial concerns and was interpreted as a biased and discriminatory attempt by Western powers to espouse Saddam's aggressive policies. The resolution's failure to denounce Iraq as the originator of war helped to further alienate Iran from the Security Council and dispose its leaders' opinion against later UN resolutions on the conflict (Parsons, 1991).

The British government's close political and military cooperation with members of the Arab Gulf Cooperation Council (GCC) might be explained by its apprehensions about their susceptibility as Britain's close regional allies to the ravages of nearby war. However, given the considerable financial and military support some GCC members— especially Saudi Arabia and Kuwait—were explicitly lending Iraq, the whole organization came to be seen by Iranian statesmen as yet another West-controlled apparatus in the region whose chief purpose was to counterbalance, if not undercut, the Islamic Republic (Lotfian, 1997; Nonneman, 2004). The principal objective of Western governments, including Britain, was to maintain the status-quo "balance of power" in the Persian Gulf, and protect their access to its "cheap oil" while they saw a recently galvanized Islamic Republic as "a superior threat" to those seminal interests rather than Saddam Hussein's "admittedly ruthless but reassuringly secular rule" (Hiltermann, 2004, p. 159). The perception might partly account for Thatcher's occasional policy of rejectionism vis-à-vis Iran during the 1980s, which, unlike its French neighbor, manifested itself more clearly in her government's adamant refusal to seek the IRI's mediation to facilitate the release of British citizens kidnapped in South Lebanon. Moreover, aggrandizing the security threat presented by the 1979 revolution to the Persian Gulf sheikhdoms could persuade them to boost their military capability by ordering equipment that would help "oil the wheels of the Western military-industrial complex," but this would fall far short of defusing "the ideological threat posed by the revolution" (Ansari, 2007, p. 110).

In spite of its official policy of neutrality, Britain tipped towards Iraq, but was also careful not to kill the slender chances of restoring its relations with Iran now that the latter had managed to repulse the invasion and the fall of the Islamic Republic. As a strong conviction for many at the outset of the war, it had been rendered an unlikely story. On the one hand, British arms dealers as well as some government officials were reportedly heavily engaged in lucrative military and commercial contracts with Iraq (Naghibzadeh, 1993; Phythian, 1997; Sweeney, 1993), and on the other, the Thatcher government allowed the National Iranian Oil Company office (*Kala*), which was seemingly arranging military equipment purchases for Iran, to operate freely in London. In 1984, when Britain was slammed by the U.S. and Iraq's Arab allies for supplying Iran with spare parts for its Chieftain tanks, Thatcher's rationale was that the equipment had been "fully paid for prior to the 1979 revolution" (as cited in Saidabadi, 1998, p. 105). Some commentators have suggested that Britain's overarching policy in the Persian Gulf after its retreat from the region was driven by a desire to hold regional states strategically at bay, hampering their independent projection of power, and at the same time, trying to retain a considerable level of relationship with them, an approach that played a significant role in informing its diplomacy towards the hostile parties during the Iran–Iraq war (Naghibzadeh, 1993).

Nonetheless, Iranian–British relations had yet to go a long way before normalization. The detention of Roger Cooper, a British citizen and a *Financial Times* journalist, in late 1985 on spying charges dealt another blow to them. Amidst the infamous "Tanker War" in the Persian Gulf and with the Iran–Iraq conflict entering a critical phase, Britain doubled its efforts to pass a mandatory resolution in collaboration with the United States and its European partners through the UN Security Council in order to bring the conflicting sides to the negotiating table and put an end to the growingly pernicious attrition. As a result of "British initiatives" in the United Nations the binding UNSC Resolution 598 was adopted on July 20, 1987, requiring Iran to end the war. As Geoffrey Howe, then UK Secretary of State for Foreign and Commonwealth Affairs, stated in the parliament:

> It was British action that secured the implementation of Resolution 598 in the first place; it was British action that therefore secured the first meeting since 1972 of Foreign Ministers of the five permanent members committed to promote action to implement it. That is why it is necessary, Iraq having accepted Security Council Resolution 598, for Iran to do likewise. If Iran does not do that, I repeat that the Security Council should proceed with a follow-up resolution to enforce compliance. (cited in Saidabadi, 1998, p. 113)

Considering the resolution a perverse Western-hatched scheme to bring the Islamic Republic to its knees, Iran resisted a year before reluctantly submitting to it on July 18, 1988 in the face of mounting international pressure, with Ayatollah Khomeini bemoaning the momentous decision as "deadlier than taking poison" (Khomeini, 2006, p. 95). The war did not definitely help to improve relations between the IRI and the UK, nor did it cause their complete severance. Iran desperately needed Britain to break out of its political and economic isolation and power its war engine through the access London provided it to international—especially European—markets. Britain did not need Iran in that sense, but by maintaining the lowest possible diplomatic ties, Britain was better able to secure its economic interests in Iran, and more significantly, its strategic stakes in the Middle East. It was politically unbecoming of such a revolutionary state as the Islamic Republic, with an established ideological identity to accept the mischief of what it had repeatedly deplored as the "Little Satan" and "wily fox." But the bitter reality of war had deeply changed the worldview of Iranian leaders, making it clear for them that the struggle for survival would have to take precedence over ideology and identity matters, especially in the short term. In a decisive letter to then Iranian President and current Supreme Leader Ali Khamenei on January 6, 1988 (approximately six months before the IRI's recognition of the UN ceasefire resolution) Khomeini had invoked the principle of "Guardianship of the Supreme Jurisprudent (*Velayat-e Faqih*)" and a curiously tailored interpretation of it to underline the survival and expedient interests (*masaleh*) of the Islamic Republic above all else, thereby prioritizing them even over the salient religious rules and fundamental precepts of Islam itself (*IRANalyst*, 2010; Shakibi, 2010).

Apart from Tehran's support for the Lebanese Hezbollah and the latter's hostage-taking of Western citizens, the last straw that would break the camel's back and throw bilateral relations entirely off course was to come soon following the publication of *The Satanic Verses* in Britain in 1988.

The Rushdie Affair and Its Implications at Home and Abroad

In the wake of Iran's acceptance of UNSCR 598, without qualification, to end the war and the resurgence of pragmatist and realist elements in its political system, its diplomatic relations with the West were set to improve. This was a development that could better serve the interests of both sides. The Iranian side needed Western knowledge, expertise, resources, and investment to reconstruct a war-stricken country; the Western side needed normal relations with Iran to deflect the increasing political and economic Soviet penetration of the region and gain a deserving share in its lucrative post-war reconstruction now that reinvigorated pragmatists in its foreign policy apparatus signaled their willingness for a reconsideration of Iran's relationship with the outside world. Thatcher's rather rejectionist policy of no negotiation with the IRI could no longer "answer," as it had particularly failed in the case of British hostages in Lebanon. Nor could Iran's revolutionary foreign policy work anymore—having been thrown into a splendid isolation in the international community.

It was against this backdrop of compromise, willingness, and hope that the Rushdie affair popped up like a poisonous magic mushroom, contaminating the whole atmosphere of Iran–West relations, radicalizing the hardly softened positions on both sides, and resurrecting the repressed conspiracy theories of the past once again. *The Satanic Verses*, a novel by Salman Rushdie—a British author born to a Muslim family in India—was published on September 26, 1988, and soon condemned by many Islamic nations including Pakistan, Egypt, Saudi Arabia, Indonesia, and Qatar, as a grave affront to the *Qur'an*, Prophet Muhammad, and generally to Islam and Muslims worldwide. There were unequivocal references in the book to the prophet of Islam whom Rushdie had dubbed "Mahound" which is considered "a derogatory name for Mohammad in medieval polemics" (Daniel, 2001, p. 226), and described as "the Devil's synonym."[4] What added fuel to the fire was that these words had been uttered and then publicized by a born Muslim. Almost five months after its publication, on February 14, 1989, Ayatollah Khomeini issued a religious edict (*fatwa*) that was publicly broadcast by Radio Tehran:

> Indeed all of us are from Allah and indeed all will return to Him. I inform the valiant Muslims all over the world that the author of the book The Satanic Verses, which has been compiled and published against Islam, the Prophet and [the] *Qur'an*, as well as [its] publishers who were aware of its contents, are sentenced to execution. I demand the valiant Muslims to execute them promptly wherever they find them so that nobody dare insult the sanctities of Muslims anymore, and everyone who is killed on the way of this cause is a martyr, Allah willing. Incidentally, if somebody has access to the author of the book, but is not himself/herself capable of executing him, s/he should introduce him to the people so that he receives the punishment for his deeds. And peace and Allah's mercy and blessings be upon you. (Khomeini, 2006, p. 263)

Apart from the official condemnations, 15 Khordad Foundation, an Iranian state-affiliated trust, offered a huge bounty for anyone who would succeed in enforcing the edict. In fact, the IRI leaders regarded the book as part of a larger project of conspiracy orchestrated by Western powers, especially Britain, to ridicule and "annihilate" the Islamic culture and revolution (Daniel, 2001; Fuller, 1991, p. 254). Issuance of a death sentence on a foreign citizen in absentia for blasphemy against Islam had a great impact on both—Iran's domestic politics and its foreign relations. It was music to the ear of Iranian hardliners as the posturing re-empowered the waning trend of Islamic idealism in the country's political ambience and revitalized the revolutionary vehemence of earlier years, once again reasserting its ideology-driven foreign policy and thwarting all pragmatic efforts to end Iran's international isolation (Ahmadi, 2008). On the international arena, the fatwa was interpreted as a radical attempt to "extend Islamic law into a predominantly non-Muslim country, Britain" (Afary & Anderson, 2005, p. 164). This meant the breach of its national sovereignty and could entail destabilizing normative as well as security implications for the West on the whole. For one, Abdullah al-Ahdal, a Belgium-based Muslim cleric who disapproved of Khomeini's decree as inapplicable outside the Islamic world, was shot to death a few weeks after the edict was publicized internationally.

Within a bigger picture, the fatwa appeared a far-reaching venture by Iran to reinforce its diminishing self-identification as "leader of the Muslim world" (Ansari, 2007, p. 127). Perhaps this was the main reason for the political disagreement its regional rivals, especially Saudi Arabia, expressed regarding the verdict. In a countermeasure to underscore its role in the Islamic world, the Saudi government held a conference of religious scholars who appealed for the formation of an Islamic court to try Rushdie before issuing a death sentence against him (Marschall, 2003). For all the diplomatic challenge it posed the Iran–West rapprochement, the fatwa helped soothe a wounded and traumatized Islamic Republic—which had been forced rather humiliatingly into succumbing to a Western-drafted ceasefire resolution and revive its diluted identity as a revolutionary state adhering to its foundation principles, however detrimental the resurfacing of such an identity proved to the nation's national interests. As a Western historian of Iranian politics construes, the fatwa inflicted "incalculable damage" on the IRI's image abroad and derailed long-term efforts to recast Islam as a tolerant religion (Daniel, 2001, p. 227). With the decree having a global reach and infringing the West's normative boundaries, 12 European Community member states joined Britain in recalling their ambassadors, while the Thatcher government withdrew its entire diplomatic mission from Tehran on February 20, 1989. In response, Iran also summoned all its diplomats from EC capitals the next day. The renewed isolation had worried the Iranian political pragmatists, but Khomeini's uncompromising stance and still unrivalled position in the country's political establishment left them no other choice than to follow his line. On February 22, two days after the EC's coordinated action, Khomeini was unmistakable in his criticism of those who still hoped to prevent the controversy from turning into an all-out diplomatic crisis:

> It is not necessary for us to go seeking to establish extensive ties because the enemy may think that we have become so dependent and attach so much importance to their existence that we quietly condone insults to our beliefs and religious sanctities. Those who still continue to believe that and warn that we must embark on a revision of our policies, principles and diplomacy and that we have blundered and must not repeat previous mistakes; those who still believe that extremist slogans or war will cause the West and the East to be pessimistic about us, and that ultimately all this

has led to the isolation of the country; those who believe that if we act in a pragmatic way they will reciprocate humanely and will mutually respect nations, Islam and Muslims, to them this [Rushdie incident] is an example. (cited in Daniel, 2001, pp. 227–228)

Significantly, the stance divulges more than anything else Khomeini's apprehensions about the future direction as well as identity of the Islamic system he had taken such great pains to build at his own discretion. He feared that, with his departure, the revolution might derail, causing the Republic to lose its "uniqueness on the global scene" (Ehteshami, 1995, p. 139). Taking advantage of the re-radicalized ambience and the fresh opportunity, however, the Islamists did not hesitate to seize the initiative, and thus entirely severed Iran's relations with the UK on March 7, 1989. For many, Iran had been reverting to its pre-war "pattern of confrontation in the international arena" (Ehteshami, 1995, p. 31). The resurgence of revolutionary sentiments and radical attitudes in Iran's political system as a consequence of the Rushdie episode exerted an adverse impact upon, and indeed substantially reduced, the speed of change Iranian pragmatists had endeavored to introduce in the country's foreign policy-making.

The lingering legacy of the incident remained even after Khomeini's death a few months later, on June 3, 1989, overshadowing bilateral ties for another considerable period of time during which Iran needed to break out of its international isolation, re-entrench itself economically, and build a republic of more modern and adaptable nature politically. The chill ground of Anglo-Iranian relations was there to stay until the ascent to power of the Reformists in Iran, headed by President Mohammad Khatami and the Labourites in Britain, and led by Prime Minister Tony Blair just before the turn of the 20th century. Although diplomatically speaking, they were restored and embassies re-opened in September 1990 during the preponderance of pragmatists under President Ali Akbar Hashemi Rafsanjani. It was only in May 1999 that for the first time since the 1979 revolution, the Islamic Republic–United Kingdom relationship was fully re-established following *diplomatic* settlement of the Rushdie affair with Nicholas Browne appointed as Britain's ambassador to Tehran and Morteza Sarmadi dispatched as Iran's envoy to London. Now over three decades after the revolution, however, Anglo-Iranian relations are formally absent and informally in a chill phase marked by insidious tension, which is arguably taking a much heavier toll on the internationally weaker side.[5]

Notes

1. The most notable instance of this historical trauma in the Iranian collective psyche is the 1953 coup d'état orchestrated jointly by the US and UK against Mohammad Mosaddeq's nationalist government in Iran.

2. For further explanation of Saddam Hussein's fears about the Iranian revolution and its political repercussions, including the activities of *al-Da'wah*, a Shi'a underground movement in Iraq that had been inspired by Ayatollah Khomeini's religious doctrine, see Dawisha, A. (2009). *Iraq: A political history from independence to occupation* (pp. 221–222). Princeton, NJ: Princeton University Press.

3. For Thatcher's views of and recollections on the menace Iran–Iraq war posed British interests in the region, see her memoir: Thatcher, M. (1993). *The Downing Street years*. London, UK: Harper Collins.

4. The 'Prophet Mahound' or the 'Messenger Mahound,' Rushdie indicated, was so dumb that Salman, his Persian "official scribe," cheated him in writing down the God-revealed verses of the *Qur'an* that Mahound recited, "pulling the word of God with my own profane language" (p. 367). "Ayesha," a wife of Prophet Mohammed, played the role of a "fifteen-year-old whore" in the novel that "was the most popular with the paying public" (p. 380). Rushdie had also brought some Islamic rules of conduct under scrutiny: "Amid the palm-trees of the oasis, Gibreel appeared to the Prophet and found himself spouting rules, rules, rules … rules about every damn thing, if a man farts let him turn his face to the wind … The revelation—the recitation—told the faithful how much to eat, how deeply they should sleep, and which sexual positions had received divine sanction, so that they learned that sodomy and the missionary position were approved of by the archangel, whereas the forbidden postures included all those in which the female was on top" (p. 363). See Rushdie, S. (1992). *The Satanic verses*. Dover, DE: Consortium.

5. For an analysis of the lowering of bilateral ties in November 2011 and an almost simultaneous takeover of the British embassy in Tehran, which finally led to its closure and virtual severance of diplomatic relations, see Behravesh, M. (2012, 19 January). Downgrading Iranian–British relations: The anatomy of a folly. *openDemocracy*. Retrieved 10 January 2013 from http://www.opendemocracy.net/ourkingdom/maysam-behravesh/downgrading-iranian-british-relations-anatomy-of-folly.

PART FOUR

MENA Women's Rights: Triumphs and Setbacks

In the earlier months of the Arab Spring, women's presence was evident in the demonstrations to oust their long-time dictators. The images of women—old and young, with head covers, veils, or none—marching in the demonstrations gave millions of Arab women hope that their lot would or could be improved with the removal of the authoritarian regimes in their respective countries. Arab women's struggle for equality and human rights and dignity has a long history dating back to the Revolution of 1919, when Egyptian women and men protested the British occupation of their country and demanded independence from the British. The wife of the Egyptian leader and revolutionary Saad Zaghlul was the first Arab woman to march with her husband in the pro-independence revolutions; and when he was arrested by the British occupiers, she led the demonstrators, and in protest took off her *hejab* (veil) signaling deviance from the status quo that imposed the *hejab* on women. In most Arab countries, women have made progress from their darkest periods of history to the present day limited progress of access to education and employment outside the home. However, these limited gains for women's rights are now being threatened by the rising tide of political Islamists and Muslim fundamentalists who want to turn back the clock.

Dr. Fredrika Malmström and Anna Hellstrand's paper explores Egyptian activists/feminists, who belong to the middle and upper classes as political actors after the Egyptian uprising(s). Their research sheds light on the complexities of global (policy) interventions, feminism, agency, and the rapid transformations of societies. Their paper attempts to provide answers to some questions about women's feelings about the recent events in their Arab homeland, and in the ways in which they react. How do Egyptian activists/feminists define feminism, and how do they interact with various actors on several levels at the same time? They elaborate on how Egyptian feminists are navigating between various actors: the global donor community "western feminism", Egyptians in general, and the new state/political Islam after the uprisings. They give examples of Egyptian political activists' intentions to translate "universal" concepts on the local level as well as to put forward processes of circulation, mediation, and transformation.

In her comparative study, Dr. Alessandra L. González explores the important roles women are playing in the middle of extreme social change and political upheaval in the traditional and religious societies of the Arab Gulf States and in what ways women's involvement in public leadership compares with the activism of women in the traditional and religious societies of Latin America. Dr. Gonzáles discusses a number of common points of interest between women in leadership in the Arab Gulf and Latin America. The paper highlights findings from a study of 35 original interviews with men and women in the Arab Gulf region on the future of women's political activism, and the relationship that religious and political affiliation have in creating a balance for women's progressive rights within traditional and religious cultures. In addition, using historical and academic sources, the paper highlights the differences and commonalities of women in business and political leadership in Latin America, and emphasizes the importance of continued comparisons between Latin America and the Arab Gulf to encounter alternative negotiation strategies for the empowerment of women and other traditionally marginalized populations. She concludes that case studies that compare women in Latin America with women in the Arab Gulf States is a perfect pairing in which to study the strategies of feminist activists who negotiate for women's rights from within their conservative and traditional cultures.

Not unlike developments in post-Arab Spring countries, where recent advancements in women's rights are being threatened by ultra-conservative Islamists and Salafists, women in Israel seem to be facing similar oppression due to the rising political clout of certain sectors of conservative and ultra-Orthodox Judaism. The study by Dr. Michal Allon of the phenomenon of the exclusion of women from the public sphere in Israel addresses the issue of the status of women in Israel which she described as "'paradoxical,' as there have been some impressive gains by women in politics, business, military and education, but there are also serious setbacks as a result of the increasing size and political and economic power of the Orthodox-Jewish population, and the extreme fundamentalism of some of its religious communities and political leaders." She describes some of the causes of this phenomenon, the impact on Israeli society, and the difficulty in confronting these causes. Dr. Allon attributes these setbacks to an accelerated process of radicalization of Orthodox Jewish fundamentalism among some religious communities and their political leaders. These trends are met with sharp, albeit mostly ineffective, opposition and demonstrations from religious and secular men and women. This conflict may be due to the lack of separation between religion and the state and the impact fundamentalism is having on women's rights. She recommends that a separation of religion and state would have a beneficial effect not only for Jewish women, but throughout the State of Israel, and would improve the lives of women of all faiths and all ethnic groups.

In their paper, Dr. Jennifer Bremer and Ola Gameel al-Talliawi examine "Gender and Leadership Style in the Middle East: Evidence from Egypt's Civil Service". They point out that while gender differentials in managerial positions and leadership style have been studied widely in the West, only rarely have they received the same treatment in the Middle East. Bremmer and al-Talliawi's study analyzes women's position in Egypt's public sector by, first, analyzing official data on female participation in public sector management positions in Egypt and, second, by comparing men's and women's leadership styles based on a survey of Ministry of Finance middle managers. The survey, which uses a variant of LBDQ XII (Leadership Behavior Description Questionnaire XII), finds no statistically significant differences based on gender. This finding supports the hypothesis that male and female leadership styles are similar and do not reflect agentic (stereotypically male) versus communal (stereotypically female) models. Their findings underscore the need to "ensure gender-neutral access to opportunities for leadership to take full advantage of Egypt's human resource assets."

Imagining the New Egypt: Agential Egyptian Activism/Feminism, Translation, and Movement

Maria Frederika Malmström
Anna Hellstrand

Abstract

This article explores Egyptian activists/feminists among the middle and upper classes as political actors after the Egyptian uprising(s). What do they think and feel about their new homeland, and in which ways do they act? The critical inquiry is to explore how these women and men combine "the old with the new" and how they deftly juggle dominant social structures of power and inequality with their personal desires in today's Cairo. Framed by their position within the broader political transformation, how do these Egyptian activists/feminists define feminism, and how do they interact with various actors on several levels at the same time? This text examines theoretically how agency is formulated in Egypt's transition in relation to how it was, how it is in the present, and how it will be in the imagined future. In order to understand this multifaceted process, we need translation and movement as analytical tools. The research throws light on the complexities of global (policy) interventions, feminism, agency, and rapid transformations of societies.

Introduction

In the current dynamics of Egypt, national activists/feminists voices are uneasy with regard to the loss of interest in women's rights. They underscore that women's rights after the uprising/s are being resisted in public discourse, in the draft constitution, and in political reforms.

Egypt has a long history of feminism, and these issues are by no means new in the national context.[1] An explicit agenda on "women's issues" was introduced into the realm of official policies in connection with foreign interests invested in the country in the middle of the 19th century. Efforts and subsequent reforms for women have taken place ever since throughout historical and political developments, although controversies on these subjects have remained (Mahmood, 2005; Ahmed, 1992). Women of the upper and middle classes in Egyptian society started to gain visibility at the end on the 19th century through articles in journals, magazines, and newspapers. In addition to writing, upper-class women started to form women's organizations and associations during the same period (Ahmed, 1992; Badran, 1995). Badran and Esfandiari (2010b) note that supporters of Egypt's nation-based secular feminism perceive their feminism as indigenous feminism—developing from within. The language of "feminism and women's rights" has strong colonial connotations, however. These colonial undertones have caused some problems for Egyptian activists/feminists as they promote their politics. Many times their ideas have been and are being dismissed as "foreign" and hence "of no relevance" to Egyptian society. The connotations with a "foreign agenda" are and have been valuable for orthodox religious groups, such as political Islamic movements. Furthermore, these Egyptian activists/feminists have not gained enough support for their politics among the poorer strata. Why? The majority of less-affluent categories of Egyptian women set themselves apart from the middle and upper classes, naming these women *afrangi/spour* (Western foreigners). The following example will be given as an illustration: in early 2003, a short, state-sponsored film (initiated by former President Mubarak's wife Suzanne Mubarak, who was the head of the National Council for Women and Children, where many Egyptian activists/feminists have been involved) was repeatedly screened on national Egyptian television. One of Malmström's interlocutors saw the film as problematic because "[t]he woman is too snobbish, an *afrangi*. Few people will recognize their own life or opportunities for their daughters in this film" (Malmström, 2009a, p. 74).

The overall aim of this article is to understand and analyze Egyptian activists/feminists as political actors after the Egyptian uprising(s). What do they think and feel about their new homeland, and how do they act? The critical inquiry is to explore how these women and men combine "the old with the new" and how they deftly juggle dominant social structures of power and inequality in today's Cairo with their personal desires. This will be explored through the following questions: How do these Egyptian activists/feminists, framed by their position within the broader political transformation, define feminism, and how do they interact with various actors on several levels at the same time? This text examines theoretically how agency is formulated in Egypt's transition in relation to how it was, how it is in the present, and how it will be in the imagined future. In order to understand this multifaceted process, we also need translation and movement as analytical tools.

This article is based upon Malmström's previous research in Egypt (Malmström, 2004, 2009a, 2009b, 2011, forthcoming; Malmström et al. 2011), and upon her former student, Anna Hellstrand's interviews and thesis (Hellstrand, 2012). Hellstrand completed interviews with 12 feminists (age range between 27 and 77 years—10 women and 2 men), as well as casual conversations and observation during the spring of 2012 (from February 1 until the end of April). The actors interviewed may be described as professionals within the strata of middle and upper classes, living in Cairo and in Alexandria, where the majority defined themselves as activists (human or women's rights), and a few as feminists.

We will use the local term "human or women's rights activist" interchangeably with the local term "feminist" (to be explained further). Feminism has a dual character as both an analytical and politically prescriptive project—because it offers both an understanding of women's situations as marginalized, subordinated, or oppressed—and an agenda for how that situation is to be addressed (Mahmood, 2005). Naturally, even though there are some common denominators of feminism, there are various orientations within feminist movements that respond differently to how women's subordination is to be understood and addressed. Furthermore, everyone does not want the liberal discourse of freedom and individual autonomy and may perceive concepts such as gender equality (as opposed to equity or complementarity) as loaded with cultural imperialism.

As a final point of this introduction, please note that this work is preliminary and what we discuss needs further extensive work to solidify our preliminary findings. At the time of this writing, the Egyptian uprising is an ongoing process. When we use the term "uprising," we refer to the series of demonstrations that took place in Egypt beginning on January 25, 2011, or to the events that caused the Mubarak regime to succumb, but in the plural "uprisings," we mean the continuous protests taking place every week in Egypt. It should be noted that the interviews were conducted at a particular moment in time, which may inform the research in general and some of the conclusions drawn.

Feminism and Women's Rights

The following section about feminism is obviously not conclusive of the various feminist conceptualizations that exist, but rather offers some views of how women's rights and feminist concerns can be understood and (re)formulated.

Feminism(s)

As mentioned, there is a wide range of feminist definitions and orientations, which can mean dissimilar things and these do not have the same connotations for everyone. A common feature among various feminism(s) is that the term denotes both a consciousness and a social movement. It is based on the awareness that women suffer discrimination because of their gender. Awareness of injustice, however, is not sufficient. The other aspect of feminism is found in the actual attempts to change these inequalities and remove constraints placed on women in favor of a more equitable gender system (Gemzöe, 2003). For the participants in this study, the term "feminism" was generally viewed as controversial, and the majority did not consider it a proper concept. The majority preferred the term "human rights activists." Some of the responses Hellstrand received when asking how they conceptualized feminism and how they related to the term were:

> Feminism in Egypt is totally different from the real feminism anywhere else. It is more "women-activism"… (Hellstrand, 2012, p. 38)

> It is a human right to be and to act—to participate.… I prefer to deal with human rights and citizen's rights. (Hellstrand, 2012, p. 38)

> I do not like it. … I prefer equality, human rights for women. (Hellstrand, 2012, p. 38)

> I never use it. … Because you know I am Egyptian. I know my society. If you say 'feminism' they think of giving complete freedom for women to do whatever they want.… (Hellstrand, 2012, p. 38)

Saba Mahmood (2005)[1] argues that a feminist agenda must be derived from the women it is targeting. Mahmood points out that in current liberal political and feminist discourses, religion in general (and Islam in particular) is often proposed as contrary to women's interests—a concept that will be developed further in the sections about dilemmas of feminism. Mahmood objects to such simplifications and suggests that women's autonomy and choices be recognized even when they occur within patriarchal frameworks. We will come back to Mahmood in the theoretical section about agency.

Committee on the Elimination of Discrimination against Women (CEDAW)

The drafting of a convention especially for women was based on the recognition that existing international legal human rights documents did not cover or satisfactorily address issues of concern for women as a group. The convention was adopted in 1979 by the General Assembly of the United Nations and has been called an international bill of rights for women. The convention defines discrimination against women and sets up an agenda for ending such discrimination. Discrimination against women is defined as:

> …any distinction, exclusion or restriction made on the basis of sex which has the effect or purpose of impairing or nullifying the recognition, enjoyment or exercise by women, irrespective of their marital status, on a basis of equality of men and women, of human rights and fundamental freedoms in the political, economic, social, cultural, civil or any other field. (Office of the United Nations High Commissioner for Human Rights, n.d.)

The convention is concerned, not only with the output on behalf of the state to end gender discrimination against women, but with the actual outcome of measures taken against such discrimination. That is, the state is obliged, not only to take measures against the discrimination, but actually to follow up their implementation and results. Also, the convention recognizes that gender discrimination against women may occur as a result of stereotypes or gender roles, a reason why measures should be taken against reproducing or reinforcing such stereotypes. Finally, the CEDAW Committee, the governing body of the convention and the main actor in its implementation, has been granted the ability to issue general recommendations applicable to all parties of the convention. The general recommendations serve both as interpretational guidelines and as elaborations of the conventional text. The recommendations are not legally binding in the same way as the conventional text, however. The ratification of the CEDAW is formally voluntary by individual states. Once ratified, though, the state binds itself to fulfill the obligations of the text. The state can make reservations upon ratification against certain articles, in theory, but not against core articles essential for the understanding of the convention (such as Articles 2 and 16); in reality, this is done nonetheless (Office of the United Nations High Commissioner for Human Rights, n.d.).

Particularism, Power, and Problems

CEDAW is a cultural product of the ideas of women's rights in Europe and the United States in the 1950–1970s, which at that time highlighted and problematized discrimination, rather than other issues, for example, violence against women. The theoretical base of the discourse that generated the international women's rights provisions was instead that "women should have the same rights as men" and that constraints on women that keep them from achieving the same things as men should be removed. Some feminists argue that social justice, instead of gender equality, ought to be based upon the recognition of gender differences. The rights of men and women could be viewed as complementary instead of competitive. Gender roles are not always conceptualized as contrary to the realization of women's rights—equity rather than equality is stressed, as mentioned earlier (Merry, 2006).

In other words, women's rights and desires may be visualized differently from how they are expressed in CEDAW. Furthermore, the international human rights law suffers from its given system. Women's rights cannot be enforced, even though they are legal in their nature and bind states to obligations. UN governing bodies lack the legal instruments, based on the current understanding of and respect for state sovereignty, to make states comply with their laws. Thus, there are no sanctions for states or governments who ignore or violate them. Moreover and ironically, the responsibility for human rights falls ultimately upon the state; at the same time the state itself is, many times, the perpetrator of human rights violations. The historical reason behind this is the identification of the state as the main violator of human rights and human dignity. The basic idea was that states would pledge a commitment to respect human rights values on a voluntary basis and (given events after World War II) would feel compelled to do so. This framework (and many of these ideas) is still the working system of the UN.

The UN and the global community are not completely out of options when it comes to sanctioning states. Their power lies in exposing states that do not show compliance with the human rights norms. Demonstrating compliance with international human rights standards is in the political interest of most states, so that they will not lose "face" in front of an international audience. How efficient such a policy is depends most likely on the status of the country in question. Countries with economic and political influence and wealth have, of course, less incentive to yield to such tactics than countries with a greater international dependency (aid, trade, or foreign investment). States can employ other tactics to avoid scrutiny, through ignoring inquiries or by referring to state sovereignty and arguing that human rights implementation conflicts with national religion, culture, tradition, or custom. Notably, states' complicity with human rights norms at this level is played out as politics and diplomacy (Charlesworth & Chinkin, 2000; Merry, 2006).

The relevance of international law as a method of advancing women's status and situation has been questioned from various feminist viewpoints. An important objection is that the international legislation covers a relatively limited space in many women's lives. Conventionally, a distinction within law has been made between what constitutes private and public life; the international legislation applies to only the public sphere of life. Thus, rights can be violated (formally) only within the public sphere. The state is the only actor answerable to human rights violations, but many of the abuses women suffer occur within the private sphere of life and by a private/known perpetrator. There have been strategies to address this dilemma, but at large and in practice this situation remains, where states may regard such cases as "too private" to be a concern of the law at all (Buss & Manji, 2005; Charlesworth & Chinkin, 2000; Merry, 2006).

Agency, Translation, and Movement

Agency as Intention and Desire

The notion of agency has been elaborated within recent gender theory, and today, many scholars have adopted an approach of more creative aspects of agency: for example, Mahmood (2001, 2005), Ahearn (2001), Ortner (2006), and McNay (2004). Abu-Lughod's (1990) understanding of resistance as diagnostic of power relations marks a vital analytical step within anthropology—to move beyond the binary of resistance/subordination and the teleology of freedom and emancipation. Saba Mahmood (2005) in turn proposes that agency does not mean only resistance to social or patriarchal norms, but resistance can occur within patriarchy. By submitting to norms that women deem positive, women may manifest their agency in practice. It is therefore necessary to question normative liberal assumptions of what agency actually means. In liberal feminist theory, an individual is considered free if she acts autonomously, which implies an understanding of working for certain predetermined goals of progressive politics. This resonates with conclusions drawn from ethnographic work about women and Islam carried out in other contexts (Malaysia and Egypt), where such active submission has been seen as an expression of female creative agency (Frisk, 2004; Mahmood, 2005). Hence, agency needs to be decoupled from any specific agenda.

Resistance is only one act among many other modes of action. Secrecy and silence may be vital components of agency, along with agency through avoidance or through endurance (Malmström, 2009a, 2009b). Overall, the discussion has turned to concepts such as creativity and imagination (Jackson, 2005). Jackson (2005) suggests that we—maybe more when acting on the world around us is restricted—"create the illusion of acting to change the world by acting on ourselves" (Jackson, p. 150). In sum, agency does not have to be against dominant norms in society, but "individuals may respond in unanticipated and innovative ways which may hinder, reinforce or catalyse social change" (McNay, 2004, p. 5).

Overall, the need to understand the complexity and dynamics of agency as the capacity to act according to the exigencies of the specific socio-cultural situation is the main premise of this article. First, in line with Abu-Lughod (1990), to be able to understand forms of resistance in specific societies, we need to analyze these acts within fields of power rather than outside of them. Second, in agreement with Mahmood (2005), agency does not mean only resistance. We need to problematize the universality of desire to be free from relations of subordination—not only in relation to the grand patriarchal plan, but in relation to state and global politics. The meaning of agency cannot be fixed in advance, but must be explored in relation to particular historical and cultural situations.

Human Rights as Culture/s

Sally Engle Merry (2006) argues that human rights are better understood as cultural practice than law. She sees the creation of human rights law itself as a production of culture, producing new visions and norms of morality with "global legality" through its processes of transnational consensus building. She also points out that "theorizing culture as an open and flexible system changes the debate about human rights and their localization and offers a more accurate framework for human rights activism" (Merry, 2006, p. 28). Merry proposes that human rights always must be translated into local contexts (at the level of local implementation), that is to say, that their "standards are tailored" to the local context. Nevertheless, we must be aware at all times of the obvious limits of unifying "universal" human rights with "particular" local meanings (Merry, 2006, p. 28).

Our point of departure in this article is that, not only in implementation, but in interpretation of human rights, the significance of cultural meanings, and the value of cultural diversity in relation to other dynamics of global power structures must be recognized (An-Na'im, 2008; Merry, 2006). This leads us to the last tool in our mode of analysis.

Human Rights as Social Worlds

Lila Abu-Lughod (2010)[2] points out that the human rights perspective must be tracked in various locales in order to understand how women's and men's rights are exceedingly differential in play. As Abu-Lughod rhetorically asks us: "What would happen if we reframed the usual questions and instead tracked…women's rights into the multiple social worlds in which they operate, paying particular attention to their mediations and transformations?" (Abu-Lughod, 2010, p. 2). An elaboration of human rights as a social fact includes an analysis of "the way both practices and talk of rights organize social and political fields, producing organizations, projects, and forms of governing as much as being produced by them" (Abu-Lughod, 2010, pp. 32–33). Abu-Lughod's approach encompasses an understanding of the various meanings of human rights (which may also accumulate meanings from numerous sources) in particular settings as well as an analysis of how human rights operate through women's lives. This perspective implies an understanding of the constant flow of various discourses in relation to women's and men's daily lived experiences (Abusharaf, 2000; Malmström, 2009a, 2009b; Wangila, 2007).

Global "Feminist" Interventions and "Elite" Feminism in the Egyptian Context

This section will elaborate Egyptian activism/feminism and its interaction with different actors: (1) the global donor community and "Western" feminism; (2) the Egyptian public; and (3) the Political Islamic movement/state.

Dilemmas of Feminism: The Global Community

Foreign funding is currently flowing into Egypt in a rapid stream in order to influence/assist Egypt to form a democratic state that respects human/women's rights and gender equality. Yet, there may be several side effects with global intervention, with its goal of emancipating women in Arab countries. First, there is an obvious risk of undermining and neglecting women's agency, from viewing the women from the Arab region once again as the "other" (cf. Abu-Lughod, 2006, 2010; Abusharaf, 2000; Kapur, 2002; Said, 1995). Colonial thoughts, through their rhetoric, have had an active part in constructing subordination as part of womanhood in the Middle East and North Africa (MENA) region (cf. Peteet, 1994—violence in relation to manhood). There is an imminent risk that implies a continuation and acceleration of this discursive production of a subordinated female subject if "proper" development—in the donor's view—does not occur. As mentioned earlier, everyone does not want the liberal discourse of freedom, and individual autonomy and/or concepts can be understood in different ways—also among women from the middle and upper classes who use the same terminology. There is, therefore, a need to study ethnographically concepts and practices such as feminism and human rights (Abu-Lughod, 2010; Merry, 2006). What do local notions and interpretations of democracy, gender equality, feminism, and human rights mean? What are the meanings of these concepts in different contexts? And how do these concepts travel and translate across various forums? As Abu-Lughod (2010) points out, we need to pay attention to both the mediation and the transformation of "universal" concepts. How people among different social strata articulate and express their voices for change in the current transformations of Egypt needs to be analyzed in its specific setting. There are reasons to be cautious when articulating "progressive politics" for "women in Egypt."

Religion in general, and Islam in particular have often been accused in Western and in liberal feminist theory of being responsible for the inferior position of women in societies and communities with a majority Muslim faith, not least in today's Egypt under President Morsi's rule (cf. Mahmood, 2005). We argue—in line with Mahmood (2005) and others—that to dismiss religious women who incorporate or inhabit values traditionally perceived as patriarchal as going against their own interests is outdated and repeats historical patterns of superiority, as well as reverts to a universalist feminist rhetoric. None of the Egyptian women interviewed regarded Islam or Christianity per se as contrary to feminist interests and demands in Egypt. This was a point that was particularly emphasized, where Farida, for example, expressed irritation toward "Western" feminists:

> If you talk to Western feminists, they obsess over religion and Islam. But these are not the issues, and they are not the pressure points of change. It is not about religion. It is about society. (Hellstrand, 2012, p. 48)

Farida questions the relevance of religion as an issue for feminist demands in Egypt. Instead, she and others suggest that the "real" issues are to be found in general societal concerns. But at the same time, as Abdelrahman (2004) indicates, in a study based on more than 50 Egyptian NGOs, feminist/activists consciously translate their priorities "to tailor their objectives to suit priorities of these agencies" (Abdelrahman, pp. 182–183).

Abu-Lughod (2010) put forward that the "production-site" of women's rights may have been disconnected from the women it actually targets. The Egyptian state, and also the Egyptian NGOs and the international donor community have been responsible, during the past years, for the drafting of the agenda of women's rights and concerns that has departed from women's own political goals—the goals of the women they were supposed to benefit (Abu-Lughod, pp. 6). This means that the state and the activists have not grasped the needs and desires of the people they have targeted. This was recognized in discussions about women's rights movements in Egypt before and after the uprising/s, as was the problem of the constant necessity to adapt to global donors' political agenda. Marwa for example, says:

> We really have to revise our approaches and methodology [after the uprising in 2011], because we have to admit we failed. We failed to reach so many women. There are many reasons for that, I mean we should not really only blame ourselves, because we were all involved into getting donors' money and that would take like 70% of our time, and then when we implement projects we have to finish it within the two years that the donors want to see something has happened—so there is no time actually to talk..." (Hellstrand, 2012, p. 45).

As illustrated here, the Egyptian activists, to be able to receive funding, have to adapt to current trends within the global donor community—hence, the global community produces specific feminist demands as universal desires (e.g., in the campaigns against female genital mutilation, where the global campaign's focus during the years has shifted from a health issue to a human rights and gender equality issue, something that can be followed in relation to the shift in the agenda of Egyptian NGOs during the same time period (cf. Malmström, 2009a). These adjustments and transformations to specific demands are not new—but what does it mean in particular in relation to building the new Egypt?

Aspects Other than Religion and Agency within Patriarchy

According to the interviewees, any political struggle taking place in transitional Egypt should relate to concrete economic and political conditions. Farida pointed out:

> I do not think ordinary women lack interest, passion or concern. It is a question of 'Do I go sell my vegetables today so I can feed my kids... so they can go to school... so I can buy them water to drink, or do I go to the Tahrir Square to discuss politics?' (Hellstrand, 2012, p. 40)

Besides the fulfilment of basic needs, the majority of the women and men underscored that even if the relevance of reforms of law—in theory and in practice—is crucial in relation to feminism, human/women's rights, and the new Egypt, the reforms are also questioned. It does not necessarily mean that reforms of legislation were dismissed as irrelevant, but that they were unsatisfactory as a method to advance women's status and situation in the new Egypt. The main problem according to the women and men was as they phrased it: "culture." Sohaila expressed:

> Things will not happen by legislation or constitution; you just need to overcome the culture. Like for example as long as someone in the street is saying a brave girl is worth a hundred men, then we still have a problem no matter what our constitution says or no matter what the law says. (Hellstrand, 2012, pp. 41-42)

All the interviewees discussed culture, or at least certain aspects of culture, as a hindrance to advance women's status. A few of the interviewees explicitly mentioned "patriarchy" or "patriarchal culture." Safa compared Egyptian and Western women's rights, emancipation, and patriarchal submission:

> It is a patriarchy, but there is a strength and autonomy in [Egyptian] women. Egyptian women have power. They are running the whole thing. Their husbands run away or they do not do anything. Women provide

for the family and raise the kids. They are running the economy … . The welfare-system has provided women with rights in Europe, but it does not mean that they are more emancipated. In Europe you have rights but there are subtle ways of submission. That is obvious here, but subtle in Europe. (Hellstrand, 2012, p. 44)

Other women framed it as a hierarchy rather than structural male dominance. Dina expressed:

We have to understand that we are a society that does not allow discussion. The father gives orders, the mother gives orders and the children obey or disobey. Afterwards, they are used to this. Look at the schools. The schools give the students orders. They go to the university—the professors at the university give orders. We are an 'army style' society …." (Hellstrand, 2012, p. 42).

The hierarchical culture, which many perceive to be patriarchal, may not be seen as an obstacle to rights and freedom, and it certainly does not exhaust the possibility of women's agency. There are subtle ways in which women may submit to, but also dominate in patriarchal structures. Karim gave an example of Egyptian women's agency, regardless of class, age, or other categories: "Women learn that women need to take their rights, not by equality, but by manipulating. They have been raised that way. You get your rights by controlling your man" (Hellstrand, 2012, p. 44). In Malmström's previous research among women from a totally different social stratum—women living in low-income neighbourhoods in Cairo—manipulation as agency was continuously brought up. Many women talked about various strategies. For example, Um Ahmed told me that her aunt taught her how to treat a man in order to get what you want in life: "I observed her and I learned everything from her." (Malmström, 2009a, p. 142). She recalled that her aunt had used a very soft voice when speaking with her husband and that she had looked into her husband's eyes with a special gaze. She was soft, smooth, and coquettish. Her husband melted, Um Ahmed remembered, because he could not resist her and he gave her everything she wanted (Malmström, 2009a). But using the body as a medium for the self (Mahmood, 2005) has political consequences. The body has the ability to act and to tell a larger story (Scheper-Huges, 2004) at the same time it signifies contradictions because it is capable of both reaffirming and transforming forms of domination.

If we, in line with Mahmood (2001, 2005), detach agency from the goals of progressive politics, it is here possible to perceive—in Karim's term—manipulation as agency. However, we prefer the concept "navigation" rather than " manipulation." Our argument here is that navigation seems to be closely connected to agency (among different categories of women)—in the private as well as in the public sphere—where "femininity/seduction/manipulation" are a conscious strategy. In sum, through agency—navigation—as a mediating category, it is possible to examine the inter-connections between identity formations and social structures: Egyptian "elite" feminists are navigating and parrying between different desires of actors on different levels—the international NGOs and European and U.S. governments, "Western" feminism, and "ordinary" women in the villages and poor suburbs of cities.

Dilemmas of Feminism and the Public

The first uprising in 2011 made it necessary for Egyptian feminist activists and organizations to reconsider their strategies and to adapt to a new political situation and in relation to new dominant political (Islamic) actors on the public scene. Political Islamic movements in Egypt have been not only well organized for a long time, but have also been very smart in—as some activists expressed it—"buying the voices of the poor through social charity" (Malmström, 2013, p. 38). That said, there is a huge, growing general mistrust towards the new government in Egypt. Also the poor, the majority of the social strata, who believed in the Muslim Brotherhood one year ago, have gradually lost their faith in the Brothers (Malmström, 2013, p. 38). Nevertheless, when these interviews were conducted, Political Islam was still perceived as more reliable among the people, which indicated changes in strategy among the Egyptian activists. Farida pointed out the necessity of new strategies such as communication and a new bottom-up approach after Mubarak's fall in 2011:

> The dialogue cannot be just among us. Activists speaking with activists will not do anything. We need to go into the local communities and address the men, women, and children there, find out about their situations and identify what they most need or want to see changed and why. How many of us go to villages? How many of us really take the patience and the time to understand and to adapt? Our visions should be representative of their passions, inspirations, and concerns. Once you can build this relationship, this trust, that you care about issues people are most concerned with, then you can begin to build campaigns and lobby for reforms needed. (Hellstrand, 2012, pp. 56-57)

As mentioned, feminist and women's rights agendas in Egypt, as they have been articulated for decades, may not resonate with the issues that many Egyptians among the poorer strata experience as problems. Poverty and unemployment (which relate to possibilities of marriage and parenthood/adulthood) are more relevant than abstract democratic or political ideals. Furthermore, the exclusive focus on women's issues may have created a distance from people in general. Marwa expressed it as a "lesson learned in the revolution."

> People in general are frustrated ... women, women, women, and women must work, and women must vote, and women ... you know. Talking about [only] women has really sort of created a reverse thing ... And I think we learned a lesson. Since the revolution, we are talking about everyone ... We are talking about equal citizenship, rights, equality and citizenship. We are talking about non-Muslims and that they too have rights. I think it is a much better way of addressing these issues now than how it was before."(Hellstrand, 2012, p. 58)

Also Sarah and Farida talked about the necessity of changing strategies:

> Now we need to build the constitution, we need to stress that it expresses the rights of humans ... We have to change our demands, asking for women's rights equals means asking for citizen's rights. It is no longer [enough] to demand specific gender rights, but to see things from a gender perspective. (Hellstrand, 2012, p. 58)

> You have to link what is happening at the parliament level to what is affecting and impacting on ordinary people and everyday issues they face. You have to make sure you address concrete issues in a way that is direct and meaningful. (Hellstrand, 2012, p. 56)

Here we can see how Egyptian feminist demands have transformed and how they are trying to navigate in relation to new situations after the fall of Mubarak. They can no longer talk about the status and situation of women only; they have to use another terminology. It is a movement from women's issues toward "see[ing] things from a gender perspective" and focusing on citizenship, which implies equality and rights for every Egyptian, irrespective of gender, class, or religion.

Dilemmas of Feminism and Political Islam

The women and men interviewed noted that nothing of substance had changed after the uprising/s or with the new political powers, or that if it had, it has not been to the advantage of women. Khaled phrased it as: "Egypt is ruled with the same mentality—it is the same men but with grown beards" (Hellstrand, 2012, p. 59). None of the interviewees expressed any appreciative opinions of the representatives in power in the first elected parliament; rather, they talked about the dangers. Yet, nearly all of the interlocutors recognized and strikingly expressed in almost the same wording that after the fall of Mubarak, the "wall of fear is gone." The parliament or government after the uprising/s was not seen as safeguarding people's rights, however. Human rights may provide a vision for political struggles, but they were not taken for granted and not presumed to be implemented by those in power. Dina expressed in mid-March 2012: "Who is the government? The government at this stage is not going to do anything. Apart from the constitution, the parliament is the main role player and the parliament is the Muslim Brotherhood and the Salafis" (Hellstrand, 2012, p. 60).

The interviewees differentiated their own interpretation of religion from how the Muslim Brotherhood and the Salafis and other Political Islamic actors many times used religion. Layla and Samia talked about gender equality within Islam and Political Islam:

> In Islam, women and men are equal; Islam gives women many rights but the Islamists misinterpret, it is not the correct Shari'a… Women are equal to men [in Islam] they have the same rights. If man is cheating, God punishes man and women in the same way. (Hellstrand, 2012, p. 48)

> In general, in Arab-Islamic cultures, when legislators are men…like anywhere in the world… women are not supposed to be on equal footing with men. This is not according to Islam. Women have rights according to Islam. It is not a religious thing. It is a cultural thing." (Hellstrand, 2012, pp. 48-49)

Hence, the women and men did not position themselves or their political views as contrary to their faith, but rather as against what they saw as the misinterpretation and misuse of religion. This misuse was perceived as emanating from a male-biased culture. They recognized that religion was used by anti-women's-rights and anti-feminist forces, such as male legislators and "Islamists." Safa expressed: "The Salafis and Muslim Brotherhood that have come to power are definitely anti-women" (Hellstrand, 2012, p. 60). However, some of the interviewees pointed out that not all "Islamists" were anti-women. Sohaila underscored that Political Islam was in fact not anti-women, but

> … it is the culture. This parliament is only a reflection of the culture. Not the culture, but the culture that has won…I think the parliament is not representing the country in any way…not just women. It is not representing young people. It is not representing the revolution. It is not a representative parliament. So I just do not care about the parliament now. They have not been representing me in any sense. (Hellstrand, 2012, p. 60)

Again, what seems to be the major problem in relation to feminism is not Islam per se but, in the view of women and men, the misinterpretation of religion. Furthermore, what is seen as the major obstacle was, in interlocutors' vocabulary, (patriarchal) culture or/and hierarchy—that is, structures in the society on every level.

It should be noted here that what was perceived as "the real" Islam was expressed as an equivalent to universal human rights. The women and men both brought up the importance of using local terminology. This means that women's (human) rights—that is to say, their values and ideals—should be advocated in a terminology accepted by the society at large; furthermore, that a foundation of such ideals was to be found in the religious sources themselves—which actually is in line with Merry's (2006) theoretical thoughts of the inevitability of translating human rights. Nehad expressed:

> We do not need to say that these concepts are from [the] UN. We need to say: It is right! It is religious! I cannot use CEDAW as a concept when I talk to normal women. No word about CEDAW. I speak in Islamic terms. The problem is not in Islam, but the theories and the stories provided by Islamists and Saudi Arabia (Hellstrand, 2012, p. 50).

Sohaila pointed out: "I would not use a controversial discourse. I would try bit by bit… You get stuck. I would try to transmit the very same ideas but in a lighter wording" (Hellstrand, 2012, p. 52).

As Merry (2006) highlights, human rights are produced in transnational settings, but understood in other ways at the local level of implementation. Nehad and Sohaila show us in the above example that (1) their intention is to translate "universal" concepts at the local level, and (2) they do not see religion as a problem, but rather a problem of incorrect interpretations and focus (the Political Islamic actors and the global donor community). We can see here processes of both mediations and transformations. As Abu-Lughod (2010) teaches us, this will be possible only if we track human rights "into the multiple social worlds in which they operate" (p. 2).

Conclusion

In the political discourse of "liberating women" it is easy to invoke and presume a specific agenda as relevant for women. In order to avoid playing into the hands of such politics and above all, to accurately and respectfully work for women's genuine interests, we need to contextualize in depth what feminist politics means according to various circumstances, intentions, and desires (cf. the classic works of Mohanty, 1988; Spivak, 2010). There is a need to recognize the autonomous lives of those women who (from the outside) may be perceived as "stuck" within patriarchal norms. Mahmood (2005) rightfully urges us to ask ourselves—as academics, as feminists, and as policy makers—do we really understand the lives of the women we so passionately want to remake? Ultimately we may need to reconsider our own imaginings of what constitutes feminism and a good life (Mahmood, 2005). As argued throughout this text, agency is both a universal human capacity for action and a socio-culturally mediated capacity (Ahearn, 2001) locally defined in social worlds (Mahmood, 2005). Without the creative aspects of agency, "we are limited in our ability to conceptualise how people come to understand themselves, and thereby act in new ways, in ways that do not fully correspond to discursive norms" (Frisk, 2004, p. 185f).

The immediate effect after the 2011 uprising may be interpreted as the beginning of a crisis in the universe of what Bourdieu refers to as doxa, "the pre-verbal taking-for-granted of the world that flows from practical sense" (Bourdieu, 1990, p. 68) among a broader layer of Egyptians, who challenged the hierarchical order in Egypt. Through the uprising in 2011, Egyptian men's and women's agency changed so they could be more "outspoken." Fear or unwillingness to criticize or oppose authority—especially authority referring to gender or age and social status, the military, and politics—was abandoned during the uprising in 2011. Temporarily—though explicitly—it challenged the norms of obedience. Women transgressed familial and social conventions of proper female behaviour and action as they participated on all fronts. However, because of the development of a new state power of Political Islam, Egyptian activists talked about how they were forced to begin to act in a smooth and silent way. They did not confront or express their activities in public to the extent they wanted, so that they could "survive" as a movement. A low profile was, as they said, a necessity in a climate where foreign influence in relation to feminism is rejected and conspiracy theories are flowing and circulating.

In this article we have elaborated how Egyptian feminists are navigating between various actors: the global donor community "Western" feminism, Egyptians in general, and the new state/Political Islam after the uprisings. They are using different strategies at the same time the feminists are being produced by the same forces. We have shown examples of Egyptian activists' intentions to translate "universal" concepts on the local level as well as to put forward processes of circulation, mediation, and transformation. Feminist politics in the new Egypt depend upon the capability of navigating, which can be very problematic, especially in relation to the current instability. It is also impossible to please all actors' (in the local, national, and global arenas) desires at the same time. As mentioned earlier, in relation to political Islam, it was recognized among the women and men interviewed that the 2011 uprising "gave a big stroke to the patriarchal kind of authority—the father's authority, the sheikhs, the *kabilah*, the big man. Hence, the hierarchical kind of authority was attacked on every level in Egyptian society. It broke with conventions and taboos in the society at large, which may give space for other forms of agency. There is a fear of criticizing or opposing authorities—especially authorities disappeared during the first uprising. The uprising in 2011 temporarily—but explicitly—challenged what the interviewees perceive as patriarchal and social norms of obedience. However, due to the developments after Mubarak's fall, it seems to be sensitive and even dangerous to act in the same way as in 2011. Although Egyptian feminists most often belong to the dominant voices in the society—voices that have the power to be heard in public—there is today an increasing dilemma that the new state silences the voices of Egyptian feminists. Furthermore, the obsession with religion in global interventions in relation to progressive politics misses the politics of Egyptian feminists as well as what people among the poor strata perceive as crucial for the new Egypt. Again, the problem, in their view, is rather the new state's incorrect interpretations of Islam and the global donor community's/"Western" feminism's obsession with Islam.

An-Na'im has directed a critique toward the assumption that Muslims educated in the West would be "unauthentic" proponents of change and their views unrepresentative of "real" Islam, which is relevant in relation to Egyptian feminists who are Muslims. These Muslims, according to An-Na'im, are dismissed both in Western and Islamic discourse as either "Westernized" or "not sufficiently Muslim"—unrepresentative of either Islam or the West. As An-Na'im (2008) states, Muslims must be allowed to be Muslims in their own right without having to fulfill Western *or* Islamic notions of who is an "authentic" Muslim. Likewise, Merry (2006) underscores that it is not possible to judge who is an internal and who is an external actor. These boundaries shift too much to be conclusive, which brings us back to the very aim of this text: how feminism and agency are formulated in Egypt's transition in relation to how it was then, how it is in the present, and how it will be in the imagined future. As we have seen throughout this article, translation and movement are crucial analytical tools. Only then can we begin to ask critical questions relevant to both academia and the policy world in relation to the new Egypt. As Abu-Lughod (2010) points out: We need to ask how human rights [and other universal concepts such as feminism] make and remake the world.

Notes

1. For an overview, see Abu-Lughod, 1998, 2010; Ahmed, 1992; Amin, 2000; Badran, 1988, 1992, 2006, 2010; Baron, 2005; el-Sadda, 2001; Nelson, 1996, 2007; Guenena & Wassef, 1999.
2. In Mahmood's former work (2001, 2005), she explores how women in the mosque movement in Cairo consciously educated themselves in Islamic "feminine" virtues in order to approximate their ideals.
3. Abu-Lughod gives several illustrative examples from her research in Palestine and in Egypt, where she had explored so-called Muslim women's rights in various locations.

Working with Patriarchy: Strategies for Women's Empowerment in Comparative Perspectives

Alessandra L. González

Abstract

What important roles are women playing in the middle of extreme social change and political upheaval in the traditional and religious societies of the Arab Gulf? In what ways do women's involvement in public leadership compare with activism of women in the traditional and religious societies of Latin America? Through academic scholarship and original fieldwork, the author discusses a number of common points of interest between women in leadership in the Arab Gulf and Latin America. The paper highlights findings from a study of 35 original interviews with men and women in the Arab Gulf region on the future of women's political activism, and the relationship that religious and political affiliation have in creating a balance for women's progressive rights within traditional and religious cultures. In addition, using historical and academic sources, the paper highlights the differences and commonalities of women in business and political leadership in Latin America, and emphasizes the importance of continued comparisons between Latin America and the Arab Gulf to encounter alternative negotiation strategies for the empowerment of women and other traditionally marginalized populations.

Introduction

This paper analyzes the relatively unexplored links between Latin America and the Arab Gulf, with particular focus on the challenges and opportunities for women's empowerment in both regions. Some of the research questions this paper addresses are: how do the efforts to empower women in both Latin America and the Gulf ameliorate shifts of political power at regional and global levels, and how can a focus on mutual efforts to encourage women's political participation contribute to a rapprochement between both regions?

The study begins by asking: What important roles are women playing in the middle of extreme social change and political upheaval in the traditional and religious societies of the Arab Gulf? In what ways do women's involvement in public leadership compare with activism of women in the traditional and religious societies of Latin America? Through academic scholarship and original fieldwork, the author discusses a number of common points of interest between women in leadership in the Arab Gulf and Latin America such as:

- How women activists set goals and approach the issue of women's rights differently by country in the Gulf;
- How relevant is the term "feminism" to an indigenous women's rights movement in the Gulf as compared to a Latin American experience;
- Lessons learned from Islamic feminist movements about the principles for women's empowerment from within traditional Muslim societies and cultures that compare with lessons from the Latin American experience;
- Practical points of cooperation and exchange between women leaders in Latin America and the Gulf (including cultural, educational, and business partnerships);
- Assessing the influence of local governments, international agencies, and NGOs on women's rights in traditional and religious societies; and
- Addressing the role that men play in facilitating women's rights both in Latin America and the Arab Gulf.

The data come from the Islamic Social Attitudes Survey (ISAS)—a study that includes 35 original interviews of men and women in Kuwait and Qatar on the future of women's political activism, and the relationship that religious and political affiliation have in creating a balance for women's progressive rights within traditional and religious cultures. In addition, the paper uses historical, academic, and media sources to highlight the differences and commonalities of women in business and political leadership in Latin America, and emphasizes the importance of continued comparisons between Latin America and the Arab Gulf to encounter alternative negotiation strategies for the empowerment of women and other traditionally marginalized populations.

This study of women's empowerment strategies from within patriarchal and religious societies strengthens the analysis of foreign policy of Latin American countries as well as those of the Arab Gulf Region—emphasizing the value of a comparative approach. This approach provides useful insights that can advance a better understanding of both the opportunities and obstacles for traditionally marginalized political actors, and increases awareness of the importance of Gulf and Latin American relationships.

Literature Review and Historical Examples of Women's Leadership in the Gulf

Women of the Arabian Peninsula historically have not had all political avenues open to them. Yet a resurgence of the popularity of universal suffrage and international pressures have emphasized full and equal political rights for women in recent years (Joseph & Najmabadi, 2005). Progressive ruling families in several Gulf countries have successfully mediated women's progress into full political participation in the last decade, notably Kuwait in 2005, Bahrain in 2002, and Qatar in 1999. However, much recent scholarship has focused on the emergence of women as political actors in Islamic contexts. Among these are studies that highlight the historical examples of women's leadership in pre-Islamic Arabia (Miles, 2001), Ethiopian Yemen (Adefris, 1998; Seunarine, 1999), and Central Arabia (al-Harbi, 2008). Such historical examples emphasize the political contributions that women have made in the past; these examples should speak to the possibilities for women's political and other leadership participation today. For example, Miles (2001) highlights early strongwomen of Islam, namely the Prophet Muhammad's wives Khadijah and 'A'isha, but also cites women warriors who took up arms in the early Islamic jihads, including Salaym bint Malhan and Arab princess Khawlah Bint al-Azwar al Kindiyyah (pp. 87-88). Among al-Harbi's conclusions, we find that women of ancient Central Arabia were educated, literate, and politically influential. They contributed financially and philanthropically to important religious and political movements in the Peninsula. Interestingly, the men in leadership who were among their relatives, including iconic figures such as Shaykh Muhammad ibn 'Abd al-Wahhab recognized and publicly appreciated the influence and support that women played in their political victories (al-Harbi, 2008, pp. 146-147). Some of the women al-Harbi cites in particular may not be easily recognized outside of the Arabic Gulf context, including women of Najd at the time that the Wahhabis forged an alliance with the al-Sauds. The fact that some of these women leaders of Central Arabia[1] are relatively unknown to mainstream feminist scholars does not mean that women leaders did not previously exist in Arabia. Rather, this highlights the lack of communication that Arabic language scholars have had with Western scholarship on the subject of religious-based feminist movements. This paper attempts to create a bridge by which some of the more recent scholarship on women's empowerment throughout the Middle East connects and contrasts with feminist movements in Latin America.

Recent literature highlights women's empowerment and progressive activism throughout the Muslim Middle East from within Islamic doctrine and tradition. Theological perspectives focus on the empowerment of women within Islamic theology and tradition (see Badran, 2009; Hafez, 2011; Wadud, 2006), while scholars in literature (Cooke, 2001), academics (Fernea, 1997) and policy activists (Coleman, 2010; Kennedy-Glans, 2009) all emphasize the empowerment of women from within their Islamic culture and traditions. Sociological studies more specific to women's movements in the Gulf include al-Mughni's account of women in Kuwait (al-Mughni, 2001), and González and al-Kazi's (2011) account of how gender and Islamic religiosity are converging in ways that depict a "co-existence" of pro-women's rights attitudes and religiosity that runs counter to a prevailing "clash of civilizations" thesis predicted by Huntington (1996) and others (George, 2001; Hunter, 1991).

Data and Methods

The data and methods for this study come from a variety of sources. In order to empirically explore the trajectory for women's progressive activism in conservative, religious societies in the Gulf, this study uses data from the Islamic Social Attitudes Survey Project (ISAS) sponsored by Baylor University Institute for the Studies of Religion. The data come mainly from 35 original semi-structured interviews with cultural elites in Kuwait and Qatar conducted in 2007 and 2008. The participants answered questions about the role of religion in promoting or inhibiting women's political leadership in their societies. The interviewees were cultural elites of various ethnic and political backgrounds, including Shi'a, Salafis, Bedouins, and urban elites. They include university professors, female parliamentary candidates, journalists, and other women's rights activists (González, 2013).

Data for women's political participation in Latin American countries come mainly from second hand sources, including statistical material compiled by various women's rights advocacy groups and available statistical sources as well as historical and academic sources. This paper is not intended to be a definite statement on the strategies of feminists in conservative, religious contexts, but rather a beginning point for future research on this topic.

Recent Findings of Women's Leadership in the Gulf

Women are increasing in public leadership positions throughout the Arab Gulf. They are breaking with cultural traditions and becoming heads of business corporations and academic departments, running for political office, and even competing in international sports competitions as archers and race car drivers.[2] Many are using strategies of negotiating for progressive rights for women from within their conservative cultural heritage and religious tradition. In my own research, I have referred to women who argue for their rights within Islam as "Islamic Feminists" for the way that they bridge the seemingly incompatible demands of modern life, while at the same time selectively preserving cultural values and traditions.

Though women have not served as heads of state in the Arabian Peninsula, an increasing number are filling strategic political positions that enable women's issues to be addressed in the general discourse (see Table 1). Where previously taboo subjects of women's health and domestic violence were left unaddressed, now various governments in the Gulf have begun to make public services available to address these unjust "inefficiencies" of Islamic governments. In my own research on politically engaged women in Kuwait and Qatar, I have found a number of both male and female activists who address women's rights in less formal and political ways. Islamic feminists in particular are prone to emphasize that political rights for women are "a means to an end" for addressing more pressing social rights such as economic independence and unfair personal status laws. Figure 1 shows some of the most pressing issues in the sample data. These denote what politically engaged elites in Kuwait have found to be of most importance. Interestingly the analysis of original interview transcripts shows differences by gender on the most frequently mentioned issues.

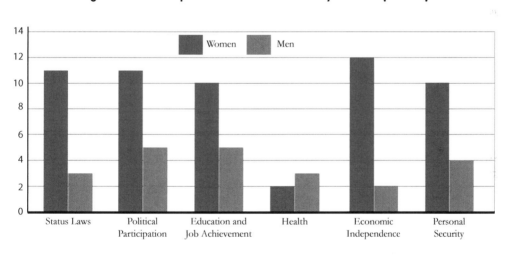

Figure 1. Most Important Women's Issues by Gender (N = 35)

Data Source: ISAS Kuwait Qualitative Interviews 2007–2008.

Table 1. Selected Women Leaders of the Gulf

Country and Year of Independence	Year of Women's Suffrage	Year of Leadership	Woman Leader	Title	Field of Leadership	National Religiosity*
Bahrain, 1971	2002	2000	Shaika Hind bint Sulman Al-Khalifa	Under-Secretary and Assistant of the Minister of Labor and Social Affairs; in 2005, Assistant Secretary in the Ministries of Social Affairs, Culture, Civil Service and the Council of Women's Affairs.	Politics	Muslim (Shi'a and Sunni) 81.2%, Christian 9%, other 9.8% (2001 census)
		2001	H.H. Shaikha Sabika bint Ebrahim Al-Khalifa, wife of the ruler of Bahrain	President of the Supreme Council for Women, holds the rank of a member of the cabinet.	Politics	
		2004-07	Dr. Nada bint Abbas Haffadh	Minister of Health	Politics	
		2005	Fatima Ahmed al-Beloushi	Minister of Social Affairs	Politics	
		2008	Shaikha Mai bint Mohammad Al-Khalifa	Minister of Culture, and Chairperson of the UN World Heritage Committee since 2010	Politics	
Kuwait, 1961	2005	1991	Sheika Rasha Al-Sabah	Undersecretary of Higher Education; Vice-Rector of University of Kuwait 1985–1991; daughter of Sheik Mahomoud Al-Jabir Al-Sabah	Politics	Muslim (official) 85% (Sunni 70%, Shia 30%), other (includes Christian, Hindu, Parsi) 15%
		1997	Amal Hamad	Undersecretary of Information	Politics	
		1999	Sara Al-Duweisan	Undersecretary of Planning	Politics	
		1999	Siham Razoogi	Undersecretary of Petrol	Politics	
		2005-06	Massouma al-Mubarak	Minister of Planning and Administrative Development; 2006–2007 Minister of Communcation; 2007 Minister of Health	Politics	
		2007-09	Nouria al-Sabih	Minister of Education	Politics	

Oman, 1650		2008-09	Mohdi Al-Homoud	State Minister for Housing and Administrative Development; 2009–2011 Minister of Education	Politics	
		2011	Amani Bouresli	Minister of Trade and Industry	Politics	
	2003	1995	Abdullah Ahmed Al-Ghazi	Advisor to the Minister of Social Affairs, Labor, Women and Children's Affairs	Politics	Ibadhi Muslim (official) 75%, other (includes Sunni Muslim, Shia Muslim, Hindu) 25%
		1997	Dr. Thuwaibah bint Ahmad Bin Isa Al-Barwani	Undersecretary for Social Affairs in the Ministry of Social Affairs, Labor and Vocational Training	Politics	
		1997–03	Dr. Fawzia bint Nasir Bin Juma Al-Farsi	Undersecretary of Education; since 2003 the eight woman in the Upper House, Majlis al-Shura	Politics	
		2003	Sheikha Aisha bint Khalfan bin Jameel al-Sayabiyah	President with the Rank of Minister of the National Authority for Industrial Craftsmanship	Politics	
		2003	Muna bint Salim al-Jardaniyah	Undersecretary of Education	Politics	
		2004	Dr. Rawya bint Saud bin Ahmed al Busaidiyah	Minister of Higher Education	Politics	
		2004	Sherifa bint Khalfan bin Nasser al-Yahiyaia	Minister for Social Development	Politics	
Qatar, 1971	1999	1996–03	Sheikha Ahmad Al-Mahmoud	Undersecretary at the Ministry of Education and Higher Education; 2003–2009 Minister of Education	Politics	Muslim 77.5%, Christian 8.5%, other 14% (2004 census)
		1998	Sheikha Mozah Bint Nasser Al Misnad	President with rank of Minister of the Supreme Council for Family Affairs; married to the Emir of Qatar since 1995; 2003 she was appointed UNESCO Special Envoy for Basic and Higher Education	Politics	
		1999	H E Sheikha Hessa bint Khalifa bin Ahmed Al-Thani	Vice-President with rank of Minister of the Supreme Council for Family Affairs; Deputy Director of the Office of the Consort of the Emir of Qatar and Director of International Affairs by the Supreme Council 1998–2002 and Special Rapporteur on Disability of the United Nations Commission for Social Development 2003–2005	Politics	

Table 1. Selected Women Leaders of the Gulf (CONTINUED)

Country and Year of Independence	Year of Women's Suffrage	Year of Leadership	Woman Leader	Title	Field of Leadership	National Religiosity*
Saudi Arabia, 1922		2006	Nada Zeidan	Competitive Athlete	Sports	
		2008–09	Sheikha Ghalia bint Mohammed bin Hammad Al Thani	Minister of Health; Member of Qatar's ruling family; former Head of the country's National Health Authority	Politics	
		2005	Mawa Al-Eifa	Competitive Athlete	Sports	Muslim 100%
	2005 (limited local suffrage); 2011	2005	Lama al-Suleiman	Boardmember of the Chamber of Commerce in Jeddah	Business	
		2005	Nashwa Taher	Boardmember of the Chamber of Commerce in Jeddah	Business	
		2009	Norah al-Faiz	Deputy Minister of Education for Women's Affairs	Politics	
UAE, 1971	2006	1996	Aisha al-Sayer	First recognized female medical doctor in UAE	Medicine	Muslim 96% (Shi'a 16%), other (includes Christian, Hindu) 4%
		1998	Moza al-Habroush	Under-Secretary of Women's Advancement	Politics	
		1999–06	Mariam Mohammed Khalfan Al-Roumi	Under-Secretary of the Labour and Social Affairs Ministry	Politics	
		2004–08	Sheikha Lubna bint Khalid bin Sultan al-Qasimi	Minister of Economic Planning	Politics	
		2005	Noora Khaleefa Salem Al-Suwaidi	Deputy Minister of Foreign Affairs	Politics	
		2008	Sheikha Lubna al-Qassemi	Minister of Foreign Trade; she is a member of the Sharjah royal family	Politics	

	2008	Dr Maitha Salem Al Shamsi	Minister of State and Head of the Marriage Fund of Abu Dhabi	Politics	
	2008	Reem Ibrahim Al Hashimi	Minister of State; A former Deputy Ambassador to the USA, she also manages the International Affairs Unit of The Executive Office of His Highness Sheikh Mohammed Bin Rashid Al Maktoum, Vice President and Prime Minister of the UAE and Ruler of Dubai and holds other positions.	Politics	
Yemen, 1962; Reunification after Civil War in 1990	1970	Amat Al-Aleem Alsoswa	Undersecretary of Information; Minister of Human Rights Ambassador to The Netherlands 2000–2003; and non-resident ambassador to Norway, Sweden and Denmark 2001–2003. Assistant Secretary-General of the United Nations and Assistant Administrator of UNDP and Director of its Regional Bureau for Arab States since 2005.	Politics	Muslim including Shaf'i (Sunni) and Zaydi (Shia), small numbers of Jewish, Christian, and Hindu
	2001–03	Wahiba Fare'e al-Fakih	Minister of State of Human Rights; former Dean of the Yemen Institute for Languages and Rector of Queen Arwa University	Politics	
	2001–07	Dr. Nafisa Al-Jaifi	Secretary-General for The Higher Council for Motherhood and Childhood and Director of The Child Development Project	Politics	
	2006	Amat Ali Razaq Ali Hamad Al-Huri	Minister of Social Affairs and Labor	Politics	
	2006–07	Khadija al-Haisami	Minister of Human Rights	Politics	
	2007–11	Huda Ali Abdellatif al-Ban	Minister of Human Rights	Politics	
	2011	Houriah Ahmed Mashhour	Minister of Human Rights	Politics	
	2011	Jawharah Hamoud Thabet	Minister of State for Cabinet Affairs	Politics	
	2011	Tawakkul Karman	Opposition activist and Nobel Peace Prize Winner	Human Rights	

*Country Religiosity Statistics, Data Source: CIA World Factbook 2012, http://www.cia.gov/library/publications/the-world-factbook/fields/2122.html.
**Leadership Data (Bahrain) Data Source: Guide2WomenLeaders, http://www.guide2womenleaders.com/female_ministers_by_country.html.

From the data set, including 35 ISAS interviews, gender differences become apparent, not just from the way that women's issues are discussed, but even in order of priority. For example, according to my analysis, women in interviews viewed the most important women's issues in their country as:

1. Economic independence;
2. Personal status laws and political participation;
3. Educational and professional achievement and personal security; and
4. Access to healthcare.

While the men listed the priority for women's issues as:

1. Political participation and educational and professional achievement;
2. Personal security;
3. Personal status laws and access to healthcare; and
4. Economic independence.

From these data, we see that women view their economic independence—that is the ability to obtain a job with sufficient wages, or a fair share of inheritance or alimony in the case of their father's death or a divorce—as their top priority. Interestingly, men list economic independence *least* frequently as a concern for women, while listing other priorities such as political rights, education, and professional achievement. It is possible that Islamic feminists view political participation as a means to other social rights for women, including economic independence and personal status, while male elites may perceive political participation of women as a marker that they have succeeded in addressing feminist grievances in their societies. What is a likely result from the increased participation of women in leadership in the Gulf is an extension of the preliminary results found among this sample of elites. That is, when women take up political leadership positions, more beneficial changes for women will occur, including increasing educational and professional opportunities, strides in personal security, and access to quality healthcare.

Women Leaders in Latin America

The approach of many women leaders in the Gulf is not unlike the path that women leaders in Latin America have forged for women to become public leaders today. Similar to the Gulf, Latin American countries have a rich tradition steeped in conservative religious beliefs. The political processes of secularization have not obliterated the influence and power of religious institutions and beliefs, in particular, as they apply to gender relations and the role of women. In fact, recently the Vatican has come out more vocally in opposition to the "radical feminist" strains of activism among some sectors of consecrated women in their fold (Tenety, 2012). In particular, women leaders in Latin America have addressed patriarchal cultural structures which have been traditionally reinforced by Christian, predominantly Catholic doctrines.

Important scholars of Latin American women's movements include Sonia Alvarez, Maxine Molyneux, Sarah Radcliffe and Sallie Westwood, among others (Alvarez, 1999; Molyneux, 1985; Radcliffe and Westwood, 1993). Cecilia Baeza suggests a possible comparison of Islamic feminism with feminist theologies of Latin American women in the mid-1980s (C. Baeza, personal communication, July 29, 2012). Baeza also offers a critique of the comparison of the social impact of Catholicism in Latin America with that of Islam in the Gulf because most governments in Latin America have secular constitutions, despite the incomplete process of secularization as compared to Europe. She notes that relative cultural secularization, despite high numbers of religious affiliation in Latin America, must be noted as a difference to the Gulf public which continues to profess high levels of religiosity in opinion surveys (González, 2011). Baeza and Galindo both offer the example of Latin American indigenous women as a possible avenue of fruitful comparison with the grassroots religious feminism of the Arab Gulf.3

Alejandra Galindo also presents some suggestions and critiques of a 'South–South' comparison of women's empowerment (A. Galindo, personal communication, July 29, 2012). She points out that the lack of political parties in the Gulf removes from the analysis a very important catalyst for women's political participation in Latin America. Galindo also points out that political processes directed by the governments of the Gulf remove some of the political competition by non-governmental organizations that Latin American women have utilized in their ascension to power. Importantly, she points out that there are many manifestations of Latin American religiosity and their relationship to the State; that a more detailed comparative analysis by countries in Latin America and the Gulf is more appropriate than the regional, macro-level theoretical approach taken in this paper. Lastly, she writes that "Islamic feminism" is a broad category and that the country by country comparison may also help to clarify and identify particular political strategies as women confront the need for social change in more localized contexts. She also points out the universal issue that once in power, women leaders do not always incorporate gender issues into their political agenda, which complicates the focus on women politicians as symbols of women's empowerment, because it is possible that by setting aside gender issues, they will inadvertently replicate the patriarchal systems that kept them from power in the first place.4 Despite these important situational differences, we continue the theoretical comparison at the macro-level to generate future research on this topic.

Presently, women have had unprecedented political power in Latin America, including serving as heads of state in Argentina and Brazil, and holding numerous ministerial and parliamentary posts (see Table 2).[5] A preliminary reading of the outstanding examples of female political leadership in Latin American brings to light several interesting observations. Like many female elites in the Gulf, we observe the importance of family, and indeed male interlocutors, for women to gain access to positions of leadership. In the Argentinian case, both female prime ministers were widows of former male presidents. In the Brazilian case, the elected female president was a strong ally of a former male president of the same political party. In the Chilean case, the elected female president had served in various cabinet positions under a male president, which arguably presented her candidacy with added legitimacy. In these examples, we observe that, as with women in politics in the Gulf, powerful male allies are essential for gaining access to leadership positions.

Despite calls from international agencies to give women full equal rights in politics, there is some evidence that the application of a quota policy to include women in the political system has not necessarily had a democratizing effect on the society because of the fact that quotas can be established by authoritarian regimes as well as leftist socialist ones (Massolo, 2007, p. 99). What was observed was that quotas helped further a general democratic effect when there was proportional representation, limiting the number of women per political district. On the other hand, quotas for local elections, where women tended to gain seats in local municipalities, appeared to have a positive effect on the perceptions of women as capable leaders, particularly in more rural districts where women had never before been seen in such public positions (Massolo, 2007, p. 100). The Latin American experience is shared with observations from women in politics in the Gulf. When women run as political candidates in rural areas, where conservative culture has not viewed women as capable leaders, they change perceptions and open pathways for future women candidates.

Of interest to the macro-level comparisons of women leaders in Latin America and the Gulf, are the cultural images within the traditional family that are held up to any emerging women leaders, namely that of mother, daughter, and sister. In the predominantly Catholic Christian tradition of Latin America, the exalted image of the Mother of Jesus Christ, Mary (whom Muslims uphold as well, as Maryam), who through her exalted virtue, gives women a model for saintly behavior. Thus religion combines with traditional values to give women prototypes to follow which differ from those of men (De Barbieri & De Oliveira, 1986, p. 23). Men may have more flexibility in terms of their image in the media, not least of which is permission to be aggressive in politics, which—unlike for women—asserts their leadership potential. Women political leaders in Latin America, like women in the Gulf, have to walk a very tight rope when facing the public scrutiny of local media. Not only do they expose themselves to media attention, but the manhood of the men that surround them (husbands, fathers, and other related males) is called into question. Similar to the Gulf countries, strict patriarchal gender norms in Latin America, often termed machismo, pervade the culture (though there is evidence to point to important variation among patriarchal attitudes in Latin

America by country). These embedded cultural frames prejudice the entry of women political leaders into public life.

It is worth noting that the sustained importance of religion in Latin American society is another point of comparison to the Gulf societies. Albeit a distinct religious tradition and theology, nonetheless, the sociological importance of reaching out to religious sensibilities is a political necessity for the female political candidate. Even in the socialist and philosophically agnostic cases, a popular appeal to mass religious sensibilities and concerns over moral and social issues is still observed. Though original qualitative research needs is necessary in order to continue to properly compare the Latin American examples with those of the Gulf, this historical analysis provides a basis with which to begin the comparison of women empowerment strategies in the realm of politics begun by women political candidates in traditional, religious, and patriarchal environments.

Analysis

The main research questions explored in this paper are: what theoretical links connect women's empowerment strategies in conservative and traditional environments of Latin America and the Arab Gulf? When women have been traditionally marginalized from positions of public authority due to religious and cultural beliefs, how do they break through cultural and deeply-held beliefs about the submission of women to male authority at home and in public life? This paper begins an exploration into the current success of women leaders in both parts of the world and compares their strategies for successful negotiation of new spaces for women.

Some of the preliminary findings from interview data of Kuwaiti and Qatari elites uncover that a critical stance towards Western feminism has spurred an indigenous, Islamic feminist approach to women's rights which holds its own distinctive characteristics. Some of these characteristics are that the Islamic Feminist agenda is part of a comprehensive Islamic worldview. In sacralized societies such as the Arab Gulf, religious meanings and symbols infuse all aspects of society where women are breaking ground, including politics. Second, an Islamic Feminist agenda is legitimated in society by a religious source—whether by sacred text or tradition. In traditions where a competing secular tradition co-exists with a religious tradition, such as the case of Latin America, it is possible that secular narratives must be discussed and debated by Christian feminists in politics. It is possible that in the Latin American case, religious voices have been largely marginalized from feminist debates, particularly when compared with the Gulf case. Third, Islamic feminists seek cultural compatibility. A similar approach was documented in studies of evangelical women in the United States, and of evangelical women in Colombia who re-shaped their communities by their pious example. Lastly, with an indigenous model of feminism that takes into account deeply held religious convictions, Islamic feminist women are succeeding in education, business, and now

Table 1. Selected Women Leaders of the Gulf

Country and Year of Independence	Year of Women's Suffrage	Year of Leadership	Woman Leader	Title	Field of Leadership	National Religiosity*
Argentina, 1816	1947	1974–1976	Isabel Martínez de Perón	President	Politics	Nominally Roman Catholic 92% (less than 20% practicing), Protestant 2%, Jewish 2%, other 4%
		2007–Present	Cristina Fernández de Kirchner	President	Politics	
Bolivia, 1825	1938; 1952	1979–1980	Lidia Gueiler Tejada	Acting President	Politics	Roman Catholic 95%, Protestant (Evangelical Methodist) 5%
Nicaragua, 1821	1955	1990–1997	Violeta Chamorro	President	Politics	Roman Catholic 58.5%, Protestant 23.2% (Evangelical 21.6%, Moravian 1.6%), Jehovah's Witnesses 0.9%, other 1.7%, none 15.7% (2005 census)
Ecuador, 1822	1929	1997	Rosalía Arteaga Serrano	Acting President	Politics	Roman Catholic 95%, other 5%
Guyana, 1966	1928	1997–1999	Janet Jagan	President	Politics	Protestant 30.5% (Pentecostal 16.9%, Anglican 6.9%, Seventh-Day Adventist 5%, Methodist 1.7%), Hindu 28.4%, Roman Catholic 8.1%, Jehovah's Witnesses 1.1%, Muslim 7.2%, other Christian 17.7%, other 4.3%, none 4.3% (2002 census)
Panama, 1821	1941	1999–2004	Mireya Moscoso		Politics	Roman Catholic 85%, Protestant 15%
Chile, 1818	1931	2006–2012	Michelle Bachelet	President	Politics	Roman Catholic 70%, Evangelical 15.1%, Jehovah's Witnesses 1.1%, other Christian 1%, other 4.6%, none 8.3% (2002 census)
Costa Rica, 1821	1949	2010–Present	Laura Chinchilla	President	Politics	Roman Catholic 76.3%, Evangelical 13.7%, Jehovah's Witnesses 1.3%, other Protestant 0.7%, other 4.8%, none 3.2%
Brazil, 1822	1934	2011–Present	Dilma Rousseff	President	Politics	Roman Catholic (nominal) 73.6%, Protestant 15.4%, Spiritualist 1.3%, Bantu/voodoo 0.3%, other 1.8%, unspecified 0.2%, none 7.4% (2000 census)

*Country Religiosity Statistics, Data Source: CIA World Factbook 2012, http://www.cia.gov/library/publications/the-world-factbook/fields/2122.html.
**Data comes from the "Chronological List of Female Presidents" by the online Worldwide Guide to Women in Leadership, http://www.guide2womenleaders.com/Presidents.htm

politics, gaining legitimacy in ways that have authority in their local contexts, and then rising as the most qualified for public leadership positions.

In addition, in the Gulf case we find that Islamic feminism is a negotiating strategy, promoting public welfare while remaining culturally sensitive. Lastly, we find that a framework of an indigenous Islamic feminism is a window into social activism in sacralized contexts where previously marginalized actors (women) are also opening up pathways to fight for the rights of other marginalized populations, such as non-citizens, and those with physical and mental handicaps, including children with special needs (González, 2013).

The preliminary analysis of indigenous feminism from the Gulf that is led by cultural elites and rooted in deeply held cultural and religious beliefs may have potential for women's rights activists in Latin America to promote women's social priorities. This would lead to economic independence, women's health and safety, and professional development, particularly among communities of women without access to such resources. In this brief survey, we find that women activists are not homogeneous or monolithic. Their political goals and approaches to the issue of women's empowerment differ by country, political ideology, and time in history. The term "feminism," however, is misunderstood and indeed relevant to the discussion of indigenous women's rights movements in both the Gulf and Latin America. The literature on women's empowerment in Latin America may be more conversant with this term because of its Western connotation, and the breadth of political spectrum in which Latin American female political leaders have operated (including secular, Leftist, and Marxist ideologies). However, the term serves as a point of reference, debate, and distinction for indigenous women's movements in the Gulf and throughout the Middle East, because it necessitates the definition of terms for women's rights activists and forces them to state their mission early on in the discussion.

Islamic feminist movements within traditional Muslim societies and cultures have both learned from, and help inform many of the feminist movements found in the Latin American experience. Women's movements of more leftist and secular natures have not succeeded in eradicating violence against women, machismo, and other social ills that they set out to address, while Islamic feminist movements seek to refine the mission of increased opportunities for women in the public sphere by addressing politics as a means toward more important social goals.

One of the commonalities arising from this study is the potential for women to benefit from participation in politics at the local level, while feeling the pressures and tensions of international agencies as they assume leadership positions in the name of social development by outside measures. Another commonality observed was the importance of male interlocutors for women's success in politics, whether they are advocates in the private or public sphere.

Questions for Further Exploration

More empirical studies of women's empowerment, both in Latin America and the Gulf, need to be conducted for a proper extension of the discussion begun here. Further comparative work on the status of women in secularizing, but previously religious contexts needs to be conducted. The case studies of women in Latin America, compared with women in the Gulf is a perfect pairing in which to study the strategies of feminist activists who negotiate for women's rights from within their conservative and traditional cultures. The second-wave feminism of the United States and Europe marginalized religious voices in feminist debates begun by women's suffragettes—of whom many were cultural conservatives—and in other respects, remained champions of "traditional" family values. In both the Arab Gulf and in many parts of Latin America, we see a resurgence of "traditional values" rhetoric among younger feminist activists who attempt to incorporate their traditional and religious beliefs, along with the pragmatic concerns of economic independence for women and due process in civil legal proceedings. In a globalizing context for academic research, further comparative work of this kind will serve to strengthen both the pedagogical and policy-driven connections that arise from cooperative academic endeavors.

Notes

1. Some women al-Harbi highlights include Moudi bint Sultan Abu Wahtan, Fatimah bint Muhammad ibn 'Abd al-Wahhab, Moudi bint Sa'ad al-Dahlawi, Maytha' bint 'Ali al-Salami, Wadha bint Muhammad ibn 'Uray'ir, Hussah bint Ahmad al-Sudairi, princess Aljawharah bint Turki ibn 'Abd Allah, Aljawharah bint Musa'ad ibn Jalawi, Sarah bint 'Ali ibn Muhammad, Nurah bint Faisal ibn Turki, and Ruqaiyah bint 'Awadh al-Hijji.

2. Qatari archer and rally driver Nada Zeidan (Vaz, 2006) and Saudi rally driver Mawa Al-Eifa (Qusti, 2005) are some recent examples.

3. Cecilia Baez cites R. Aída Hernández Castillo (2010), "The Emergence of Indigenous Feminism in Latin America," *Signs*, *35*(3), 539-545.

4. Galindo cites Molyneux (2003). *Movimientos de mujeres en América Latina: Estudio teórico comparado*. Madrid, ES: Ediciones Cátedra; Stephen (1997). *Women and social movements in Latin America: Power from below*. Austin, TX: Texas University Press; Lebon, Maier, & Norma (2010). *Women's activism in Latin America and the Caribbean: Engendering social justice, democratizing citizenship*. Austin, TX: Texas University Press; Speed, Castillo, & Stephen (2006). *Dissident women: gender and cultural politics in Chiapas. Austin, TX: Texas University Press*; Espinosa Damián. G. (2009). *Cuatro vertientes del feminismo enMéxico:Diversidad de rutas y cruce de caminos*. México, D.F.: UAM-Xochimilco. Dahlerup, D. (Ed.) (2006). *Women, quotas, and politics*. New York, NY: Routledge.

5. Argentina's Head of State is Cristina Fernández de Kirchner, wife of former Argentinian president Néstor Kirchner, and the only woman to serve as President in Argentina since Isabel Martinez de Perón in 1974–1976. Brazil's current President Dilma Rousseff (since 2011) is the only woman to serve as Brazil's head of state. See Table 1 for more historical examples of women leaders in Latin America.

Gender Segregation, Effacement, and Suppression: Trends in the Status of Women in Israel

Michal L. Allon

Abstract

The aim of this paper is to analyze the phenomenon of the exclusion of women from the public sphere in Israel. The paper describes some of the causes of this phenomenon, its impact on Israeli society, and the difficulty in confronting it. Israeli women have made impressive gains on many fronts, but the exclusion of women from the public sphere as a result of the influence of the growing Ultra-Orthodox minority, which imposes its norms on the general public, raises serious concerns. The exclusion of women manifests itself in several forms: gender, segregation in public spaces, the effacement of women's images from the public sphere, and the suppression of women's voices. The infiltration of Orthodox Jewish fundamentalism into Israeli society may cause the regression of advancements previously made in women's rights in Israel. The paper points to the limitations of the treatment of this phenomenon within a theory of multiculturalism, and suggests an alternative framework of discourse, which relies on concepts that are drawn from the literature on environmental ethics, public rights, and public ownership of space and resources.

Introduction

The status of women in Israel is paradoxical. On the one hand, there have been impressive gains in the advancement of women in many domains, while on the other, there have recently been serious setbacks in their status. These setbacks are due to an accelerated process of radicalization of Orthodox Jewish fundamentalism among some religious communities and their political leaders.[1] These trends are met with sharp, albeit mostly ineffective, opposition and demonstrations from women and men, both religious and secular.

The literature on gender inequity and discrimination against women in various societies and cultures is abundant. Much of the discussion is conducted within the framework of a theory of multiculturalism (see Kukathas, 1992; Kymlicka, 1995, 1997; Okin, 1997; Shachar, 2000). However, in the case of Israel, a theory of multiculturalism does not capture the complexity and ramifications of gender inequity.

I will start by reviewing the advances made by women in the decades following the establishment of the State of Israel in 1948. I will briefly describe the complex relationships between state and religion, and the challenges they pose to the liberal model of a modern society. I will then describe the relatively recent regression, which is the focus of this paper. I will review some treatments in the literature of the challenge of multiculturalism to a liberal society, and examine the applicability of the multicultural model to the Israeli phenomenon in question. Finally, I will suggest an alternative framework of discourse, which relies on concepts that are familiar in the literature on environmental ethics, public rights, and public ownership of space and resources. This approach better accounts for the Israeli phenomenon of gender exclusion, and thereby allows for a more tractable ethical perspective on the matter.

Women's Gains

Israel belongs to the exclusive club of countries where a woman served as head of government as early as over 40 years ago. In politics, business, academia, and the military, women have made considerable and continual progress in asserting their participation in more, as well as higher positions. In the January, 2013 general elections in Israel, four center-left opposition parties were headed by women; the number of women in the Knesset (the Israeli parliament) is the highest since the establishment of the state. The former Chief Justice of the Supreme Court was a woman, as are 4 out of 15 justices on the present court, including the Deputy Chief Justice. The CEO's of many major companies and banks are women. In 2009, an Israeli female scientist, Professor Ada Yonath, won the Nobel Prize in chemistry, and there are female presidents of universities, scientists, and researchers in universities and research institutions. Women have also made considerable gains in the military. The Head of Personnel—a Major General in rank—is a woman, and there are now female pilots, marine officers, and combat soldiers. It is worth noting that the latter achievement—the participation of women in different roles in the military, which had been previously restricted to men—came only after the intervention of the courts, which forced the armed forces to adopt a more egalitarian, bias-free recruitment policy. Notable was the case of Alice Miller, an aeronautical engineer, who sued the Minister of Defense for refusing to allow her to take the Israeli Air Force pilot training exams on account of her gender (Greenberg, 1994).

Barriers and Problems

Needless to say, women in Israel face the same barriers as in other countries. The numbers cited above demonstrate this. Indeed, there are two women who are presidents of major universities in Israel, but only two out of eight university presidents. There are now 27 female parliament members, more than ever before, but they comprise only 22% of the assembly members. In addition, women have to struggle with a myriad of serious problems that confront women all over the world: prostitution and human trafficking, sexual harassment, and domestic violence, to name a few. Arab women, and especially Bedouin women, endure additional hardships like honor killing, female genital mutilation, forced marriages, and limited educational and employment opportunities. The additional specific hardships and discrimination endured by women of non-Jewish ethnic minorities, and especially Muslim women, are beyond the scope of this paper.

The Hold of Official Religion

Established religion is an integral part of the government in Israel, and it plays a central role in its politics. Religious parties invariably take part in the coalition which forms the government, and are very influential in determining the political and public agenda. There is no separation of religion and state, and the state sees it as its duty to provide free religious services to its citizens. The major religions are subsidized by the government, and the clergy (priests, imams, and rabbis) are on the state payroll, as are judges in the respective religious courts for religious and family matters. These courts constitute a parallel and separate judiciary system. Moreover, from its inception, the State of Israel surrendered its role in the area of marriage and divorce to the respective religious sects. As a result, 64 years after the establishment of Israel, there is no civil marriage or divorce, intermarriage between people of different religions is impossible inside Israel, and some people are prevented from marrying a person of their choice altogether, because of religious restrictions. Similar problems of the right to marry and to divorce and the conflict between religious law and civil law face societies in other countries as well (Douglas, Doe, Gilliat-Ray, Sandberg, & Khan, 2011). Since the offices of the various religious establishments are male-dominated, women—religious and secular alike—suffer discrimination, humiliation and hardship when they are in need of the services of these institutions. Needless to say, women cannot serve as judges in the religious courts which have jurisdiction over them. Barzilai (2003) claims that Israel cannot be regarded a liberal democracy because of the lack of separation between state and religion. It should also be noted that most of the religious political parties officially exclude female candidates and female parliament members, a practice which has been challenged in court (see Warton, 2012).

All religions, like all male-dominated institutions, discriminate against women in some form or another. Some argue that gender discrimination is not sanctioned by the "true" religion, and stems from a misinterpretation of its scripture. Be that as it may, when there is no constitutional separation between state and religion, the dictates of religion are forced upon those who do not wish to conform to them.

The history of public discussion in Israel abounds with conflicts between religion and the liberal secular way of life of the majority of the population. In many cases, these conflicts have evolved around issues concerning the proper observance of the Jewish day of rest. The public manifestation of the Sabbath—i.e., the lack of public transportation, the closing of major transportation arteries, and the mandatory closure of businesses on Saturday—has been a continual locus of political and public debate and friction. These debates are outside the scope of this paper.

The Religious Source of Gender Segregation

Traditionally, Jewish men and women pray separately in synagogues of the Orthodox stream of Judaism, which is the only stream which is officially recognized by the State of Israel. Hence, in Orthodox synagogues, there is a separate (and very often inferior) section for women.

Gender separation is not restricted to places of worship. For reasons of modesty and the observance of certain religious restrictions, some observant Jews avoid exposing their bodies in mixed company. So in order to cater to these special requirements, there are several beaches and swimming pools which keep separate hours and days of the week for men and for women, in order to enable gender-separated bathing. There is an ongoing battle about the extent of these provisions. Orthodox Jews continue to advocate for more and more gender-segregated beaches, swimming pools, gymnasia, etc., and for assigning them for the use of the religious sector of the population. On the other side, there are pressures from the general secular public and civil rights groups to limit these provisions, as they restrict access of the general public to national and public resources. I will elaborate on this conflict later in my discussion of the enclosures of the commons.

The requirements of modesty, the extent and the manifestations of which are often open to interpretation and debate, is understood as a requirement to avoid any physical contact between a man and a woman who are not married. Orthodox Jewish men also refrain from shaking hands with a woman, or being in the same room with one, without a third person being present.

Jewish Fundamentalism and the Process of Radicalization

The above-mentioned customs have been undergoing a gradual process of radicalization within the Orthodox Jewish community, but as long as they remained restricted to the community which accepted them as its normative way of life, they were met with relative tolerance from the rest of society.

Religious leaders are constantly dictating new, more radical limitations, more stringent prohibitions, and increasingly modest dress codes, especially for women and even young girls (Nahshoni, 2012).

It should be noted, however, that not all Orthodox women, and not all men, accept all of these restrictions willingly. There are groups within the Orthodox community, albeit few and small, who try to challenge some of the dictates of extreme modesty.

Forms of Exclusion: Gender Segregation, Effacement, and Repression

The focus of this paper, however, is not only a relatively recent phenomenon of radicalization among certain sectors of Orthodox Judaism, but also increasingly, the slippage or infiltration of this phenomenon into the general public sphere in Israel. The custom of segregation of the sexes, and its various manifestations, has taken an alarming turn. It has been gradually exceeding its traditional and historical boundaries, becoming more and more extreme, transcending religious communities and neighborhoods, and infiltrating the streets, the means of transportation, and the public venues which are frequented by the general population. Religious extremism is strengthening its hold in the public sphere, thus affecting religious and secular people alike.

This form of fundamentalism manifests itself in three ways: one is gender segregation; the second is the effacement of women's images from the public sphere; and the third is the repression of their voice. The rationales for these practices are modesty, and the religious requirement to avoid sexual stimulation in men. The result is that women, both secular and religious, are excluded from being seen or heard in public.

Israeli society is witnessing a transgression of practices and norms which had been restricted to the Orthodox community and places of worship, onto Israeli society at large. These restrictions are leading to discrimination, harassment, and even physical violence against women. The restrictions on women are often enforced by self-appointed zealots, but the official authorities stand by, or even cooperate, for political gains.

The unique structure of Israeli politics hampers attempts to battle this process or reverse it, despite continual attempts by women's organizations and civil rights groups. Appeals to the courts have yielded some decisions against these practices, but the enforcement of these decisions has been lacking.

Gender Segregation

The following are some examples of gender segregation which have become more common in recent years:

Tourist attractions and national landmarks, which are considered places of worship, have increasingly been monopolized as religious sites, which must, in the minds of the religious, conform to the standards of Orthodox synagogues, and have thus made their requirements for strict gender separation and modest dress code more visible and more strictly observed. The Western Wall (also known as "The Wailing Wall"), the most sacred place for Jews over the ages, is an example of a site with a dual function. It used to be a place where people came to visit, hold parties and ceremonies, pay their respects to an important landmark in their history, as well as pray. There are documents and photographs which clearly show that historically there was no separation between men and women there. Today, a tall fence separates the entire square, and gender segregation is strictly enforced. Tourists, youth groups, and school children, who until recently were able to visit the square, are now prevented from approaching the Western Wall unless they conform to the newly enforced rules of modesty of attire and to gender separation. The same phenomenon can be observed in other places which are historical sites and tourist attractions, as well as places of worship. The religious use has hijacked the secular use, preventing families and tourist groups from visiting those places together.

There are cemeteries in which women are not allowed to approach the grave during the burial, or to eulogize their loved ones. Hence, family members, who wish to stay together and support each other in their hour of grief, are forced to be separated during the funeral. The reason that is sometimes given for this prohibition is that women are "impure" because they "menstruate, and according to Jewish religion, are prohibited from walking amongst the graves" (Saraga, 2009, para. 5).

Next to synagogues and yeshivas (institutions for Jewish religious studies) signs have been put up which instruct the public to walk on separate sides of the street according to gender, and specifically, women are instructed to distance themselves or even hide themselves, so as not to be seen by men. Needless to say, although these phenomena are mainly seen in predominantly religious neighborhoods, streets and sidewalks are public spaces which should be open to everybody, and this restriction of access is not sanctioned by Israeli law (Ettinger & Kyzer, 2009).

The separation of men and women has infiltrated public transportation as well. The phenomenon started on a small scale: In 1997, the largest public bus company started operating two bus lines which were used by observant Orthodox Jews in two cities with a large Orthodox population. In these busses women board and sit in the rear and men sit in the front of the bus. The practice has since expanded and currently there are dozens of such segregated bus lines. Women who refuse to sit in the assigned zone are sometimes bullied and attacked. The public bus company, which has the monopoly over nationwide mass transportation, complies silently with the ever increasing demands of the most extreme segments of the population to enforce this gender segregation. The arrangement—which used to be restricted to busses which serve neighborhoods with a large Orthodox population—has gradually expanded to include intercity lines which serve the population at large. The practice had been challenged in court and the courts have ruled that gender segregation on busses is illegal, unless it is voluntary. However, the practice not only continues, but has indeed become more widespread.

In some localities, there are separate ticket booths for busses and trains. There are also separate lines in post offices and police stations, and in 2009 there were attempts to influence the national airline, El-Al, to conform to this trend and have separate flights for the Orthodox population in which there would be separate sections for men and women, with only male flight attendants to serve the men (Nahshoni, 2009). These pressures have so far met with resistance from the airline. A recent phenomenon which has become increasingly common involves Ultra-Orthodox people who approach passengers on El-Al flights, requesting them to switch seats so that they do not have to sit next to a passenger of the opposite sex (Twersky, 2012).

In compliance with demands from extremists in the Orthodox community, there are more public health clinics that treat men and women in separate sections, and patients are guaranteed medical treatment by staff of the same sex.

Some private businesses have also started to conform to these practices. There are shops with different entrances for men and women. In some supermarkets, there are separate cash registers for men and women, and in others all the female cashiers have been replaced by male workers.

During holidays in which, traditionally, there is a large assembly of people in the streets, pedestrian streets in Jerusalem are partitioned, so as to enforce gender segregation. As always, the purported justification is that extramarital physical and visual contact between men and women ought to be prevented. In some religious neighborhoods, segregated sidewalks are now the norm.

These phenomena are usually restricted to neighborhoods populated by Orthodox Jews, and the "rules" are usually enforced by self-appointed zealous hoodlums. Many people, both men and women of these communities do not condone these practices, but are usually reluctant to stand up against them, for fear of seeming "liberal" or less pious.

Furthermore, the population in some of these neighborhoods is mixed, and some religious communities are adjacent to other neighborhoods with diverse populations. The streets, the public spaces, the shops, as well as the means of transportation cater to a diverse population, for which these practices seem not only inconvenient (e.g., parents cannot stay with their children, husbands and wives cannot shop together, etc.) but also alien, offensive, and degrading to women. It should be stressed that these places are public, legally open to all, and maintained by taxes paid by the populations that are being limited.

The Effacement of Women's Images

The rationale behind these restrictions is the desire to avoid sexual stimulation of men, and consequently the possibility of sin, whether actual or in thought. However, the responsibility and the limitations are placed on women rather than on men, who are supposedly unable to control their desire. Hence, women and girls dressed in modern attire, which is often considered immodest by Orthodox Jews, are often verbally and physically attacked when entering Orthodox neighborhoods or means of transportation dominated by Orthodox communities.

The restriction of looking at women who are not modestly dressed is gradually and increasingly understood by some to be a restriction of looking at women in general, even the most modest ones, and in its extreme form—at photos, pictures, images, and even garments and artifacts of women. This is one of the most salient manifestations of the exclusion of women from the public sphere. There has been ongoing and increasing pressure from extremists to remove the images of women from billboards, busses, commercials, official publications, catalogues, etc.[2] Busses and billboards which display pictures of women are often damaged and defaced, and bus stops with ads containing images of women have been burnt and vandalized. This has led to advertisers capitulating to the extremists, and to the disappearance of such images from the streets in predominantly religious localities. The national bus company faces an added difficulty because, unlike billboards, busses are not stationary, and there are lines that traverse both religious and secular neighborhoods. Recently, the bus company has decided not to display women's pictures on its busses. This decision was challenged in court; the court declared this business policy illegal, and the company was instructed not to discriminate against women. Nevertheless, the bus company, obliged by the court decision, while fearing extremist vandalism, has since decided to stop posting ads with images of both men and women on its busses in Jerusalem.

The prohibition against images of women gradually encompasses a prohibition against any visual representation of the female body or face, however subtle, stylized, or artistic. Photos and drawings of women have also been removed from commercials, food packages, and websites of public services.

The dictated prohibition of women's images has become evidently more than merely an aesthetic or commercial issue when women who ran for office were not allowed to post their pictures as part of their political campaign, while men's pictures were posted. This was the case in the elections to the city council in Jerusalem (see Kelner, 2011) and to a student union in a religious college (Zilberman, 2012). This is a particularly serious infringement on the civil rights of women, since it hampers their ability to effectively participate in the political discourse of the country.

The Suppression of Women's Voices

In addition to the restrictions on public images of women, the Orthodox rules of modesty are now commonly understood as prohibiting men from even listening to women's voices. The original religious decree is to refrain from listening to erotic and seductive singing (Makovi, 2010). It is a recent radical interpretation of this decree which extends the prohibition to women's voices in general. Religious figures have interfered in the form and content of artistic performances in official ceremonies by dictating the dress, the music and the participants in the performance. Official ceremonies and festivities which used to include performances by female singers and dancers have been censored and altered (see Medzini, 2008). Contrary to tradition, in the parliament, the military, as well as in municipal and national ceremonies, only male singers are invited to sing for fear of offending the attending rabbis and the scrupulously observant audience members.

Women scientists were prevented from going on stage to receive an official prize of the Ministry of Health, so as not to offend attending rabbis. The women were asked to send a man to receive the prize on their behalf, while their male peers accepted the prize in person, on stage, from the Deputy Minister of Health, an Orthodox Jew (Goldberg, 2011). Similarly, the former mayor of Jerusalem, an Orthodox Jew, refused to shake hands with female laureates of the prestigious Israel Prize, shaking hands with the male laureates only.

Since in Israel there is general conscription at age 18 for men and women, the military is an important locus of integration and social mobility, especially for the Jewish population. There has been a continual attempt by women to be allowed to occupy the full array of significant jobs and positions in the military, and the efforts have resulted in significant gains for women. This progress, however, has recently been countered by pressure from religious leaders and servicemen to apply ever stricter standards of gender segregation. The army often complies with demands from religious figures to establish separate units for male and female soldiers, and enforces strict rules of modesty of dress on female soldiers, far exceeding the military dress code. There have been reported cases of religious soldiers who refuse to be taught by female instructors and commanders.

Religious cadets, who refused to remain present when female soldiers sang in a military ceremony, were expelled from the training course (Bar-Zohar, 2012; Harel, 2011; Leibowitz, 2011). This led to a parliamentary bill to ensure that male soldiers are not penalized in the future for such acts of disobedience (Lees & Bar-Zohar, 2011).

Reactions and Protests by Women and Civil Rights Organizations

Most of these practices have been deemed illegal when contested in court, but the authorities have been reluctant to enforce the law. Moreover, commercial chains and businesses violate the law by caving in to extremists' demands, trying to avoid confrontations for fear of violence and subsequent financial losses.

Feminist organizations and civil rights groups protest against the exclusion of women, their images, and their voice from the public sphere, but these protests are met with demands to accept and respect the Orthodox way of life in the name of multiculturalism.

Even within the religious communities, there are those who are alarmed by the extremist trends. A group of religious women who are known as "Women of the Wall," have been trying to protest against the monopoly of the extremists dictates by defiantly praying at the Western Wall, wearing praying shawls. They have been harassed, accused of disturbing the peace, and even arrested by the police (Goldenberg, 2012).

Multiculturalism

Proponents of multiculturalism argue for the right of minority groups to live their lives as they see fit. The motto "live and let live" captures the driving principle behind this approach. Within the religious community, the process of radicalization is ignored and denied, defended as a positive change toward a more modest society, or deemed as an inevitable backlash due to the increasing immodesty and liberalism of the surrounding secular world.

The argument for allowing the exclusion of women from the public sphere can be examined from the viewpoint of multiculturalism. Advocates of cultural diversity and multiculturalism defend the rights of minority groups to maintain their culture and their customs, even in cases where the majority of the society within which they live finds these customs objectionable and indeed illegal. The degree of justifiable intervention by the state in the self-government of cultural minorities is a topic of debate (Herr, 2004; Okin, 1997; Shachar, 2000).

There are other gender-related practices in Israeli society that are illegal but still practiced, to the detriment of women, and the authorities do not go out of their way to stop them. Polygamy, forced marriage of minors, and female genital mutilation (also known as clitoridectomy) are still practiced in the Bedouin community. Most advocates of multiculturalism do not go so far as to include these practices among those which deserve the tolerance and protection of a liberal state. There are those, however, who take a pragmatic stand and claim that it is better for women in certain societies to "play by the rules" and accept such injurious practices because this is their only way to remain members of their community and of their culture (Lennahan, 2004).

The Israeli phenomenon in question is usually less violent, but it raises similar questions. Multiculturalism, and the tolerance in which a liberal society treats its minorities, very often comes at the expense of the most vulnerable members of the minority group. The purported right to live according to a traditional or religious code is often exploited as license to discriminate and harm a minority within it, or its women. Much of the criticism of the multiculturalist approach hinges on these adverse implications (Okin, 1997).

Following Susan M. Okin, one can ask whether, in adopting the multicultural attitude, and accepting the right of the Orthodox minority to maintain the social values it chooses, we do not sacrifice the rights of women—unquestionably a vulnerable minority within the Orthodox minority—to live a life free from discrimination and oppression.

The liberal dilemma is difficult to resolve. On the one hand, the liberal state is committed to allowing and enabling a community to maintain its social structure according to its own cultural norms, and to uphold its values and practices even if they violate basic tenets of a liberal society. A liberal society may indeed find these values and practices abhorrent. On the other hand, the state is obligated to protect the weak and vulnerable members of society, including members of the minorities. Whether multiculturalism and feminism are allies or rivals is an ongoing debate among philosophers of law and ethics. Does respecting a minority culture necessarily entail respecting and allowing the most odious aspects of it?

The Inadequacy of the Multicultural Model

There are inherent difficulties in treating the problem within the framework of multiculturalism. Firstly, since the community is a conservative patriarchal society, whose values and regulations are determined by men, and since the religious legal code (*halacha*) was written by men, women's interests and wishes are usually not reflected in them. The norms which place women in their "proper place" in the domestic rather than the public sphere were constructed by men, and therefore cannot be considered representative of the wishes and the interests of women.

Another debated issue is whether the apparent consent of oppressed individuals within the minority can be understood to be genuine, free, and informed consent. The voices of women in the Orthodox sector are not properly heard, and whether or not they wish to be silenced, muted, and absent from the public sphere is hard to determine. The issue is further complicated because from a very young age Orthodox girls are raised to accept their inferior role as natural and desirable. Women who are segregated, assigned separate sections, hidden, and silenced may say that they have no complaint with these traditions, but can we take this complacency at face value? Does not society have the duty to protect these women even if they seem not to seek such protection?

Thirdly, there is a problem in treating the Orthodox religious community as monolithic. Even if most women, when asked, agree to the practices and restrictions described here, and even if we accept that their consent is informed and voluntary, it does not follow that *all* the women in the community agree and condone them.

The above tension between liberalism and multiculturalism notwithstanding, there remains serious criticism of the adequacy of the multicultural model when referring to the Israeli phenomenon in that it does not capture the complexity and the problematic ramifications of this phenomenon. The infiltration of the practices of gender segregation and the effacement of women from the public sphere affect not only the Orthodox community, but the general public. The question is no longer the extent of freedom granted to a minority to practice illiberal rituals in the private sphere, but rather this minority's demand to impose illiberal standards and values on the public sphere of a liberal society. The multicultural discourse typically deals with the rights of minorities vis-à-vis the culture of the majority, but it does not address the right of the majority to preserve its way of life and to protect its members from injustice and oppression. Therefore, an analysis within the framework of multiculturalism seems inadequate.

The Commons, Enclosure, and Reclaiming the Commons

The term *commons* was historically used to refer to land and other natural resources which are collectively owned by society. In his seminal and controversial paper "The Tragedy of the Commons," biologist Garrett Hardin "revived" the term as a metaphor for the public sphere. In his paper, he refers to the pollution of the commons, not only with chemical pollutants, but also with noise, advertising, and other disturbances to mental health and to pleasure (Hardin, 1968). In contemporary debate over intellectual property, the term *commons* is often used to refer to more abstract resources such as technological and digital information; creative resources such as open source technologies; and online educational resources such as Wikipedia. The term *enclosure* has been used to refer to the process of enclosing and privatizing land (Monbiot, 1994). In current environmental discourse, these terms are widely used to describe the privatization, marketing, and abuse of natural resources (Mishori, 2010).

I would like to adopt this terminology for the discussion of the phenomenon which I have described here, and to suggest that it captures the debate surrounding it, as well as the ethical ramifications of its propagation. The commons is the public sphere which belongs to everybody and to nobody in particular. The conceptual counterpart of the commons is the enclosure. The exclusion of women from certain locations constitutes an enclosure of a space which should be open to everybody, men and women. Just as parks, beaches, clean air, and water are seen as commons, so are more abstract spaces in which people, men and women, have an equal right to be heard and seen.

Each of the manifestations of the exclusion of women I have described above can be viewed as cases of enclosure. Gender segregation is, in effect, an enclosure of the public space and a restriction of access to the commons for some of the commoners, i.e. women. The effacement of women and their image, and the suppression of their voice, rob women of access to the commons. As a result, their right to be active members of the society is being increasingly limited.

Hence, when women are prevented from running for office effectively, from utilizing all the means of campaigning, persuasion, and publicity that are available to men, such as appearing and speaking in public and having their picture displayed, they are deprived of their right to participate in the democratic process (see Sen, 1999). They are thereby denied access to the political commons. Likewise, when female artists are discriminatorily prevented from performing in public, where men are not, they are denied access to the artistic commons.

Mishori (2010) describes a recent controversy in Israel over advertising on billboards alongside a highway in metropolitan Tel Aviv. One of the arguments for the removal of the billboards draws from "mental environmentalism" claiming that the public has rights over public space, which should not be polluted by advertisements. In this sense, the public tried to reclaim the commons, i.e., the public sphere.[3]

Ironically, proponents of the exclusion of women use arguments similar to those employed by environmentalists. They claim their right to have the commons free of mental pollutants such as pictures of women, which they do not wish to see, or of a women's voice, which they do not wish to hear. The problem with such arguments is that they are used discriminatorily, and only women's images and voices are considered pollutants, while those of men are not.

Gender segregation is an injurious enclosure of the commons in many other ways, some rather subtle. Every time a gender segregated health clinic opens, or a segregated bus line starts running, a parallel service, which is not gender segregated needs to be made available to the general public which does not wish to be so segregated. This "extravagance" results in redundancy, over-spending, and excessive exploitation of public resources, over and above the injustice to women inherent in the practice itself.

Bollier (2002) calls for the "reclaiming" of the commons. In the case of exclusion of women from the public sphere, this means banning all forms of gender segregation, prohibiting the effacement or repression of women, their images and their voice.

Conclusion

I have restricted the discussion in this paper to the Jewish sector, and have shown that religious fundamentalism has a detrimental effect on the lives and status of women. It is at least partly due to the lack of separation between religion and the state that this form of fundamentalism is able to have such a strong effect.

I believe that a separation of religion and state would have a beneficial effect, not only for Jewish women, but throughout the State of Israel, and would improve the lives of women of all faiths and all ethnic groups.

The focus of this paper has been the exclusion of women from the public sphere, sometimes in blatant violation of the law. A small, but ever growing Ultra-Orthodox minority imposes its norms on the general public, demanding consideration and respect for its way of life.

Many in Israel see the worrisome phenomenon of the exclusion of women from the public sphere as harmful and dangerous, and as adversely affecting all members of society. We seem to be sliding down a slippery slope of deterioration of the rights of the public at large. The current trend amounts to the trading of minority rights for the right of the general public, whose core values are in danger. The exclusion of women from the public sphere transcends the boundaries of the Orthodox community; hence, it poses a clear threat to the way of life of women and men who do not belong to the Orthodox community, who do not share its values and norms, but who do share the same public space.

The manifestations of this exclusion-gender segregation, the effacement of women's images, and the suppression of the female voice, all amount to enclosures of the commons, and they deprive women access to the public sphere. If universal values of equality, the right to dignity, to equal representation, and to equal protection of the law, are important to Israeli society, it must take measures to reclaim the commons.

Notes

1. Throughout the paper I will use the terms "religious" and "Orthodox" interchangeably to refer to the Ultra-Orthodox Jewish sector, which is sometimes referred to in Israeli Hebrew as *Haredim*. This is an over simplification of a very complex variety of religious sects and levels of religiosity. The terminology and the classification which are used in communities outside of Israel are often different. In the United States, they are often labeled "Hasidic Jews."

2. Israel is not the only country where women are excluded from the public sphere. See Molin (2012) for the story of the exclusion of women from IKEA catalogues designated for distribution in Saudi Arabia.

3. Unfortunately, this case was lost in favor of profit. Following a court ruling in favor of the environmentalists' appeal, the Israeli parliament changed the law to allow for advertising along the Ayalon Highway.

Gender and Leadership Style in the Middle East: Evidence from Egypt's Civil Service

Jennifer Bremer
Ola Gameel Al-Talliawi

Abstract

Gender differentials in managerial positions and leadership style have been studied widely in the West, but only rarely in the Middle East. This study analyzes women's position in Egypt's public sector by first, analyzing official data on female participation in public sector management positions in Egypt and, second, by comparing men's and women's leadership styles based on a survey of Ministry of Finance middle managers. The survey, which uses a variant of the Leadership Behavior Description Questionnaire XII (LBDQ XII), finds no statistically significant differences based on gender. This finding supports the hypothesis that male and female leadership styles are similar and do not reflect agentic (stereotypically male) versus communal (stereotypically female) models. The findings underscore the need to ensure gender-neutral access to opportunities for leadership to take full advantage of Egypt's human resource assets.

Introduction

The governmental transformation sweeping the Middle East places new demands on government and opens new opportunities for reform. It thus increases the premium on leadership to enable public agencies to respond to greatly increased popular pressure for better performance. To meet these demands, Middle East governments must make effective use of all their human resource assets by addressing the under

utilization of women in management and leadership positions. While global research on gender workplace differences demonstrates widespread patterns of inequality, the Middle East faces special challenges in overcoming historical and cultural biases against women in management roles.

The need to take full advantage of women managers reflects human rights concerns: all productive citizens have the right to equal participation and representation (Noble & Moore, 2006). It is also a practical issue of human resource management (HRM). The negative evaluation of women in leadership roles can decrease individual well-being and undermine HRM (Stelter, 2002), wasting capabilities in ways that hard-pressed developing countries can ill afford. Gender discrimination has been proven to negatively affect professional advancement and job satisfaction among female workers (Newman, Guy, and Mastracci, 2007), thus depriving organizations of needed talents and perspectives (Appelbaum, Audet, & Miller, 2003).

Egypt, like other developing countries, urgently needs to utilize all its human potential. The landmark first Arab Human Development Report (UNDP, 2002) argued strongly that overall development in the Arab world is severely impaired by low female participation in public life, the economy, and politics (UNDP, 2002).

The need to ensure full participation by women in public life, including public service has taken on greater importance in the wake of Islamist electoral victories in Egypt's 2012 elections. Although few women candidates ran in Egypt's first open parliamentary elections in decades, and fewer still won office, women constitute about a quarter of the senior-level positions in the Egyptian bureaucracy. The ability of women public sector managers to exercise leadership will therefore be a critical factor in defining how the revolution shapes women's (and men's) lives and the scope for women to participate in setting and implementing government policies for post-revolutionary Egypt.

A better understanding of the status of women in public service and the factors shaping their effectiveness as leaders is therefore needed to inform strategies that can ensure representation of women's perspectives at the decision-making table and to redress gender imbalances in income, services, and opportunities. Very little is known about women's leadership roles in the Egyptian public sector, however. The primary aim of this study is to contribute to filling this gap.

The study proceeds in four steps. It first presents the main schools of thought on gender leadership style differentials, which take competing views as to whether such differences exist and, if so, whether they are beneficial or detrimental to organizational performance. The next part examines gender roles in Egypt's public sector, offering an analysis of the roles of men and women in Egypt's public sector as a whole with regard to employment, wage differentials, and the status of men and women in government versus private sector employment. This is followed by a case study of the Ministry of Finance (MOF), examining how gender issues are reflected in its roles as an employer and as a key actor in the distribution of government resources. This analysis examines recent efforts to promote gender equality in the ministry itself and through the ministry's work on the national budget, and presents the results of a survey of middle manager's leadership style characteristics, using a variant on the LBDQ XII. The final section draws conclusions for policy-makers and points toward future directions for research on gender workplace issues in Egypt in particular, and the Middle East more generally.

While literally hundreds of studies have examined gender-based leadership style differentials outside the Middle East, the present study is believed to be the first conducted in a Middle Eastern public sector setting. At this juncture, when gender roles are expected to come under renewed examination in the region, this study seeks to shed light on the relative potential for men and women to contribute to coming reforms in public governance.

Schools of Thought on Gender and Leadership: an Increasingly Global Debate

Two main schools of thought have emerged in the gender and leadership literature, but numerous studies conducted over the years have failed to determine which school has the strongest case (Porterfield & Kleiner, 2005). The competing schools of thought, briefly summarized below, are referred to here as the "complementary contribution" school and the "equality-based" school. The debate initiated in the United States and Europe however, has since spread to non-Western societies, although it remains much less developed in the latter areas.

At the core of this debate are two questions: 1) do differences exist between male and female leadership styles and, 2) if so, do these differences have an impact on the relative leadership effectiveness of males and females and the organizations in which they work? Among those scholars who argue that differences exist, there is a further debate as to whether such differences promote or impede women's leadership at the personal and institutional level and whether differences are personality-based, gender-based, a product of organizational environment, or shaped by a mix of these factors.

The "complementary contribution" school holds that there are male–female leadership style differences, but that these styles are complementary, each contributing to organizational effectiveness in different ways. Trinidad and Normore (2005) for example argue that "the integration of women in leadership roles is not a matter of 'fitting in' the traditional models, but 'giving in' the opportunities for them to practice their own leadership styles" (p. 574) and matching candidate skills with what is needed for organizational success.

Some researchers have extended this debate further to argue that women's leadership styles are not only different from men's, but more effective. They provide evidence that women's leadership styles align with the transformational or charismatic style of leadership, generally regarded as more effective than the transactional or laissez faire leadership styles. Eagly (2007) presents the case for this position, differentiating between leadership style and actual effectiveness in diverse organizational settings and summarizing evidence that higher participation by women in leadership roles is associated with greater organizational effectiveness.

The competing "equality-based" paradigm holds that gender is not a useful construct for distinguishing among individuals with regard to performance or capabilities. This model recognizes that there are differences between men and women as individuals, but those similarities between men and women, and differences within genders make it impossible to generalize about male–female leadership differences.

The equality-based school finds more frequent expression in the literature. It serves as the ground floor for many gender advocates, who argue that any barriers to the leadership of women do not reflect an underlying leadership capability differential with men, but rather spring discrimination, unfairly hindering women's progress up the career ladder.

Both schools frame the discussion around sets of leadership characteristics that may (or may not) be differentiated by gender. Gibson (1995) classifies these differences into two leadership styles, agentic and communal. Agentic leadership qualities, seen as stereotypically male, include assertiveness, self-reliance, dominance, directness, decisiveness, aggressiveness, ambition, and self-sufficiency. Communal, stereotypically female qualities include concern for the welfare of others and awareness of their feelings; nurturance, affection, and sympathy; ability to devote oneself to others; emotional expressiveness; and helpfulness.

Other terms have since come into use based on a conceptually similar distinction, although differing on the specific set of behaviors identified. Thus, agentic leadership traits are also found in the transactional or authoritative/directive leadership style. These styles have been found by some researchers (but by no means all) to be comparatively more common among men than women. By contrast, the communal leadership traits overlap with the transactional or charismatic leadership style, associated with stereotypically female behaviors (Ashkanasy & Tse, 2000; Bass & Avolio, 1994; Eagly, 2007; Groves, 2005; Klenke, 2002; Mandell & Pherwani, 2003).

A large body of empirical studies has attempted to test these propositions, without reaching a firm conclusion. Three meta-analyses have been conducted to review this literature as a whole, covering well over 200 studies. Dobbins and Platz (1986) concluded that, on the basis of leadership characteristics such as initiating structure, consideration, and subordinate satisfaction, leaders' sex did not affect any of the dependent variables. Eagly and Johnson (1990) in their subsequent meta-analysis reached the opposite conclusion, finding that differences "occurred in the tendency for women to adopt a more democratic or participative style and for men to adopt a more autocratic or directive style" (p. 233), a finding broadly in line with the communal-agentic classification, and thus with the complementary-contribution thesis. Where differences were found, they were not always significant and tended to be low, however. Finally, Eagly, Johannesen-Schmidt, and van Engen (2003), and van Engen and Willemsen (2013) report a meta-analysis of more recent literature, reaching broadly similar results to the earlier Eagly and Johnson study.

Though extensive, this literature has given comparatively little attention to public sector settings outside the education sector, despite the importance of government employment in most countries, particularly for women. Eagly and Johnson (1990) report that only 19 out of a total 370 gender style comparisons were made in governmental organizations, excluding schools and universities, while eight out of 72 of the comparisons in van Engen and Willemsen (2013) were in government organizations. The vast majority of these studies were in industrialized countries, primarily the United States and Europe. Van Engen and Willemsen report the location of the 23 studies for their meta-analysis, of which only two are in developing countries (both surveys of students in India).

The setting of the present study, in a Middle Eastern government organization, thus addresses two gaps in the gender-based leadership style literature: the limited study of leadership in the public sector, and developing country settings. As discussed below, only one earlier study could be identified that examined workplace gender differences in leadership style in the Middle East, and this did not address the public sector workplace.

Gender and Leadership in the Middle East: Review of an Emergent Literature

Neal, Finlay, Catana, and Catana (2007) call attention to the need to extend the inquiry of gender differentials in leadership capabilities to the Arab world, where women are gaining influence in government, education, and business spheres, making it essential to understand their aptitudes so as to equip them for leadership roles in the public and corporate worlds.

Field research is only beginning to respond to this need, however. While the stereotypical view of women's position and leadership roles in Middle Eastern society is clearly one of subservience to men (if not absent from the world outside the home altogether), only a handful of studies have sought to measure the views of Middle Eastern managers on women's leadership. Mostafa's 2003 study of attitudes toward women's work in Egypt confirmed that women were more favorable to women's work than were men, but found no significant generational gap in these views, leading him to conclude that Egyptian and Arab culture are still dominated by patriarchal values and that "while Arab women are willing to accept additional responsibilities in the occupational, educational, and social spheres, men are not ready to share these responsibilities with them" (p. 260).

Arabsheibani's (2000) study of male–female earnings differentials among Egyptian university graduates found a relatively small wage differential of only 7% in this group, which may be attributed at least in part to the predominance of public sector employment within the sample: approximately 95% of each group were employed in the public sector. Although published in 2000, her analysis is based on data collected in 1979 (a fact itself suggestive of the data deficiencies that inhibit research in the region). Her analysis found that "just over one-quarter of the gross earnings differential between men and women remains unexplained [by differentials in such characteristics as education or experience], which is usually taken to be the result of discrimination" (p. 129). She also found that the private sector paid relatively higher wages to male graduates than to female graduates, with a premium of 38% and 30% above the public sector monthly earnings, respectively.

The Global Leadership and Organizational Behavior Effectiveness research project (GLOBE) focuses on inter-country differences, and thus its data do not directly measure male–female leadership style differences (GLOBE, 2010). However, they do capture attitudes toward gender egalitarianism as one of the nine core societal cultural dimensions analyzed, along with such leadership style constructs as humane orientation, power distance, and community orientation (Kabasakal & Bodur, 2002).

Kabasakal and Bodur (2002) report the GLOBE findings from the Middle East region cluster, which includes Turkey, Egypt, Morocco, Kuwait, and Qatar. GLOBE data confirmed that middle managers in this region attach less importance to gender egalitarianism overall compared to the average for the remaining eight regional clusters. Managers surveyed assessed current gender egalitarianism at 2.95 out of a possible 7, the lowest score in any regional cluster. Egypt's score of 2.81 fell below the regional mean.

Those surveyed were relatively more favorable to gender egalitarianism as an ideal to be pursued, assessing the desired level of this trait among leaders at 3.65 out of 7. The score assigned by Middle East managers to the gender egalitarianism of current leaders fell short of this ideal and trailed the average in other geographic clusters by 0.45, the largest negative difference of any characteristic. The gap in the ideal leader's level of gender egalitarianism was even greater, falling below the average for non-Middle East clusters by 0.92, again the largest negative gap for any value, with Egypt's score of 3.18 also the lowest in its cluster. These results lend support to the stereotype that Middle East society places a low value on having leaders who value gender equity.

Only a handful of studies provide quantitative analyses of women's leadership roles in the Middle East. Metcalfe (2008) calls attention to this deficit, noting that "[a] major problem for women in the ME region is a lack of information about women's leadership and women's global achievement" (pp. 91-92). She provides a broad overview of women's position in private sector leadership in the region, concluding that "there have been significant achievements in advancing women in leadership and political roles, but that there are still institutional and cultural barriers embedded in business systems" (p. 85).

Neal et al. (2007) compare the leadership styles of women—but not men—in two Arab countries (Oman and Lebanon) to those in two European countries (Romania and the United Kingdom), based on a survey of 425 female business students in the four countries. They find that the Lebanese and Omani women were closer to each other, in general, than to one or both of the European country groups in the four authority prototypes in leadership that they explored (the rational-legal, interactive, traditional, and charismatic). The rational-legal prototype was the most strongly supported by all four national groups, however, suggesting that the differences are more nuanced than absolute.

Only one study, Yaseen (2010), was identified that directly compares men's and women's leadership styles in the Middle East based on survey data. This study uses the Multifactor Leadership Questionnaire developed to explore differences between male and female leaders in the United Arab Emirates. The survey was administered to a sample of 100 Arab middle managers and their supervisors, peers, and colleagues, predominantly in the United Arab Emirates, of whom 40% were women.

Yaseen (2010) argues that stereotypes themselves may shape male–female differences in leadership style. Women may use communal leadership strategies because they have "learn[ed] that they are more effective when they employ" such styles or because they have internalized the stereotype that this is how women are "supposed" to behave, regardless of whether they would choose communal approaches in the absence of gender role stereotypes (p. 65). His study finds that women were more likely to use transformational leadership approaches, while men preferred transactional approaches, with "70 percent of Arab men indicat[ing] that they focus their attention on dealing with mistakes, complaints, and failures" (p. 68).

Gender Parity in Egypt's Public Administration: a National Perspective

Female participation in the Egyptian labor force is low by international standards. The World Bank (2007) reports that only 22% of women participate in the labor force. Consistent with this, women accounted for just 22% of non-agricultural labor force participants aged 15–64 in 2004. While many women choose not to be economically active for social or family reasons, women's unemployment rates are more than three times those of men (Livani, 2007).

A recent analysis by Egypt's Central Agency for Public Mobilization and Statistics (CAPMAS, the official statistical agency) indicates that Egyptian women are nearly twice as likely as men to work for the government, reflecting a preference for public sector employment that may be attributable to both social and economic factors, as discussed below. Whereas 39% of women were employed in government organizations in 2008, only 24% of men worked in the public sector (CAPMAS, 2009).

Despite women's relative and absolute preference for public sector work, men predominate in the public sector because of women's low labor force participation rates. Overall, women accounted for 27% of the public sector workforce in 2007 (CAPMAS, 2009). This considerably overstates women's role in the public sector as a whole, however, because women teachers and health workers account for nearly three-quarters of this total, more than 1 million of the 1.4 million women in public sector employment (CAPMAS, 2009 and authors' calculations). By contrast, 38% of male government employees work in local education and health services, although they overwhelmingly dominate another category of low-level service workers, that is, the one million local police and security workers, 98% of whom are men. In urban areas, where government jobs are concentrated and where women are more likely to work outside the home, 64% of women work in the public sector, as shown in Table 1 below.

Table 1. Distribution of Total Workforce by Sector, Location, and Sex, 2008

Sector	Percentage of employees					
	Urban		Rural		Total	
	M	F	M	F	M	F
Central government	21.9	60.9	19.2	21.5	20.3	37.5
Other public sector	5.7	3.1	2.7	.4	3.9	1.5
Private/other	72.4	36.0	78.2	78.1	75.7	61.1
Total	100	100	100	100	100	100

Source: CAPMAS, 2009.

Egyptian public administration heavily favors promotion based on seniority rather than merit, providing some protection for women against discrimination (Abdelhamid & El-Baradei 2010). Because women entered senior civil service ranks comparatively recently, the share of females who have risen to decision making and leadership positions in government is still low compared to men, although greatly increased over the past three decades. In 1988, women accounted for only 7% of those in the upper management cadre, but this proportion reached 21% in 2000 and 24% in 2008, as shown in Table 2 (CAPMAS, 2009). The rate of increase over this period has been highest at the top, in the two ranks just below ministerial grade.

Table 2. Percentage of Senior-level Positions in the Egyptian Civil Service Held by Women (by grade, 1988–2008)

Category of employee	1988	1996	2000	2003	2005	2008	2008 share as multiple of 1988 level
Ministerial	1.4	2.6	2.9	3.8	3.8	2.5	1.8
Vice-ministerial	3.0	3.2	—	—	7.1	18.2	6.1
Superior grade	0.9	3.3	5.2	9.0	13.4	14.3	15.9
Upper grade	4.3	8.5	15.2	15.9	21.7	20.9	4.9
General manager	8.8	17.5	23.3	23.3	15.4	25.5	2.9
Total	7.3	15.3	21.5	23.5	16.2	24.1	3.3

Source: CAPMAS, 2009 and authors' calculations.

Table 3. Proportion of Government Leadership Positions Held by Women, Selected Sectors

Sector	Percentage of leadership-level employees who are women
Social protection	36.5
Housing and community utilities	31.9
Health	29.3
Public general services	28.4
Education	25.5
Public discipline and safety affairs	23.3
Environment protection	21.0
Entertainment, culture, and religion	17.5
Economic affairs	17.0
Defense, security, and justice	1.3
Total	28.4

Source: CAPMAS, 2009 CAPMAS (2009) reports that the proportion of leadership positions held by women varies considerably by sector, as shown in Table 3.

Women occupy about the same share of upper-level government positions as they hold in the civil service overall (27%); thus, the gender gap in the civil service is concentrated in the very highest ranks. Analysis of average pay rates in the public sector, comparing them to private sector rates of pay, provides further insight into why women prefer public sector employment. Egyptian labor law requires equal pay for equal work and forbids discrimination based on gender in both the public and private sectors, but, as in many countries, the actual situation does not always conform to this requirement (CAPMAS, 2009). Official data show that a pay gap does indeed exist between men and women in the public sector, but it is in favor of women.

CAPMAS data on average weekly earnings collected in late 2007 show that the average male working in the public sector earned LE (Egyptian pound) 300/week (about US$50 at current exchange rates), while the average woman earned LE 331 (US$55). Contrary to stereotypes, average public sector earnings exceeded those in the private sector: the average private sector male worker earned LE 182 (US$30) per week and the average female worker just LE 128 (US$21), equivalent to only US$1,100 on an annualized basis.

Thus, women in Egypt's public sector earn more on average than their male peers and more than twice what their sisters earn in the private sector. Even these differentials understate the relative attractiveness of public sector employment, particularly for women, because of the non-cash benefits of government employment. Not only is the public sector social protection package much more attractive than that in the private sector, but women in the public sector also benefit from the more family-friendly work hours, lifetime job security, and a work environment that is considered more suitable and respectful for women than many private sector workplaces (Barsoum, 2004). As discussed by Yaish and Stier (2009), this pattern is also common across governments in the industrialized world.

Recent hires in Egypt's public sector have often been contractual in an effort to reduce the country's six million-strong bureaucracy and thus do not enjoy the full benefit package. They are nonetheless in a much better situation than private sector workers in the informal sector, who account for more than half of all private employment and very rarely receive social benefits (Wahba, 2009).

There is considerable sectorial variation within this broad picture. Table 4 shows public wages in monetary terms, male–female wage differentials in each sector, and the public–private wage differential within each gender, ranked by the magnitude of the male–female public sector earnings differential.

Table 4. Comparison of Male and Female Earnings in Selected Economic Activities, Public Sector versus Private Sector

Economic Activity	Weekly public sector earnings (Egyptian pounds)		Public sector earnings/ Private sector earnings		Male/Female weekly earnings	
	Men	Women	Public Sector	Private Sector	Men	Women
Transport, storage, and communications	287	399	1.39	1.18	1.15	1.36
Community, social, and personal services	151	185	1.23	.78	1.16	1.83
Manufacturing	299	351	1.17	0.65	1.85	3.34
Utilities	341	391	1.15	1.30	1.19	1.05
Construction	254	290	1.14	1.19	1.20	1.16
Education	NA	NA	NA	0.90	NA	NA
Brokerage	328	324	0.99	1.14	0.73	0.63
Restaurants and hotels	131	128	0.98	1.13	0.88	0.76
Wholesale and retail trade	259	224	0.86	0.73	1.12	1.33
Real estate	191	147	0.77	1.14	0.84	0.56
Health and social work	417	100	0.24	0.68	3.00	1.05
Total	300	331	1.10	0.70	1.65	2.59

Source: CAPMAS (2009) and authors' calculations; LE 1 = approx. US$5.5.

Although these data reflect average earnings across all types of workers within the sector, from highly skilled professionals to cleaning staff, the patterns, nonetheless, offer insight into the relative position of women in government and business. First, there is a moderately strong relationship across the sexes (r = 0.46) with regard to which economic activities pay better in the private sector than in the government. In other words, in sectors where the private sector market offers a better wage for men than does the public sector, women's private sector wages also tend to be higher. This suggests that employers see sufficient substitutability to enable women to bargain for higher wages. Second, the public–private differentials are higher overall for women. Women in the public sector earn on average 2.6 times what women earn in the private sector. The comparable differential for men, while still favoring the public sector, is only 1.6. Third, the earnings of men and women working in the same economic sector are moderately correlated within the public sector (r=0.44) and almost perfectly correlated in the private sector (r=0.97). Finally, at the economic sector level, gender pay gaps are correlated within each sector between public and private workplaces (r=0.36).

Given this situation, it is hardly surprising that women prefer government jobs even more than do men. Although promotion in the Egyptian public service is only very weakly related to performance, it is noteworthy in the context of women's rise to leadership positions that women participate disproportionately in government training programs. Newman (1993) notes that limiting women's access to training indicates a failure to invest in women, but this limitation would not appear to prevail in Egypt's public sector.

CAPMAS data show that women accounted for 27% of the government workforce but 41% of central administration trainees in 2007/2008, receiving proportionately better access to training than did men. The proportion of women trainees relative to men did not vary substantially by type of training; women accounted for 38% of those trained in supervisory skills, for example. With regard to training in leadership skills specifically, women's share corresponds closely to their share in the leadership cadre: women made up 27% of participants in such programs in 2003, compared to their 28% share in leadership positions, though it is not possible to say whether those receiving leadership training were drawn from the upper-level cadre (CAPMAS, 2009).

Case Study of the Ministry of Finance

Egypt's Ministry of Finance (MOF) offers an example of how government units are beginning to address both programmatic and human resource aspects of gender in public service. The ministry has made substantial internal efforts to develop women leaders and to build skills in managing workplace diversity. More recently, it has begun to implement gender-responsive budgeting (GRB) and to analyze the gender equity of public sector expenditure.

Incorporating Gender into the Ministry's Workforce Development and Programming

Women represented 37% of MOF employees in 2006 (the most recent available), well above the average for all government employment. Women accounted for 30% of the MOF leadership and managerial positions in the same year (EOU, 2006), a level that rose to 40% in 2009 (EOU, 2009). These levels exceeded government-wide figures, discussed above.

The rapid increase may reflect in part the role of the Equal Opportunity Unit (EOU) established within the Ministry as well as increased attention to the role of women more generally across the Egyptian government and demographic factors within the civil service. It may also reflect a preferential bidding away of men with financial analysis and management skills to join Egypt's rapidly expanding private financial and accounting sectors or to take financial management jobs in the broader private sector (suggesting an avenue for further research).

To promote gender equity in the ministry and its work, the MOF established an Equal Opportunity Unit in 2001. The unit went through a long incubation period and only became fully active in 2005, following issuance of a ministerial decree to promote equal opportunities for men and women employees within the ministry.

The EOU links the ministry to the National Council for Women, a high-profile body formerly chaired by Egypt's then-powerful first lady, Suzanne Mubarak. As of early 2010, the EOU had six staff members and a network of representatives within each of the 18 MOF departments. The EOU has promoted gender-responsive budgeting in the state budget, developed employees' awareness and understanding of gender-sensitive issues in the workplace, and documented women's status in the MOF. It has organized staff training on monitoring and evaluation, leadership, and team building and worked to correct gender stereotypes (EOU, 2006; SMEPOL, 2007). In 2008/2009, more than 1,200 MOF employees attended EOU seminars and workshops, evenly divided between males and females (EOU, 2009).

The EOU collaborates actively with donors and international funders, such as the United Nations Development Fund for Women (UNIFEM). Its core funding now comes from the ministry budget, an important step toward sustainability and institutional integration.

The EOU's work in gender-responsive budgeting (GRB) is part of Egypt's move to a program and performance-based budget (PPBB) within a broader public finance reform. The EOU worked with the National Planning Institute and CAPMAS to increase the production of gender-differentiated data (including the CAPMAS study cited above, the first to provide detailed information on this topic).

An initial pilot GRB was developed for the 2009/2010 budget, which was also the first where the official budget circular required gender disaggregation of the budget (Al-Sheikh & Khattab, 2009). Detailed estimates were prepared of the share of expenditures allocated by gender, disaggregated by ministry and, for 5 of the 27 governorates (provinces), developed estimates of gender-disaggregated spending for social service delivery in five sectors.

Al-Sheikh and Khattab's (2009) analysis of the GRB results finds significant gender bias, with an average of only 43% of government expenditures allocated to women. The estimated women's share of government expenditures ranged from a low of 29.3% for youth, culture, and religious affairs to a high of 48.7% for subsidies and social protection. Both education and health services showed considerable inequality, with about 40% of expenditures allocated to women in both areas. It is too early to say how this initiative will be affected by the January 25th Revolution, which brought the parliament under the control of Islamist parties.

The Ministry of Finance offers an appropriate venue to explore leadership styles in Egypt's public sector, for three reasons. First, as discussed above, the ministry's Equal

Opportunity Unit has been a leader in promoting gender equity and was both ready and able to facilitate the survey, a key consideration in Egypt's closed bureaucratic culture. Second, the MOF has a higher share of women employees both overall and in leadership positions than the typical government agency, with the share of such positions occupied by women about 10 percentage points higher than the government-wide average (see discussion above). Thus, the MOF is much less male-dominated than other Egyptian government settings, a factor identified as favoring the development of women leaders (Eagly, 2007). Third, while the MOF can be characterized as "women-friendly," it is not a "gender ghetto" traditionally dominated by women, such as education, social work, or programs specifically focused on women's issues. It would thus be expected to be more representative of women's roles across the government.

Results of a Survey of Gender Differentials in Leadership Style among Ministry Middle Managers

To explore gender leadership styles in the MOF, a survey of middle managers was conducted, using the LBDQ XII (Stogdill, 1963). Although developed originally by the Fisher School of Business at Ohio State University in the 1960s, this questionnaire continues to be one of the most widely used survey instruments for assessing individual leadership styles, particularly in an international context (see Judge, Piccolo, & Ilies, 2004; and Littrell, 2002). The LBDQ XII's demonstrated reliability and validity, direct comparability to a large volume of other studies, and its simple, unbiased, and broadly acceptable language made it a logical choice for this application.

While LBDQ XII measures 12 dimensions of leadership, the MOF survey was reduced to six aspects with five, rather than eight questions for each aspect, so as to increase the survey's acceptability in a Middle Eastern context, where such research is rare. The resulting 30-question survey was translated into Arabic. The six dimensions included three agentic dimensions—initiation of structure, role assumption, and production emphasis, and three communal dimensions, tolerance and freedom, consideration, and integration.

The sample population consisted of managers of Egyptian nationality in a supervisory position within the MOF. Respondent selection was based on convenience sampling, reflecting the difficulty of administering a questionnaire within a government office in Egypt. For every female surveyed, a male peer was included in the original sample with equivalent authority and job responsibilities.

Even with this simplified instrument and the full cooperation of the MOF EOU over several weeks, only 99 questionnaires could be collected, of which 79 were complete and usable. This sample was judged to be acceptable under the circumstances and is in line with the average sample of 88 reported by Eagly and Johnson (1990).

The central findings are straightforward: (1) there were no significant differences between male and female managers on any of the six dimensions measured, (2) male and female managers did not differ significantly on the agentic versus communal dimension, and (3) the measured levels of all the constructs measured were toward the low end of the scale for both male and female managers. Table 5 summarizes the results of the survey on the six LBDQ XII dimensions measured and on the agentic/communal dimension.

Table 5. Leadership Style Survey Results					
		Percent of sample			
Leadership characteristic	Leadership style category	Male (n = 33)		Female (n = 46)	
		High	Low	High	Low
Production emphasis	Agentic	49	52	50	50
Consideration	Communal	39	61	46	54
Tolerance and freedom	Communal	33	67	39	61
Initiation of structure	Agentic	33	67	35	65*
Role assumption	Agentic	42	58	33	67*
Integration	Communal	21	79**	17	83**
Overall leadership style:					
Agentic		52	49	54	46
Communal		46	55	50	50

Source: Authors' survey
Note: none of the male–female differences shown are statistically significant at the 95% level.
On a within-gender basis, the null hypothesis that the high and low levels of the leadership style characteristic are equal is rejected for those measures indicated with * (5% confidence level) and ** (1% confidence level).

Although none of the between-gender differences are statistically significant at the 5% level, the null hypothesis that the population is equally divided between those with a high level of the characteristic and those with a low level is rejected at the 5% level for four gender-dimension pairs, with more than half of the sample population falling in the "low" range for each of these dimensions. These include three dimensions for the female population, initiation of structure (A), role assumption (B), and integration (C), and one for the male population, integration (C). A higher proportion of women were classified at the "high" level in four of the six areas, while men were more likely to be classified as "high" in two areas. These areas were equally divided between agentic and communal characteristics for both groups. These differences were not statistically significant, however.

Across both genders, middle managers in the Egyptian Ministry of Finance do not display high levels of leadership characteristics, whether agentic or communal. If anything, they are more likely to be classified as having a low level of leadership characteristics, but a more reasonable conclusion from the data collected would be that they are neither high nor low This suggests a need for leadership development in order to meet the urgent need for reform of public sector management, a topic further explored in the conclusions section.

The survey found that women supervise fewer employees on average than do men. Whereas 32% of the men surveyed supervised at least 32 employees (the sample median) only 7% of the females supervised this many. This difference might reflect the recent entry of women into the workforce, with their consequent lower seniority, but it may also reflect stereotypes about women's leadership skills or other gender bias. This difference was significant at the 1% level, using Pearson's chi-square.

Overall, the study findings thus support the equality hypothesis over the complementary contribution hypothesis. No significant differences were found between the leadership styles of male and female middle managers in the Ministry of Finance. This finding is consistent with earlier U.S.-based analysis reported in Newman 1994 that women who rise to leadership positions tend to be similar to their male counterparts.

Conclusion: Implications for Building Women's Leadership in Public Governance in the Middle East

The findings of this exploratory study do not support stereotypical expectations of male–female leadership style differences in the Middle East and are thus consistent with many (but by no means all) similar studies conducted elsewhere. The results refute the concept that Egyptian men are more likely to display agentic, more stereotypically "masculine" qualities, and females to show more communal or "feminine" qualities.

The findings thus suggest that the observed gender gap among those holding leadership positions reflects other factors, such as prior or continuing discrimination, lack of opportunities for capacity development, including mentoring, or application of outdated preconceptions, and support a need to challenge the biased delegation of reponsibilities. Available organizational mechanisms, exemplified by the MOF's Equal Opportunity Unit, can play a critical role in addressing inequalities within the public sector and can contribute to making government programs more gender-neutral by working at both the human resource and policy levels.

Additional gender-unbiased mechanisms should be developed to foster leadership in ways that equally address the needs of women and men and overcome bias inherent in the relatively recent entry of women into more senior positions in the Egyptian civil service. A gender-neutral approach to selection and preparation for leadership positions would also contribute to a more effective workforce that reflects the nation's citizens and models a fairer workplace, promoting the value of social justice that emerged with such prominence during the Arab Spring revolution.

Effective action to increase gender equity in public sector leadership will require further research to build a greater understanding of gender differences in leadership roles and styles in the Middle East and to determine the sources of the inequality observed, whether based in stereotype, differential access to opportunities, inappropriate personnel policies, or cultural bias. More analysis is needed to confirm whether men in other agencies are also given more important leadership roles, as suggested by their assignment to lead larger units at the MOF, and whether the parity in leadership styles found in this survey stands up under broader examination. The differential in assignments may signal greater opportunities for men to demonstrate and build their leadership and supervisory skills through better access to mentoring or other factors. If so, mechanisms should be instituted to nurture promising female employees to prepare them to move up in greater numbers.

The study's findings, although preliminary, point to important research questions for future study. These include: What specific barriers limit women's advancement in Egyptian public organizations? How do existing policies and procedures limit their promotion and success? What policy efforts are needed to overcome such barriers and to facilitate women's more equal career advancement? Such studies should address soft skills and competencies in emotive leadership as well as other aspects of leadership, including cultural orientation and organizational climate.

Overall, there is a need not only to expand and extend the study of gender and leadership in the Middle East, but also to examine institutional and historical factors in the workplace, in education, and in the broader society that may prevent Middle East societies from fully utilizing the capabilities of female citizens. This need is particularly great in the public sector, where women have proportionately more opportunities and where the need for leadership is even more urgent than it was before the Arab Spring.

REFERENCES

PART 1

Democracy and Islamist Violence: Lessons from Post-Mubarak Egypt*

*This research was made possible by a grant from the Swiss National Science Foundation (SNSF).

References

Bjørgo, T. (2005). *Root causes of terrorism: Myths, reality and ways forward*. Abingdon, UK: Routledge.

Burgat, F. (2003). *Face to face with political Islam*. London, UK: I. B. Tauris.

Burgat, F., & Dowell, W. (1993). *The Islamic movement in North Africa*. Austin, TX: Center for Middle Eastern Studies, University of Texas at Austin.

Calvert, J. (2010). *Sayyid Qutb and the origins of radical Islamism*. New York, NY: Columbia University Press.

Hafez, M. M. (2003). *Why Muslims rebel: Repression and resistance in the Islamic world*. Boulder, CO: Lynne Rienner.

Hamad, A. (n.d.) *Muraja'at hawl al-Muraja'at* (Revisions on the revisions). Retrieved from http://www.tawhed.ws/r?i=8ja7dzs2.

Hoffman, B., Rand Corporation, & Worldwide Department of Defense Combating Terrorism Conference. (1993). *"Holy terror," the implications of terrorism motivated by a religious imperative*. Santa Monica, CA: RAND.

Juergensmeyer, M. (2000). *Terror in the mind of God: The global rise of religious violence*. Berkeley, CA: University of California Press.

Juergensmeyer, M. (2008). *Global rebellion: Religious challenges to the secular state, from Christian militias to al-Qaeda*. Berkeley, CA: University of California Press.

Lia, B., & Skjolberg, K. (2004). *Causes of terrorism: An expanded and updated review of the literature*. FFI Report RT-2004/04307. Retrieved from http://rapporter.ffi.no/rapporter/2004/04307.pdf.

Morgan, M. J. (2004). The origins of the new terrorism. *Parameters, 34*(1), 29–43.

Pelham, N., & Royal Institute of International Affairs. (2012). *Sinai: The buffer erodes*. London, UK: Chatham House.

Rapoport, D. C. (2004). The four waves of modern terrorism. In A. K. Cronin, & J. M. Ludes (Eds.), *Attacking terrorism: Elements of a grand strategy* (pp. 46–73). Washington, DC: Georgetown University Press.

Schmid, A. P. (Ed.). (2011). *The Routledge handbook of terrorism research*. Abingdon, UK: Routledge.

Selengut, C. (2008). *Sacred fury: understanding religious violence.* Oxford, UK: Rowman & Littlefield.

Stern, J. (2004). *Terror in the name of God: Why religious militants kill.* New York, NY: HarperCollins.

Tucker, D. (2001). What's new about the new terrorism and how dangerous is it? *Terrorism and Political Violence, 13*(Autumn 2001), 1–12.

In Between the Glorious Past and Wounded Self-Image: What does Turkey Have to Offer for the Middle East?*

*The author wishes to thank his mentors Mehmet Şahin, Professor of International Relations, Abdülkadir Çevik, Professor of Psychiatry, and his colleague Rifat S. İlhan, M.D. for their valuable comments and support.

References

Abou-el-Fadl, R. (2012). Arab perceptions of contemporary Turkish foreign policy: Cautious engagement and the question of independence. In K. Öktem, A. Kadıoğlu, & M. Karlı (Eds.), *Another empire? A decade of Turkey's foreign policy under the justice and development party* (pp. 231–257). İstanbul: Bilgi.

Ahmad, F. (2008). *From empire to republic: Essays on the late Ottoman Empire and modern Turkey–Volume 2.* İstanbul, TR: Bilgi University Press.

Alford, F. C. (1994). *Group psychology and political theory.* New Haven, CT: Yale University Press.

Altunışık, M. B., & Tür, Ö. (2005). *Turkey: Challanges of continuity and change.* London, UK: Routledge.

Awad, G. (2003). The minds and perceptions of 'the others.' In S. Varvin & V. D. Volkan (Eds.), *Violence or dialogue? Psychoanalytic insights on terror and terrorism* (pp.153–176). London, UK: IPA.

Barkey, H. J. (2010). Turkey and the great powers, In C. Kerslake, K. Öktem & P. Robins (Eds.), *Turkey's Engagement with Modernity* (pp. 239–257). London, UK: Palgrave MacMillan.

Çevik, A. (2009). *Politik psikoloji* (Political psychology). Ankara: Dost.

Çevik, B. S. (2012). Restoring regional humiliation: Mending the psychological wounds of the Middle East. *Akademik Ortadoğu, 6*(2), 135–155.

Çiftçi, K. (2010). *Türk dış politikası: Tarih, kimlik ve eleştirel kuram bağlamında* (Turkish foreign policy: In the context of history, identity and critical theory). Ankara, TR: Siyasal.

Davutoğlu, A. (2011). *Stratejik derinlik* (Strategic depth) (73rd Ed.). İstanbul, TR: Küre Yayınları.

Deringil, S. (2004). *Turkish foreign policy during the Second World War: An active neutrality.* Cambridge, UK: Cambridge University Press.

Dinç, C. (2011). Turkey as a new security actor in the Middle East: Beyond the slogans. *Perceptions, 16*(2), 61–77.

Dinçer. O. B., & Kutlay, M. (2012). *Turkey's power capacity in the Middle East: Limits of the possible* (USAK Center for Middle Eastern and African Studies. Report No. 12-04). Ankara, TR: USAK.

Erikson, E. (1968). *Identity: Youth and crisis*. New York, NY: W. W. Norton.

Freud, A. (1993). *The ego and the mechanisms of defense* (Rev. ed.). London, UK: Karnac Books.

Freud, S. (1949). *Group psychology and the analysis of the ego* (5th imp.). London, UK: International Psychoanalytic.

Hashemi, N. (2011). The Arab revolution of 2011: Reflections on religion and politics. *Insight Turkey, 13*(2), 15–21.

Inbar, E. (2001). The strategic glue in the Turkish–Israeli alignment. In B. Rubin, & K. Kirişci (Eds.), *Turkey in world politics: An emerging multiregional power* (pp. 115-127). Boulder, CO: Lynne Rienner.

Karpat, K. H. (1992). Turkish foreign policy: Some introductory remarks. *International Journal of Turkish Studies*, 6(1–2), Madison, 1992–4.

Karpat, K. H. (2001). *The politization of Islam*. Oxford, UK: Oxford University Press.

Karpat, K. H. (2012). *Türk dış politikası tarihi* (The history of Turkish foreign policy). İstanbul, TR: Timaş.

Keyman, E. F., & Öniş, Z. (2007). *Turkish politics in a changing world*. İstanbul, TR: Bilgi University Press.

Kirişci, K. (2001a). The future of Turkish policy toward the Middle East. In B. Rubin, & K. Kirişci (Eds.), *Turkey in world politics: An emerging multiregional power* (pp. 93–114). Boulder, CO: Lynne Rienner.

Kirişci, K. (2011). Turkey's demonstrative effect and the transformation of the Middle East. *Insight Turkey, 13*(2), 33–55.

Larrabee, S. (2007). Turkey rediscovers the Middle East. *Foreign Affairs, 86*(4), 103–114.

Larrabee, S. (2011). The new Turkey and American–Turkish relations. *Insight Turkey, 13*(1), 1–9.

Mack, J. E. (1990). The enemy system. In V. D. Volkan, D. Julius, & J. V. Montville (Eds.), *The psychodynamics of international relationships, Vol. I* (pp. 57–69). Lexington, MA: Lexington Books.

Moisi, D. (2009). *The geopolitics of emotion: How cultures of fear, humiliation and hope are reshaping the world*. Ireland: Bodley Head.

Moses, R. (1996). The perception of the enemy: A psychoanalytic view. *Mind and Human Interaction, 7*(1), 37–43.

Oğuzlu, T. (2011). Ortadoğu'da demokratikleşme ve Türkiye model Olabilir mi Tartışması: Evet, ama! (Democratization in the Middle East and 'Could Turkey be a model' dispute: Yes, but!). *Ortadoğu Analiz, 27*(3), 73–79.

Oran, B. (2012). TDP'nin Temel İlkeleri (The basic principles of Turkish foreign policy). In B. Oran (Ed.), *Türk dış politikası, cilt 1* (Turkish foreign policy, Volume 1), (pp 46–53). İstanbul, TR: İletişim.

Orsam Minutes. (2012). *Egypt in transition and Turkey and Egypt relations in new era*. No.14.

Ross, M. H. (2000). Culture and ethnic conflict. In S. A. Renshon, & J. Duckitt (Eds.), *Political psychology: Cultural and cross-cultural foundations* (pp. 146–157). New York, NY: NYU Press.

Şahin, M. (2010). Anadolu kaplanları Türkiye'yi Ortadoğu ve Afrika'da Etkili Kılıyor (Anatolian tigers are enforcing Turkey's influence in the Middle East and Africa). *Ortadoğu Analiz, 17*(2), 94–99.

Şahin, M. (2011). Tunus olayları, Ortadoğu ve Türkiye deneyimi (Tunisian events, The Middle East and Turkey experience). *Ortradoğu Analiz, 26*(3), 8–14.

Shaw, S. J., & Kural-Shaw, E. (1977). *History of the Ottoman Empire and modern Turkey Volume II*, Cambridge, UK: Cambridge University Press.

Stein, H. F. (1990). The indispensible enemy and American–Soviet relations. In V. D. Volkan, D. Julius & J. V. Montville (Eds.), *The psychodynamics of international relationships, Vol. I* (pp.71–89). Lexington, MA: Lexington Books.

Tajfel, H., & Turner, J. C. (2004). The social identity theory of intergroup behavior. In J. T. Jost, & J. Sidanius (Eds.), *Political psychology* (pp. 276–293). New York, NY: Psychology Press.

Teazis, C. (2010). *İkincilerin cumhuriyeti: Adalet ve Kalkınma Partisi* (The Republic of the seconds: The Justice and Development Party). İstanbul, TR: Mızrak.

Uysal, A. (2011). *Ortadoğu'da Türkiye Algısı: Mısır Örneği*. (The perception of Turkey in the Middle East: The case of Egypt). Ankara, TR: Stratejik Düşünce Enstitüsü.

Uzgel, İ. (2012). TDP'nin Oluşturulması (The construction of Turkish foreign policy). In B. Oran (Ed.), *Türk dış politikası,cilt 1* (Turkish foreign policy, Vol. 1) (pp. 73–93). İstanbul: İletişim.

Volkan, V. D. (1990). An overview of psychological concepts pertinent to interethnic and/or international relationships. In V. D. Volkan, D. Julius, & J. V. Montville (Eds.), *The psychodynamics of international relationships, Vol I* (pp.31-46). Lexington, MA: Lexington Books.

Volkan, V. D. (1994). *The need to have enemies and allies*. Northvale, NJ: Aronson.

Volkan, V. D. (1997). *Blood lines: From ethnic pride to ethnic terrorism*. New York, NY: Farrar, Straus and Giroux.

Volkan, V. D. (2004). *Blind trust: Large groups and their leaders in times of crisis and terror*. Charlottesville, VA: Pitchstone.

Volkan, V. D. (2006). *Killing in the name of identity: A study of bloody conflicts*. Charlottesville, VA: Pitchstone.

Volkan, V. D. (2007). On Kemal Atatürk's psychoanalytic biography. In B. Tezcan, & K. K. Barber (Eds.), *Identity and identity formation in the Ottoman World* (pp. 229–241). Madison, WI: Center for Turkish Studies, University of Wisconsin Press.

Volkan, V.D., & Itzkowitz, N. (1984). *The immortal Atatürk: A psychobiography*. Chicago, IL: University of Chicago Press.

Volkan, V. D., & Zintl, E. (1993). *Life after loss: The lessons of grief*. New York, NY: Charles Scribner MacMillan.

Yılmaz, T. (2011). Arap İsyanları ve Arap Ortadoğu'sunun Siyasal Dönüşümü (Arab uprisings and political transformation of the Arabian Middle East). *Akademik Ortadoğu, 6*(1), pp. 63-75.

Zürcher, E. J. (2010). The importance of being secular: Islam in the service of the national and pre-national state. In C. Kerslake, K. Öktem, & P. Robins (Eds.), *Turkey's engagement with modernity* (pp. 55-69). London, UK: Palgrave MacMillan.

The Wall of Fear and the Intelligence Apparatus in Syria

References

Human Rights Watch. (2011a, 1 June). *We've never seen such horror: Crimes against humanity by Syrian security forces*. Retrieved from http://www.hrw.org/sites/default/files/reports/ syria0611webwcover.pdf

Human Rights Watch. (2011b, 15 December). *By all means necessary! Individual and command responsibility for crimes against humanity in Syria*. Retrieved from http://www.hrw.org/sites/default/files/reports/syria1211webwcover_0.pdf

Syria's Intelligence Services: A primer. (2000, 1 July). *Middle East Intelligence Bulletin*. Retrieved from http://www.meforum.org/meib/articles/0007_s3.htm

Ziadeh, R. (2011). *Power and policy in Syria: The intelligence services, foreign relations and democracy in the modern Middle East*. London, UK: I. B. Tauris.

Iran and the Syria Crisis: Policies, Problems, and Prospects*

*The author acknowledges the sponsorship offered by the Swedish foundation Stiftelsen Karl Staaffs Fond for this project.

References

Abdo, G. (2011, 25 August). How Iran keeps Assad in power in Syria: The weapons, technology, and expertise Tehran sends Damascus. *Foreign Affairs*. Retrieved from http://www.foreignaffairs.com/articles/68230/geneive-abdo/how-iran-keeps-assad-in-power-in-syria

Amnesty International. (2011, July). Crackdown in Syria: Terror in Tell Kalakh. Retrieved from http://www.amnestyusa.org/sites/default/files/mde240292011en_1.pdf

Bakri, N. (2011, 27 August). Iran calls on Syria to recognize citizens' demands. *The New York Times*. Retrieved from http://www.nytimes.com/2011/08/28/world/middleeast/28syria.html?_r=0

Ball, J. (2012, 27 July). Syria has expanded chemical weapons supply with Iran's help, documents show. *The Washington Post*. Retrieved from http://articles.washingtonpost.com/2012-07-27/world/35489623_1_chemical-weapons-chemical-plants-president-bashar

Batrawy, A. (2012, 18 September). Egypt: Iran's support for Syria hinders relations. *The Associated Press*. Retrieved from http://news.yahoo.com/egypt-irans-support-syria-hinders-relations-151711339.html

Black, I. & Sherwood, H. (2012, 23 October). Qatari Emir's visit to Gaza is a boost for Hamas. *The Guardian*. Retrieved from http://www.guardian.co.uk/world/2012/oct/23/qatari-emir-welcome-gaza-visit

Bozkurt, B. (2012, 23 December). Turkish minister Şahin slams Iran for providing support to PKK/KCK. *Today's Zaman*. Retrieved from http://www.todayszaman.com/news-302004-turkish-minister-sahin-slams-iran-for-providing-support-to-pkkkck.html

Cave, D. & Saad, H. (2012, 5 August). 48 captives are Iran 'thugs,' rebels say. *The New York Times*. Retrieved from http://www.nytimes.com/2012/08/06/world/middleeast/syrian-rebels-say-hostages-are-iranian-guards.html

Charbonneau, L. (2012, 19 September). Exclusive: Western report – Iran ships arms, personnel to Syria via Iraq. *Reuters*. Retrieved from http://www.reuters.com/article/2012/09/19/us-syria-crisis-iran-iraq-idUSBRE88I17B20120919

Coughlin, C. (2011, 12 August). Iran agrees to fund Syrian military base. *The Telegraph*. Retrieved from http://www.telegraph.co.uk/news/worldnews/middleeast/iran/8699077/Iran-agrees-to-fund-Syrian-military-base.html

Crilly, R. (2012, 15 August). Iran snipers in Syria as part of crackdown. *The Telegraph*. Retrieved from http://www.telegraph.co.uk/news/worldnews/middleeast/syria/8702466/Iran-snipers-in-Syria-as-part-of-crackdown.html

Dehghan, S. K., & Harding, L. (2012, 30 August). Egyptian leader stuns Iran with plea to back Syrian rebels. *The Guardian*. Retrieved from http://www.guardian.co.uk/world/2012/aug/30/egyptian-leader-iran-syrian-rebels

DeYoung, K., & Warrick, J. (2013, 10 February). Iran and Hezbollah build militia networks in Syria in event that Assad falls, officials say. *The Washington Post*. Retrieved from http://articles.washingtonpost.com/2013-02-10/world/37026054_1_syrian-government-forces-iran-and-hezbollah-president-bashar

Ephron, D. (2013, 30 January). Did Israeli strike target Syrian chemical weapons? *The Daily Beast*. Retrieved from http://www.thedailybeast.com/ articles/2013/01/30/did-israeli-strike-target-syrian-chemical-weapons.html

Fassihi, F. (2012a, 8 August). Tensions rise over Iranian Hostages. *The Wall Street Journal*. Retrieved from http://online.wsj.com/article/SB10000872396390443792604577575221903873222.html

Fassihi, F. (2012b, 27 August). Iran said to send troops to bolster Syria. *The Wall Street Journal*. Retrieved from http://online.wsj.com/article/SB10000872396390444230504577615393756632230.html

Fisk, R. (2010, 16 September). Robert Fisk: Freedom, democracy and human rights in Syria. *The Independent*. Retrieved from http://www.independent.co.uk/voices/commentators/fisk/robert-fisk-freedom-democracy-and-human-rights-in-syria-2080463.html

Golovnina, M. & Perry, T. (2013, 10 January). Syria overshadows Iran charm offensive in Egypt. *Reuters*. Retrieved from http://www.reuters.com/article/2013/01/10/us-egypt-iran-idUSBRE9090VZ20130110

Gordon, M. R. (2012, 5 September). U.S. presses Iraq on Iranian planes thought to carry arms to Syria. *The New York Times*. Retrieved from http://www.nytimes.com/2012/09/06/world/middleeast/us-presses-iraq-on-iranian-planes-thought-to-carry-arms-to-syria.html?_r=0

International Institute for Strategic Studies (IISS). (2012, August). IISS strategic comments: Unease grows over Syria's chemical weapons, Vol. 18, comment 25. Retrieved from http://www.iiss.org/EasySiteWeb/ getresource.axd?AssetID=68491&type=full&servicetype=Attachment

Iran, Syria relations main axis of resistance against Israel: Lawmaker. (2012, 5 November). *Press TV*. Retrieved from http://www.presstv.ir/ detail/2012/11/05/270563/iran-syria-ties-main-resistance-axis/

Khamenei, A. (2011, 1 July). Dast-e Amrika va Esra'il dar havades-e Souriyeh ashkar ast [The hand of

America and Israel is evident in the Syrian events]. *Fars News Agency*. Retrieved from http://www.farsnews.com/newstext.php?nn=9004100204

Lappin, Y. (2013, 27 January). IDF deploys Iron Dome battery to Haifa area. *The Jerusalem Post*, Retrieved from http://www.jpost.com/Defense/Article.aspx?id=301124

Meshaal: Erdogan is not only Turkey's leader; he is also a leader of the Muslim world. (2012, 1 October). *Sabah*. Retrieved from http://english.sabah.com.tr/national/2012/10/01/meshaal-erdogan-is-not-only-turkeys-leader-he-is-also-the-leader-of-the-muslim-world

Miller, E. (2013, 14 January). Assad and family said to be living on a warship. *The Times of Israel*. Retrieved January 15, 2013 from http://www.timesofisrael.com/assad-and-family-said-to-be-living-on-a-warship/

Moʻaven-e vezarat-e kharejeh-ye Iran: Souriyeh az bohran'e amniyati obour kardeh [Iran deputy foreign minister: Syria has left security crisis behind]. (2012, 15 October). *British Broadcasting Corporation (BBC) Persian Service*. Retrieved from http://www.bbc.co.uk/persian/iran/2012/09/120925_l23_syria_iran_.shtml

Oweis, K. Y. & Abbas, M. (2012, 7 November). Syrian rebels fire at, miss Assad's palace. *Reuters*. Retrieved from http://in.reuters.com/article/2012/11/07/syria-damascus-bombs-idINDEE8A603020121107

Reed, J. (2013, 28 January). Israel shifts Iron Dome battery north. *Financial Times*. Retrieved from http://www.ft.com/cms/s/0/d6944780-6925-11e2-9246-00144feab49a.html#axzz2JkS3Fb7T

Report says Assad residing on warship. (2013, 14 January). *United Press International (UPI)*. Retrieved from http://www.upi.com/Top_News/World-News/2013/01/14/Report-says-Assad-residing-on-warship/UPI-95401358162184/

Rezaee, M. (2011, 20 October). Mohsen Rezaee: Souriyeh, Hamas va Hezbollah khatt-e ghermez-e Jomhouri-ye Eslami hastand [Mohsen Rezaee: Syria, Hamas and Hezbollah are the Red Line of the Islamic Republic]. Jonbesh-e Rah-e Sabz (*Jaras*). Retrieved from http://www.rahesabz.net/story/44081

Salami, L. (2013, 29 January). 'Fetneh-ye Sham'; Negah-e nahadha-ye Irani be bohran-e Souriyeh [The 'Sham Sedition'; Iranian institutions' view of the Syrian crisis]. *British Broadcasting Corporation (BBC) Persian Service*. Retrieved from http://www.bbc.co.uk/persian/iran/2013/01/130129_an_syria_iran.shtml

Smith, M. (2013, 28 January). Al-Assad's grip on power 'slipping away,' Medvedev says. CNN. Retrieved from http://edition.cnn.com/2013/01/27/world/europe/russia-syria/?hpt=hp_t3

Tisdall, S. (2011, 9 May). Iran helping Syrian regime crack down on protesters, say diplomats. *The Guardian*. Retrieved from http://www.guardian.co.uk/world/2011/may/08/iran-helping-syrian-regime-protesters

US Department of the Treasury. (2011, 18 May). Administration takes additional steps to hold the government of Syria accountable for violent repression against the Syrian people. Retrieved from http://www.treasury.gov/press-center/press-releases/Pages/tg1181.aspx

Williams, C. (2012, 17 February). Syrian situation is complex and unpredictable. *The Sydney Morning Herald*, Retrieved from http://www.smh.com.au/opinion/politics/syrian-situation-is-complex-and-unpredictable-20120216-1tbs2.html

WikiLeaks. (2006, 20 June). Viewing cable 06PARIS4218, AUSTRALIA GROUP: 2006 INFORMATION EXCHANGE (IE). Retrieved from http://wikileaks.org/cable/2006/06/06PARIS4218.html#

WikiLeaks. (2008, 17 April). Viewing cable 08PARIS735, AUSTRALIA GROUP: 2008 INFORMATION EXCHANGE (IE). Retrieved from http://wikileaks.org/cable/2008/04/08PARIS735.html#

Yek bank-e Irani yek milyard dolar khatt-e etebari be Souriyeh ekhtesas dad [An Iranian bank allocated a 1-billion-dollar line of credit to Syria]. (2012, 21 January). *Mardomak*. Retrieved from http://www.mardomak.org/story/75807

"God save the King?"
The Evolution of Protest in Jordan in Light of the Arab Spring

References

Adely, F. (2013). The emergence of a new labor movement in Jordan. *Middle East Research and Information Project*. Retrieved from www.merip.org/mer/mer264/emergence-new-labor-movement-jordan

al-Hourani, H. (2013). The Jordanian Labour Movement–Part 3. Retrieved from library.fes.de/fulltext/iez/01144002.htm#E10E1

Al-Jazeera. (2013). Jordan's king calls for national unity. Retrieved from www.aljazeera.com/news/middleeast/2011/03/2011327203224334931.html

Amman. (2012). Labor protests in Jordan during 2011. *Jordan Labor Watch*, *264*(1).

Barrett, R. (2011). How a broken social contract sparked Bahrain protests. *The Christian Science Monitor*. Retrieved from www.csmonitor.com/World/Middle-East/2011/0221/How-a-broken-social-contract-sparked-Bahrain-protests

Choucair, J. (2006). Illusive reform: Jordan's stubborn stability. *Carnegie Endowment for International Peace*. Democracy and Rule of Law Project, No. 76 (December 2006).

Cuomo, K. K. (2013). Speak truth to power–telling stories. Personal communication. Retrieved from www.pbs.org/speaktruthtopower/rana.html

Goode, L. (2013) Cultural citizenship online: The Internet and digital culture. Retrieved from https://researchspace.auckland.ac.nz/handle/2292/18292

Hattar, M. (2013). 'Rape-law' triggers fury in Jordan. Retrieved from http://www.google.com/hostednews/afp/article/ALeqM5gZmvi2qU1sDyMSFomYTKL6hREBlA

History of Jordan (n.d.). In *Wikipedia*. Retrieved February 10, 2013. Retrieved from en.wikipedia.org/wiki/History_of_Jordan

IRIN. (2013). Honour killings still tolerated. *Humanitarian News and Analysis*. Retrieved from www.irinnews.org/Report/70634/JORDAN-Honour-killings-still-tolerated

Jordan Labor Watch (2012). Labor protests in Jordan during 2011. *Jordan Labor Watch* (1).

Levs, J., Al-Assad, A., Razek, R., Alkhshali, H., & Karadsheh, J. (2013). Jordanian protesters make rare move: Speak out against King Abdullah. CNN. Retrieved from www.cnn.com/2012/11/14/world/meast/jordan-gas-prices

Lynch, M. (2013). Jordan, forever on the brink. *Foreign Policy* [Weblog]. Retrieved from lynch.foreignpolicy.com/posts/2012/05/07/jordan_forever_at_the_brink.

National Public Radio. (2013). Some Jordanians say gerrymandering makes for an unfair election. *All Things Considered*. Retrieved from www.npr.org/2013/01/23/170101076/ some-jordanians-say-gerrymandering-makes-for-an-unfair-election

National Public Radio. (2011, 22 September). King Abdullah: Jordan needs 'Stable Middle Class.' *National Public Radio*. Retrieved from http://www.npr.org/2011/09/22/140670554/king-abdullah-jordan-needs-stable-middle-class

Pearlman, A. (2013). Outrage over Jordan's draconian rape law. Retrieved from www.globalpost.com/dispatches/globalpost-blogs/rights/outrage-over-jordans-draconian-rape-law.

RT. (2013). Jordan engulfed in protests over fuel price hike. [Photos]. Retrieved from rt.com/news/jordan-protests-fuel-hike-452/

Rudoren, J. (2013). Jordan faces protests after gas-price proposal. *NYTimes.com*. Retrieved from www.nytimes.com/2012/11/14/world/middleeast/jordan-faces-protests-after-gas-price-proposal.html?pagewanted=all&_r=0

Schwedler, J. (2013). The politics of protest in Jordan. *Foreign Policy Research Institute*. Retrieved from https://www.fpri.org/articles/2012/03/politics-protest-jordan

Tal, L. (1995). Britain and the Jordan crisis of 1958. *Middle Eastern Studies*, *31*(1), 39–57.

Tobin, S. A. (2012). Jordan's Arab Spring: The middle class and anti-revolution. *Middle East Policy, XIX* (1), 96–109.

United Nations High Commissioner for Refugees. (2013). Syria regional refugee response. Retrieved from data.unhcr.org/syrianrefugees/country.php?id=107

Arab Spring and Modernization of Islam: A Major Step toward the Unification of Human Civilization

References

ANI. (2013, 21 January). Most weapons used by al-Qaeda terrorists in Algeria hostage came from Libya. Retrieved from http://in.news.yahoo.com/most-weapons-used-al-qaeda-terrorists-algeria-hostage-075352848.html

Armstrong, K. (1992). *Muhammad: A biography of the prophet*. San Francisco, CA: Harper SanFrancisco.

BBC News. (2012, October 8). Saudi weapons seen at Syria rebel base. Retrieved from http://www.bbc.co.uk/news/world-middle-east-19874256

Bernama. (2006, 3 January). Late Everest climber Moorthy promoted to sergeant posthumously. *Malaysian National News Agency*. Retrieved from http://www.bernama.com/bernama/v3/printable.php?id=173804

Blustein, P. (2005, 19 November). U.S. trade deficit hangs in a delicate imbalance. *Washington Post*. Retrieved from http://www.washingtonpost.com/wp-dyn/content/article/2005/11/18/AR2005111802634.html

Butler, D. (2012, 9 December). Georgia details nuke black market investigations. *AP*. Retrieved from http://news.yahoo.com/georgia-details-nuke-black-market-investigations-153216292.html

Crawford, D. (2005, 7 December). West's relations with Saudis face growing strains: German hosts are furious as militant Islam is taught at Saudi diplomatic school. *Wall Street Journal*.

Deccan Herald. (2012, 31 March). Pak foils terror plot to attack parliament: Malik. Retrieved from http://www.deccanherald.com/content/238546/ipl-2012.html

Farley, R. (2012, 7 August). Militants pose corrosive threat across Afghan border. *Global Times*. Retrieved from http://www.globaltimes.cn/content/725660.html

Ferguson, N. (2010, 1 December). In China's orbit. *www.niallferguson.com*. Retrieved from http://www.niallferguson.com/journalism/finance-economics/in-chinas-orbit

Fisher, M. (2013, 4 February). Clinton: Syria rebels getting 'messages' from Pakistan region known as Qaeda haven. *Washington Post*. Retrieved from http://www.washingtonpost.com/blogs/worldviews/wp/2013/02/04/clinton-syrian-rebels-getting-messages-from-pakistan-region-known-as-qaeda-haven/

Friedman, T. L. (1999). *The lexus and the olive tree*. New York, NY: Farrar, Straus and Giroux.

Friedman, T. L. (2005). *The world is flat*. New York, NY: Farrar, Straus and Giroux.

Fukuyama, F. (2006). *The end of history and the last man*. New York, NY: Free Press.

Hall, J. (2013, 4 February). Saudi preacher who 'raped and tortured' his five-year-old daughter to death is released after paying 'blood money.' *Independent* (UK). Retrieved from http://www.independent.co.uk/news/world/middle-east/saudi-preacher-who-raped-and-tortured-his-five-yearold-daughter-to-death-is-released-after-paying-blood-money-8480440.html

Harden, B., & Cha, A. E. (2008, 20 September). Japan, China locked in by investments. *Washington Post*. Retrieved from http://articles.washingtonpost.com/2008-09-20/world/36864825_1_central-bank-japanese-banks-japan-s-nikkei/2

Hersh, S. M. (2009, 16 November). Defending the arsenal. *New Yorker*. Retrieved from http://www.newyorker.com/reporting/2009/11/16/091116fa_fact_hersh

Hirschler, B. (2012, 28 March). Tens of billions of habitable worlds in Milky Way. *Reuters*. Retrieved from http://www.reuters.com/article/2012/03/28/us-planets-milkyway-idUSBRE82R0EI20120328

Homer-Dixon, T. F. (1991). On the threshold: Environmental changes as causes of acute conflict. *International Security*, *16*(2), 76–116.

Hourani, A. (1991). *A history of the Arab peoples*. Cambridge, MA: Belknap Press of Harvard University Press.

Howden, D. (2006, 19 April). Shame of the House of Saud: Shadows over Mecca. *Independent* (UK). Retrieved from http://www.independent.co.uk/news/world/middle-east/shame-of-the-house-of-saud-shadows-over-mecca-474736.html

Huntington, S. P. (1993). A clash of civilizations? *Foreign Affairs. 72*(3), 22–49.

Huntington, S. P. (1996). *The clash of civilizations and the remaking of working world order.* New York, NY: Touchstone.

Hussain, Z., & Solomon, J. (2004, 19 August). Al Qaeda gaining new support. *Wall Street Journal.* Available at http://online.wsj.com/article/0,,SB109287072274195388,00.html.

Juster, J. (1912). *La condition legale des Juifs sous les sous rois Visigoths.* Paris: Geuthner. Retrieved from http://archive.org/details/laconditionlga00just

Krugman, P. (2010, 27 June). The third depression. *New York Times.* Retrieved from http://www.nytimes.com/2010/06/28/opinion/28krugman.html?_r=0

Kumar, S. (1995, 15 December). Christian vs. Islamic civilization—Another Cold War? *Global Times.* Retrieved from http://www.susmitkumar.net/index.php?option=com_content&view=article&id=58:christian-vs-islamic-civilization

Kumar, S. (1996, October). Forgotten victims of U.S. crusades to save the world from communism. *Global Times.* Retrieved from http://www.susmitkumar.net/index.php?option=com_content&view=article&id=63:forgotten-victims-of-us-crusades-to-save-the-world-from-communism

Lewis, B. (2002). *What went wrong?* New York, NY: Oxford University Press.

Lewis, B. (2003). *The crisis of Islam.* New York, NY: Modern Library.

MacFarquhar, N. (2001, 19 October). Anti-Western and extremist views pervade Saudi school. *New York Times.* Retrieved from http://www.nytimes.com/2001/10/19/international/middleeast/19SAUD.html?pagewanted=all

Mason, R. (2013, 25 January). Britain is experiencing 'Worse slump than during Great Depression.' Retrieved from *Telegraph* (UK). http://www.telegraph.co.uk/news/9826857/Britain-is-experiencing-worse-slump-than-during-Great-Depression.html

Mayer, A. E. (1999). *Islam and human rights.* Boulder, CO: Westview.

Mearsheimer, J. J. (1990). Back to the future: Instability in Europe after the Cold War. *International Security, 15*(1). 5–56.

Mearsheimer, J. J., & Walt, S. M. (2007). *The Israel lobby and U.S. foreign policy.* New York, NY: Farrar, Straus and Giroux.

Michael, M. (2012, 10 May). Egypt seizes heavy weapons from arms smuggler. *AP.* Retrieved from http://news.yahoo.com/egypt-seizes-heavy-weapons-arms-smugglers-153044450.html

Monbiot, G. (2008, 18 November). Clearing up this mess. [Weblog]. Retrieved from http://www.monbiot.com/2008/11/18/clearing-up-this-mess/

Montgomery, L. (2009, 3 January). U.S. debt expected to soar this year. *Washington Post.* Retrieved from http://articles.washingtonpost.com/2009-01-03/politics/36920649_1_national-debt-treasury-survey-rates-on-treasury-bills

Murphy, D. (2011, 5 December). Hillary Clinton compares parts of Israel to Jim Crow south. *Christian Science Monitor*. Retrieved from http://www.csmonitor.com/World/Backchannels/2011/1205/Hillary-Clinton-compares-parts-of-Israel-to-Jim-Crow-south

Norris, F. (2010, 17 December). The Euro's uneven benefit in Europe. *New York Times*. Retrieved from http://www.nytimes.com/2010/12/18/business/18charts.html.

Rahman, F. (1983). Status of women in the *Qur'an*. In G. Nashat (Ed.), *Women and revolution in Iran* (pp. 37–54). Boulder, CO: Westview Press.

Rowland, B. M., & Brittain, W. H. (Eds.). (1976). *Balance of power or hegemony: The interwar monetary system*. New York, NY: New York University Press.

Rumbelow, H. (2011, 20 August). Pentagon prepares for economic warfare. *Australian*. Retrieved from http://www.theaustralian.com.au/news/world/pentagon-prepares-for-economic-warfare/story-e6frg6so-1226118380617

Shakir, F. (2006). Bush administration's pre-9/11 focus was missile defense, not terrorism. *Think Progress*. Retrieved from http://thinkprogress.org/politics/2006/09/26/7689/not-focused/?mobile=nc

Shanmuga, K. (2005, 29 December). A summary of the case and related events of Kaliammal Sinnasamy v Islamic Religious Affairs Council of the Federal Territory, Director Kuala Lumpur General Hospital & Government of Malaysia. *The Malaysian Bar*. Retrieved from http://www.malaysianbar.org.my/bar_news/berita_badan_peguam/re_everest_moorthy_.html

Simon, M. (1986). *Versus Israel: A study of the relations between Christians and Jews in the Roman Empire (AD 135–425)*. H. McKeating (Trans.). Oxford, UK: Littman Library of Jewish Civilization.

Spencer, R. (2013, 6 February). Tunisia in turmoil as prime minister offers to dissolve parliament. *Telegraph* (UK). Retrieved from http://www.telegraph.co.uk/news/worldnews/africaandindianocean/tunisia/9853938/Tunisia-in-turmoil-as-prime-minister-offers-to-dissolve-parliament.html

Strauss, V., & Wax, E. (2002, 25 February). Where two worlds collide. *Washington Post*. Retrieved from http://wwrn.org/articles/3740/?&place=north-america&section=islam

Taylor, J. (2012, 26 October). Medina: Saudis take a bulldozer to Islam's history. *Independent* (UK). Retrieved from http://www.independent.co.uk/news/world/middle-east/medina-saudis-take-a-bulldozer-to-islams-history-8228795.html

Traynor, I. (2012, 18 September). EU heavyweights call for radical foreign and defence policy overall. *Guardian* (UK). Retrieved from http://www.guardian.co.uk/world/2012/sep/18/eu-foreign-defence-policy-overhaul

Washington Times (2005, 14 November). Saudi jailed for discussing the Bible. Retrieved from http://www.washingtontimes.com/news/2005/nov/14/20051114-015138-3548r/

Webb, J. (2011, 25 June). Don't be distracted by Greece: Americans must also face financial facts. *Telegraph* (UK). Retrieved from http://www.telegraph.co.uk/news/worldnews/us-politics/8598451/Dont-be-distracted-by-Greece-Americans-must-also-face-financial-facts.html

Weiner, E. J. (2010, 6 October). China's giant economic sway. *Los Angeles Times*. Retrieved from http://articles.latimes.com/2010/oct/06/opinion/la-oe-weiner-china-20101006

World Bank. (2010). www.worldbank.org

Wright, R. (2004, 1 April). Top focus before 9/11 wasn't on terrorism. *Washington Post*. Retrieved from http://www.washingtonpost.com/wp-dyn/articles/A42287-2004Apr1_2.html

Ye'or, B. (2002). *Islam and Dhimmitude: Where civilizations collide.* M. Kochan & D. Littman (Trans.). Madison, NJ: Fairleigh Dickinson University Press.

Part Two

Arab Gulf Investments into Non-Inclusive Urban Development in the Middle East: A Partial Precursor to the Arab Spring

References

Adham, K. (2005). Globalization, neoliberalism, and new spaces of capital in Cairo. *Traditional Dwellings and Settlements Review, 17*(1), 19.

Adely, F. (2012). The emergence of a new labor movement in Jordan. *Middle East Report, 264*. Retrieved from: http://www.merip.org/mer/mer264/emergence-new-labor-movement-jordan

Aly, R. (2011). Rebuilding Egyptian media for a democratic future. *Arab Media & Society, 14*(1) 1–7.

Boyle, M. & Rogerson, R. J. (2001). Power, discourses and city trajectories. In R. Paddison (Ed.), *Handbook of urban studies* (pp. 402–416). London, UK: Sage.

Byrne, D. (1999). *Social exclusion*. Buckingham: Open University Press.

Clarke, J. A., et al. (2004). Using simulation to formulate domestic sector upgrading strategies for Scotland. *Energy and Buildings, 36* (8), 759–770.

Daher, R. F. (2008). Amman: disguised genealogy and recent urban restructuring and neoliberal threats. In Y. Elsheshtawy (Ed.), *The evolving Arab city: Tradition, modernity, and urban development* (pp. 37–68). New York, NY: Routledge.

Eberhard, J. P. (2007). *Architecture and the brain: A new knowledge base from neuroscience*. Atlanta, GA: Greenway Communications.

Eid, F. & Paua, F. (2003). Foreign direct investment in the Arab world: The changing investment landscape. *World Economic Forum*. Retrieved from https://members.weforum.org/pdf/Global_Competitiveness_Reports/Reports/AWCR_2002_2003/FDI.pdf

Hertog, S. (2011). The evolution of rent recycling during two booms in the Gulf Arab States: Business dynamism and society stagnation. In M. Legrenzi & B. Momani (Eds.), *Shifting geo-economic power of the Gulf: Oil, finance and institutions* (pp. 55–74). London, UK: Ashgate.

Hvidt, M. (2011). Economic diversification in the Gulf Arab States. In M. Legrenzi & B. Momani (Eds.), *Shifting geo-economic power of the Gulf: Oil, finance and institutions* (pp. 39–54). London, UK: Ashgate.

International Monetary Fund. (2011). *Economic transformation in MENA: Delivering on the promise of shared prosperity.* G-8 Summit, May 27, Deauville, France.

Kantor, P. (1987). The dependent city: The changing political economy of urban economic development in the United States. *Urban Affairs Quarterly, 22*, 493–520.

Keyder, C. (2005). Globalization and social exclusion in Istanbul. *International Journal of Urban and Regional Research, 29*(1), 124–134.

Khalaf, R., & England, A. (2008, January 19). Gulf oil boom spreads to poorer lands. *Financial Times*. Retrieved from http://www.ft.com/intl/cms/s/0/849d1898-c61f-11dc-8378-0000779fd2ac.html#axzz2MoGXBWpN

Lawrence, D. L., & Low, S. M. (1990). The built environment and spatial form. *Annual Review of Anthropology, 19*, 453–505.

Lauria, M. (1997). *Reconstructing urban regime theory: Regulating urban politics.* Thousand Oaks, CA: Sage.

Logan, J., & Molotch, H. (1987). Urban fortunes: The political economy of place. Berkeley, CA: University of California Press.

Madanipour, A. (1998). Social exclusion and space. In A. Madanipour, G. Cars, & J. Allen (Eds.), *Social exclusion in European cities* (pp. 75–94). London, UK: Jessica Kingsley.

Mohamed, S. E., & Sidiropoulos, M. G. (2010). Another look at the determinants of foreign direct investment in MENA countries: An empirical investigation. *Journal of Economic Development, 35*(2), 75–95.

Momani, B. (2010). The GCC oil exporters and the future of the dollar. *New Political Economy.* Retrieved from http://www.arts.uwaterloo.ca/~bmomani/documents/ NPE_GCC_Oil_Exporters.pdf

Momani, B. (2011). Shifting Gulf Arab investments into the Mashreq: Underlying political economy rationales. In M. Legrenzi, & B. Momani (Eds.), *Shifting geo-economic power of the Gulf: Oil, finance and institutions* (pp. 163–182). London, UK: Ashgate.

Onyeiwu, S. (2008). Does investment in knowledge and technology spur "optimal" FDI in the MENA region: Evidence from logit and cross-country regressions. Paper presented at the *African Economic Development Conference Organized by ADB and ECA.* Tunis, November 12–14. Retrieved from http://www.afdb.org/fileadmin/uploads/ afdb/Documents/Knowledge/30753785-EN-2.3.4-ONYEIWU-TECHNOLOGY-AND-FDI-IN-THE-MENA-REGION.PDF

Sadik, A. T., & Bolbol, A. A. (2001). Capital flows, FDI, and technology spillovers: Evidence from Arab countries. *World Development, 29* (12), 2111–2125.

Schwedler, J. (2012). The political geography of protest in neoliberal Jordan. *Middle East Critique, 21*(3), 259–270.

Shafik, N. (2012, 10 May). Making sure Middle East growth is inclusive. *iMFdirect*. Retrieved from http://blog-imfdirect.imf.org/2012/05/10/making-sure-middle-east-growth-is-inclusive/

Siddiqi, M. (2009). Global crunch presents stiff challenges to FDI despite new incentives. *Middle East, 398*, 34–38.

Smith, P. (2007). Gulf investors focus on Arab and African neighbours. *The Middle East, 381,* 38–43.

Tripp, C. (Speaker). (2012, 23 February). The politics of resistance and the Arab uprisings. *Middle East Centre Arab Uprisings Lecture Series.* Retrieved from http://www2.lse.ac.uk/publicEvents/events/2012/02/20120223t1830vHKT.aspx

Vischer, J. C. (2008). Towards a user-centred theory of the built environment. *Building Research and Information, 36*(3), 231–240.

World Bank. (2009, 10 February). What is inclusive growth? Retrieved from http://siteresources.worldbank.org/INTDEBTDEPT/Resources/468980-1218567884549/WhatIsInclusiveGrowth20081230.pdf

Citizenship, National Identity, and the Future of "UAE, Inc.": Confronting the Fragility Thesis

References

Abdullah, M. M. (1978). *The United Arab Emirates: A modern history.* London, UK: Croom Helm.

Al-Abed, I., & Hellyer, P. (Eds.) (2001). *The United Arab Emirates: A new perspective.* London, UK: Trident.

Al-Qassemi, S. (2012, January 26). Reform in Arab Gulf regimes is unattainable – for now. *The Guardian.* Retrieved from http://www.guardian.co.uk/commentisfree/2012/jan/26/reform-arab-gulf-regimes-unattainable

Ali, S. (2010). *Dubai: Gilded cage.* New Haven, CT: Yale University Press.

B'huth Dubai. (2013). Proprietary public opinion polling conducted regularly in the United Arab Emirates. Dubai, UAE: B'huth Dubai.

Bremmer, I., & Keat, P. (2010). *The fat tail: The power of political knowledge in an uncertain world.* New York, NY: Oxford University Press.

Business Monitor International. (2013). United Arab Emirates Business Forecast Report. Retrieved from http://store.businessmonitor.com/em/bf/unitedarabemirates.html?campaign=em&utm_source=Adestra&utm_medium=email&utm_term=BFR&utm_content=1stPara&utm_campaign=Feb2013%20-%20BFR%201%20-%20MEAF%20-%20%282%2F2%29

Chase-Dunn, C. (1975). The effects of international economic dependence on development and inequality: A cross-national study. *American Sociological Review, 40*(6), 720–738.

Cincotta, R. (2012). Life begins after 25: Demography and the societal timing of Arab Spring. *Foreign Policy Research Institute E-note* (Philadelphia).

Clinton, H. R. (2011, January 30). Interview with David Gregory of NBC's Meet The Press. *U.S. Department of State.* Retrieved from http://www.state.gov/secretary/rm/2011/01/155585.htm

CNN. (2011, December 6). Emirates leader discounts fear of Iranian bomb. http://edition.cnn.com/2011/12/05/world/meast/iran-nuclear-uae

Crystal, J. (1990). *Oil and politics in the Gulf: Rulers and merchants in Kuwait and Qatar.* New York, NY: Cambridge University Press.

Dahl, R. A. (1961). *Who Governs? Democracy and power in an American city.* New Haven, CT: Yale University Press.

Davidson, C. M. (2008). *Dubai: The vulnerability of success*. London, UK: Hurst.

Davidson, C. M. (2012). *After the Sheikhs: The coming collapse of the Gulf monarchies*. London, UK: Hurst.

El-Beblawi, H., & Luciani, G. (Eds.) (1987). *The rentier state*. New York, NY: Croom Helm.

Fain, H. (1987). *Normative politics and the community of nations*. Philadelphia, PA: Temple University Press.

George, B. (2003). *Authentic leadership: Rediscovering the secrets of creating lasting value*. San Francisco, CA: Jossey-Bass.

Hudson, M. (1979). *Arab politics: The search for legitimacy*. New Haven, CT: Yale University Press.

Hunter, S. T., & Malik, H. (Eds.) (2005). *Islam and human rights: Advancing a U.S.-Muslim dialogue*. Washington, DC: Center for Strategic and International Studies.

Jay, A. (1996). *Management and Machiavelli: A prescription for success in your business*. New York, NY: Simon & Schuster.

Khalaf, A., & Luciani, G. (Eds.) (2006). *Constitutional reform and political participation in the Gulf*. Gulf Research Center, Dubai, United Arab Emirates. Retrieved from http://www.princeton.edu/~gluciani/pdfs/Constitutional%20Reform%20and%20Political%20Participation.pdf

Krane, J. (2009). *Dubai: The story of the world's fastest growing city*. London, UK: Atlantic Books.

Kubálková, V., Onuf, N., & Kowert, P. (Eds.) (1998). *International relations in a constructed world*. Armonk, NY: M. E. Sharpe.

Lévinas, E. (1999). *Alterity and transcendence*. Michael B. Smith, (Trans.). New York, NY: Columbia University Press.

Lienhardt, P. (2001). *Shaikhdoms of Eastern Arabia*. New York, NY: Palgrave.

Lipset, S. M. (1960). *Political man: The social bases of politics*. New York, NY: Doubleday.

Lyons, J. (2009). *The house of wisdom: How the Arabs transformed Western civilization*. London, UK: Bloomsbury.

Mameli, P. (2013, February 21). *Under new management: What the Arab Spring tells us about leadership needs in the Middle East and North Africa*. Paper presented at Middle East Dialogue 2013, Washington, DC. Abstract retrieved from http://domes.uwm.edu/2013/PeterMameli.pdf

Rashid, A. (2013, March 11) UAE state security case adjourned: Judge orders defendants to undergo medical check-ups as lawyers make new demands. *Gulf News*. Retrieved from http://gulfnews.com/news/gulf/uae/crime/uae-state-security-case-adjourned-1.1156865

Reisman, W. M., & McDougal, M. S. (1981). *International law in contemporary perspective: Public Order of the World Community*. Eagan, MN: The Foundation Press.

Reus-Smit, C. (1997). The constitutional structure of international society and the nature of fundamental institutions. *International Organization, 51*(4), 555–590.

Rosenau, J. N. (1990). *Turbulence in world politics: A theory of change and continuity*. Princeton, NJ: Princeton University Press.

Ruggie, J. G. (1998). *Constructing the world polity: Essays on international institutionalization.* New York, NY: Routledge.

Terry, R. W. (1993). *Authentic leadership: Courage in action.* San Francisco, CA: Jossey-Bass.

United Nations Development Program. (2012). *Arab knowledge report 2010/2011: Preparing future generations for the knowledge society.* Retrieved from http://www.undp.org/content/rbas/en/home/library/huma_development/arab-knowledge-report-2010-2011/

United States CIA. (2010, 2011, 2012). World Factbook. https://www.cia.gov/library/publications/the-world-factbook/geos/ae.html

Wise, K. L. (1997). The constitutional requirements of citizenship in the global polity. In *Science and Technique of Democracy, No. 21* (pp. 137–159). Germany: Council of Europe Publishing.

Wise, K. L. (1998). Review of Heater, Derek. *World citizenship and government: Cosmopolitan ideas in the history of western political thought.* Retrieved from http://www.h-net.org/reviews/showrev.php?id=1598

Zahlan, R. S. (1979). *The origins of the United Arab Emirates: A political and social history of the trucial states.* New York, NY: St. Martin's Press.

Middle East Union (MEU): A Futuristic Approach for Democratic Transition and Economic Development

References

BBC News. (2012). Profile: Gulf Cooperation Council. *World News Feature,* 1–2. Retrieved from http://news.bbc.co.uk/2/hi/middle_east/country_profiles/4155001.stm

Bellin, E. (2012). Research opportunities post Arab Spring: Mobilization and contentious politics. Project on Middle East Political Science, 7.

DeAngelis, T. (2009). Understanding terrorism. *Journal of the American Psychological Association, 40*(10), 1–2. Retrieved from http://www.apa.org/monitor/2009/11/terrorism.aspx

Foxman, A. (2011, 9 March). Seizing new Middle East opportunities. *The Forward.* Retrieved from http://www.adl.org/ADL_Opinions/International_Affairs/20110310-Op-ed+Forward.htm

Hammond, A. (2012, 17 May). Analysis: Saudi gulf union plan stumbles as wary leaders seek detail. *Thomson Reuters,* ,1–2. Retrieved from http://www.reuters.com/assets/print?aid=USBRE84G0WN20120517

Hunter, S. (2012). Sunni–Shi'a tensions are more about politics, power and privilege than theology. Edmund A. Walsh School of Foreign Service, Georgetown University. Retrieved from http://acmcu.georgetown.edu/135390.html

Legal Information Institute. (2010). Civil rights: An overview. *Cornell University Law School.* Retrieved from http://www.law.cornell.edu/wex/civil_rights

Lynch, M. (2012). Arab uprisings: New opportunities for political science, introduction. Project on Middle East Political Science, 3–6.

Masters, M. (2012, 26 January). The Arab League. *Council on Foreign Relations*, p. 1–6. Retrieved from http://www.cfr.org/middle-east/arab-league/p25967

Naggar D. (2006, 19 April). Sustaining gains in poverty reduction and human development in MENA requires new approaches. *The World Bank*, 1–2. Retrieved from http://go.worldbank.org/LFPHZE72S0

Roudi, F. (2011). Youth population and unemployment in the Middle East and North Africa: Opportunity or challenge. *United Nations Population Division, Population Division, Department of Economic and Social Affairs* (pp. 1–14). New York, NY: United Nations Secretariat.

United Nations. (1948). The Universal Declaration of Human Rights. *Human Rights Law*, 1–8. Retrieved from http://www.un.org/en/documents/udhr/index.shtml.

Ignorance, Lobby Power, and the Formulation of U.S. Foreign Policy

References

Agence France Presse (2007, 27 April). *Khatami says "Radical Warmongers" drive US policy*. Retrieved from http://www.commondreams.org/headlines02/0427-03.htm

Amirahmadi, H. (2000, 22 December). The time is now. *The Iranian*. Retrieved from http://iranian.com/Opinion/2000/December/Time/index.html

Fitchett, J. (2002, 27 April). Khatami sees Bush influenced by 'warmongers': Iran leader assails U.S. policies. *New York Times\International Herald Tribune*. Retrieved from http://www.nytimes.com/2002/04/27/news/27iht-iran_ed3_.html

Granitsas, A. (2005, 24 November). Americans are tuning out the world. *YaleGlobal Online*. Retrieved from http://yaleglobal.yale.edu/content/americans-are-tuning-out-world

Herman, E. S., & Chomsky, N. (1988). *Manufacturing consent: The political economy of the mass media*. New York, NY: Pantheon.

Holsti, O. (2004). *Public opinion and American foreign policy* (Rev. ed.). Ann Arbor, MI: University of Michigan Press.

Kennan, G. F. (1967). *Memoirs 1925–1950*. [Atlantic Monthly Press]. Boston, MA: Little, Brown.

Kennan, G. F. (1977). *The cloud of danger: Current realities of American foreign policy*. Boston, MA: Little, Brown.

Lindsay, J. M., & Boot, M. (2004). On foreign policy, red and blue voters are worlds apart: Commentary on the Council/Pew Poll. *Council on Foreign Relations*. Retrieved from http://www.cfr.org/world/foreign-policy-red-blue-voters-worlds-apart-commentary-councilpew-poll/p7259

Pew Research Center for People and the Press. (2004). Cable and Internet Loom Large in Fragmented Political News Universe: Perceptions of Partisan Bias Seen as Growing, Especially by Democrats. Retrieved January 11 from http://www.people-press.org/2004/01/11/cable-and-internet-loom-large-in-fragmented-political-news-universe/

Sanger, D.E. (2000). U.S. ending a few of the sanctions imposed on Iran. *New York Times.* Retrieved March 18 from http://www.nytimes.com/2000/03/18/world/us-ending-a-few-of-the-sanctions-imposed-on-iran.html?pagewanted=all&src=pm

Stoppard, T. (1972). *Jumpers.* New York, NY: Grove Press.

Trubowitz, P. (2000). Domestic Politics are Gaining Ground in Presidential Foreign Policy Decisions. *Public Affairs Report, University of California–Berkeley 41*(3).

PART 3

Socioeconomic Rights: A Dialogue with Islam*

*The author wishes to express his many thanks to Hartley Dean and Timur Kuran for their comments and also to Ashley McKinless and Jesse Spafford for their research assistance on this paper.

References

Adib-Moghaddam, A. (2012, 11 April). *Islamutopia: A very short history of political Islam.* Retrieved from http://blogs.lse.ac.uk/ideas/2012/04/islamutopia-a-very-short-history-of-political-islam/

Ahmad, W., & Mohamad, S. (2012). Classical jurists' view on the allocation of zakat: Is zakat investment allowed? *Middle-East Journal of Scientific Research, 12*(2), 195–203. Retrieved from http://idosi.org/mejsr/mejsr12(2)12/9.pdf

Akan, T. (2011). Responsible pragmatism in Turkish social policy making in the face of Islamic egalitarianism and neoliberal austerity. *International Journal of Social Welfare, 20,* 367–380.

Amara, T. (2012, October 12). Tunisia's financial push has political echoes. *Reuters.* Retrieved from http://www.reuters.com/article/2012/10/10/tunisia-islamic-finance-idUSL6E8L2ESJ20121010.

Arieff, A. (2012). Morocco: Current issues. *Congressional Research Service,* 11. Retrieved from http://www.fas.org/sgp/crs/row/RS21579.pdf

Berman, S. (2003). Islamism, revolution, and civil society. *Perspectives on Politics, 1*(2), 257–272. Retrieved from http://www.jstor.org/stable/3688899?seq=1

Bielefeldt, H. (2000). "Western" versus "Islamic" human rights conceptions? A critique of cultural essentialism in the discussion on human rights. *Political Theory, 28*(1), 90–121. Retrieved from http://www.jstor.org/stable/pdfplus/192285.pdf

Bonner, M. (2005). Poverty and economics in the Qur'an. *Journal of Interdisciplinary History, 35*(3), 391–406.

Bonner, M., Ener, M., & Singer, A. (2003). *Poverty and charity in Middle Eastern contexts.* Albany, NY: SUNY Press.

Center for Social and Economic Rights. (2013) *United States.* Retrieved from http://www.cesr.org/section.php?id=26

Council on Foreign Relations. (2011, 30 November). *Tunisia's challenge: A conversation with Rachid al-Ghannouchi.* Retrieved from http://www.cfr.org/tunisia/tunisias-challenge-conversation-rachid-al-ghannouchi/p26660

Dean, H., & Khan, Z. (1997). Muslim perspectives on welfare. *Journal of Social Policy, 26* (2), 193–209.

Etzioni, A. (2007). *Security first: For a muscular, moral foreign policy.* New Haven, CT: Yale University Press.

Haqqani, H., & Fradkin, H. (2008). Going back to the origins. *Journal of Democracy, 19*(3), 13–18. Retrieved from http://www.worde.org/wp-content/uploads/2011/12/ fradkin-islamist-parties.pdf

Hamzawy, A. (2007, 11 September). *The 2007 Moroccan parliamentary elections: Results and implications.* Retrieved from https://www.carnegieendowment.org/ files/moroccan_parliamentary_elections_final.pdf.

Handler, J. (2004). *Social citizenship and workfare in the United States and Western Europe: The paradox of inclusion.* Cambridge, UK: Cambridge University Press.

Harrigan, J. (2009, 29 March). Economic liberalisation, social welfare and Islam. *Development Viewpoint, 25.*

Harrigan, J., & el-Said, H. (2009). *Economic liberalisation, social capital and Islamic welfare provision.* New York, NY: Palgrave Macmillan.

Heper, M., & Sule, T. (2003). Islam, modernity, and democracy in contemporary Turkey: The case of recep tayyip erdoğan. *The Muslim World, 93*(2), 157–185. Retrieved from http://onlinelibrary.wiley.com/doi/10.1111/1478-1913.00019/pdf

Justice and Development Party. (2013). *Party Programme.* Retrieved from http://www.akparti.org.tr/english/akparti/parti-programme#bolum

Knickmeyer, E. (2007, 7 September). Islamic party confident in Morocco. *The Washington Post.* Retrieved from http://www.washingtonpost.com/wp-dyn/content/article/2007/09/06/AR2007090602547.html

Kunkle, F (2011, 8 April). In Egypt, Muslim Brotherhood's charitable works may drive political support. *Washington Post.* Retrieved from http://www.washingtonpost.com/world/in-egypt-muslim-brotherhoods-charitable-works-may-drive-political-support/2011/04/07/AF7wWM2C_story.html

Kuran, T. (1989). On the notion of economic justice in contemporary Islamic thought. *International Journal for Middle East Studies, 21,* 171–191.

Nathan, A. (2012, 16 November). *How human rights became our ideology.* Retrieved from http://www.tnr.com/article/books-and-arts/magazine/110197/how-human-rights-became-our-ideology?page=0,0

Narveson, J. (2001). *The libertarian idea.* Peterborough, ON: Broadview.

Önis, Z., & Keyman, E. (2003). A new path emerges. *Journal of Democracy, 14*(2), 95–107.

Pepinsky, T., & Welbourne, B. (2011). Piety and redistributive preferences in the Muslim world. *Political Research Quarterly, 64*(3), 491–505. Retrieved from http://prq.sagepub.com/content/64/3/491.full.pdf html

Piccard, A. (2010). The United States' failure to ratify the international covenant on economic, social and cultural rights: Must the poor be always with us? *The Scholar: St. Mary's Law Review on Minority Issues*, *13*(2), 221–272.

Pryor, C. (2011). Looking for bedrock: Accounting for human rights in classical liberalism, modern secularism, and the Christian tradition. *Campbell Law Review, 33,* 609–640.

Said, A. (1979). Precept and practice of human rights in Islam. *Universal Human Rights*, *1*(1), 63–79.

Said, A., Abu-Nimer, M., & Sharify-Funk, M. (2006). *Contemporary Islam: Dynamic not static.* New York, NY: Routledge.

Saif, I., & Abu Rumman, M. (2012, May). *The economic agenda of the Islamism parties.* Retrieved from http://carnegieendowment.org/2012/05/29/economic-agenda-of-islamist-parties/b0fh

Shogimen, T., & Nederman, C. (Eds.). (2009). *Western political thought in dialogue with Asia.* Lanham, MD: Lexington Books.

Singer, A. (2006). Soup and sadaqa: Charity in Islamic societies. *Historical Research*, *79*(205), 306–324.

Taşpınar, Ömer. (2012, April). *Turkey: The new model.* Retrieved from http://www.brookings.edu/research/papers/2012/04/24-turkey-new-model-taspinar

Willis, M. (2004). Morocco's Islamists and the legislative elections of 2002: The strange case of the party that did not want to win. *Mediterranean Politics*, *9*(1), 53–81.

Re-approaching-Not Merely Reproaching-Religious Sectarianism within a Tumultuous Middle East

References

Abd-Allah, U. F. (1983). *The Islamic struggle in Syria.* Berkeley, CA: Mizan Press.

Akhtar, S. (2008). *The Qur'an and the secular mind.* New York, NY: Routledge.

Arango, T. (2012, 7 December). Fears of deeper sectarian strife in Syria. *The New York Times,* p. A6.

Bar-Asher M., & Kofsky A. (2012). *Kitab al-ma'arif by abu sa'id maymun b. Qasimal-tabarani:* Critical Edition with an Introduction. Brussels, BE: Peeters. Retrieved from http://www.peeters-leuven.be/boekoverz_print.asp?nr=8994

Barnard, A. (2013, 7 January). Syria President's defiant words are another roadblock of peace. *The New York Times,* pp. A1–A7.

Chulov, M. (2013, 17 January). Syria crisis: al-Qaida fighters revealing their true colours, rebels say. *The Guardian.* Retrieved from http://www.guardian.co.uk/world/ 2013/jan/17/syria-crisis-alqaida-fighters-true-colours

Crone, P. (2012). *The nativist prophets of early Islamic Iran: Rural revolt and local zoroastrianism.* Cambridge, UK: Cambridge University Press.

Dabashi, H. (2011). *Shi'ism: A religion of protest.* Cambridge, MA: Belknap Press.

Dabashi, H. (2013a). *Being a Muslim in the world.* New York, NY: Palgrave Macmillan.

Dabashi, H. (2013b, February 12). Wresting Islam from Islamists. AlJazeera English. Retrieved from http://www.aljazeera.com/indepth/opinion/2013/02/ 201326124432686900.html

Davis, E. (2008). Pensée 3: A sectarian Middle East? *International Journal of Middle East Studies, 40*(4), 555–558.

Dawson, L. (2009). Church—sect—cult: Constructing typologies of religious groups. In P. B. Clarke (Ed.), *The Oxford handbook of the sociology of religion* (pp. 525–544). Oxford, UK: Oxford University Press.

Dubuisson, D. (2003). The Western construction of religion: Myths, knowledge, and ideology. W. Sayers (Trans.). Baltimore, MD: Johns Hopkins University Press.

Eisenstadt, S. N. (1993). Religion and the civilizational dimensions of politics. In S. A. Arjomand (Ed.), *The political dimensions of religion* (pp. 13–41). Albany, NY: SUNY Press.

Eisenstadt, S. N. (1999). *Fundamentalism, sectarianism, and revolution: The Jacobin dimension of modernity.* Cambridge, UK: Cambridge University Press.

Eisenstadt, S. N. (2012). The axial conundrum between transcendental visions and vicissitudes of their institutionalizations: Constructive and destructive possibilities. In R. N. Bellah, & H. Joas (Eds.), *The axial age and its consequences* (pp. 277–293). Cambridge, MA: Belknap Press.

Esposito, J. (2003). *The Oxford dictionary of Islam.* Oxford, UK: Oxford University Press.

Fahim, K., & Saad, H. (2013, 9 February). A faceless teenage refugee who helped ignite Syria's war. *The New York Times,* pp. A1, A8.

Fernández, B. (2011). *The imperial messenger: Thomas Friedman at work.* New York, NY: Verso.

Fernandez, Y. (2013, 14 January). Turkey, Qatar sectarian plots will fail in Iraq. *Press TV.* Retrieved from http://presstv.com/detail/2013/01/14/283441/turkey-qatar-sectarian-plots-fail-in-iraq/

Fisk, R. (2009). *The age of the warrior: Selected writings.* London, UK: Harper Perennial.

Fisk, R. (2010, 6 November). Our actions in the Middle East are what is endangering our security. *The Independent.* Retrieved from https://www.commondreams.org/ view/2010/11/06-2

Fox, R. (2011). *The Tribal imagination: Civilization and the savage mind.* Cambridge, MA: Harvard University Press.

Friedman, T. L. (2013, 10 February). Any solution to Syria? *The New York Times,* p. 11.

Governance and Social Development Resource Center. (2011, April 27). Helpdesk Research Report: Understanding sectarianism in MENA countries. Retrieved from www.gsdrc.org/docs/open/HD766.pdf

Gray, J. (2007). *Black Mass: Apocalyptic religion and the death of Utopia.* New York, NY: Farrar, Straus and Giroux.

Haddad, F. (2011). *Sectarianism in Iraq: Antagonistic visions of unity.* London, UK: Hurst.

Hassan-Yari, H. (2012). "Clashology within Islam: Not civilizational, but political." In M. Mahdavi, & W. A. Knight (Eds.), *Towards the dignity of difference? Neither 'End of History' nor 'Clash of Civilizations'* (pp. 71–82). Farnham, UK: Ashgate.

Inside Sectarianism: News, thoughts, and resources on Sectarian relations and related issues with a focus on Islam and Pakistan. Retrieved from http://insidesectarianism.blogspot.ca/

Joseph, S. (2008). Pensée 2: Sectarianism as imagined sociological concept and as imagined social formation. *International Journal of Middle East Studies, 40*(4), 553–554.

Juergensmeyer, M. (2008). *Global rebellion: Religious challenges to the secular state, from Christian militias to al-Qaeda.* Berkeley, CA: University of California Press.

Kostiner, J. (2011). GCC "perceptions of collective security in the post–Saddam era." In M. Kamrava (Ed.), *International politics of the Persian Gulf* (pp. 94–119). Syracuse, NY: Syracuse University Press.

Lockman, Z. (2010). *Contending visions of the Middle East: The history and politics of Orientalism* (2nd ed.). Cambridge, UK: Cambridge University Press.

Makdisi, U. (2000). *The culture of sectarianism: Community, history, and violence in nineteenth-century Ottoman Lebanon.* Berkeley, CA: University of California Press.

Makdisi, U. (2002). Revisiting sectarianism. In T. Scheffler (Ed.), *Religion between violence and reconciliation* (pp. 179–191). Beirut, LB: Ergon Verlag Würzberg in Kommission.

Makdisi, U. (2008). Pensée 4: Moving beyond Orientalist fantasy, sectarian polemic, and nationalist denial. *International Journal of Middle East Studies, 40*(4), 559–560.

Masters, B. (2004). *Christians and Jews in the Ottoman Arab world: The roots of sectarianism.* Cambridge, UK: Cambridge University Press.

Nasr, V. (2007). *The Shi'a revival: How conflicts within Islam will shape the future.* New York, NY: W.W. Norton.

Nasr, V. (2013). *The dispensable nation: American foreign policy in retreat.* New York, NY: Doubleday.

Occhiogrosso, P. (1996). *The joy of sects: A spirited guide to the world's religious traditions.* New York, NY: Image.

Oliver, P. (2012). *New religious movements: A guide for the perplexed.* London, UK: Continuum.

Oudat, B. (2012, 12 November). Dangers of sectarianism. *Al-Ahram Weekly.* Retrieved from http://weekly.ahram.org.eg/News/510/-/-.aspx

Partridge, C., ed. (2004). *New religions: A guide. New religious movements, sects and alternative spiritualities.* New York, NY: Oxford University Press.

Peteet, J. (2008). Pensée 1: Imagining the 'New Middle East.' *International Journal of Middle East Studies, 40*(4), 550–552.

Press TV. (2009, 15 February). "Iran prosecutor: Bahais, Israeli agents." Retrieved from http://edition.presstv.ir/detail/85798.html

Qur'an. (1992 [1909]). M. Pickthall (Trans.), New York, NY: Alfred A. Knopf.

Raslan, R., & Sabbagh, H. (2013, 30 January). Jamil: Political solution is only way out of crisis in Syria. *SANA: Syrian Arab News Agency.* Retrieved from http://www.sana-syria.com/eng/22/2013/01/30/464475.htm.

Rieff, D. (2012). History resumes: Sectarianism's unlearned lessons. *World Affairs, 175*(2), 29–38.

Ruthven, M. (2011a). Storm over Syria. *The New York Review of Books, 58*(10), 16–20.

Ruthven, M. (2011b). The revolutionary Shias. *The New York Review of Books, 58*(20), 89–96.

Saigol, L. (2013, 11 January). Q & A: Sectarian violence in Pakistan. *Financial Times.* Retrieved from http://www.ft.com/cms/s/0/576ab642-5c14-11e2-ab38-00144feab49a.html#axzz2LIzKHoI

Sanasarian, E. (2006). *Religious minorities in Iran.* Cambridge, UK: Cambridge University Press.

Tadros, M. (2012). *The Muslim brotherhood in contemporary Egypt: Democracy redefined or confined?* New York, NY: Routledge.

The Economist. (2012, 12 May). Sunni-Shia strife: The sword and the word. *403* (8784), 66-67.

United Nations High Commissioner for Human Rights. (2012, 20 December). *Independent International Commission of Inquiry on the Syrian Arab Republic established pursuant to United Nations Human Rights Council Resolutions S-17/1, 19/22 and 21/26: Periodic Update.* http:// Retrieved from www.ohchr.org/Documents/Countries/SY/ColSyriaDecember2012.pdf

United Nations Regional Information Centre for Western Europe. (2012, 20 December). "*Syria: UN Commission paints a bleak picture.*" Retrieved from http://www.unric.org/en/latest-un-buzz/28119-syria-confict-increasingly-sectarian-in-nature

van Dam, N. (2011). *The struggle for power in Syria: Politics and society under the Baa'th Party* (4th ed.). London, UK: I. B. Tauris.

Weber, M. (1958 [1904-5]). *The protestant ethic and the spirit of capitalism,* T. Parsons (Trans.), New York, NY: Charles Scribner's Sons.

Wilson, B. (1990). *The social dimensions of sectarianism: Sects and new religious movements in contemporary society.* Oxford, UK: Clarendon Press.

Zubaida, S. (2009). Sects in Islam. In P. B. Clarke (Ed.), *The Oxford handbook of the sociology of religion* (pp. 545–561). Oxford, UK: Oxford University Press.

Christian–Muslim Relations in Egypt in the Wake of the Arab Spring

References

Ahram Online. (2013). Coptic Pope Tawadros II criticizes Egypt's Islamist leadership, new constitution. Retrieved February 5 from http://english.ahram.org.eg/NewsContent/1/64/64135/Egypt/Politics-/Coptic-Pope-Tawadros-II-criticises-Egypts-Islamist.aspx

Al-Arabiya News. (2011). Ex-minister suspected behind Alex church bombing. Retrieved February 7 from http://www.alarabiya.net/articles/2011/02/07/136723.html

Al-Aswany, A. (2011). *On the state of Egypt.* New York, NY: Vintage.

Arab West Report. (2011). Statement by the [Coptic Orthodox] Church [Patriarchate]. Retrieved February 7 from http://www.arabwestreport.info/year-2011/week-8/7-statement-coptic-orthodox-church-patriarchate

BBC News. (2005). Three killed in Egypt church riot, October 22. Retrieved from http://news.bbc.co.uk/2/hi/middle_east/4366232.stm

Brynen, R., Moore, P.W., Salloukh, B. F., and Zahar, M.-J. (2012). *Beyond the Arab Spring: Authoritarianism and democratization in the Arab world.* Boulder, CO: Lynne Rienner.

Carnegie Endowment for International Peace. (2012). Results of Egypt's people's assembly election. Retrieved from http://egyptelections.carnegieendowment.org/2012/01/25 /results-of-egypt%E2%80%99s-people%E2%80%99s-assembly-elections

Casper, J. (2011a). Interview with the Maspero Youth Union. *A Sense of Belonging.* Retrieved September 29 from http://asenseofbelonging.org/2011/09/29/interview-with-the-maspero-youth-union/

Casper, J. (2011b). Analyzing video evidence from Maspero: Bloody confrontations following the Coptic protest of October 9, 2011. Center for Intercultural Dialogue and Translation, October 26. Cairo, EG.

Casper, J. (2012). Can Egypt's Christian Assistant President get democracy back on track? *Christianity Today.* Retrieved from http://www.christianitytoday.com/ct/2012/november-web-only/can-egypts-christian-assistant-president-get-democracy-back.html

Coptic Youth Channel. (2012). Interview with H.G. Bishop Tawadros of Beheira. Retrieved October 22 from http://www.youtube.com/watch?feature=player_embedded&v=8zBzWoVPU9c

Egypt Independent. (2011). State TV: Pope Shenouda calls for end to Protests. Retrieved February 5 from http://www.egyptindependent.com/news/state-tv-pope-shenouda-calls-end-protests

el-Gundy, Z. (2012). Coptic FJP leader and presidential advisor quits political life. *Ahram Online.* Retrieved December 6 from http://English.ahram.org.eg/NewsContent/1/64/59931/Egypt/Politics-Coptic-FJP-leader-and-presidential-advisor-quits-p.aspx

el-Rashidi, Y. (2011). Egypt: Why are the churches burning?" *NYR Blog.* Retrieved May 17 from http://www.nybooks.com/blogs/nyrblog/2011/may/17/egypt-why-are-churches-burning/

Farah, N. R. (1986). *Religious strife in Egypt.* New York, NY: Gordon and Breach.

Hasan, S. S. (2003). *Christians versus Muslims in Egypt: The century-long struggle for Coptic equality.* Oxford, UK: Oxford University Press.

Ibrahim, E. (2012). Justice denied: Egypt's Maspero massacre one year on. *Ahram Online.* Retrieved October 9 from http://english.ahram.org.eg/NewsContent/1/64/54821 /Egypt/Politics-/Justice-denied-Egypts-Maspero-massacre-one-year-on.aspx

Kirkpatrick, D. (2012). Coptic Church chooses Pope who rejects political role. *The New York Times.* Retrieved November 4 from http://www.nytimes.com/2012/11/05/world/middleeast/coptic-church-chooses-pope-who-rejects-politics.html?pagewanted=all&_r=0

Leila, R. (2011). Church fire fires up Copts. *Al-Ahram Weekly.* Retrieved October 6–12 from http://weekly.ahram.org.eg/2011/1067/eg6.htm

Makari, P. (2007). *Conflict and cooperation: Christian-Muslim relations in contemporary Egypt.* Syracuse, NY: Syracuse University Press.

McCallum, F. (2007). The political role of the patriarch in the contemporary Middle East. *Middle Eastern Studies, 43* (6), 923-940.

Nkrumah, G. (2012). Shenouda's lost flock. *Al-Ahram Weekly.* Retrieved March 22 from http://weekly.ahram.org.eg/2012/1090/fr1.htm

Reuters. (2011). Egypt church blast death toll rises to 23. Retrieved January 4 from http://www.reuters.com/article/2011/01/04/us-egypt-church-idUSTRE7010M020110104

Reuters. (2011). Egyptian Christians protest over a church burning. Retrieved March 7 from http://www.reuters.com/article/2011/03/07/us-egypt-christians-idUSTRE7266C520110307

Rowe, P. S. (2001). Four guys and a fax machine? Diasporas, new information technologies, and the internationalization of religion in Egypt. *Journal of Church and State, 43* (1), 81-92.

Rowe, P. S. (2007). Neo-millet systems and transnational religious movements: The *Humayun* decrees and church construction in Egypt. *Journal of Church and State, 49* (2), 329-350.

Scott, R. (2010). *The challenge of political Islam: Non-Muslims and the Egyptian state.* Stanford, CA: Stanford University Press.

Shalaby, E. 2012. Coptic presidential assistant decides to resign, presidential team holds urgent meeting. Daily News Egypt. Retrieved November 23 from http://www.dailynewsegypt.com/2012/11/23/coptic-presidential-assistant-decides-to-resign-presidential-team-holds-urgent-meeting/

Politics of Conflict in Pakistan's Tribal Areas Vulnerability Reduction in Violence-Prone Complex Adaptive Systems

References

Adger, W. N. (2006). Vulnerability. *Global Environmental Change, 16*(3), 268–281.

Berkes, F., & Folke, C. (1998). *Linking social and ecological systems: Management practices and social mechanisms for building resilience.* Cambridge, UK: Cambridge University Press.

Folke, C. (2006). Resilience: The emergence of a perspective for socialecological systems analyses. *Global Environmental Change, 16*(3), 253–267.

Fussel, H. M., & Klein, R. (2006). Climate change vulnerability assessments: An evolution of conceptual thinking. *Climatic Change, 75*(3), 301–329.

Gunderson, L. H. (2000). Resilience in theory and practice. *Annual Review of Ecology and Systematics, 31,* 425–439.

Holling, C. S. (1973). Resilience and stability of ecological systems. *Annual Review of Ecology and Systematics, 4,* 1–23.

Janssen, M. A, Schoon, M. L, Ke, W., & Börner, K. (2006). Scholarly networks on resilience, vulnerability and adaptation within the human dimensions of global environmental change. *Global Environmental Change, 16*(3), 240–252.

Kasperson, J. X., & Kasperson, R. E. (2001). *International workshop on vulnerability and global environmental change.* SEI Risk and Vulnerability Programme Report 2001–01, Stockholm, SE: Stockholm Environment Institute.

Kates, R. W., Clark, W. C., Corell, R., Hall, J. M., Jaeger, C. C., Lowe, I., Mooney, H. (2001). Environment and development—sustainability science. *Science, 292*(5517), 641–642.

Koliba, C., Meek, J., & Zia, A. (2010). *Governance networks in public administration and public policy.* New York, NY: CRC Press.

O'Brien, K., Leichenko, R., Kelkar, U., Venema, H., Aandahl, G., Tompkins, H., . . . West, J. (2004). Mapping vulnerability to multiple stressors: Climate change and globalization in India, *Global Environmental Change, 14,* 303–313.

Chill Ground: Iranian–British Relations during Khomeini–Thatcher Years

References

Afary, J., & Anderson, K. B. (2005). *Foucault and the Iranian revolution: Gender and the seductions of Islamism.* Chicago, IL: University of Chicago Press.

Ahmadi, H. (2008). The dilemma of national interest in the Islamic Republic of Iran. In H. Katouzian, & H. Shahidi (Eds.), *Iran in the 21st century: Politics, economics and conflict* (pp. 28–40). London, UK: Routledge.

Ansari, A. M. (2007). *Confronting Iran: The failure of American foreign policy and the next great crisis in the Middle East.* New York, NY: Basic Books.

Carter, J. (1982). *Keeping faith: Memoirs of a president.* London, UK: Harper Collins.

Daniel, E. L. (2001). *The history of Iran.* Westport, CT: Greenwood Press.

Dobson, A. P. (1995). *Anglo-American relations in the twentieth century: Of friendship, conflict and the rise and decline of superpowers.* New York, NY: Routledge.

Ehteshami, A. (1995). *After Khomeini: The Iranian second republic.* London, UK: Routledge.

Farber, D. (2005). *Taken hostage: The Iran hostage crisis and America's first encounter with radical Islam.* Princeton, NJ: Princeton University Press.

Freedman, L. (2008). A choice of enemies: America confronts the Middle East. New York, NY: Public Affairs.

Fuller, G. E. (1991). *The center of the universe: The geopolitics of Iran.* Oxford, UK: Westview Press.

Fry, G. K. (2008). *The politics of the Thatcher revolution: An interpretation of British politics, 1979–1990.* Basingstoke, UK: Palgrave Macmillan.

Herring, G. C. (2008). *From colony to superpower: U.S. foreign relations since 1776*. Oxford, UK: Oxford University Press.

Hiltermann, J. R. (2004). Outsiders as enablers: Consequences and lessons from international silence on Iraq's use of chemical weapons during the Iran-Iraq war. In L. G. Potter, & G. G. Sick (Eds.), *Iran, Iraq and the legacies of war* (pp. 151–166). Basingstoke, UK: Palgrave Macmillan.

Houghton, D. P. (2001). *US foreign Policy and the Iran hostage crisis*. Cambridge, UK: Cambridge University Press.

IRANalyst. (2010, October 19) The power politics of demonization in Iran: The 'necessitated' enemy and its functions. *e-International Relations*. Retrieved from http://www.e-ir.info/2010/10/19/the-power-politics-of-demonization-in-iran-the-necessitated-%E2%80%98enemy%E2%80%99-and-its-functions/

Jones, H. (2001). *Crucible of power: A history of American foreign Relations from 1897*. Lanham, MD: Rowman & Littlefield.

Karsh, E. (2002). *The Iran-Iraq war 1980–1988*. Oxford, UK: Osprey Publishing.

Khomeini, R. M. (1385/2006). *Sahifeh-ye Emam [Collection of Imam Khomeini's guidelines]* (vol. 21). Tehran, IR: The Institute for Compilation and Publication of Imam Khomeini's Works.

Lotfian, S. (1997). Taking sides: Regional powers and the war. In F. Rajaee (Ed.), *Iranian perspectives on the Iran-Iraq war* (pp. 13–28). Gainesville, FL: University Press of Florida.

Marschall, C. (2003). *Iran's Persian Gulf policy: From Khomeini to Khatami*. London, UK: Routledge.

Matin-Asgari, A. (2004). From social democracy to social democracy: The twentieth-century odyssey of the Iranian Left. In S. Cronin (Ed.), *Reformers and revolutionaries in modern Iran: New perspectives on the Iranian left* (pp. 37–64). London, UK: Routledge.

McLachlan, K. (1993). Analyses of the risks of war: Iran-Iraq discord, 1979–1980. In F. Rajaee (Ed.), *The Iran-Iraq war: The politics of aggression* (pp. 24–31). Gainesville, FL: University Press of Florida.

Mesbahi, M. (1993). The USSR and the Iran-Iraq war: From Brezhnev to Gorbachev. In F. Rajaee (Ed.), *The Iran-Iraq war: The politics of aggression* (pp. 69–102). Gainesville, FL: University Press of Florida.

Naghibzadeh, A. (1993). Collectively or singly: Western Europe and the Iran-Iraq war. In F. Rajaee (Ed.), *Iranian perspectives on the Iran-Iraq war* (pp. 39–48). Gainesville, FL: University Press of Florida.

Naji, K. (2008). *Ahmadinejad: The secret history of Iran's radical leader*. Berkeley, CA: University of California Press.

Nonneman, G. (2004). The Gulf states and the Iran-Iraq war: Pattern shifts and continuities. In L. G. Potter, & G. G. Sick (Eds.), *Iran, Iraq and the legacies of war* (pp. 167–92). Basingstoke, UK: Palgrave Macmillan.

Nunn, H. (2002). *Thatcher, politics and fantasy: The political culture of gender and nation*. London, UK: Lawrence and Wishart.

Parsons, A. (1989). Iran and Western Europe. *The Middle East Journal, 43*(2), 218–29.

Parsons, A. (1990). Iran and Western Europe. In R. K. Ramazani (Ed.), *Iran's revolution: The search for consensus*. Bloomington, IL: Indiana University Press.

Parsons, A. (1991). Iran and the United Nations, with particular reference to the Iran-Iraq war. In A. Ehteshami & M. Varasteh (Eds.), *Iran and the international community* (pp. 7–30). London, UK: Routledge.

Pelletiere, S. C. (1992). *The Iran-Iraq war: Chaos in a vacuum.* New York, NY: Praeger.

Phythian, M. (1997). *Arming Iraq: How the U.S. and Britain secretly built Saddam's war machine.* Boston, MA: Northeastern University Press.

Rajaee, F. (1993). Introduction. In F. Rajaee (Ed.), *The Iran-Iraq war: The politics of aggression* (pp. 1–10). Gainesville, FL: University Press of Florida.

Saidabadi, M. R. (1998). *Iranian-British relations since 1979* (Unpublished doctoral dissertation). Canberra, Australia: Australian National University.

Sajjadpour, K. (1997). Neutral statements, committed practice: The USSR and the war. In F. Rajaee (Ed.), *Iranian perspectives on the Iran-Iraq war* (pp. 29–38). Gainesville, FL: University Press of Florida.

Shakibi, Z. (2010). *Khatami and Gorbachev: Politics of change in the Islamic Republic of Iran and the USSR.* London, UK: I. B. Tauris.

Shokrani, M. (1372/1993). *Amalkard-e yazdahsaleh-ye dolat-e mohafezekar-e Margaret Tacher* [*The eleven-year performance of Margaret Thatcher's conservative government*]. Tehran, Iran: Iranian Foreign Ministry Publications.

Smith, G. (1990). *Reagan and Thatcher.* London, UK: Bodley Head.

Sweeney, J. (1993). *Trading with the enemy: Britain's arming of Iraq.* London, UK: Pen Books.

Tehrani, I. A (1993) Iraqi attitudes and interpretation of the 1975 agreement. In F. Rajaee (Ed.), *The Iran-Iraq war: The politics of aggression* (pp. 11–23). Gainesville, FL: University Press of Florida.

PART FOUR

Imagining the New Egypt: Agential Egyptian Activism/ Feminism, Translation, and Movement

References

Abdelrahman, M. (2004). *Civil society exposed: The politics of NGOs in Egypt.* London, UK: I. B. Tauris.

Abu-Lughod, L. (1990). The Romance of resistance: Tracing transformations of power through Bedouin women. *American Ethnologist, 17*(1), 41–55.

Abu-Lughod, L. (1998). *Remaking women: Feminism and modernity in the Middle East.* Princeton, NJ: Princeton University Press.

Abu-Lughod, L. (2006). 'Orientalism' and Middle East feminist studies. *Feminist Studies, 27*(1), 101-113.

Abu-Lughod, L. (2010). The active social life of "Muslim women's rights": A plea for ethnography, not polemic, with cases from Egypt and Palestine. *Journal of Middle East Women's Studies, 6*(1), 1-45.

Abusharaf, R. M. (2000). Revisiting feminist discourses on infibulation: Responses from Sudanese feminists. In B. Shell-Duncan, & Y. Hernlund (Eds.), *Female 'circumcision' in Africa: Culture, controversy, and change* (pp. 151–166). London, UK: Lynne Rienner.

Ahearn, L. M. (2001). Language and agency. *Annual Review of Anthropology, 30*(1), 109–37.

Ahmed, L. (1992). *Women and gender and Islam: Historical roots of a modern debate.* London, UK: Yale University Press.

Amin, Q. (2000). *The liberation of women and the new woman: Two documents in the history of Egyptian feminism.* Cairo, EG: American University Press.

An-Na'im, A. A. (2008). *Islam and the secular state: Negotiating the future of Shari'a.* Cambridge, MA: Harvard University Press.

Badran, M. (1988). Dual liberation: Feminism and nationalism in Egypt 1870–1925. *Gender Issues, 8*(1), 17–19.

Badran, M. (1992). From consciousness to activism, feminist politics in early twentieth century Egypt. In J. P. Spagnolo (Ed.), *Problems of the Middle East in historical perspective* (pp. 27–48). Ithaca, NY: Cornell University Press.

Badran, M. (1995). *Feminists, Islam, and nation: Gender and the making of modern Egypt.* Princeton, NJ: Princeton University Press.

Badran, M. (2006). *Women and radicalization.* DIIS Report 2006, no. 5, Danish Institute for International Studies, Copenhagen, DK.

Badran, M. (2010). Feminist activism for change in family laws and practices: Lessons from the Egyptian past for the global present. In M. Badran, & H. Esfandiari (Eds.), *Middle East program. Occasional paper series* (pp. 6–9). Washington, DC: Woodrow Wilson International Center for Scholars.

Badran, M., & Esfandiari, H. (2010). Introduction to Islamic feminism and beyond: The new frontier. In M. Badran & H. Esfandiari (Eds.), *Middle East program. Occasional paper series* (pp.1–5). Washington, DC: Woodrow Wilson International Center for Scholars.

Baron, B. (2005). *Egypt as a woman: Nationalism, gender, and politics.* Berkeley, CA: University of California Press.

Bourdieu, P. (1990). *The Logic of Practice.* Cambridge, UK: Polity.

Buss, D., & Manji, A. (Eds). (2005). *International law, modern feminist approaches.* Portland, OR: Hart Publishing.

Charlesworth, H., & Chinkin, C. (2000). *The boundaries of international law: A feminist analysis.* Manchester, UK: Manchester University Press.

el-Sadda, H., Abu-Ghazi, I., Usfur, J., *Masirat al-mar'a al-Misriyya: `Alamat wa mawaqif.* Cairo, EG: National Council for Women. Trans. 2001 into English by Hala Kamal as *Significant moments in Egyptian women's history.* Cairo, EG: The National Council for Women.

Frisk, S. (2004). *Submitting to God: Women's Islamisation in urban Malaysia* (Doctoral dissertation). Göteborg, SE: Göteborg University.

Gemzöe, L. (2003). *Feminism.* Stockholm, SE: Bilda Förlag.

Guenena, N., & Wassef, N. (1999). Unfulfilled promises: Women's rights in Egypt. *Population Council.* Retrieved from http://www.popcouncil.org/pdfs/unfulfilled_promises.pdf

Hellstrand, A. (2012). *Feminist perspectives on the Egyptian revolution.* (Master's thesis). Uppsala, SE: Uppsala University. Retrieved from

http://uu.diva-portal.org/smash/get/diva2:556212/FULLTEXT01.pdf

Jackson, M. (2005). *Existential anthropology: Events, exigencies & effects.* New York, NY: Berghahn.

Kapur, R. (2002). The tragedy of victimization rhetoric: Resurrecting the "Native" subject in international/post-colonial feminist legal politics. *Harvard Human Rights Journal, 15,* 1–37.

Mahmood, S. (2001). Feminist theory, embodiment, and the docile agent: Some reflections on the Egyptian revival. *Cultural Anthropology, 6*(2), 202–236.

Mahmood, S. (2005). *Politics of piety: The Islamic revival and the feminist subject.* Princeton, NJ: Princeton University Press.

Malmström, M. F. (2004). Omskärelse är sött. Mat, kropp och kvinnlig omskärelse i Kairo, Socialmedicinsk Tidskrift, *6,* 512–519.

Malmström, M. F. (2009a). *Just like couscous: Gender, agency and the politics of female circumcision in Cairo* (Doctoral dissertation). Göteborg, SE: Göteborg University.

Malmström, M. F. (2009b). Bearing the pain: Changing views of the meaning and morality of suffering. In A. Schlyter (Ed.), *Body politics and women citizens – African eExperiences* (pp. 104–114). Stockholm, SE: Sida Studies 24. Retrieved from http://www.sida.se/Documents/Import/pdf/Sida-Studies-No-24-Body-Politics-and-Women-Citizens.pdf

Malmström, M. F. (2011). Gender, agency, and embodiment theories in relation to space in Gender, cities and local governance. In S. Denéfle & S. Monqid (Eds.), *Gouvernance locale dans le monde arabe et en Méditerranée: Quels rôles pour les femmes? Égypt/Monde Arabe 9/3e* (pp. 21–36). Cairo, EG: Centre d'Études et de Documentation Économiques, Juridiques et Sociales.

Malmström, M. F. (2013). Ihbaat again? Ihbaat – frustration – is one of the emotions in play as Egyptian people try to cope with their new political circumstances. In *Development Dilemmas. Annual Report 2012.* Uppsala, SE: The Nordic Africa Institute. Retrieved from http://www.nai.uu.se/about/organisation/annualreport/NAI_2012AnnualReport_HighRes.pdf

Malmström, M. F. (forthcoming). The production of sexual mutilation among Muslim women in Cairo. *Global Discourse, 3* (1). Retrieved from http://global-discourse.com/contents

Malmström, M. F., Diop, N. J., Moneti, F. Donahue, C., Toure, A., & Haug, W. (2011). UNFPA-UNICEF Joint Programme on female genital mutilation-cutting: Accelerating change. *Annual report 2010. Nurturing change from within.* New York, NY: UNFPA-UNICEF. Retrieved from http://www.unfpa.org/gender/docs/2010_Annual_Report_2.pdf

McNay, L. (2004). Agency and experience: Gender as a lived relation. *Sociological Review. 52*(2), 173–190.

Merry, S. E. (2006). *Human rights and gender violence: Translating international law into local justice.* Chicago, IL: University of Chicago Press.

Mohanty, C. T. (1988). Under Western eyes: Feminist scholarship and colonial discourses. *Feminist Review 30,* 61–88.

Nelson, C. (1996). *Doria Shafik, Egyptian feminist: A woman apart.* Gainsville, FL: University Press of Florida.

Nelson, C. (2007). *Pioneering feminist anthropology in Egypt: Selected writings from Cynthia Nelson* (*Cairo Papers in Social Science Vol. 28.2/3*). M. Rieker (Ed.), L. Abu-Lughod, & J. E. Tucker (Contributors). Cairo, EG: American University in Cairo Press.

Office of the United Nations High Commissioner for Human Rights. (n.d.). *Committee on the Elimination of Discrimination against Women Convention.*

Retrieved from http://www2.ohchr.org/english/bodies/cedaw/convention.htm

Ortner, S. (2006). *Anthropology and social theory: Culture, power, and the acting subject.* Durham, NC: Duke University Press.

Peteet, J. M. (1994). Male gender and rituals of resistance in the Palestinian intifada: a cultural politics of violence, *American Ethnologist 21*(1), 31–49.

Said, E. W. (1995). *Orientalism.* London, UK: Penguin Books.

Scheper-Huges, N. (2004). Who's the killer? Popular justice and human rights in a South African squatter camp. In N. Scheper-Huges, P. Bourgois, & P. Malden (Eds.), *Violence in war and peace: An anthology* (pp. 747–762). Malden, MA: Blackwell.

Spivak, G. (2010). Can the subaltern speak? (Rev. ed.). In R. C. Morris (Ed.), *Can the subaltern speak? Reflections on the history of an idea* (pp. 21–80). New York, NY: Colombia University Press.

Wangila, M. N. (2007) Beyond facts to reality: Confronting the situation of women in "Female Circumcising" communities. *Journal of Human Rights, 6*(4), 393–413.

Working with Patriarchy: Strategies for Women's Empowerment in Comparative Perspectives*

*An earlier version of this paper was presented to the Third Gulf Research Meeting (GRM), Cambridge, July 2012, organized by the Gulf Research Center Cambridge (GRCC) at the University of Cambridge. Excerpts from the paper were presented to the Kuwait University Women's Research Center Conference, March 2013, Kuwait City. Thanks to Cecilia Baeza and Alejandra Galindo for their invaluable comments.

References

Adefris, A. (1998). *The betrayal of Ethiopia.* Springfield, VA: American Ethiopian Press.

al-Harbi, D. M. (2008). *Prominent women from Central Arabia.* Reading, UK: Ithaca.

al-Mughni, H. (2001). *Women in Kuwait: The politics of gender.* London, UK: Saqi.

Alvarez, S. E. (1999). Advocating feminism: The Latin American feminist NGO 'boom'. *International Feminist Journal of Politics, 1*(2), 181–209.

Badran, M. (2009). *Feminism in Islam: Secular and religious convergences*. Oxford, UK: Oneworld.

Coleman, I. (2010). *Paradise beneath her feet: How women are transforming the Middle East*. New York, NY: Random House.

Cooke, M. (2001). *Women claim Islam: Creating Islamic feminism through literature*. New York, NY: Routledge.

De Barbieri, T., & De Oliveira, O. (1986). Nuevos sujetos sociales: La presencia política de las mujeres en América Latina. *Nueva Antropología, 8*(30), 159-185.

Fernea, E. W. (1997). *In search of Islamic feminism: One woman's global journey*. New York, NY: Doubleday.

George, R. P. (2001). *Clash of orthodoxies: Law, religion, and morality in crisis*. Wilmington, DE: Intercollegiate Studies Institute.

González, A. L. (2011). Measuring religiosity in a majority Muslim context: Gender, religious salience, and religious experience amongst Kuwaiti college students – A research note. *Journal for the Scientific Study of Religion, 50*(2), 339–350.

González, A. L. (2013). *Islamic feminism in Kuwait: The politics and paradoxes*. New York, NY: Palgrave Macmillan.

González, A. L., & al-Kazi, L. (2011). Complicating the 'Clash of Civilizations': Gender and politics in contemporary Kuwait. In P. Michel and E. Pace (Eds.), *Annual Review of the Sociology of Religion: Volume 2: Religion and politics* (pp. 64–84). Boston, MA: Brill Academic Publishers.

Hafez, S. (2011). *An Islam of her own: Reconsidering religion and secularism in women's Islamic movements*. New York, NY: New York University Press.

Hunter, J. D. (1991). *Culture wars: The struggle to control the family, art, education, law, and politics in America*. New York, NY: Basic Books.

Huntington, S. P. (1996). *The clash of civilizations and the remaking of world order*. New York, NY: Simon & Schuster.

Joseph, S., & Najmabadi, A., (Eds.), (2005). *Encyclopedia of women and Islamic cultures: Family, law and politics*. Boston, MA: Brill Academic.

Kennedy-Glans, D. (2009). *Unveiling the breath: One woman's journey into understanding Islam and gender equality*. Canada: Pari.

Massolo, A. (2007, June). Participatción política de las mujeres en el ámbito local en América Latina. Report prepared for the UN-INSTRAW. Retrieved from http://www.congreso.gob.pe/I_organos/mujeres_parlamentarias2009/imagenes/Documentos-paridad-representacion/AL_participacion_politica_mujer.pdf

Miles, R. (2001). *Who cooked the last supper? The women's history of the world*. New York, NY: Three Rivers Press.

Molyneux, M. (1985). Mobilization without emancipation? Women's interests, the state, and revolution in Nicaragua. *Feminist Studies, 11*(2), 227–254.

Qusti, R. (2005, 13 March). Saudi champ rallying for drive for development. *Arab News*. Retrieved from http://archive.arabnews.com/?page=8&section=0&article=60372&d=13&m=3&y=2005

Radcliffe, S.A., and S. Westwood. (Eds.). (1993). *'Viva': Women and popular protest in Latin America*. London, UK: Routledge.

Seunarine, L. (1999). *Ethiopian women of power*. New York, NY: Imani.

Tenety, E. (2012). Vatican: U.S. Catholic Sisters, Nuns making serious theological errors. *The Washington Post*. Retrieved April 18 from http://www.washingtonpost.com/blogs/under-god/post/vatican-report-us-catholic-sisters-nuns-hold-serious-theological-errors/2012/04/18/gIQAWSarRT_blog.html

Vaz, A. (2006). Qatari women at the Asian games: Cultural differences on display in conservative Muslim City. *Ohmy News*. Retrieved December 12 from http://english.ohmynews.com/articleview/article_view.asp?menu=c10400&no=334125&rel_no=1

Wadud, A. (2006). *Inside the gender Jihad: Women's reform in Islam*. Oxford, UK: Oneworld.

Gender Segregation, Effacement, and Suppression: Trends in the Status of Women in Israel*

The author is indebted to Dr. Daniel Mishori for fruitful and insightful discussions and helpful suggestions, and also like to thank Etan J. Tal, Einam Livnat, and Lisa Ratz for perceptive and useful comments on earlier drafts of this paper.

References

Bar-Zohar, O. (2012, 31 May). Israeli advocacy group urges Haredi draft must not be at expense of women soldiers: Groups cite numerous examples of service of ultra-Orthodox men causing detrimental changes in the service of women soldiers. Haaretz (English edition). Retrieved from http://www.haaretz.com/news/diplomacy-defense/israeli-advocacy-group-urges-haredi-draft-must-not-be-at-expense-of-women-soldiers-1.433471

Barzilai, G. (2003). The different among us: Law and political boundaries of religious fundamentalism. *Iyunei Mishpat, 27*(2), 1–51. Retrieved from http://faculty.washington.edu/gbarzil/courses/Final.pdf. English abstract retrieved from http://faculty.washington.edu/gbarzil/pubs/21_DifferentAmongUs_englabst.pdf.

Bollier, D. (2002). Reclaiming the commons. *Boston Review, 27*(3–4). Retrieved May 2, 2007 from http://www.boston review.net/BR27.3/bollier

Douglas, G., Doe, N., Gilliat-Ray, S., Sandberg, R., & Khan, A. (2011). *Social cohesion and civil law: Marriage, divorce and religious courts—report of a research study funded by the AHRC*. Cardiff, UK: Cardiff University.

Ettinger, Y., & Kyzer, L. (2009, 27 October). Haredi teargases woman for using 'men only' sidewalk. *Haaretz (English edition)*. Retrieved from http://www.haaretz.com/print-edition/news/haredi-teargases-woman-for-using-men-only-sidewalk-1.5374

Goldberg, J. J. (2011, 20 December). Women honorees barred from science award stage. *Forward The Jewish Daily*. Retrieved from http://blogs.forward.com/forward-thinking/tags/israeli-ministry-of-health/

Goldenberg, T. (2012, 15 December). To pray like men: Women of the Wall endure taunts, arrests and even plastic chairs thrown at them by angry worshippers, all to worship as they wish at Judaism's holiest site. *The Times of Israel*. Retrieved from http://www.timesofisrael.com/to-pray-like-men/

Greenberg, J. (1994, 3 November). Israeli woman sues for chance to be a combat pilot. *New York Times*. Retrieved from http://www.nytimes.com/1994/11/03/world/israeli-woman-sues-for-chance-to-be-a-combat-pilot.html

Hardin, G. (1968). The tragedy of the commons. *Science, 162*(3859), 1243–1248. Retrieved from http://www.cs.wright.edu/~swang/cs409/Hardin.pdf

Harel, A. (2011, 23 November). IDF must bar soldiers from leaving events over women's singing; officer says decision of Maj. Gen. Orna Barbivai, head of the Israel Defense Forces' Personnel Directorate, expected to contradict wishes of many rabbis. *Haaretz (English edition)*. Retrieved from http://www.haaretz.com/print-edition/news/idf-must-bar-soldiers-from-leaving-events-over-women-s-singing-officer-says-1.397170

Herr, R. S. (2004). A third world feminist defense of multiculturalism. *Social Theory and Practice, 30*(1), 73–103.

Kelner, V. (2011, 24 November). Will women disappear from the public sphere? Not if it is up to Rachel Azaria. *Globes*. Retrieved from http://www.globes.co.il/news/article.aspx?did=1000700239

Kukathas, C. (1992). Are there any cultural rights? *Political Theory, 20*(1), 105–139. Retrieved from http://www.jstor.org/stable/191781

Kymlicka, W. (1995). *Multicultural citizenship: A liberal theory of minority rights*. Oxford, UK: Clarendon. Retrieved from http://www.scribd.com/doc/52506863/W-KYMLICKA-MULTICULTURAL-CITIZENSHIP

Kymlicka, W. (1997). Do we need a liberal theory of minority rights? Reply to Carens, Young, Parekh and Forst. *Constellations: An International Journal of Critical & Democratic Theory, 4*(1), 72–87.

Lees, J., & Bar-Zohar, O. (2011, 29 November). Proposed bill: Male soldiers will be exempt from women singing [my translation]. *Haaretz*. Retrieved from http://www.haaretz.co.il/news/politics/1.1579140

Lennahan, J. B. (2004, March). Do we know consent when we see it? Female genital mutilation and the dilemmas of consent. Western political science association 2004 conference, Portland, Oregon. Retrieved from http://citation.allacademic.com/meta/p_mla_apa_research_citation/0/8/2/9/2/p82929_index.html

Leibowitz, A. R. (2011, 27 November). It ain't over 'til the IDF soldier sings: The question of whether Orthodox soldiers should be forced to listen to female singers has exploded into a public scandal—what does this say about the shifting commitments on both sides? *Haaretz* (English edition). Retrieved from http://www.haaretz.com/jewish-world/it-ain-t-over-til-the-idf-soldier-sings-1.398037

Makovi, M. (2010, 1 February). *A new hearing for Kol Ishah*. Retrieved from http://www.jewishideas.org/articles/new-hearing-kol-ishah

Medzini, R. (2008, 26 June). Council meeting erupts in yells: Jerusalem is not Iran. *Ynet*. Retrieved from http://www.ynetnews.com/articles/0,7340,L-3560965,00.html

Mishori, D. (2010). Conceptualizing the commons: Reflections on the rhetoric of environmental rights and public ownership. In O. F. von Feigenblatt (Ed.), Development and Conflict in the 21st Century (pp. 105–127). Bangkok, TH: JAPASS Press. Retrieved from http://www.japss.org/upload/developmentconflict21st.pdf

Molin, A. (2012, 1 October). IKEA regrets cutting women from Saudi ad. *The Wall Street Journal*. Retrieved from http://online.wsj.com/article/SB10000872396390444592404578030274200387136.html

Monbiot, G. (1994). The tragedy of the enclosure. *The Social Contract*, Spring, 1–2. Retrieved from http://www.thesocialcontract.com/pdf/four-three/monbiot.pdf

Nahshoni, K. (2009, 1 December). El-Al to launch kosher flights for Haredim. *Ynet*. Retrieved from http://www.ynetnews.com/articles/0,7340,L-3654758,00.html

Nahshoni, K. (2012, 30 December). The modesty code of Rabbi Aviner: This is how you will dress from age 3 [This author's translation]. *Ynet*. Retrieved from http://www.ynet.co.il/articles/0,7340,L-4326091,00.html. English version in Kolech Magazine: http://www.kolech.com/english/show.asp?id=56745

Okin, S.M. 1997. Is multiculturalism bad for women? *Boston Review*. http://www.bostonreview.net/BR22.5/okin.html

Saraga, N. (2009. [Weblog post], 11 March). Women prevented from crying, mourning, approaching graves, by Haredim in Yavne, Israel: Women are "impure" because of menstruation and according to the "Jewish religion" are prohibited from approaching graves. Retrieved from http://failedmessiah.typepad.com/failed_messiahcom/2009/03/women-prevented-from-crying-mourning-approaching-graves-by-Haredim-in-Yavne-israel.html

Sen, A. 1999. Democracy as a Universal Value. *Journal of Democracy, 10* (3), 3–17.

Shachar, A. 2000. "On Citizenship and Multicultural Vulnerability." *Political Theory, 28* (1), 64–89. Retrieved from http://www.jstor.org/stable/192284

Twersky, M. 2012. "Ultra-Orthodox Jews Increasingly Refuse to Sit Near Women on El-Al Flights." *Haaretz* (English edition), March 23. Retrieved from http://www.haaretz.com/weekend/anglo-file/ultra-orthodox-jews-increasingly-refuse-to-sit-near-women-on-el-al-flights-1.420298

Warton, L. 2012. "A Petition to the Central Elections Committee for the 2013 Elections to the Israeli Parliament." *Disqualifying parties for exclusion of women* [This author's translation]. Retrieved from http://www.bechirot.gov.il/elections19/heb/law/request12.pdf.

Zilberman, Y. (Writer) 2012. Did the exclusion of women reach the academia? (This author's translation) [Television series episode]. In *Hadashot-2* MAKO. Retrieved from http://www.mako.co.il/news-israel/local/Article-822f9944081ea31004.htm

Gender and Leadership Style in the Middle East: Evidence from Egypt's Civil Service

References

Abdelhamid, D., & El-Baradei, L. (2010). Reforming the pay system for government employees in Egypt. *International Public Management Review, 11*(3). Retrieved from http://www3.imp.unisg.ch/org/idt/ipmr.nsf/ac4c1079924cf935c1256c76004ba1a6/0a6bc377c4552cd9c12577d1005957ea/$FILE/Abdelhamid%20and%20El%20Baradei_IPMR_Volume%2011_Issue%203.pdf

Al-Sheikh, S., & Khattab, A. S. (2009). *Gender-responsive budgeting in Egypt: An analytical reading of the contributions of a number of ministries.* Cairo, EGt: Egyptian Ministry of Finance, Equal Opportunity Unit.

Appelbaum, S. H., Audet, L., & Miller, J. C. (2003). Gender and leadership? Leadership and gender? A journey through the landscape of theories. *Leadership and Organizational Development Journal, 24*(1), 43–51.

Arabsheibani, G. (2000). Male–female earnings differentials among the highly educated Egyptians. *Education Economics, 8*(2), 129–139.

Ashkanasy, N. M., & Tse, B. (2000). Transformational leadership as management of emotion: A conceptual review. In N. Ashkanasy, C. E. J. Härtel, & W. J. Zerbe (Eds.), *Emotions in the workplace: Research, theory, and practice* (pp. 221–235). Westport, CT: Quorum Books.

Barsoum, G. (2004). The employment crisis of female graduates in Egypt, an ethnographic account. Cairo Papers 25. Cairo, Egypt: American University in Cairo Press. Retrieved from http://www.aucegypt.edu/huss/CairoPapers/Pages/BackVolumes.aspx

Bass, B. M., & Avolio, B. J. (1994). Shatter the glass ceiling: Women may make better managers. *Human Resource Management, 33*(4), 549-560.

CAPMAS (Arab Republic of Egypt, Central Agency for Public Mobilization and Statistics). (2009). *The status of man and woman in Egypt.* Cairo, Egypt. Retrieved from http://www.capmas.gov.eg/Default.aspx?lang=2 (Arabic version, Wad' al-mar'a w'il-ragil fi misr, Retrieved from http://www.capmas.gov.eg/pages_ar.aspx?pageid=503

Dobbins, G. H., & Platz, S. J. (1986). Sex differences in leadership: How real are they? *The Academy for Management Review, 11*(1), 118–127.

Eagly, A. H. (2007). Female leadership advantage and disadvantage: Resolving the contradictions. *Psychology of Women Quarterly, 31*(1), 1–12.

Eagly, A. H., & Johnson, B. T. (1990). Gender and leadership style: A meta-analysis. *Psychological Bulletin, 108*(2), 233–256.

Eagly, A. H., Johannesen-Schmidt, M. C., & van Engen, M. L. (2003). Transformational, transactional, and laissez-faire leadership styles: A meta-analysis comparing women and men. *Psychological Bulletin, 129*(4), 569–591.

Engen, M. L. van, & Willemsen, T. M. (2013, 12 April). Gender and leadership styles: a review of the past decade. WORC Paper 001009, 1–33. *Tilburg University.* Retrieved from http://ideas.repec.org/p/dgr/kubwor/20006.html

EOU (Equal Opportunity Unit). (2006). Arab Republic of Egypt, Ministry of Finance Equal Opportunity Unit. *Non-periodic newsletter, Issue 1 (Nashra qheyr dawriyya tusdir 'an wehda takafu' al-furus).*

EOU (Equal Opportunity Unit). (2009). Arab Republic of Egypt, Ministry of Finance Equal Opportunity Unit. *Non-periodic newsletter, Issue 5 (Nashra qheyr dawriyya tusdir 'an wehda takafu' al-furus).*

Gibson, C. B. (1995). An investigation of gender differences in leadership across four countries. *Journal of International Business Studies. 26*(2), 255–279.

GLOBE. (2010). GLOBE Project. *New Mexico State University, College of Business.* Retrieved from http://business.nmsu.edu/programs-centers/globe/

Groves, K. S. (2005). Gender differences in social and emotional skills and charismatic leadership. *Journal of Leadership and Organizational Studies. 11*(3), 30–46.

Judge, T. A., Piccolo, R. F., & Ilies, R. (2004). The forgotten ones? The validity of consideration and initiating structure in leadership research. *Journal of Applied Psychology. 89*(1), 36–51.

Kabasakal, H., & Bodur, M. (2002). Arabic cluster: a bridge between East and West. *Journal of World Business, 1*(37), 40–54.

Klenke, K. (2002). Cinderella stories of women leaders: Connecting leadership contexts and competencies. *Journal of Leadership and Organizational Studies, 9*(2), 18–28.

Littrell, R. (2002). Desirable leadership behaviors of multi-cultural managers in China. *Journal of Management Development. 21*(1), 5–74.

Livani, T. (2007). Middle East and North Africa: Gender overview. *World Bank.* Retrieved from http://siteresources.worldbank.org/INTMENA/Resources/MENA_Gender_Overview_2007.pdf.

Mandell, B., & Pherwani, S. (2003). Relationship between emotional intelligence and transformational leadership style: A gender comparison. *Journal of Business and Psychology, 17*(3), 387–404.

Metcalfe, B. D. (2008). Women, management and globalization in the Middle East. *Journal of Business Ethics, 83*(1), 85–100.

Mostafa, M. M. (2003). Attitudes towards women who work in Egypt. *Women in Management Review, 18*(5), 252–266.

Neal, M., Finlay, J., Catana, J. G., & Catana, D. (2007). A comparison of leadership prototypes of Arab and European females. *International Journal of Cross Cultural Management, 7*(3), 291–316.

Newman, M. (1993). Career advancement: Does gender make a difference? *American Review of Public Administration, 23*(4), 361–384.

Newman, M. (1994). Lowi's thesis and gender. *Public Administration Review, 54*(3), 277–284.

Newman, M., Guy, M., & Mastracci, S. (2007). Beyond cognition: Affective leadership and emotional labor. *Public Administration Review. 69*(1), 6–20.

Noble, C., & Moore, S. (2006). Advancing women and leadership in this post feminist, post EEO era: A discussion of the issues. *Women in Management Review, 21*(7), 598–603.

Porterfield, J., & Kleiner, B. H. (2005). A new era: Women and leadership. *Equal Opportunities International. 24*(5/6), 49–56.

SMEPOL. (2007). Newsletter. Issue 13. Cairo, Egypt: Small and Medium Enterprise Policies Project, Ministry of Finance.

Stelter, N. Z. (2002). Gender differences in leadership: current social issues and future organizations. *Journal of Leadership and Organizational Studies, 8*(4), 88–99.

Stogdill, R. (1963). Manual for the leadership behavior description questionnaire—Form XII. *Ohio State University*. Retrieved from http://fisher.osu.edu/supplements/10/2862/1962%20LBDQ%20MANUAL.pdf

Trinidad, C., & Normore, A. H. (2005). Leadership and gender: A dangerous liaison? *Leadership and Organization Development Journal. 26*(7), 574–590.

UNDP. (2002). Arab human development report 2002: Creating opportunities for future generations. *United Nations Development Programme Arab Fund for Economic and Social Development*. Retrieved from http://hdr.undp.org/en/reports/regionalreports/arabstates/RBAS_ahdr2002_EN.pdf

Wahba, J. (2009). The impact of labor market reforms on informality in Egypt: Gender and work in the MENA region. *Working Paper Series, No. 3*. Cairo, EG: Population Council.

World Bank. (2007). The status and progress of women in the Middle East and North Africa. Retrieved from http://siteresources.worldbank.org/INTMENA/Resources/MENA_Gender_BW2007.pdf

Yaish, M., & Stier, H. (2009). Gender inequality in job authority: a cross-national comparison of 26 countries. *Work and Occupations, 36*(4), 343–366.

Yaseen, Z. (2010). Leadership styles of men and women in the Arab world, education, business and society. *Contemporary Middle Eastern Issues, 3*(1), 63–70.

ABOUT THE AUTHORS

Michal L. Allon, PhD is senior teacher at the Division of Foreign Languages at Tel Aviv University, Israel. She is the coordinator of English courses in the Faculty of Social Science, where she teaches English and academic literacy. She received her BA in Philosophy and English Linguistics from the Hebrew University of Jerusalem, Israel. Her MA and PhD in Linguistics are from the University of Illinois, USA, where she wrote her dissertation on "Focus Constructions in Somali". Her article "Disempowerment by Design: The Trials and Tribulations of Language Teachers at Tel Aviv University" was published in the book *Precarious Employment - Systematic Exclusion and Exploitation in the Labor Market* (Edited by Mishori and Maor in 2012). In this chapter she recounted her experience and her activities as a member of the Union of Junior Academic Staff, and a member of the negotiation team with the management of Tel Aviv University. **Part 4, p. 293.**

Ola Gameel Al-Talliawi, MPA received her Master of Public Policy and Administration from the American University in Cairo, Egypt. Her thesis title was "Gender and Leadership in Egypt's Public Sector: the Case of the Ministry of Finance." **Part 4, 307.**

Mohammed M. Aman, PhD is Professor of Information Studies at the University of Wisconsin-Milwaukee (UWM) and Editor-in-Chief of the peer-reviewed Wiley/PSO journal, *Digest of Middle East Studies (DOMES)*, and *Middle East Media and Book Reviews (MEMBR)*. He received his BA (with Hons) from Cairo University, Egypt, MS from Columbia University and his PhD from the University of Pittsburgh. He has held a number of academic leadership positions including Dean of the School of Information Studies at UWM (1979-2002); Interim Dean of the School of Education and Vice Chancellor for Partnership in Education (2000-2002); Dean of the School of Information Sciences at Long Island University (1976-79); Director and Professor, St. John's University, New York, Division of Information Sciences (1972-76); Information Officer, Arab League Mission to the United Nations, consultant to UNESCO, UNIDO, UNDP, Arab League, US State Department, and various Arab and African governments. He is the author of more than 200 articles and 15 books—among them: *The Gulf War in World Literature*; *Islamic Books*; *Information Systems and Services*; and *Academic Library Management*. **Editor.**

Mary Jo Aman, MLIS is Associate Editor of the peer reviewed Wiley/PSO journal, *Digest of Middle East Studies (DOMES)* and the *Middle East Media and Book*

Reviews (MEMBR). She received her BA from Fisk University and MLIS from Clark Atlanta University, Atlanta, GA. She held several positions in New York—among them Director of Library Promotion at the Viking Press; Consultant, Nassau County, N.Y Library System; Assistant Coordinator, Brooklyn Public Library; Member of the Board of International Board of Books for Young People (IBBY) and Editor of IBBY's *Newsletter*; and most recently Coordinator of Outreach, School of Continuing Education and Outreach; Director, Department of Technology, Division of Student Services; and Director, Education and Curriculum Library at the University of Wisconsin-Milwaukee. She lectured in Egypt and Kuwait and taught at St. John's University in New York, and Cardinal Stritch University in Fox Point, Wisconsin. Mrs Aman is the recipient of several awards including citations of merit from the Milwaukee Board of Supervisors and the Wisconsin State Senate, and the University of Wisconsin-Milwaukee's Spaights Award for Outstanding Contributions to UWM. **Editor.**

Maysam Behravesh is PhD Candidate, Political Science at Lund University, Sweden, with an MA (with Hons.) in British Studies from the University of Tehran in Iran. He has been on the editorial board of the international politics website *e-International Relations* (e-IR) since February 2011, and is also a contributing editor for the peer-reviewed journal *Asian Politics & Policy* (APP). Among his publications are "A Crisis of Confidence Revisited: Iran-West Tensions and Mutual Demonization" (*APP*, 2011), "The Formative Years of Anglo-Iranian Relations (1907-1953): Colonial Scramble for Iran and Its Political Legacy" (*DOMES*, 2012), "Downgrading Iranian-British Relations: The Anatomy of a Folly" (*OpenDemocracy*, 2012), "Revolt in Syria: An Alternative View from Iran" (*IR Diplomacy*, 2011), and "Iran's Syria Gamble: Losing the War, Losing the Peace" (e-IR, 2012). **Part 1, p. 45; Part 3, p. 237.**

Jennifer Bremer, PhD is an international development professional with more than 30 years of professional practice and academic experience in the field. Her career has focused on mobilizing private sector resource for development and facilitating inter-sectoral partnerships'. Most recently, she led the knowledge management function at DAI, a leading international consulting firm. She also holds the position of professor of practice at the American University in Cairo, where she served as founding chair of the Department of Public Policy and Administration. From 1990 to 2006, she led the Kenan Institute Washington Center, a unit of the University of North Carolina Kenan-Flagler Business School, developing collaborative programs to engage the private sector in development. She holds an MPP and Ph.D. in public policy from the Harvard Kennedy School, an MA in development economics from Stanford University, and a BA in political science from Barnard College. Dr. Bremer is the Vice President of the Association for Middle Eastern Public Policy and Administration (AMEPPA), and Chair of its 2011 Inaugural Conference in Ifrane, Morocco. **Part 4, 307.**

Bahar Senem Çevik, PhD is Assistant Professor at Ankara University's Center for the Study and Research of Political Psychology and has been focusing on Turkish identity politics during the Arab Uprisings. She attended several programs on media and terrorism at the NATO COE-DAT and holds a certificate from the Stanford University Political Psychology Summer Program. Çevik is an associate member of the International Dialogue Initiative (IDI) and has contributed to the bi-annual IDI reports. In 2008, as a project assistant, she participated in a field research on the socio-political perceptions of the south-eastern population in Turkey; and in 2009, another research on Turkish immigrants in Belgium—both conducted by Bahçeşehir University. She has edited three books in Turkish, the most recent being "The New World Order, Arab Spring and Turkey." Dr. Çevik recently co-authored a published report on the psycho-politics of the Turkish-Syrian conflict. **Part 1, p.19.**

Lawrence Davidson, PhD is Professor of History, West Chester University in Pennsylvania. His academic work is focused on the history of American foreign relations with the Middle East. Many of Dr. Davidson's recent articles have appeared in *Logos*, an on-line journal for which he is a contributing editor. His book *Cultural Genocide* was published by Rutgers University Press in March 2012. His other books include: *Islamic Fundamentalism-An Introduction* (Greenwood Press, and a third edition, by ABC-Clio); *Privatizing America's National Interest* (University Press of Kentucky, 2009); *America's Palestine: Popular and Official Perceptions from Balfour to Israeli Statehood* (University Press of Florida, 2001); and with Arthur Goldschmidt, published the eighth edition of *A Concise History of the Middle East* (Westview Press, 2006 and 2012). The *Concise History...* is probably the most widely used textbook on Middle East history in the United States. At Georgetown University, Dr. Davidson studied modern European intellectual history under the Palestinian ex-patriot Professor Hisham Sharabi. Many of Dr. Davidson's articles appear in the early issues of the *Journal of Palestine Studies*, edited by Professor Sharabi. **Part 2, p. 167.**

Jerome Drevon is a doctoral candidate at Durham University in the United Kingdom where he specializes in the study of Islamist armed groups in the Middle East. He is a Junior Research Fellow of the Swiss National Science Foundation (SNSF); his research interests lie in Security Studies and Social Movement Studies. He is currently focusing on the evolution of Islamist armed groups in ideologies and practices. His PhD is centered in particular on the evolution of two Egyptian militant groups, the *al-Jama'ah al-Islamiyah* (Islamic Group) and *al-Jama'ah /Tandhim al-Jihad* (The Jihad Group/Organization). He interviewed most of their leaders and senior members during his stay in Egypt, as well as dozens of militants and sympathizers. He has recently presented preliminary results of his research in conferences in several British universities and in Australia and plans to publish them shortly. Before joining academe, Jerome extensively travelled the region and lived in Egypt, Lebanon, the occupied Palestinian territories, and Syria. In this context, he worked in several NGOs and research centers in Europe and in the Middle East, where he acquainted himself with the academic study of armed violence as well as with Human Rights law. **Part 1, p. 5.**

Amitai Etzioni, PhD is University Professor, Professor of International Affairs, and Director of the Institute for Communitarian Policy Studies at George Washington University. In 2001, he was named among the top 100 American intellectuals as measured by academic citations in Richard Posner's book, *Public Intellectuals: A study of Decline*. After receiving his PhD in Sociology from the University of California, Berkeley in 1958, Etzioni served as a Professor of Sociology at Columbia University for 20 years—part of that time as the chairman of the department. He was a guest scholar at the Brookings Institution in 1978 before serving as a Senior Advisor to the White House (1979-1980). He has served as the Thomas Henry Carroll Ford Foundation Professor at the Harvard Business School, as the president of the American Sociological Association, and was the founding president of the International Society for the Advancement of Socio-Economics. In 1990, he founded the Communitarian Network, a not-for-profit, non-partisan organization dedicated to shoring up the moral, social and political foundations of society. He was the editor of *The Responsive Community: Rights and Responsibilities* (1991-2004), and has authored 24 books. In 1991, the press began referring to Dr. Etzioni as the "guru" of the communitarian movement; he can be seen and heard frequently in the media. **Part 3, p. 183.**

Alessandra I. González, PhD is ISR Research Fellow, Baylor University and Post-Doctoral Research Associate, John Jay College, CUNY. Her latest book, *Islamic Feminism in Kuwait: The Politics and Paradoxes* appeared in 2013 (Palgrave Macmillan Press). In 2011, González became a research fellow at the Institute for the Studies of Religion at Baylor University in central Texas. She received her PhD and MA degrees in Sociology from Baylor University and received a BA in Sociology and Policy Studies from Rice University. She is the principal investigator of the Islamic Social Attitudes Survey Project, a study in conjunction with Baylor's Institute for the Studies of Religion on Islamic Religiosity and Social Attitudes, including Women's Rights Attitudes in the Arab Gulf Region. She has forthcoming book chapters in "Women's Encounter with Globalization" (Frontpage Publications) and "Islam and International Relations: Mutual Perceptions" (Cambridge Scholars Publishing), publications in the *Journal for the Scientific Study of Religion*, the *Annual Review of the Sociology of Religion*, and an op-ed on Islamic Feminism in the *Dallas Morning News*. She has presented her research at the Center for the Study of Islam and Democracy's Conference on "The Rights of Women in Islam;" the American Council for the Study of Islamic Societies; the Dialogue of Civilizations Conference hosted by the Institute for Interfaith Dialogue in Houston; the Gulf Research Conference at the University of Exeter; and other academic settings. **Part 4, p. 275.**

Kashif Hameed, MSc is Executive Director of the Center for Research Communication and Dialogue in Islamabad, Pakistan. He received his MSc in urban and regional planning from the University of Engineering and Technology, Lahore. **Part 3, p. 223.**

Anna Hellstrand, MA, has a degree of Bachelor of Science in Peace and Conflict Studies and a degree of Master of Arts in Theology with Human Rights as the main field of study. Within these fields of interest she is engaged in Women's Human Rights and Feminist perspectives, exploring origins, expressions and goals of Women's Rights and Feminist activists and academics, with particular concern to the Middle East. Anna Hellstrand is also an active member of the Feminist Party in Sweden. **Part 4, p. 257.**

Susmit Kumar, PhD, is President of Kumar Consultancy, U.S. He received his doctorate in 1992 from Pennsylvania State University. Before coming to the United States, he was selected in the prestigious Indian Administrative Service and trained at the Lal Bahadur Shastri National Academy of Administration, Mussoorie, India. He is the author of *The Modernization of Islam and the Creation of a Multipolar World Order* (Booksurge, January 2008), *Casino Capitalism: The Collapse of the US Economy and the Transition to Secular Democracy in The Middle East* (iUniverse, 2012), and *Karma, Mind, and Quest for Happiness: The Concrete and Accurate Science of Infinite Truth* (iUniverse, 2012). The first book was an extension of his 1995 article published in *Global Times*, Denmark. **Part 1, p. 71.**

Maria Frederika Malmström, PhD is a researcher for North Africa in the Conflict, Security and Democratic Transformation cluster at the Nordic Africa Institute. She is also a Senior lecturer at School of Global Studies University of Gothenburg. Since 2010, she has been a visiting scholar (2010-2012) at the Center for the Study of Gender and Sexuality at New York University; and from 2012, at Performance Studies, Tisch School of the Arts. Additionally, she is a gender consultant (UNFPA, UNICEF and others), and member of several academic/policy networks, e.g. Think Tank for Arab Women and the Nordic Network—FOKO—Research about female circumcision. Malmström received her PhD from the School of Global Studies, Social Anthropology, and University of Gothenburg, Sweden (2009), and a MA, Social Anthropology, Department of Social Anthropology, University of Gothenburg, Sweden 2000. Her dissertation examined how female gender identity is continually created and re-created in Egypt through a number of daily practices, of which female circumcision is central. The study explored how the subject is made through the interplay of global hegemonic structures of power and the most intimate sphere, which has been exposed in the international arena. **Part 4, p. 257.**

Bessma Momani, PhD is Associate Professor at the Balsillie School of International Affairs at the University of Waterloo. Dr. Momani is a Fellow at both the Brookings Institution and the Centre for International Governance and Innovation, prominent think tanks on global governance. She is a Fulbright Scholar and a visiting associate at Georgetown University's Mortara Center. Momani has received a number of awards and prizes for her research, funded by Canada's Social Sciences and Humanities Research Council (SSHRC). She is the recipient of a numerous awards on her publications, including the University of Waterloo's Lois Claxton Humanities and Social Sciences Endowment Fund Award. Dr. Momani has authored and co-edited several books, including: *Targeted Transnationals: The State, the Media, and Arab Canadians* (UBC Press, 2013); *Shifting GeoEconomic Power of the Gulf* (Ashgate, 2011); *From Desolation to Reconstruction: Iraq's Troubled Journey* (Wilfrid Laurier University Press, 2010). She is also the author of over 45 scholarly journal articles and book chapters that have examined the IMF, the World Bank, the Financial Stability Board, petrodollars, regional trade agreements in the Middle East and economic liberalization throughout the Arab Gulf and the Middle East. **Part 2, p. 119.**

Alan Moss, PhD is forensic economist and author of books of non-fiction and fiction. As Senior Consultant for Employment Research Corporation of Ann Arbor, Michigan, Dr. Moss has directed teams concerning requirements of the Fair Labor Standards Act, prevailing wage statutes, and the development and use of labor market information. He has prepared and delivered expert reports and testimony on behalf of attorneys representing corporate clients and workers. Prior to his work in forensics, Dr. Moss was Chief Economist and Director of Wage Determinations for the U.S. Department of Labor's Wage and Hour Division, and Chief of Labor Market Information for the Labor Department's Employment and Training Administration. Moss received his PhD in the Economics of Human Resources, with a Minor in Political Science, from the Catholic University of America. His non-fiction offerings include *Selling-Out America's Democracy* (Praeger, 2008) and *Employment Opportunity: Outlook, Reason, and Reality* (Prentice Hall, 2000); *Island of Betrayal* (Gauthier, 2010); and *Insidious Deception* (Whiskey Creek Press, March, 2013). **Part 2, p. 153.**

Paul Rowe, PhD is Associate Professor and Chairman, Department of History, Geography, and Political and International Studies at Trinity Western University (TWU) and coordinator of the International Studies program. Prior to his appointment at TWU, he taught at the University of Western Ontario and Queen's University. His areas of expertise include: Middle Eastern Politics; Religion and Politics; Developing World Politics, International Politics; and Christian Minorities in the Middle East. His most recent book, *Religion and Global Politics* (Oxford University Press Canada), was published in 2012. Dr. Rowe grew up in Ontario, Canada and completed degrees at the University of Toronto and Dalhousie University prior to doctoral work in Political Science at McGill University, which he completed in 2003. His doctoral dissertation focused upon the politics of Christian minority communities in Middle Eastern states. He has spent extended time in the Middle East and South Asia and continues to study the politics of religious groups in developing countries and at the global level. He comments on a variety of issues in international politics, the developing world, the Middle East, and the politics of religion. **Part 3, p. 209.**

Sarah Tobin, PhD is a Mellon Post Doctoral Fellow in Islamic Studies, Department of Anthropology at Wheaton College, Norton, MA. Her expertise is in Islam, economic anthropology, and gender in the Middle East. Ethnographically, her work focuses on Islamic piety in the economy, especially Islamic Banking and Finance during times of economic shifts. She is the author of *Everyday Piety: Islam and the Economy in Amman, Jordan*, which is currently under review at Cornell University Press. It draws on 21 months of participant observation in Amman, Jordan, including the first ethnographic study conducted inside an Islamic bank. She is the editor of a volume in progress entitled, *Faith and Finance: Anthropological and Sociological Perspectives on Islamic Banking and Finance*. This project spans anthropology, sociology, banking and finance, and Islamic studies as the first volume to explore the social and cultural implications of this new movement. Her latest manuscript in progress, *Branding Islam: Islamic Symbols in Jordanian Newspapers Published in the 20th Century*, traces a history of the usage of symbols of Islam in print newspapers in Amman, Jordan, and then puts focus on how Islam is used to "brand" given products or services, reflecting the integration of both the consumption of an authentic Islam and images of contemporary life and lifestyles. **Part 1, p. 57.**

Andrew Wender, JD, PhD is a Continuing Sessional Instructor in the University of Victoria's Department of Political Science, where he has taught since 2006, and in UVic's Department of History, where he has taught since 2001. He holds an Interdisciplinary PhD (2006) from the University of Victoria, which he completed while a Fellow at UVic's Centre for Studies in Religion and Society. Prior to undertaking his PhD, Dr. Wender completed a JD (1997) at the Seattle University School of Law, and became a member of the Washington State Bar. Wender's teaching—for which he received UVic's 2011 Gilian Sherwin Alumni Award for Excellence in Teaching—and writing focus on the historical and contemporary interconnections between politics and religion, the politics and history of the Middle East, political theory, and world politics and history. Special teaching projects also include his fall 2012 course for UVic's Religious Studies Program, "Religious Sectarianism in the Contemporary World," and the ongoing "Religion in Society" course that he offers for UVic's Department of Sociology. Dr. Wender has published in such journals as the *Digest of Middle East Studies* (including the recent 2012 article, "Learning Through Upheaval: Strategies for Analyzing and Construing Emerging Socio-Political Transformations in the Middle East"), *Implicit Religion,* and *Capitalism, Nature, Socialism.* **Part 3, p. 195.**

Kenneth L. Wise, **PhD** is Director of B'huth's (Dubai Consultancy Research & Media Centre) Policy Research Division and an advisor in the UAE's Watani social development program. He directs B'huth conferences on national security and treating terrorism, participated in a tribal reconciliation in Yemen, and designed campaign workshops for candidates in the UAE's first election—Federal National Council in 2006. Dr. Wise, now a member of the emeritus faculty, taught political science and international relations at Creighton University (Omaha, USA). His teaching and research specialties were U.S. foreign policy, diplomacy, international geostrategy, political conflict and resolution, international law, new sovereigns and global citizenship, global governance policy process, and international studies paradigms. He holds a BA in History (cum laude) from Midland Lutheran College (USA), an MA in International Law and Organization, and a PhD in International Studies (with distinction) from the School of International Service of The American University, Washington, D.C. For 25 years he was Director of the Omaha Committee of the Council on Foreign Relations. He is an Academic Associate of the Atlantic Council of the United States—a Washington, D.C., think tank; member of the Middle East Institute, American International Law Society, International Studies Association, American Political Science Association, Inter-University Seminar on Armed Forces and Society; and reviewer for Harvard University Press, McGraw-Hill, Dushkin Publishing Group, Pearson-Longman, *The Journal of Armed Forces and Society, Policy Studies Review, Perspective—Review of International Affairs,* and the *International Studies Journal.* **Part 2, p. 131.**

Asim Zia, PhD is Associate Professor at the Department of Community Development and Applied Economics at the University of Vermont. He received his PhD from the Georgia Institute of Technology. His research is focused on the development of computational and complex-systems based approaches for Policy Analysis, Governance Informatics and Adaptive Management. His published research spans the substantive policy domains of transportation, air quality and land-use planning; climate policy; and international development and biodiversity conservation. In January 2013, Routledge Press published his recent book *Post-Kyoto Climate Governance: Confronting the Politics of Scale, Ideology and Knowledge*. **Part 3, p. 223.**

Radwan Ziadeh, PhD is Visiting Scholar at Lehigh University and Fellow at the Institute for Social Policy and Understanding (ISPU) in Washington D.C. Since the Syrian uprising started in March 15, 2011, he has been involved in documenting all human rights violations, testifying at the UN Human rights council in Geneva, and serving as Director of Foreign Relation Office for the Syrian National Council (SNC). Among positions held by Dr. Ziadeh are: visiting scholar at Dubai Initiative at Kennedy School of Government at Harvard University; visiting scholar at The Institute for Middle East Studies (IMES) in the Elliot School of International Affairs, George Washington University; Prins Global Fellow at Hagop Kevorkian Center for Near Eastern Studies at New York University; and Visiting Scholar at The Center for Contemporary Arab Studies (CCAS) at Georgetown University. He is the founder and director of the Damascus Center for Human Rights Studies in Syria and co-founder and Executive Director of the Syrian Center for Political and Strategic Studies in Washington, D.C. He also writes a bi-monthly op-ed for leading Arab newspapers, such as *Al-Hayat*. Dr. Ziadeh is the author/editor of several publications including his most recent *Power and Policy in Syria: Intelligence Services, Foreign Relations and Democracy in the Modern Middle East* (I. B. Tauris, 2011). **Part 1, p. 37.**

Made in the USA
Middletown, DE
07 February 2016